Bolivia's
Radical Tradition

Bolivia's

Radical Tradition

Permanent Revolution in the Andes

S. Sándor John

the university of arizona press   tucson

THE UNIVERSITY OF
ARIZONA PRESS

© 2009 The Arizona Board of Regents
All rights reserved
First issued as a paperback edition 2011

www.uapress.arizona.edu

Library of Congress Cataloging-in-Publication Data
John, S. Sándor, 1955–
Bolivia's radical tradition : permanent revolution in the Andes /
S. Sándor John.
p. cm.
Includes bibliographical references and index.
ISBN 978-0-8165-2764-9 (hardcover : alk. paper)
ISBN 978-0-8165-1678-0 (pbk. : alk. paper)
1. Communism—Bolivia—History. 2. Bolivia—Politics and
government—20th century. 3. Bolivia—Politics and government—21st century. 4. Partido Obrero Revolucionario (Bolivia)
5. Movimiento Nacionalista Revolucionario (Bolivia) 6. Chaco
War, 1932–1935—Influence. 7. Bolivia—History—Revolution,
1952—Influence. 8. Political culture—Bolivia—20th century.
9. Political culture—Bolivia—21st century. I. Title.
HX188.5.J64   2009
984—dc22   2009016375

Manufactured in the United States of America on acid-free,
archival-quality paper and processed chlorine free.

16   15   14   13   12   11   8   7   6   5   4   3

To the miners of Bolivia.
To the men and women who shared their story.
And to Roy John (1924–2009).

Contents

Abbreviations used in the text and notes are explained in the Glossary and References.

Illustrations

Acknowledgments

My biggest debt is to the participants—named and anonymous, those still living and the many who died in recent years—who trusted me with their recollections. My admiration for their courage and perseverance has deepened in the course of this project.

I thank Herbert S. Klein for encouraging me to write this history and extend it into the present; my patient, encouraging, and knowledgeable advisers Mario Miranda Pacheco (Universidad Nacional Autónoma de México) and José Luis Rénique (City University of New York); CUNY professors Margaret Crahan, Gerald Markowitz, and Alfonso Quiroz, who gave generously of their time; and New York University professor Sinclair Thomson, who shared his critical insight on Bolivian social movements.

My appreciation goes to University of Arizona Press editors Patti Hartmann and Nancy Arora for their belief in this book; to the two anonymous reviewers whose suggestions made it a better one; to Seth Miller at Matrix Productions; and to Kay Mikel for copyediting. Among family members, Andi and Penny made editing suggestions; Horacio made the map; Leslie worked many hours with me on photos; Laura helped with the bibliography; Paul and Vicky gave me *carne adobada*, Bushmill's, and a place in their adobe to work. . . . Irina pitched in with great doses of patience, movies, and sympathy. Myriad other siblings, in-laws, babies, and pets provided encouragement, entertainment, or both. Roy, who taught me to ask *why*, painstakingly read multiple drafts and made crucial suggestions; to my sorrow, he did not live to see the final product. Vera helped me understand the creative process, contributing insight at each phase of this one. Stan, too long ago now, taught me to listen; I hope that I have, at least something like the way he did.

In Bolivia, I received inestimable assistance from many people, including Susana Bacherer, Bolshia Bravo and André Gautier, Elizabeth Espinoza,

Ana María Núñez, Comibol archive director Huracán Ramírez and the indomitable history-rescuers he leads, Cecilia Salazar, Edgar and Sonia, Yanchi, and others. Luis Oporto, Rolando Alvarez, and Ludmila Zeballos of the Archivo del Congreso were amazingly hospitable and helpful, as was Marcela Inch of the Archivo Nacional in Sucre.

CUNY colleagues and friends too numerous to list made useful suggestions, as did Richard Bucci and members of North America's small confraternity of Bolivia scholars such as Brooke Larson and Ann Zulawski. Sarah Hines generously allowed me to quote from her valuable interviews, and Nadezhda Bravo Cladera conducted two important ones for me in Stockholm. Loretta Valero helped enormously with preliminary work on this project, and Jan Norden gave time and expertise to help with graphic materials. CUNY's Center for Latin American, Caribbean, and Latino Studies provided a summer research grant.

Map of Bolivia. (Courtesy of Horacio Cocchi)

In Nanterre, Geneviève Dreyfus-Armand of the Bibliothèque de Documentation Internationale Contemporaine provided great assistance, as did Dale Reed of the Hoover Institution archives at Stanford. I would also like to thank the personnel of other libraries and archives consulted in the course of this project, in Buenos Aires, Cochabamba, La Paz, Mexico City, New York, Paris, Quito, and Santiago de Chile.

Bolivia's

Radical Tradition

Introduction

In December 2005, Bolivian peasant leader Evo Morales became the first Indian president in South American history. More than any event since Che Guevara's death four decades earlier, his election put the isolated Andean country on the map for people around the world. Garlanded in coca leaves, Morales and his running mate—Álvaro García Linera, a former "Indianist" guerrilla leader—took office to the tune of the *morenada*, a dance portraying black slaves and subterranean devils, traditionally performed by Bolivian miners in homage to the Virgin of the Mineshaft.

The election of the leftist coca-grower Morales followed a series of convulsive social upheavals. For Bolivia, the millennium began with the "Water War" of 2000 against the privatization of water services in Cochabamba. Three years later, a bloody "Gas War" on the *altiplano* (high plateau) overthrew the neoliberal president who was one of Washington's regional favorites. In 2005, "Gas War II" took the country to the brink of civil war again, overthrowing another president and opening the way for Morales's election.

Although Bolivia has made front-page headlines in recent years, it remains little studied and less understood. Legend has it that Queen Victoria took out her map of the world and drew a big X across Bolivia when a *caudillo* president humiliated Britain's envoy. For subsequent generations, it might have been summed up as the land of coups, coca, and Che. To many, its fragmented, convulsive history seemed incomprehensible.

Today, Bolivia symbolizes new shifts in Latin America that have occurred under the impact of social movements of the poor, the dispossessed, and indigenous peoples once crossed off the maps of "official" history. Bolivian radicalism, however, has a distinct genealogy; and it does not fit into ready-made patterns of the Latin American left. This book was born from a desire to understand a place where miners spoke in Quechua-inflected Spanish of Leon Trotsky's "permanent revolution" while offering coca leaves and cigarettes to El Tío, a pre-Inca deity of the world beneath the world. Why was Bolivia home to the most persistently, heroically combative labor movement in the Western Hemisphere? How did the Andean altiplano foster a movement born from distant disputes over Marxist doctrine in Soviet Russia? This movement, "Bolivian Trotskyism," has played a central role in shaping the tradition of Bolivian radicalism.

A Distinctive Radical Tradition

In many vital ways, the country is markedly different. Some differences are extreme expressions of tendencies common to much of Latin America; others are unique. Bolivia is one of the very poorest countries in the hemisphere, and also the most Indian, far outstripping even Guatemala: two-thirds of the population describes itself as indigenous. It is one of the most volatile places in a region often marked by upheaval. Upper Peru's Tupac Katari rebellion of 1781 was one of the most powerful indigenous risings in the Spanish empire. When Spain was driven out in 1825, Bolivia was named after South America's "Liberator," Simón Bolívar. Yet independence brought further turmoil, civil wars, loss of the seacoast in a disastrous war with Chile, and so many military takeovers that other Latin Americans nicknamed it *Golpilandia* (Coup-Land).

Bolivia's economy long revolved around production of one key commodity, first silver, then tin; later gas and oil (and at some points coca). As tin became a strategic metal in the early twentieth century, miners drawn from the indigenous countryside acquired an exceptionally important influence on national life. Centered on their union, Bolivia's labor movement became the most politicized and radical in the hemisphere, developing traditions of struggle deeply colored by miners' class identity and culture (see figure I.1).

Concentrated in the mine camps of the altiplano, these workers played a central military and political role in the Bolivian Revolution of 1952, one of the most extensive social upheavals in Latin American history. The regional impact of this revolution owed much to the political prominence of Indian miners and peasants in the destruction of the old order and the conflict-ridden construction of its successors.

The miners' militancy, facing civilian and military regimes' attempts to crush their resistance, made them a reference point for activists throughout the continent. A year after the 1952 revolution, a young Ernesto Guevara

Figure I.1 La Paz, June 2005: miners march during the "Gas Wars." (Photo by author)

passed through Bolivia, where he encountered armed miners returning from a demonstration. The experience made such an impression on the future "Che" that he wrote two poems dedicated to the Bolivian miners, "mole-warriors" who emerged into the sun to explode "a thousand thunders" of dynamite as they marched to commemorate the revolution.[1]

After Guevara's death in 1967, his then-follower Régis Debray castigated the Bolivian working class for its "overweening self-confidence," while noting that Bolivia "re-created" classical Marxist concepts because they seemed "profoundly expressive of the life of the country." In particular, "the continuing Trotskyist tendency among rank-and-file workers . . . has set its seal on the thinking of the trade-union movement from its beginnings," because key aspects of Bolivian society "illustrate the theories of permanent revolution outlined by [Leon] Trotsky."[2]

Until now, there has been no full-length study explaining how and why Bolivia became the Western country where Trotskyism has had the deepest and longest-lasting impact. This movement achieved comparable influence only in Sri Lanka and (from the 1930s to the 1940s, when it was wiped out) in Vietnam. Students of Bolivia have long recognized Trotskyism's influence there but rarely sought to explain it. "One of the curiosities of Bolivia is that it has produced one of the most long-lived and influential Trotskyist parties in the world," write two prominent political scientists, noting that the movement "had an ideological influence on the Left far beyond its actual numbers."[3] Some see it as a picturesque feature of the landscape, the political equivalent of the vicuña, a wild high-Andes relative of the furry llama. Yet to understand Bolivian Trotskyism and its place in the country's radical tradition, we must grasp the appeal of its ideas, tracing their connections to broader political, social, and cultural history.

Why did this movement take root so deeply and so stubbornly, like a red *kantuta*, Bolivia's hardy national flower, on the wind-swept altiplano? What does this tell us about the 1952 Revolution and the explosive developments of more recent years and decades? To answer these questions, we must piece together a fragmented past to show a part of Latin American radical history overlooked for too long.

Trotskyism and Bolivian History

This book is about a political vanguard that exercised long-lasting effects by producing ideology that helped forge the identity of radical miners, peasants, and intellectuals. It acquired surprising influence in a society split by class, ethnicity, region, and an inequality spectacular even by Latin American standards. This movement helped indigenous miners forge a worldview that vindicated their central role in the nation's life, providing it with an international context and historical mission. The collective memory the miners treasured would, the movement taught, enrich the class consciousness of all the world's workers. No longer to be derided and despised, the rich cultural production of Bolivia's poor would be part of the struggle for a different, better world.

Seventy years before "Evo," this movement proudly proclaimed the Andean, indigenous, pre-Columbian, Inca (and pre-Inca) roots of a national majority locked out of political power. It organized Quechua and Aymara peasants to take their masters' land, and their own fate, into their own hands. It taught that isolated, "backward" Bolivia could take its place in the vanguard of a worldwide revolution of the poor. It appealed to Indian miners to emerge from their *socavones*, the hell-hot mineshafts that turned their lungs to dust, to lead the exploited and oppressed in a final "assault on heaven." This would not be another in the endless series of military coups and nationalist *pronunciamientos*, but a permanent revolution opening the way to a classless society. This movement is Bolivian Trotskyism.

Guillermo Lora, whose striking Aymara features were a fixture of Bolivian politics for decades as leader of the Partido Obrero Revolucionario (POR; Revolutionary Workers Party), liked to claim that *Bolivia es un país trotskizado*: "Bolivia is a Trotskyized country." Quite a boast, and one that could be made nowhere else. For decades, the movement was interlocutor, half-willing partner, specter, and rival to ruling parties and presidents. In what other country would the President of the Republic find it necessary to warn the people that a "Trotskyist government" could only be short-lived?[4]

Amidst seventy years of turbulent history, Bolivian Trotskyism posed, and sought to answer, fundamental questions about revolutions and how they are made; about interactions of class and ethnicity involving the cities, mines, and countryside; and about class alliances and social movements' relations with the state. Disputes within the movement and with other political groupings centered on these issues, which concerned and sometimes tormented those who sought not merely to interpret, but to change, what they saw as a profoundly oppressive and unjust society. Neither arcane nor abstract, these debates dealt with political issues that repeatedly, in a starkly literal sense, acquired life-and-death importance.

At crucial junctures, Bolivia was a laboratory for competing ideologies, many of which influenced large sections of Latin American society. Bolivian revolutionaries had to contend with the oligarchic liberalism of the early twentieth century, "military socialism" in the 1930s, "revolutionary nationalism" in the 1940s and 1950s, Pentagon-promoted counterinsurgency from the 1960s through the early 1980s, followed by the 1982–85 "popular front" of nationalists and Communists, then a two-decade onslaught of "neoliberalism."

On the left, the Trotskyist movement defined and redefined itself in relation to a wide range of political currents. These included radical "indigenism," as the movement's founders, challenging the oppression of the Indian majority, repeatedly harked back to the Incas; the official Communist movement, which they saw as betraying the promise and program of the Russian October; Guevara-style guerrilla warfare; and state-based populism, whose co-optive appeal has been shown anew in recent years. Today, they face the government of Evo Morales, viewing him not as an engineer on the locomotive of revolution, but a fireman trying to put out the flames of revolt.

A Legacy of Rebellion

In a colloquium on the Bolivian left, Carlos Mesa, then the country's best-known historian, summed up the impact of the Trotskyist party formed in the 1930s: it was "very significant in the field of ideas and the radicalization of grassroots, labor and political movements' positions."[5] In June 2005, Mesa became the latest Bolivian president to be overthrown by radicalized movements of miners, peasants, and slum dwellers.

Mesa was the successor to the previous overthrown president, Gonzalo Sánchez de Lozada. Known as el gringo Goni, Sánchez de Lozada signed away the country's gas and oil wealth to international energy cartels. Educated in the United States, Goni enjoyed a special closeness with North American elites. During the October 2003 Gas War, he used U.S.-supplied tanks and machine guns to massacre protesters. Yet even when his troops left the highway to La Paz strewn with the bodies of peasants, workers, and youth from the slums of El Alto, Goni was unable to stop the rebellion. Driven into exile in Miami, he left his office in the Palacio Quemado to the ill-fated Mesa, who lasted less than two years.

The decisive moment in Goni's fall occurred when troops blocking the highway to La Paz allowed truckloads of miners to proceed to the capital. The decisive moment in Mesa's fall occurred when miners led columns of peasants advancing on the city of Sucre, to which parliament had fled after miners besieged it in La Paz. The assassination of a mine leader by an army sharpshooter took the country to the brink of civil war, a situation defused only when Evo Morales, leader of the Movimiento Al Socialismo (MAS; Movement Toward Socialism), helped arrange an "orderly transition" to an interim president, the head of the Supreme Court. This was the prelude to Morales's election as president at the end of 2005.

How are these recent events connected to Bolivia's traditions of radicalism? Several months after Morales took office, a perceptive analysis of his election began with the life story of Sacarías Flores, a vice president of

Morales's party. A former tin miner, he was among the thousands of workers "relocated" to the tropics after the government closed state-owned mines in the 1980s. "Armed with a miner's long militant tradition," he transformed a local mutual-aid society into "a radical union" that helped found a national peasant union federation and, eventually, the MAS.

The particular Bolivian tradition of mineworker radicalism, noted author Alma Guillermoprieto, bore a distinctive relation to international currents of revolutionary thought: "The miners, having come under the influence of Trotskyism in the only country in Latin America in which this variant of Marxism was dominant, coalesced into a notably resistant and militant labor union, which survived the long string of military dictatorships that ended in the 1980s." Flores told her: "Our brother workers in the mines created a document back in 1946, called the Theses of Pulacayo." Until then, miners had protested for one or another change in their conditions, "but the theses talked about taking power." In the 1980s, "We said to ourselves, 'Why not take these beautiful theses of our compañeros and make them a reality?'" [6]

When the world market price of tin fell drastically in 1985, neoliberal policy makers seized the opportunity to break the power of the miners' union, ordering the firing of twenty thousand workers and a program to relocate them to agricultural areas. "History," Guillermoprieto noted, "would eventually find a use for thousands of organized, militant, enraged miners, Flores among them, who were left unmoored, and joined the migrant stream to the jungles. The miners brought with them not only their formidable organizing skills but [an effective] form of protest . . . the roadblock," which they had often used to stop transport to La Paz from Oruro, the mine districts' most important city. Now protests by peasant-union *bloqueadores* (blockaders) began to cut the highway from Bolivia's breadbasket, Cochabamba, to the capital city. In the Cochabamba Water War, a signal role was played by bloqueadores from the coca-growing region of the Chapare, where the unions were led by Evo Morales.[7] Internationally, critics of neoliberal-style capitalism hailed protests that reversed the plans to turn over the city's water system to an affiliate of the Bechtel Corporation. The historical and social background to recent struggles is less widely known.

Many neighborhoods in urban Cochabamba are made up of former miners. Often, they are named for particular mine districts or events from labor history. The renowned Trotskyist union militant Cirilo Jiménez, who moved to Cochabamba after being "relocated" from the Siglo XX mine, told a North American researcher: "The Water War was started by the ex-miners. We came from the mines to . . . areas where there was no water, no basic sewage services, nothing, and we miners orient ourselves perfectly, since we have been educated by our struggles over the course of many years."[8]

Another area where many ex-miners settled is El Alto, the Aymara city just above La Paz that was the epicenter of struggles in 2003 and 2005. Here, too, "traditions of mobilization . . . memory and organizational habits," particularly experiences of miners' and peasants' unions, shaped social movements, as leading Bolivian sociologists note in a recent study.[9] The many recorded casualties of miners bore witness to the crucial role they played in the Gas Wars. When disciplined contingents of miners took the lead in driving out first Goni and then Mesa, the parties that had made their living upholding the "Washington consensus" fell by the wayside. So too did the postmodern nostrum that neoliberalism had made Bolivia's working class a thing of the past.

From Prinkipo to Pulacayo

When Leon Trotsky was exiled from the Soviet Union, the first place he found refuge was the Turkish isle of Prinkipo. Expelled from one country after another, he spent his last years in Coyoacán, Mexico, where Stalin's agent killed him in 1940. Shortly thereafter, "Trotskyism" began to find an echo in the mineshafts of far-off Bolivia. That it did so, with such far-reaching effects, is "a unique and exceptional phenomenon" in Latin American radical history.[10]

As dynamite-wielding miners toppled presidents at the beginning of the twenty-first century, the slogan ¡Viva la Tesis de Pulacayo! appeared on the walls of La Paz, Cochabamba, Oruro, and other towns. Prominent labor leaders proclaimed that the time had come to "return to the Thesis of Pulacayo." The Thesis is a programmatic document written by the POR under the inspiration of Trotsky's theory of permanent revolution and approved by the Mine Workers Federation in 1946. Calling for the Indian miners to lead peasants and the urban poor in social revolution, it "became the ideological cornerstone of the miners' identity." Today, a tourism Web site invites visitors to stop in Pulacayo, "a significant town in Bolivian social history, for here the famous Tesis [sic] of Pulacayo was formulated."[11]

Thus, it was perfectly logical that in 2006, when ex-miner Flores wanted to explain Bolivia's radical traditions to a foreign journalist writing about Evo Morales, he talked about the Pulacayo Thesis. Morales's government promises not permanent revolution but a reformed "Andean capitalism," but as Guillermoprieto notes, it was "under the tutorship of a leading Trotskyist organizer from the mines" that he became the foremost leader of the coca-growing peasants. She is referring to Filemón Escóbar (half-brother of POR head Lora and a former Mine Federation leader), who became Morales's "mentor" after concluding that "the revolution will come from the Chapare" coca-growing region, where many laid-off miners were sent in the 1980s.[12]

That ideas associated with the exiled organizer of Russia's revolution and Red Army made the journey from Prinkipo to Pulacayo is remarkable; even more so is their enduring impact. British political scientist Laurence Whitehead notes that it was here that "dissident Marxists . . . gained signifi-cant influence and established a tradition of Trotskyism more ineradicable than elsewhere in Latin America," perhaps because, he suggests, they were "closer to the aspirations of Bolivian workers" than "orthodox" pro-Moscow leftists. U.S. government agencies and their friends in the press made sure to follow the movement's activities. When the Andean nation was swept by labor protests in the late 1950s, *Time* magazine wrote: "Bolivia is the brightest jewel in the crown of the Fourth International, the 'true,' workers-of-the-world-unite Communists who oppose the Russian Reds."[13]

This book's story begins with a handful of young Bolivian radicals who rebelled against an *ancien régime* in which a tiny, complacent, "white" elite lived off the life-crushing labor of indigenous miners and peasants. Plung-ing into the eclectic intellectual experimentation of early twentieth-century Latin America, they drew inspiration from Incas and Bolsheviks, Peruvian Marxist *amauta* (sage) José Carlos Mariátegui, Mexican and Chilean Com-munists, and an astonishing range of others. In the midst of the Great Depression, their own society entered a profound and traumatic crisis. Shaken by the conflict with Paraguay in the Chaco War (1932–35), Bolivia experienced a wave of radicalization in the late 1930s. Young antiwar intel-lectuals were attracted to slogans and concepts derived from the platform of Trotsky's International Left Opposition, precursor to the Fourth Inter-national he founded shortly before World War II. "Trotskyism" opposed the program of Stalin's Communist International, which called for Latin American workers to ally with the "national bourgeoisie" in a two-stage revolution (first "bourgeois-democratic," later "proletarian-socialist"). It gave theoretical grounding to the idea that Bolivia's mine proletariat could spearhead a class upheaval mobilizing the Indian peasantry in a decisive showdown (a "permanent revolution") with the "tin baron" elite and its Anglo-American backers.

The alliance that young POR activists forged in the 1940s with mine union leaders was a crucial element conditioning the impact of the Bolivian Trotskyist movement. The radicalism of their program, and their emphasis on the miners' leading role, struck a deep chord among workers in the nation's central industry. Bolivian Trotskyism was, moreover, a nationally specific ideology, which began by combining elements of *indigenismo* ("Indianism") with aspects of international Marxist thought.

After World War II, the growth in Trotskyist influence was often reported as an index of rising labor radicalism: "A crucial event took place involving Bolivia's miners' groups" in 1946, one U.S. historian wrote. "In a special congress held at Pulacayo, they adopted the Trotskyite philosophy of class struggle." From then on, "the lines were clearly drawn" between Bolivia's working class and the country's old regime. North America's preeminent Bolivia scholar, Herbert Klein, underlines that the Thesis provided the "official ideology" of the miners' union. Despite his antipathy to Trotskyism, Régis Debray notes that in Bolivia "the theory of permanent revolution gained authority and credibility with a large section of the workers' movement," calling the Thesis of Pulacayo "the Founding Charter" of Bolivian labor.[14]

However, this influence came at a price: fortifying the militant image of the labor wing of the Movimiento Nacionalista Revolucionario (MNR) of Víctor Paz Estenssoro. The objectives of this nationalist party were distant indeed from those of Marxian socialism. "Left" MNR spokesmen like Juan Lechín, legendary head of the Mine Workers Federation, played a double game.

The 1952 Bolivian Revolution was unleashed by miners, factory workers, and Indian peasants, the very forces in which the Trotskyists had placed their hopes. Soon, POR cadres found themselves in positions of leadership in the new nationwide labor federation and among peasants in Bolivia's breadbasket, the Cochabamba Valley. Under the impact of miners' mobilizations and peasant land seizures, the new government acceded to demands for the nationalization of the mines and an extensive land reform, seemingly echoing slogans the Trotskyists had raised since the time of the Chaco War. A year and a half after the April 1952 uprising, the Paris *Le Monde* ran a front-page headline: "The Bolivian Revolution between Wall Street and Trotsky."[15]

Yet the MNR, to which the miners' and peasants' leaders had turned over power, promised not to overstep the Cold War limits laid down by Washington. Soon enough the Revolution turned to the right, leading eventually to a new military dictatorship. Over the following decades Bolivia's history continued to be tumultuous, from Guevara's short-lived guerrilla struggle in 1967 and the revival of labor-based radicalism in 1970–71 to the hard-line dictatorship of Hugo Banzer, the "popular front" experiment of 1982–85, and then the MNR's return to power in its new role as paladin of neoliberalism on the altiplano.

As will be shown in the pages that follow, Bolivian Trotskyists played a significant role in each of these phases, contributing—in ways that would undoubtedly have surprised them when they set out on their path—to "state formation" in their country. To understand this history, we will examine patterns of political activity established before and during 1952. Continuing to play themselves out, these patterns led to the repeated frustration of popular aspirations and, with them, the objectives the Bolivian Trotskyists had set out to accomplish. This dénouement is a tragedy of missed opportunities. Nonetheless, if anything can be said with certainty about Bolivia's future, it is this: the story of its revolutions is far from over.

Trotskyism and Bolivian Culture

To situate Bolivia's radical tradition in its social context, we must question artificial distinctions between "proletarians" and "Indians." Since silver and then tin chained its fate to the world market, most of its proletarians have been of indigenous origin. While some distinguished themselves from *los indios*, most grew up in Quechua- or Aymara-speaking homes; many retained close links to family members in indigenous communities. During layoffs or political firings in the mines, radical mine unionists often returned to the countryside. As far back as the 1940s, these ex-miners played a central role in organizing peasant unions.

In Bolivia, as elsewhere, the history of class formation is embedded in language. The lexicon of mining is filled with English terms like "block caving" and "sink and float," together with Quechua and (to a lesser extent) Aymara words. A day's work is a *mita*, the Inca term for draft labor; a type of drilling is *huallpa-chaki* (chicken foot), ore-stealers are *jucos* (owls), job categories include *khoyanchos*, *makipuritas* (full- and part-timers), and *chasquiris* (from the Inca term for messenger). Events may require a *ch'alla* (offering) or *huajta* (cleansing ceremony), and breaks always involve *pijcheo* (coca-chewing).[16]

Listening to the miners' radio stations, which played a crucial role in strikes, protests, and resistance to military coups, one heard news in Quechua, Aymara, and Spanish; music of many descriptions; and scores from soccer teams like "El Club the Strongest de La Paz." Cultural syncretism is integral to miners' identity, as shown in the pioneering studies of June Nash. Llamas are sacrificed in the mines with the goal of increasing production and warding off accidents. Bolivian short story writer and memoirist René

Figure I.2 Left: Trotskyist miner Angel Capari, to left of effigy of El Tío, Siglo XX mine, 1980 (Courtesy of Angel Capari). Right: Meeting of Trotskyists at Siglo XX, early 1960s. On banner, portrait of Trotsky and symbol of Fourth International. (Courtesy of Cesar Escóbar)

Poppe—some of whose writings first appeared in the Trotskyist weekly *Masas* during the 1970s—draws the reader into the worldview of miners attuned to both "El Tío" and Trotsky (see figure I.2).[17]

Argentine activist/historian Adolfo Gilly recalled his surprise, during a political visit to Bolivia, when he learned that a Trotskyist union leader was missing an important meeting because he had to dance in the *diablada*, the "devil dance" performed by miners' fraternities in the Oruro Carnival. "In Oruro, the POR comrades were miners and railway workers," Gilly said. "Paulino Joaniquina was the leader of the San José mine. . . . One day, Paulino didn't show up because he was in the diablada. . . . Imagine that: a Marxist, a Trotskyist, in the diablada. I went to have a look, and there he was with his devil mask, jumping and dancing. . . . Paulino didn't dance because of the *entrada* [procession in honor of the Virgin], but because you have to dance in the diablada!" At one point the POR even had its own Carnival dance group in La Paz, Los Pacochis.[18]

In Bolivia, as elsewhere, miners' songs help transmit group memory. Today, market stalls throughout the country sell innumerable music videos of these songs, whose lyrics reflect the class-conscious radicalism of the milieu. The versions are sometimes traditional, sometimes updated with electric instruments and faster tempos. Accompanying images depict the mines, the workers, their tools, their marches and the massacres in which so many of them died.

Over the years, Trotskyist militants participated in creating or adapting such songs to commemorate historic milestones, from the Pulacayo Thesis to the Cuban Revolution, important strikes, or the murder of union and party activists.[19] Due to their role in labor struggles and national history, Trotskyists also appear in cartoons in the daily papers, satirical verses by popular singers, and television news programs. Not long before he became president, Carlos Mesa narrated a televised history of the Bolivian Revolution. He used one "talking head" more than any other: POR leader Guillermo Lora, featured both as a protagonist of the events and the foremost expert on them.[20]

Trotskyism took root in the artistic as well as political culture of Bolivia. Vibrant graphics were a crucial part of the movement's tradition, and mainstream culture also bore its imprint: the country's leading muralist, Miguel Alandia Pantoja, was also a leader of both the POR and the Bolivian Labor Federation (COB). One of the movement's founders (José Aguirre Gainsborg) was the grandson of the "father of Bolivian letters," Nataniel Aguirre; the other (Tristán Marof) was a prolific novelist as well as a pamphleteer. The movement's literary traditions also were embodied in the work of the noted writer Alfonsina Paredes, a cousin of the country's main *costumbrista* (author of vignettes on national customs), Antonio Paredes Candia. Sucre POR leader Agar Peñaranda, daughter of another famous man of letters, organized cultural *tertulias* (gatherings) frequented by the leading lights of music and the arts. As for the ever-prolific Lora, his writings include not only political and historical works but literary and art criticism, as well as a 600-page dictionary of politics, history, and culture.

Revolution and Collective Memory

History seemed to erupt through the earth's crust in the Gas Wars of 2003 and 2005, as workers and peasants faced off against the army and police in the colonial plazas of the capital. In Bolivia, the past is never far from the surface of the present. To put it another way, it refuses to remain in the past, as historical memory keeps entwining with daily life.[21] This was brought home in myriad ways wherever the research for this book took me, from the living rooms of Chaco War "defeatists" to the kitchen tables of "relocated" Trotskyist miners, the old age home where an old insurrectionist told of chairing the Pulacayo Congress, and the El Alto archive built from scratch by ex-miners who quite literally rescued from the garbage heap the priceless records of the nation's mining industry.

"The rich have stolen everything from us, all the way back to the Age of Silver" under the Spanish empire, a retired miner told me in the central square of La Paz during the 2005 revolt against President Mesa. In a middle-class neighborhood near the infamous San Pedro prison (where many of those interviewed for this study spent years behind bars), I witnessed another invocation of history and cultural tradition. "Remember the Tupac Katari rebellion!" a speaker cried out to the *vecinos* (residents):

> Today marchers have blockaded La Paz, and some people say we should not support them. But during the Tupac Katari rebellion [of 1781], the city was even more cut off than it is now. Some people said the *paceños* should be against the Indians and support the rulers of that time. But a *vecino* came out with his little statue of Ekeko [the pre-Inca deity of abundance]. You all give offerings to Ekeko, don't you? [His listeners nodded.] Well, people did back then too. So he said, "Who is the real Ekeko? The real Ekeko is the *campesino*, the Indian, who brings us our *chuño* [dried potatoes], our vegetables, our meat. He is the real god of abundance." And they all agreed. It is still true. Today we must support the *campesino* marchers, because the *campesino* is the real Ekeko.

The speaker's appeal to memory swayed the crowd; listeners called out, "Yes, he's right."

Collective memory has been crucial to the identity of Bolivian workers. As the leftist intellectual René Zavaleta wrote, the Bolivian proletariat developed "the best historical sense of any of the continent's working classes."[22] During the 2005 protests, miners addressing huge crowds in the central plaza often referred to mine workers' role in the 1952 Revolution, in battles against a grim procession of military dictators, and in the overthrow of the hated Goni in 2003. Seeing it as their own, huge crowds of peasants and slum dwellers applauded this history. Unionists from Huanuni marched near the Palacio Quemado (presidential palace), singing "We have returned!" As I watched them descend to the central plaza, a well-dressed elderly woman yelled to onlookers, "*¡Aplaudan, aplaudan, son los mineros, ellos son los que hicieron este país!*" (Applaud, applaud, it's the miners! They are the ones who made this country!)

The concept of "the memory of the working class" is of particular importance to Trotskyists, who (following Trotsky himself) see its highest expression in the formation of a revolutionary party. Precisely for this reason, social memory is a field of struggle and polemic with implications for the present and future. Participants in the events discussed in this book shared their personal recollections as elements in the collective work of remembering, viewing this as crucial to the different future they had given so much of themselves to make. What did they have to say about Trotskyism's impact on their country? When asked for a capsule explanation, they gave different kinds of answers. Amadeo Vargas was a leading activist for decades, but when we spoke in 2004 he was sapped by untreated diabetes and tired after a life of sacrifice. He wondered if Trotskyism might have taken root in Bolivia for the simple reason that "it was a novelty." This is not the view of former Potosí miner Julio García. Now the leader of the Bolivian Retirees' Association, he says: "The Trotskyist is respected because he understands revolutionary theory and gives the best orientation in the political struggle."

Retired miner Pastor Peláez, from Llallagua-Siglo XX, has a simpler explanation, at least for the origins of his own convictions. His father was a Chaco War veteran who died young, "leaving me in diapers." This was "because he got a sickness in the mine called silicosis," from breathing mineral-laden dust every day. "Poverty has always existed in this country, and that is what made me become a Trotskyist. It was the situation of the miners that made me have my revolutionary ideas."[23]

Organization

Interviews are the heart of this book, together with manifestos, letters, leaflets, and polemics dug out of public archives and private collections from El Alto to Palo Alto, Paris to Potosí. It begins with the origins of the radical tradition known as Bolivian Trotskyism and its role in shaping the generation that would carry out the National Revolution of 1952. The first chapter traces radicals' debates on the oppression of the Aymara and Quechua peoples, the revolutionary potential of indigenous miners and peasants, and the meaning of the social and political catastrophe touched off by the Chaco War.

The battle of ideas resonated powerfully in a society forced to question its own foundations. Defeat on the battlefield gave birth to a new revolutionary movement, whose fitful beginnings are discussed in the book's second chapter. During the early populist experiment known as "military socialism," Bolivian Trotskyism foundered, presaging the difficulties experienced by much of the Latin American left under populist regimes. "Refounded" in the provincial city of Cochabamba, it beat a path to the mines during and after World War II. The third chapter discusses Bolivian Trotskyism's bitter struggle to survive when a coalition of pro-Washington and pro-Moscow parties inaugurated a period of severe political repression.

In the crucial years preceding the 1952 Revolution, the POR authored the Pulacayo Thesis, was elected to Congress (and banished from it) as part of the Miners Parliamentary Bloc, and attempted to forge an "anti-imperialist front."

The alliances formed in this period helped shape the political contours of the National Revolution that broke out in 1952. The fourth chapter explores the complex role of the nation's most influential leftist movement in this new period of Bolivian history, when a decidedly bourgeois regime, born of an unmistakably proletarian insurrection, rested atop the bayonets of workers' and peasants' militias, proclaiming anti-imperialism while seeking (and gaining) Washington's favor. Entangled with these contradictions, Bolivian Trotskyism confronted the government as both adviser and antagonist. Quechua "ultra-leftists" brought revolution to the countryside, while many party leaders joined the MNR outright, and factional warfare engulfed the POR.

Bolivia's place in the Cold War is the background to the fifth chapter, which describes mass disillusionment with the MNR, struggles against U.S.-sponsored "structural adjustment," and the impact of the Cuban Revolution. Rebuilt with American dollars, mentored by the Pentagon as a new age of counterinsurgency was dawning, the army took power, made a "military-peasant pact" against labor radicalism, and drove the unions underground. Symbolizing, for many, the martyred heroism of the mine proletariat itself, Trotskyist workers paid a fatal price for resistance. It was in this deadly period that Guevara's guerrillas evoked solidarity from the miners, whom the military punished en masse on the bloody St. John's Night of 1967.

As Bolivian radicals debated the guerrilla warfare strategy, mass protests brought a short-lived opening in the political situation and the formation of the left-nationalist regime of Juan José Torres in 1970. The upsurge that followed, discussed in the sixth chapter, culminated in what some in the Trotskyist movement called "the first soviet of the Americas," only to be cut short when a new coup d'état helped inaugurate a refurbished "Southern Cone model" of repression, coordinated region-wide through the fearsome Operation Condor. POR leaders responded with an ill-fated attempt to unite leftists with the deposed Torres in a "Revolutionary Anti-Imperialist Front."

Through the experience of radical activists, the final chapter traces the convulsions of Bolivian society from the hard-line junta through the election of Evo Morales. A desperate hunger strike by radical miners' wives sparked mass protests against the dictatorship. After the savage interregnum of a surreal "cocaine junta," a popular front of nationalists and pro-

Moscow Communists took office, detonating a new explosion when it imposed austerity measures decreed by the International Monetary Fund. As twelve thousand miners occupied La Paz chanting "Workers to power," the permanent revolution seemed close at hand.

Instead, the labor leadership retreated, giving way to a right-wing backlash that inaugurated two decades of neoliberal rule. Faced with large-scale privatizations and stringent anti-union legislation, labor and the left underwent a painful process of recomposition and defensive struggles. New peasants' and slum dwellers' movements emerged, strongly influenced by the radical mine workers' traditions that Bolivian Trotskyism helped to shape.

In 2003 and 2005, miners, indigenous peasants, and slum dwellers launched new revolts that many participants believed were putting revolution on the agenda once again. This was averted largely through the intervention of Evo Morales, who channeled hopes for fundamental change into a landslide electoral victory. Announcing a "democratic and cultural revolution," his government promised moderation and stability. Instead, social polarization has continued, and regional conflicts threaten to pull the country apart. For Bolivian workers and peasants, the ideals expressed at Pulacayo remain to be realized.

Before taking up the story of this radical movement, a word is in order about my own sympathies: rarely would a historian decide on a project like this without having some of his or her own. I admire the courage, determination, and self-sacrifice shown by the activists of the Bolivian Trotskyist movement. Moreover, I am sympathetic not only to their ideals, but specifically to the concepts and program formulated by Leon Trotsky. This very sympathy heightens my duty as a historian to approach Bolivian Trotskyism with a critical eye (and in this book I use the term "Trotskyist" for those who called themselves that, even when they diverged significantly from the views Trotsky advocated). If solidarity is not to be an empty phrase, it demands critical thinking and learning from experience. The results are for the reader to judge.

Between Tupac Amaru and Trotsky

When Francisco Pizarro's conquistadors entered the altiplano in the late 1530s, the land they called Upper Peru was pushed into the world economy to produce a single commodity: silver. Indigenous miners dug a seemingly endless supply from the Cerro Rico (Rich Mountain) of Potosí. African slaves helped mint it, long providing much of Europe's coinage. The countryside furnished a plentiful supply of hands, through a system based on the Incas' *mita*, together with food, coca leaf, and draft animals (see figure 1.1). Miners learned that their labor made the colony a source of unimaginable wealth for kings across the sea. Yet the deeper they burrowed into the mountains, it seemed, the closer they got to hell. The centrality of their labor and the hellishness of their existence constituted a powerful contradiction.

When Bolívar's forces ended Spanish rule in 1825, they brought their triumph to Potosí. The Liberator, for whom the new country was named, climbed the mountain and made an impassioned speech, paying tribute to generations of miners. The new Republic would need them too, but it did not put an end to the inferno of life underground. Nor did it view Indians as citizens. As Florencia Mallon observes, "More than anywhere else in Latin America, except Haiti, it was in the Andes that the painful contradiction between nationalism's inclusionary promise and exclusionary practice earliest became clear." [1]

Even silver could not reign forever: as the nineteenth century drew to a close, world market prices collapsed. In 1883, national catastrophe arrived: defeated in the War of the Pacific, Bolivia lost its entire seacoast. With the ruling Conservatives disgraced, the Liberal Party mobilized Indian communities against its rivals, only to subjugate them without mercy or compunction

Figure 1.1 Mariátegui's *Amauta* often featured images of rural indigenous life. Bolivian radical Tristán Marof became a contributor to the journal. (Courtesy of Biblioteca y Archivo Histórico del Congreso)

once victory was won. Entrenched in power, the Liberal oligarchy inaugurated the new Age of Tin. Wars made the boom: increasingly, the great powers needed this baser metal to make armaments and can food for their troops. Bolivia had it in quantity, often in the same mountains that had yielded so much silver.

Indian Miners versus Tin Barons

By the early years of the twentieth century, tin was Bolivia's economic raison d'être. By 1929, Bolivia was one of four nations providing 80 percent of the world's supply, and tin represented almost three-quarters of its exports. The men who dug it from the mountains were concentrated in settlements on the high plateau, as Bolivia's lode mining system depended on a high "density" of workers.[2] Like silver before it, they knew the "devil's metal" meant misery and early death for them.

Amidst extremes of heat and cold, they wielded dynamite, picks, and heavy perforators, loading ore into heavy carts they pushed by hand. Accidents were frequent, often deadly; enveloped in clouds of dust, most succumbed to silicosis. One activist recalls that in the 1940s, when he first sought work in the Potosí mines, "it was rare for a miner to reach the age of forty." Six decades later, the *New York Times* reported: "By their 40's most are finished. Few live past 50. . . . Some 'older' miners, in their 30's and 40's, spend their last few months in the pulmonary wing [at the hospital], gasping for breath."[3]

The *mal de mina* (mine sickness) became a symbol for injustice, *escupir sangre* (spitting blood) a metaphor for exploitation. Son of a Potosí miner who died of silicosis, Grover Alejandro spent decades as a Trotskyist activist in the miners' union. His voice breaks when he quotes the old saying, *"Minero boliviano, venas de estaño, sangre de copagira"* (Bolivian miner, your veins are made of tin, your blood of the poisoned water in the mines). Oruro mine workers' leader Felipe Vásquez lay dying in a public hospital as he spoke quietly of his struggles for the Fourth International, laughing sometimes despite his pain. Exiled in Stockholm for the past three decades, Dionicio Coca marvels that he will soon reach the age of seventy: "We miners usually die before we're 40 or 45, like my father, who died of tuberculosis." How did he become a revolutionary? "Experiencing life in the mines, it's like you feel the class contradictions, that Marxist idea, with your own hands."[4]

In 1940 a miner earned half an American dollar in the average *mita* (day's work). Five years before the 1952 Revolution, his wages could buy only 20 percent of what a five-member family needed to live.[5] In the countryside, "white" landowners held Indian peasants in a system of personal servitude known as *pongueaje,* although some communities were able to fend off destruction of their *ayllus* (the kinship-linked socioeconomic units of Andean village life). For "modernizing" elites, Indians were the obstacle to progress. Excluded from suffrage on the grounds of illiteracy, they found public squares off-limits when they ventured into the cities. Newspapers routinely ran photos of Indians chained together, en route to jail for one or another infraction, together with warnings that the *indianada* (Indian horde) was poised to revolt.

At the top, a tiny sector voted, while an even more exclusive nucleus made the real decisions. Tin had reconfigured Bolivia's ruling sectors into a "ring"—*La Rosca,* in popular parlance—centered on the three principal tin companies, the politicians and newspapers they controlled, and the landowning interests with which they allied. "Tin barons" Simón Patiño, Mauricio Hochschild, and Carlos Aramayo depended on European and U.S. firms to process their tin—Bolivia had no smelters—and to market it, and the army to protect their power. Like loans to keep the treasury afloat, the weapons came from abroad.

For underground miners, solidarity is essential to survival. As a modern labor movement emerged, Bolivian miners, at the center of the nation's economy, began to see themselves as the advance guard of the laboring poor. Growing class consciousness was expressed in Spanish and Quechua songs like the still-popular Andean *huayño* dedicated to the *pobre obrero explotado,* the poor worker exploited by "capitalists without shame."

Just as "the mine proletariat synthesized the history of capitalism in Bolivia," a recent study notes, the industry tied together "other forms of exploitation," in the "countryside, haciendas, enterprises [and] mercantile circuits" (figure 1.2). While giving voice to an increasingly militant syndicalism, Bolivian miners remained in close touch with rural society. "I was in the mines," a Trotskyist sympathizer recalls, "but after all, we came from the countryside, so we kept in contact with the peasant *compañeros.*" What he learned in the miners' union helped him organize peasant unions after the 1952 Revolution.[6]

Nor did the miners lose touch with their pre-Columbian (and pre-Inca) roots. Ideological syncretism mirrored the cultural world of miners who prayed to the Virgin above ground before descending to the realm of "El Tío (uncle) of the Mines." Also called Supay, this deity requires regular tribute in coca, alcohol, and tobacco, was called *diablo* by the Spaniards, and is, in turn, intolerant of Christian symbols.

Figure 1.2 Mine owners' association ad, 1949: "Mineral production fuels Bolivia's economy!" (Courtesy of Biblioteca y Archivo Histórico del Congreso)

As in other parts of the world, the years at the close of World War I brought a wave of labor agitation. Factory and transport workers protested; miners launched strikes in 1917, 1918, and 1919. Matters came to a head in June 1923, when the army shot down striking miners at Uncía. This massacre became a symbol of government repression in the service of the mine magnates. Company documents show the Patiño firm paid for "the mobilization and feeding of the troops" and "dissolution of the [local union] Federation." The clash also became a symbol of miners' resistance, a landmark in their historical memory, and an important episode in their increasing politicization. By the time the old regime was finally overthrown, two decades after the Uncía Massacre, the "mine-workers had proved themselves to be the most powerful force in the country."[7]

The Early Communist Movement

How did this happen? Bolivian writer Víctor Montoya puts it this way: "As they spit out their lungs, hardened by silicosis, the miners knew the tin they extracted from the mountains' bowels came back to the nation converted into weapons and money, which the rich used for massacres and coups. Seizing the most advanced revolutionary doctrines, they fought to better their conditions, throwing themselves into harsh struggles that the rulers tried to drown in blood."[8]

The politicization of Bolivian workers followed a unique path. Like most of Latin America, the country was *terra incognita* for the Socialist, or "Second," International. Not until 1914 was an ephemeral Socialist Party founded in La Paz. Pioneering trade unionists—artisans, skilled tradesmen, women culinary workers, La Paz labor federation leaders—often identified with anarchism, and some of this influence undoubtedly rubbed off on mine union organizers. By the time the core of the Bolivian proletariat entered the field, however, anarchism was in decline in most of Latin America, and its Bolivian branch never reached the levels of allegiance and organization attained in Argentina, Mexico, and Brazil.

Under the impact of the Bolshevik Revolution, the 1920s saw the emergence of significant, sometimes powerful Communist parties in much of Latin America. In Bolivia, a number of groupings and individuals, generally from the anarchist milieu, were attracted to the Communist International (Comintern or CI). Several first encountered Communism as exiles in Chile. In Mexico, meanwhile, the exiled Bolivian writer Gustavo Navarro ("Tristán Marof") became a popular speaker at rallies of the Comintern-sponsored Anti-Imperialist League.

By 1926, Communist circles had formed in La Paz and other cities, and Comintern supporters were active in several unions as well as in locally limited, short-lived efforts to form socialist and labor parties. Most significantly, in 1929 the tailor Carlos Mendoza Mamani represented the La Paz labor federation (Federación Obrera del Trabajo; FOT) at the Comintern-sponsored Latin American Trade Union Conference in Montevideo.

Campaigning for unionization, secularization, and Indian rights, the FOT's journal *Bandera Roja* (Red Flag) combined the written word with bold, attention-grabbing graphics, setting a pattern for future publications of the Bolivian left. Some articles showed an anarchist bent, but others were close enough to the Comintern's line to be reproduced in its Latin American organ, *La Correspondencia sudamericana*. On the ninth anniversary of the Bolshevik Revolution, *Bandera Roja* featured a woodcut and biographical sketch of the organizer of "the great and powerful Red Army," Leon Trotsky. With striking naïveté, it reported that while "a small distancing" had occurred "between him and his fellow Soviet commissars," in a recent congress "all difficulties were resolved."[9]

Despite this rosy picture, Joseph Stalin had spent years making Trotsky's name anathema and rewriting the history of the Communist movement. Formed in 1923, Trotsky's Left Opposition was pitted against Stalin's doctrine of "socialism in one country," bureaucratization of the Soviet party, and the CI's alliance with such "bourgeois nationalists" as China's Chiang Kai-shek. The man *Bandera Roja* accurately described in 1926 as Lenin's comrade-in-arms would be deported less than three years later to Prinkipo, where he established the International Left Opposition, precursor of the Fourth International (see figure 1.3).

"In Bolivia, the Proletariat Is Indigenous"

In Bolivia, any serious radical movement had to come to grips with the subjugation of the indigenous majority. Although early Bolivian Communists faced intractable organizational obstacles, part of their legacy was an emphasis on programmatically addressing "the Indian question." This effort involved the Peruvian Marxist José Carlos Mariátegui, with whom Tristán Marof, later a founder of Bolivian Trotskyism, established a working relationship.

The facile presumption is too often made that Marxist movements overlooked "non-class" forms of oppression. In seeking to address the exclusion of Bolivia's indigenous peoples, the early Communist movement aimed to follow Lenin's dictum that a revolutionary party must be a "tribune of the

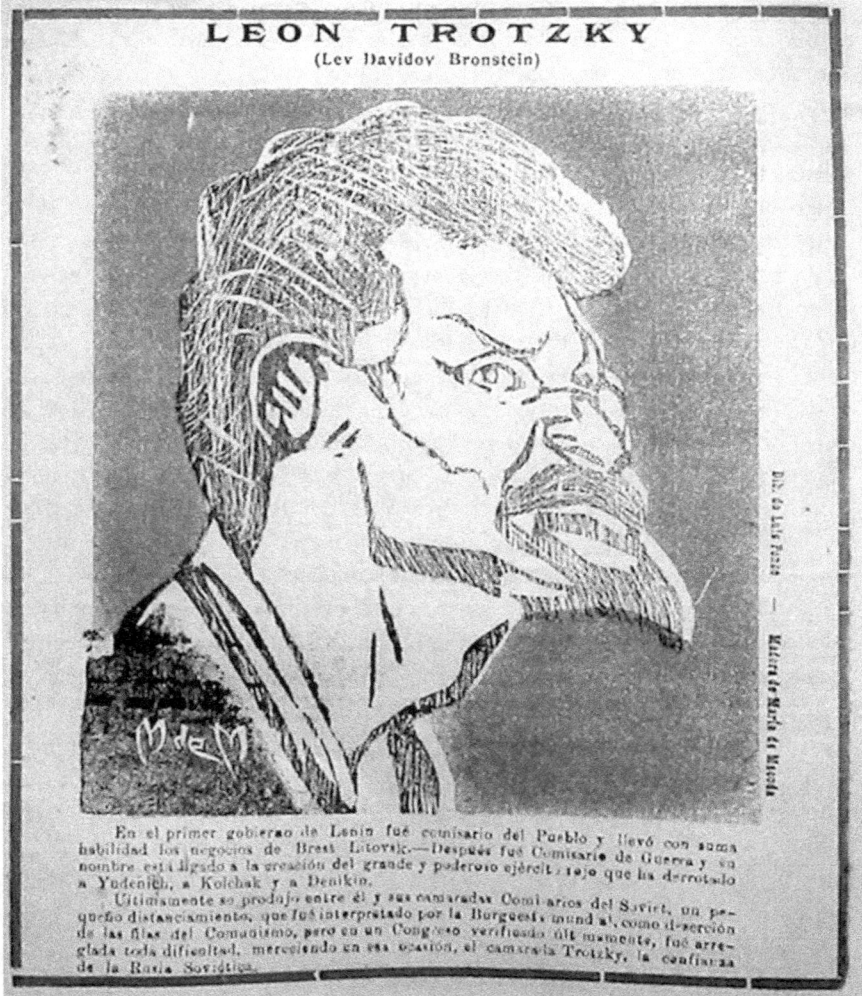

LEON TROTZKY
(Lev Davidov Bronstein)

En el primer gobierno de Lenin fué comisario del Pueblo y llevó con suma habilidad los negocios de Brest Litovsk.—Después fué Comisario de Guerra y su nombre está ligado a la creación del grande y poderoso ejército rojo que ha derrotado a Yudenich, a Kolchak y a Denikin.

Ultimamente se produjo entre él y sus camaradas Comisarios del Soviet, un pequeño distanciamiento, que fué interpretado por la Burguesía mundial, como deserción de las filas del Comunismo, pero en un Congreso verificado últimamente, fué arreglada toda dificultad, mereciendo en esa ocasión, el camarada Trotzky, la confianza de la Rusia Soviética.

Figure 1.3 Woodcut of Trotsky from *Bandera Roja*, 1926. (Courtesy of Biblioteca y Archivo Histórico del Congreso)

people," mobilizing the working class against all forms of oppression. Latin American CI spokesmen reported with pride that "our grouping in La Paz" emphasized "the Indian question, completely ignored by the 'left' intellectuals, downplayed and misunderstood by the anarchist intellectuals and . . . [non-revolutionary] union leaders." [10]

In 1928, the Comintern's Sixth World Congress noted that "Indian tribes play a very important role in the social structure of the Latin-American countries, especially in the Bolivian [i.e., Andean] countries." The 1929 Latin American Communist Conference called on the region's parties to overcome any "indifference . . . regarding the race issue in Latin America" and "devote all their energy to a conscientious study of the race question's characteristics in each particular country." In addition to discrimination against blacks in Brazil, it highlighted "the countries where the Indian question involves the great majority of the population: Mexico, Peru, Bolivia, Ecuador, Guatemala." "In Bolivia, where the economy is based on the mines," it noted, "the proletariat is indigenous."[11]

Mariátegui contributed a conference document on Latin America's "race question," written with Peruvian fellow Communist Dr. Hugo Pesce (whose later hospitality to Che Guevara was portrayed in *The Motorcycle Diaries*). The region's ruling classes "feel the same disdain toward Indians, blacks and mulattoes as the white imperialists do," they noted. "Racial solidarity, or prejudice, joins with class solidarity to make the national bourgeoisies docile instruments of Yankee or British imperialism. This sentiment extends to a large part of the middle classes, which imitate . . . this contempt for plebeian people of color, despite the fact that they themselves are *mestizos* [of mixed race]."[12]

In Bolivia, Peru, and Ecuador, the fact that the Indian population "is the basis of production and capitalist exploitation" is of "fundamental importance" for revolutionary politics, as "the *race* factor is intertwined with the *class* factor" and "the Quechua or Aymara Indian sees his oppressor in . . . the white man." Mestizos' "habit of disdain and repugnance toward Indians can only be destroyed by class consciousness." Yet even among "self-proclaimed revolutionaries," the authors noted, it is "not uncommon to encounter the prejudice that Indians are inferior."

If the revolutionary movement systematically trained "Indian propagandists," they continued, its program could "take root quickly among the indigenous masses." The urbanized Indian in danger of becoming "an auxiliary to those who exploit his race" would instead see "his own value as an instrument of emancipation of this race, oppressed by the same class that exploits the worker in the factory, in whom he will discover a class brother." Bolivian miners "constitute a strong Indian proletariat."[13]

At the 1929 conference, Bolivian delegate "Mendizábal" noted the "combative and courageous" spirit of his country's "rebellious" Aymara population. He described what indigenous people "have to put up with in our country": "Indians are put in a situation of complete inferiority toward whites, and are humiliated. For example, they have to . . . prostrate themselves in front of any white person. They cannot enter places where whites live. They are not allowed to use the same utensils, etc." [14]

The attempt to root Marxism in the indigenous reality of the Andes would be a central concern of the Bolivian Trotskyist movement that arose in the mid-1930s. This was manifested in slogans like *Tierras al indio* (land to the Indian) as well as in some of the names and symbols (such as Tupac Amaru and the Andean condor) it used in its formative period.

Absence of a Structured Communist Party

Bolivia proved to be a frustrating place for the Comintern, as its efforts to cohere groups of sympathizers into a stable, structured party repeatedly failed. At its 1929 Latin American conference, delegate Mendizábal stressed that to create "real revolutionary consciousness," it was necessary "in the first place to form a real Communist Party." Yet the body could report only the existence of a "sympathizing" organization in his country. In 1932, as Bolivia entered the Chaco War, the Comintern noted that its Communist movement was still "incipient," in the "beginnings of gestation." In 1934, CI supporters formed the Agrupación Comunista (Communist Grouping), as if to emphasize the absence of a genuine party, and the following year they formed a "Provisional Secretariat of Bolivian Communist Groups." These difficulties reflected Bolivia's isolation, relative "underdevelopment," and the geographical dispersion of the most important working-class nuclei. Repression also intervened, as the authorities mounted a series of "Communist trials" in the early 1930s. And while the CI wanted a section in Bolivia, it gave higher priority to Mexico and the "ABCs" (Argentina, Brazil, Chile). [15]

The absence of a stable, functioning Communist Party was one of the conditions for the rise of Bolivian Trotskyism, in contrast to the United States, China, France, Spain, and other countries where Trotskyism emerged when established Communist parties purged groups of cadres for sympathy with the Left Opposition. In those countries, Trotskyists tried to wrest the most radical sections of politicized workers away from established parties. In Bolivia, as the miners organized on a national scale, they entered the political field when no such hegemonic party of the left existed.

The party closest to Soviet "Stalinism" would be the Partido de la Izquierda Revolucionaria (PIR; Party of the Revolutionary Left), but the PIR was formed only in 1940. Bolivian workers were growing more militant, but by this time Stalin's followers had grown considerably less so under the Popular Front policy the Comintern inaugurated in the mid-1930s. With the approach of World War II, "in Bolivia as in Argentina," Alan Knight notes, "the Stalinist left joined in alliance with the pro-Ally (*ergo* 'democratic') oligarchy." When the PIR aligned with tin companies supplying this strategic metal to Moscow's allies, many miners viewed it as a craven handmaiden to their bosses. It is in this context that Whitehead makes his observation that the Trotskyists were "closer to the aspirations of Bolivian workers." [16]

The Chaco Cataclysm

"War is the mother of revolution," and Bolivia was no exception. Its Trotskyist movement arose amidst the worldwide turmoil of the Great Depression, Hitler's rise, and the regional conflicts prefiguring World War II. Strife reached Latin America when Bolivia and Paraguay faced off in the Chaco War (1932–35), a watershed in political, social, and cultural life. This conflict caused more casualties—100,000 Bolivian and Paraguayan dead—than any in the Western Hemisphere since the U.S. Civil War. Twenty-one thousand Bolivian soldiers were taken prisoner,[17] among them Miguel Alandia Pantoja, who would become the country's leading muralist and an influential Trotskyist. Creating the climate for "one of the most powerful, independent and radical labor movements in the Americas," [18] the war was a defining experience in the lives of many protagonists of Bolivia's 1952 Revolution.

Marking the death throes of the *ancien régime*, it gave birth to political parties that would play important roles in the ensuing period. The most powerful would be the Movimiento Nacionalista Revolucionario, but six years before the MNR's foundation (and five before that of the Stalinist PIR), the Trotskyist Partido Obrero Revolucionario was established as a direct consequence of the Chaco debacle.

The war's causes continue to be debated. The contested region was not merely inhospitable but virtually uninhabited. Two years before war broke out, an internal Comintern report noted: "In the Chaco Boreal, there is no population which can determine its own fate, as there is nothing but mosquitoes, crocodiles and oil." [19] Many came to believe that oil was the real prize, even that Bolivia and Paraguay were little more than stand-ins for Standard Oil and Royal Dutch Shell.

Bolivian historian René Zavaleta called the Chaco carnage "a kind of self-cannibalism" and "absurd . . . mass duel" between the losers of two nineteenth-century wars: those of the Pacific, when Bolivia lost its seacoast, and of the Triple Alliance, when Brazil, Argentina, and Uruguay devastated Paraguay. After Chile and Peru made a new and unfavorable territorial arrangement

Figure 1.4 Bolivian soldiers entering the Chaco, 1932. Second from left: Fernando Bravo. (Courtesy of Emma Bolshia Bravo Cladera)

in the late 1920s, another study notes, Bolivia "turned toward the Paraguay River as its most feasible outlet to the sea." The North American Trotskyist press observed at the time that while U.S.- and British-backed oil companies had a stake in the conflict, the Chaco's reported oil deposits were "of secondary importance." More relevant was Standard Oil's "virtual monopoly over the immense oil deposits of Bolivia proper," located "at the eastern base of the Andes [where] piping of the oil over a mountain range more than 11,000 feet high is too expensive to be a practical undertaking." For these deposits to be developed, the "natural outlet" was "by pipe line to some point on the Paraguay River, accessible to ocean steamers."[20]

Domestic politics provided further motives. As one founder of Bolivian Trotskyism told me, "When the United States sneezes, the countries of Latin America catch a cold. . . . With the economic crisis that began in 1929, many Bolivian workers came home from Chile," swelling the ranks of the unemployed. For Bolivia's president Daniel Salamanca, concerned that the resulting turmoil posed a "red threat," war served as a powerful antidote (see figure 1.4). POR founder José Aguirre Gainsborg wrote that the war served as a "platform for all the traditional parties seeking political advantage," while "the ingenuous chauvinist education of the people" contributed an additional "psychological factor."[21]

The first weeks and months were filled with the heady illusion of a quick and easy victory. Even leftist-minded youth were caught up in jingoistic fervor, as another future Trotskyist recalled: "We went out into the street to shout, 'On to Asunción! Asunción for the Bolivian army!' I remember one fellow going into the plaza and yelling, 'I'm a communist, but we have to go to the Chaco to defend the *patria* (fatherland)!'" Soon, however, Bolivian forces bogged down in the Chaco's "Green Hell." As one setback followed another, the government's failures began to be seen as a crisis of the old regime itself. As the promised lightning campaign turned into a demoralizing quagmire, Bolivia increasingly "lived the war as a defeat," embodying "the failure of the liberal republic, the violent, sudden frustration of [the nation's] association with imperialism."[22]

Instead of dampening the flames of discontent, the war wound up fanning them into a conflagration. Among the contradictions it laid bare, none was more glaring than the clash between Bolivia's traditional exclusion of the Indian majority and its reliance on ever-larger numbers of indigenous conscripts, who were "supposed to defend 'their fatherland' . . . which had always considered them either stateless or second-class citizens."[23] As thousands of peasants from remote villages were forcibly incorporated into national life, intellectuals, artisans, and laborers were radicalized by the evident bankruptcy of the ruling elite.

Ten years old when the conflict began, Eduardo Mendizábal remembers demobilized soldiers marching by, as well as "hiding behind my mother's skirt as she wrote letters for people with a brother or a husband in the army," who felt "the whole force of the war crashing down on the lower classes."[24] After decades as a Trotskyist militant, the memory is vivid still.

Aguirre Gainsborg and the "Defeatists"

As bellicose euphoria gave way to despair, the government lashed out at "agitators" and "communists" both real and imagined. Blaming subversives for the enormous number of deserters from the front (10,000 of whom sought refuge in Argentina) and war-weariness in the rear, it promulgated a "Law of Social Defense" and a state of siege. Sensational headlines denounced radicals for inciting rebellion among Indian villagers and planning an antiwar trade union congress in Montevideo, while trials made for lurid articles on "The Attempted Communist Conspiracy in the Army." In late 1932, a military court tried leftists charged with promoting communism in the armed forces and receiving "subversive letters" from exiled radical writer Tristán Marof (Gustavo Navarro). Tried separately in absentia,

Marof—soon to be a key founder of the Trotskyist movement—was sentenced to six years in prison.[25]

The government's fears were not entirely baseless. Small groups of Communist and anarchist sympathizers, sometimes joined by leftist labor groups, spoke out against the war. "On May Day 1932, I gave a speech in the main plaza in Sucre," an Indian lawyer recalled after the 1952 Revolution, in which he called the war "a stupid and evil business." Soon, "everyone was yelling 'Down with the war, down with the war! Long live the proletariat, long live the social revolution!'" The police intervened, "I spent two months in jail," and three of his brothers were sent to the front. A broader phenomenon was the growth of "defeatism" among young men drafted into the army. The daily press warned ever more stridently of the danger this represented. Indeed, Eduardo Arze recalled: "In the Chaco, anybody considered a communist, any student, could be condemned to death. . . . It was very simple: give them a dangerous assignment, send them to a place where the Paraguayan soldiers were deployed, and that would be that."[26]

"Defeatism" had a specific meaning in the Communist movement, based on Lenin's dictum: "During a reactionary war a revolutionary class cannot but desire the defeat of its government."[27] Bolivia's press used the term for anything from "demoralization" about the prospects for victory to explicit condemnation of the government's objectives. More a milieu than an organized opposition movement, "defeatists" were mainly youth in an early, ideologically undefined stage of rebellion. Increasingly, however, they saw the war as a symptom of deeper problems in Bolivian society. Among them were young intellectuals who would help found the Trotskyist movement.

A few "defeatists" were already committed revolutionaries when the government targeted them for repression, most importantly José Aguirre Gainsborg, grandson of the social novelist Nataniel Aguirre and son of a diplomat who became Education Minister in Hernando Siles's nationalist government. Born in 1909, the young Aguirre attended the Instituto Americano in La Paz, a high school established by North American Methodists, where Siles's son Hernán—who became José's political associate and eventually president himself—also studied.[28] When Latin America's university reform movement reached Bolivia in the late 1920s, Aguirre became labor liaison secretary of the La Paz Student Federation and then secretary of relations for Cochabamba's University Student Federation.

Bolivian writer Porfirio Díaz Machicao describes meeting Aguirre not long before the outbreak of the Chaco War. "Vibrant, ardent" and blue-eyed, with the broad forehead of a "dreamer," he emanated both brilliance and simplicity. Aguirre, Díaz, and their friend Guillermo Viscarra moved into an old house in the Cochabamba countryside, where they lived "like Franciscan monks," "practicing vegetarianism and sun therapy . . . reading the new Russian writers out loud." Using charcoal from the stove, Aguirre drew a huge portrait of Lenin.

They "visited labor unions to give friendly chats," met with workers "at night, by candlelight in their humble homes," and, after dancing the *cueca* with women cooks in La Paz, helped them set up their own labor union. Bolivia's bourgeoisie would "pardon us for everything except leading their cooks astray," since "it's bad news when the Social Revolution walks in through the kitchen." Neighbors began to call the young men "communists, enemies of God" who "don't love the *patria*."[29]

Aguirre reportedly joined a clandestine Communist organization in 1930, and in early 1932, during a Cochabamba labor federation protest against the war, gave a speech so "energetic and vibrant," according to a local journal, that bystanders "applauded wildly." In response to such protests, Aguirre later wrote, the "repressive apparatus" sought to "crush . . . revolutionary thought and organization." Arrested under the state of siege, he was sentenced to "confinement" in a small mining village because, the Interior Ministry explained, "at this extremely delicate moment in international affairs, he is making communist propaganda and seeking to carry out acts of defeatism openly counterposed to Bolivian patriotism."[30]

Aguirre was eventually transported to La Paz with Viscarra, future PIR leader Ricardo Anaya, and Díaz, who recalls: "We defeatists arrived in La Paz. Broad, hungry and Satanic, the prison doors opened. . . . The sounds reached the [cells] where we were growing numb: '¡Abajo el Paraguay!' The wave grew, answering with fury: '¡Abajo!' José Aguirre Gainsborg and Ricardo Anaya read. Viscarra took long drags from his cigarette. The screams of the mob ebbed and flowed. . . . Blindfolded, the unfortunate Bolivian people were being taken to the slaughterhouse." An officer requested that President Salamanca send the prisoners to the Chaco to be shot "on the field of battle," but Díaz and others were sent into internal exile, where they were greeted with cries of "Death to the defeatists! Death to the traitors!" As for Aguirre Gainsborg, his family convinced the Chilean government to accept him as a political exile.[31]

In Chile, under the pseudonym M. Fernández, Aguirre joined one of the hemisphere's oldest and deepest-rooted Communist parties, soon becoming a member of its Central Committee. The Bolivian revolutionary had arrived at a crucial juncture, as the party was in the process of splitting between a "Stalinist" wing and a large dissident faction led by Manuel Hidalgo and sympathetic to "Trotskyism." When police broke up a clandestine party congress, "the debates continued in jail." Siding with the "Hidalguistas," Aguirre was expelled from the party for "refusing to abide by [its] decision" to ban "hostile" activity and "Trotskyist propaganda."[32]

In March 1933, the dissidents formed a new organization called Izquierda Comunista (Communist Left), choosing the same name as the group in Spain led by Comintern veteran Andrés Nin, then the foremost voice of the Left Opposition in the Spanish-speaking world. Assigned to write "theses" on the Chaco War, Aguirre called for a "plan of effective action" uniting workers throughout the region. Applying concepts from the Bolsheviks' struggle against World War I, he wrote: "Every blow that the working class delivers to the bourgeoisie of Argentina and Chile will become not only a blow against the Chaco War, but support to the workers of Bolivia and Paraguay, who must reverse the terms of the present struggle by turning it into a war against their own bourgeoisies." Criticizing South American Stalinists for "tailing behind" the Chaco events instead of posing precise slogans, he denounced the Soviet government for promoting illusions in the League of Nations while declaring that it would allow weapons for Bolivia to be transported through its territory.[33]

Aguirre's Chaco War writings are the pioneer documents of Bolivian Trotskyism. Exiled revolutionaries were gaining invaluable "international experience," he noted, raising hopes for "a Bolivian section of the nascent Fourth International," given the "degeneration . . . of Stalinism on an international scale." Commenting on a letter from the Chaco by "Comrade Keswar" (Alipio Valencia), he stated: "The comrades of Bolivia and Paraguay can count on our internationalist collaboration: the clear and consistent path of the Fourth International."[34] Sadly, neither clarity nor consistency would characterize Aguirre's path in the few years remaining before his untimely death.

From the Izquierda Comunista to the Izquierda Boliviana

If Aguirre Gainsborg was the first to introduce Trotskyism to Bolivia, it is important to see what kind of organization introduced Aguirre to Trotskyism. The political confusion of early Bolivian Trotskyism may be traced in part to Aguirre's formative experiences in the Izquierda Comunista (IC). The Chilean IC was one of the movement's two "foremost Latin American sections" (the other was the sizable group in Cuba), reported Mexican co-thinkers in 1934, "strongly linked to the masses, occupying a front-line position in workers' struggles." The IC led important construction and peasant unions; Hidalgo had been elected to the Chilean Senate and another IC leader to the House of Representatives. Hidalgo was so popular, in fact, that the *Herald Tribune* claimed he might win the presidential elections.[35]

Yet despite its declared sympathy with Trotsky, the IC's adherence to the platform of Trotsky's International Left Opposition was far from clear. Like its Iberian namesake, the Chilean group was far more conciliatory toward "reformist" leaders than the international movement considered permissible. These included spokesmen for moderate socialist currents and followers of the "military socialist" Marmaduke Grove, a picturesque adventurer who decreed a short-lived "Chilean Socialist Republic" after a June 1932 military coup. In fact, the Communist Party's resolution expelling Aguirre accused him of seeking a "united front" with "Grove, [liberal ex-president] Alessandri, Hidalgo, etc."[36]

In 1935 the Izquierda Comunista joined the Left Bloc, immediate predecessor to Chile's Popular Front, one of whose spokesmen was future president Salvador Allende. The International Secretariat of the world Trotskyist movement noted that "the disagreements with the Chilean comrades" were "analogous to those with the Spanish comrades," who broke with the international movement and soon joined Spain's Popular Front.[37] For Trotsky, the Popular Front was an instrument of class collaboration; to join it meant preparing the victory of right-wing reaction. The breach was permanent: the Chilean IC dissolved into the Socialist Party, with a small group splitting off to remain loyal to the Trotskyist movement.

Aguirre began to organize a Bolivian group while he was still a member of the Chilean IC. His first recruit was a young Bolivian studying in Santiago, Eduardo Arze. Having met Aguirre once, before coming to Chile, Arze recognized him on the street. They became close friends, and Aguirre decided to share Arze's lodgings. "We shared very meager meals," Arze recalled decades later, and "discussed what we should do, what was going to happen with Bolivia. The war would finish the traditional parties. . . . Socialism was the only way. So we studied it."

Soon enough, "We decided to organize a communist party. How? With a manifesto." Before long, Arze was arrested, so all their revolutionary literature must "still be in Santiago's Investigaciones (secret police) files." Most of the propaganda was written by Aguirre, and the two called their exile group Izquierda Boliviana, seeing it as "the first step toward a party." Yet something was lacking: "we needed a leader . . . someone with enough prestige, whom we could trust. And so Aguirre, who was a Don Quixote, said . . . Tristán Marof."[38] This decision would be fateful indeed.

Caudillo in a Red Cravat

The author of a biographical pamphlet on José Aguirre Gainsborg believes his "great error was to make Tristán Marof the head of the new party, with the misguided idea of capitalizing on his prestige as a 'fearsome revolutionary.' . . . The entire revolutionary movement has paid very dearly for this mistake." [39] Marof was certainly famous: Aguirre had written political theses for small leftist publications, but Marof was a celebrated author. Today, the U.S. Library of Congress calls him "Bolivia's most important Indianist." From 1928 to 1940 he was "Bolivia's best-known socialist leader," his name becoming a "synonym for social revolution and national liberation," especially after his military trial in absentia for Chaco War "defeatism." [40]

Herbert Klein notes that as "the outstanding figure among the older generation of extreme radicals, [Marof] combined a strong current of European Marxism with a deep commitment to American *indigenismo*." Yet far from "a scientific political militant," he was "an adventurous novelist with a flair for pamphleteering." The model of a romantic "red," with his pipe and beard, red cravat, and long record of voyages and exiles, it is said that in his native Sucre, pious women would cross themselves and mutter *"Supay chayamushan"* (here comes the devil) when they saw him coming down the street.[41] This prolific and talented writer was also an indefatigable self-promoter whose works often dwelt on his own adventures. Nonetheless, they allow us to trace the development of key themes in the Bolivian radical tradition, and this path will soon take us back to Aguirre, Arze, and their quest for revolutionary leadership in the struggle against the Chaco War.

Tristán Marof was the pen name of Gustavo Adolfo Navarro. Almost a decade older than Aguirre Gainsborg, he was born in Sucre in 1898, the son of a lawyer and military officer. His literary career began early: by the age of nineteen he was publishing a journal called *Renacimiento altoperuano* (Upper Peru [Bolivian] Renaissance). After a tour of South America, he published a pamphlet on the continent's "Poet-Idealists and Idealisms," with a prologue by the Chilean poet Gabriela Mistral. In a text no less lyrical than its title, he "exalts" the Cuban José Martí, the Peruvian Manuel González Prada, and Bolivian "masters" such as the politicians Daniel Salamanca, Bautista Saavedra (both of them future presidents) and Franz Tamayo. An important literary figure, Tamayo is praised as "a cultural representative of the genuinely American race." [42]

Together with "Americanist" nationalism, the pamphlet voices a theme that would be central in Marof/Navarro's work: idealization of the pre-Columbian past. It reprints his lecture to the Domingo Sarmiento Society (ironically named after Argentina's preeminent anti-Indian ideologue), on "The Concept of American Civilization among the Quechua." Here Navarro speaks of the Inca Empire's supposed "communism," "carried out with ineffable sweetness and strategic suavity," an example for "all those who suffer today, whose impoverished fists pound the gates of capital." [43]

"Ineffable sweetness" was not the order of the day when Navarro, then twenty-two, became part of another tradition: the coup d'état, joining the July 1920 "revolution" of Republican Party caudillo Bautista Saavedra. Navarro co-authored a "chronicle" of the coup, later reminiscing that "Don Bautista chose me to carry out a number of difficult roles." In 1921, he was named Bolivian consul in Italy and Belgium. The turmoil of postwar Europe, where the Russian Revolution reverberated powerfully, deepened his interest in radical ideas. In 1922 he published a volume on "The Naïve American Continent," which he later called "a harsh . . . critique of South American society," featuring a foreword by renowned French leftist Henri Barbusse. Soon thereafter he came out with a picaresque satire, *Suetonio Pimienta*— pseudo-memoirs of a diplomat from the "Republic of Zanahoria"—under the exotic, Franco/Russian-tinged *nom de plume* Tristán Marof. In a 1928 review, Miguel Ángel Asturias called the book a hilarious slap in the face to pretentious Latin American diplomats. [44]

Marof was now moving in the circles of Latin American intellectuals who discovered their own continent abroad. Attending the 1925 Paris conference of the "Latin American Union" with the Guatemalan Asturias, the Mexican José Vasconcelos, the Peruvian Víctor Raúl Haya de la Torre, and others, he joined the confraternity of intellectuals who spoke of the true American race and the unification of Hispanic America. [45] Vasconcelos's *Cosmic Race* was published that year, and Haya de la Torre had just founded his American Popular Revolutionary Alliance (APRA), which mixed Marxist-flavored rhetoric, nationalist goals, and romanticization of "Indo-American" roots.

In July 1928 the local Communist paper *El Machete* reported Marof's impassioned speeches to meetings of the Comintern-inspired Anti-Imperialist League in Mexico City, where he joined Cuban revolutionary Julio Antonio Mella, and the brother of Nicaraguan rebel Augusto Sandino, in whose honor the "Corrido de Nicaragua" was sung. Further color was added by former Hungarian president Count Károlyi and the ever-flamboyant Diego Rivera. Marof later said the muralist "liked to lie a lot, and painted with a .45 pistol sticking out of his pants." After Rivera's then-wife Lupe took Marof rowing at Xochimilco, "Diego tried to scare me with the pistol but . . . Lupe told me he'd never fired a shot."⁴⁶

A key connection was the one Marof made with Peruvian Marxist Mariátegui. "Beginning with Manuel González Prada . . . and flowing . . . into the original Peruvian socialism of José Carlos Mariátegui," Florencia Mallon notes, "a strand of radical thought in the first half of the twentieth century looked for inspiration in the deep traditions of Andean peasants and their collectively organized communities." Given that "the masses—the working class—are four-fifths Indian," Mariátegui insisted, "our socialism would not be Peruvian—nor would it be socialism—if it did not establish its solidarity principally with [the demands of] the Indian." Much the same could be said of Bolivia. Equally relevant was Mariátegui's observation that "antiimperialism cannot, in itself, constitute a political program," as it "does not annul the antagonism between classes." Thus, "our mission is to . . . demonstrate to the masses that only a socialist revolution can oppose the advance of imperialism with a real, definitive barrier."⁴⁷

The claim that Marof "anticipated Mariátegui's . . . ideas on Indians' role in the social revolution" is debatable, but when the two met in Lima in 1927, the Peruvian was impressed. This "Don Quixote of American politics and literature," he announced, was "born to make history." In a less serious vein, "apropos of Tristán Marof's beard," Mariátegui promised to develop a "theory of the beard" and its functions in different historical epochs. Soon, Marof was contributing articles on politics, economics, literature, and art to Mariátegui's influential journal Amauta. One, with the impassioned vagueness that often characterized his writing, argued that "only a group of fanatics, lovers of the people" could do away with the "colonial mentality," "ignorance," and "archaic" structures of Bolivian society; only "an essentially revolutionary youth" could "rouse the masses from their obscurantism and slavery." Another affirmed: "Our America, fertile in blood and forces, is a field of experiences which will give rise to a new civilization."⁴⁸

Back home, Marof's "Inca Justice" manifesto was one of the popular writings that attracted Bolivian youth to leftist ideas. Its motto "Land to the people, mines to the state"—alternately formulated as "Land to the Indian, mines to the state"—was soon adopted by other Bolivian radicals. A 1927 workers' congress in Oruro was the first of many to take up this "magic formula." Peppered with some references to Marx and Lenin, La justicia del Inca espoused an isolationist nationalism while proclaiming that "the honestly communist idea is nothing new in America": the Incas had practiced it "with the greatest success," forming "a happy people surrounded by abundance." The task was to "organize the last descendants of the Inca and return to

Figure 1.5 Two views of Tristán Marof in the 1930s. Portrait of Marof (Courtesy of Archivo y Biblioteca Nacionales de Bolivia) and caricature of Marof seated. (Courtesy of Biblioteca y Archivo Histórico del Congreso)

fraternity." Thus, Marof presented an outlook akin to utopian socialism, not with the intricate blueprints of Fourier's phalansteries, but in the regal attire of Manco Cápac, mythic founder of the Inca dynasty. "For emotional reasons," he "interpreted Marx with the idea that Bolivian communism should be a continuation of the Inca empire," notes historian Juan Albarracín. Yet for Marx, preindustrial life was "not an 'idyllic society,' 'golden age' or 'happy era' of mankind . . . and could not be the model for any modern society to which one should aspire." Marof's terminology shows he was more "a populist leader of the day than an orthodox Marxist." [49] (See figure 1.5.)

In 1927, Marof ran on the ticket of the short-lived Partido Socialista and joined other radicals in supporting a rebellion by Indian ayllus in the Sucre region. Mariátegui's *Amauta* reported that he had "taken up [the] arduous task" of bringing together Bolivia's disparate but "valuable revolutionary forces." The government claimed that Marof and a "Council of Ten" union leaders and leftists were hatching a "communist plot" to seize power. Joined by the leftist journal *Bandera Roja* (which the government soon closed down),

Marof denounced this as a fabrication.[50] Undeterred, the government exiled him to Argentina. Over the next ten years, his exile odyssey would take him to Panama, Mexico again, Cuba, Peru, Brazil, and other countries, then back to Argentina, before he returned to Bolivia in 1937.

Exile brought Marof closer to the international left, as he returned to the pages of *Amauta* to argue that mine nationalization must be "a revolutionary phenomenon," not the action of "governments interested in upholding a parasitic minority," like that of Bolivia, where democracy was a "fiction." Briefly, he served as "Latin American Anti-Imperialist Editor" for the New York *Labor Defender*, organ of the Communist-led International Labor Defense. In a column on a bitter textile strike in Gastonia, North Carolina, where the "proletariat—black and white—are together fighting against their exploiters," Marof voiced the hope that "the American proletariat will fight with greater impetus than in any other part of the world." He wrote too of "the Indian workers of Bolivia"—"A brilliant past is theirs. The Incas were their forefathers"—and warned of war between Bolivia and Paraguay, in which "those who will pay dearly will be the workers and peasants who will go, fooled or by force, to defend territory for foreign companies."[51]

By now, Marof had aroused considerable interest within the Comintern. The Communists he worked with in Mexico hoped to send him to the Lenin School for Cadres in Moscow and were acutely disappointed when he traveled to Argentina instead. When Mexico expelled him as a "subversive" in 1930, one of its diplomats in the USSR wrote that "the Soviet press has been reporting on the expulsion of foreigners, citing, among others, the writer Tristán Marof." The next year, Marof published *Wall Street y hambre* (Wall Street and Hunger), a lively *novela picaresca* about a Latin American leftist's adventures in New York, describing the customs (real or invented) of the city's immigrant and African American residents, Ellis Island officials, "Irish cops," "agile and skinny poor Jews," bars, 42nd Street "fairy shows," flophouses, and Communist headquarters. Like many of Marof's books, it cultivates his own myth: the introduction compares his beard to Christ's and his hands to those of El Greco, lauding the author as an "artist, revolutionary, and citizen of the world."[52]

Marof's next book sought to draw lessons from the Mexican Revolution. In correspondence with Mariátegui, he argued: "Mexico stands at the head of our countries. . . . We have to make a revolution very similar to the one Mexico carried out in 1910; perhaps ours will have greater social content and a broader overall vision, but this is only the result of experiences obtained from Mexico." Building on this idea, *México de frente y perfil* (Portrait of Mexico) combined descriptions of Mexico's politics, economics, and culture with a radical critique of the frustration of the Revolution by Mexico's "bourgeois" regime. Criticizing "narrow nationalism," he declared that the "only party which can lead the masses to final victory, without compromises with the bourgeoisie or deals with imperialism, is the communist party." He criticized Latin American Communists, however, for "putting forward slogans that are not clearly understood by the masses" and appearing to imitate "all that comes from Europe." Mexico had "given the Latin American proletariat an invaluable lesson": in "the Americas as in China . . . , the proletariat that does not know how to maintain its independence of action" will "awake to find itself betrayed and subjected to a harsher oppression." Still, revolutions in the Americas would not be "strictly communist." First the masses must destroy "the feudalist regime" and "annihilate foreign imperialism as far as possible," even "inaugurate governments of workers, peasants and soldiers." Yet "all this does not mean carrying out a 'socialist revolution'," the "historic destiny" which the proletariat would fulfill at some later time.[53]

Marof's schema was closer to early-1930s variants of Stalin's "two-stage" revolution (first against "feudalism" and imperialism, later against capitalism) than to Trotsky's theory of permanent revolution. For Latin American Trotskyists, the Mexican experience validated this theory, as did the disaster that occurred when Stalin subordinated Communists to Nationalists in China. In Trotsky's view, "tasks" like liberating the nation from imperialist control, emancipating the rural population from landlord domination, and overcoming the oppressed majority's disfranchisement could be carried through only by the proletariat seizing power, led by a genuine communist party and supported by the poor peasants. Yet a "workers' and peasants' government" could not maintain power unless it expropriated the capitalist class and extended the revolution to the richer, dominant capitalist countries. (For further explanation, see Appendix.)

The Grupo Tupac Amaru and the Chaco War

As the Chaco War approached, Marof the Bohemian radical declared himself a Marxist-Leninist but operated outside of Comintern control. Still, relying more on evocative language than programmatic clarity, his political conceptions remained distant from Trotskyism.

It was Marof's activity during the war that would lead José Aguirre Gainsborg to propose an alliance to build a new party. Around the beginning of the war, Marof and other Bolivian exiles established the Grupo Tupac Amaru (GTA) in the northern Argentine city of Córdoba, "publishing

manifestos that reached the ranks of Bolivian and Paraguayan combatants."
The GTA was "the most important link between the pre-war radical left in
Bolivia and the post-war groups," Klein states, with a network of agents able
to distribute its appeals on the front lines. Guillermo Lora tells the story of
the student draftee Raúl de Bejar, who "entered the history of the Bolivian
left as a mythic character." Bejar was executed in December 1932 after officers discovered a notebook in which he had written: "Fortunately, up until
now I have not fired at any Paraguayan brother." It is said that after digging
his own grave, he stood before the firing squad shouting, "Long live the
socialist revolution! Long live the Grupo Tupac Amaru!"[54]

Aguirre wrote that in addition to Marof, the GTA was led by "comrade
Ivan Keswar, who is equally deserving of our confidence and has had important experience at the front." Keswar (Alipio Valencia) became a leftist as
a university student before being drafted into the army and then deserting.
Another GTA leader was Luis Peñaloza, a former army lieutenant who also
deserted and years later became a leader of the MNR. In a manifesto for
May Day 1932, the GTA denounced "landowners, bosses and exploiters"
who, in "partnership with foreign capital, exploit Bolivia like an hacienda."
It called on "the united proletariat, organized under the eye of a trained
vanguard," to "lead the masses to the genuine revolution." The document
continued to occupy a programmatic no man's land somewhere between
indigenism and Stalin's "two-stage" schemas:

> At first, the revolution must confine itself to the latifundia [landed
> estates] and the elimination of feudalism . . . giving land to the Indi-
> ans, using their communities as cells to build vast agricultural estab-
> lishments using the most modern techniques . . . instructing and edu-
> cating the Indians, the basis of our nationality and 85 percent of our
> population, in a socialist way; nationalizing the mines and exploiting
> them scientifically for the benefit of the Republic, reviving the coop-
> erative feeling cut short by the Spanish conquest, and making Bolivia
> a country for all those who labor, without distinction of classes and
> castes; establishing fraternal links with the proletariat of the Americas
> and the world, as the anti-imperialist agrarian revolution could con-
> ceivably win the sympathy of the great powers.[55]

As a "soldier" of the GTA, in 1934 or early 1935 Marof published one
of his most influential works, *La tragedia del altiplano* (The Tragedy of the
Altiplano), which declared: "We fight to transform the war . . . into revolution, with a social character, to tear down four centuries of slavery borne
by the Indian people of Alto Peru [Bolivia], under the various colonial
and republican regimes." Demonstrating Marof's talents (and limits) as a

radical publicist, the book cataloged the ills of Bolivian society, appealing to a generation awakening to political life under the impact of the war. It features an "Open Letter" to Bolivian workers, stating: "The Chaco lands are a shameful trap laid by the rulers of Bolivia and Paraguay in order to lead to their death two valiant peoples, whose energy and courage should be used to free themselves from all imperialist tutelage." The proletariat will "spill its blood for nothing, and the soil of the Americas will be covered with spoils, misery and tears" unless the working class "learns to rebel in time, with audacity and energy." The text ends with a call to action:

> This absurd war presents the proletarians of Bolivia and Paraguay with a series of questions. They have the arms in their hands and can rebel. The bayonets should be plunged not into the chest of their exploited brother, but of the exploiter. Bolivians and Paraguayans have a destiny to fulfill if they know their own interests.
>
> There is no reason to waver. War on behalf of the imperialist masters means a slaughter of those who are most wretched. The rich do not fight. The war is a business for arms dealers and food provisioners. The imperialists are preparing a banquet with the skin of Bolivians and Paraguayans. [The rulers of both countries] are entrepreneurs of death, trading soldiers' valor and heroism on the stock exchange.
>
> The proletariat of both countries can shed its blood only for its freedom and economic independence. Its struggle can have one goal: to strip the feudal lords of their privileges and expel the foreign companies from both countries.
>
> Down with this criminal war! Long live insurrection and the establishment of councils and committees of workers, students, peasants and soldiers![56]

The book includes a declaration of principles of the GTA. Composed of "students, intellectuals, workers, soldiers and indigenous people," the group sought to "see its country free of all slavery and subjection to foreign imperialism" through a "proletarian and anti-imperialist revolution . . . to give freedom to the oppressed, land to the Indians, and destroy the barbarous feudalism that still exists on the Bolivian *altiplano*." The text explained the group's name (while confusing the Tupac Amaru revolt of Lower Peru with the 1781 siege of La Paz led by Tupac Katari):

> [The GTA] has taken the name of that great Indian, so strong and audacious, who paralyzed the city of La Paz for 159 days, leading 200,000 Indians in revolt with the goal of regaining their lands. He was the

first to understand the rights of his class under Spanish domination. Today, insurrection is required not only against the domestic landowning master, but against the imperialist finance capital that backs him, resolutely fighting until we tear Bolivia away from their yoke and its inferior position as a colonial country.

The declaration calls on "the working classes, students and soldiers, professionals and small business people, miners and indigenous people, to . . . organize in a united front, forming the 'Workers Party of Bolivia,'" and ends with the slogan "VICTORY OR DEATH."

The document is noteworthy for its calls to "constitute the first socialist government in South America" and to "destroy" the "Bolivian army that serves the imperialists and the feudal class," replacing it with an "army of the revolution . . . in the service of the working class." *La tragedia del altiplano* urged radicals to speak to indigenous peoples "in their own language," advocating struggle against their ethnic, cultural, linguistic, and economic oppression, within the framework of social revolution. Landed estates would be "distributed among the soldiers and indigenous people, forming large communities, using the broadest techniques, so that the Quechua, Aymara and mestizo peoples may form their free organizations, develop their life and elevate their culture." The old order "must be destroyed by the Indians themselves, allied with . . . artisans in the cities, students and the proletarians of the mines." Indians needed to "strengthen their community organizations, coordinate their links, establish contacts between those of the north and the south, between Quechuas and Aymaras, elect their representatives to workers' congresses and follow a single line of conduct." What would happen to Bolivian capitalists' property in a revolution against what Marof called "feudal" society remained unclear. The indigenous population is described as a single "class" (to which the noble Tupac Amaru apparently belonged). The GTA is called "national in its methods of work" and, vaguely, "international in its relations."[57]

I have dwelt at some length on Marof's ideas for two reasons: they synthesized concepts and slogans that profoundly influenced political thinking in subsequent years, and they manifested contradictions that shaped Bolivian Trotskyism during its gestation. The GTA's publications were building blocks of the leftist regroupment that arose from the Chaco disaster. Marof's *Tragedia* proclaimed: "The Chaco War is the liquidation of the old, feudal, cacique-dominated Bolivia, so long as there is courage and decisiveness among the soldiers, students and workers; so long as a proletarian vanguard, prepared and energetic, arises amidst the pain and the blood." Among "Bolivians exiled in Chile and Argentina" who had taken up the struggle against the war, Marof approvingly mentioned José Aguirre Gainsborg.[58]

And so we return to Eduardo Arze's account of what happened when Aguirre proposed that Marof be "the leader" of the party the two young friends wanted to found.

> I have a certain Indian malice, and I said: The name sounds nice, but what kind of man is he? Are we going to show up and say, "Marof, Marof, we've become Trotskyists"? At that point Aguirre Gainsborg didn't have many arguments that could convince me.
>
> But then a manifesto from Argentina reached Chile, from the Grupo Tupac Amaru in Córdoba, where Tristán Marof was living. Alipio Valencia was with him, as well as other Bolivians and some Argentines too, because of Marof's personality. . . . And we compared their manifesto with our own: one seemed like the copy of the other, they were so similar.

Nonetheless, Arze wanted to clear up the long-standing accusation that Marof had abused prisoners taken during the 1920 Saavedra coup. "So Aguirre Gainsborg and I went to visit Don Bautista Saavedra, former President of the Republic and illustrious Bolivian exile," who was living in Santiago's Hotel Victoria. Noting that Marof had broken from him after becoming a socialist, Saavedra vouched for his good character. The accusations were false, he told Aguirre and Arze, who "was convinced, and so we decided that [Marof] would be our leader."[59] The two young revolutionaries' visit to the ex-president and embodiment of Rosca power—Saavedra headed the government during the 1923 Uncía mine massacre—may seem like political surrealism, or sheer naïveté. Above all, however, it showed how isolated they still were from the Bolivian workers they aspired to lead.

Bolivia's humiliation in the Chaco highlighted and deepened the country's class, ethnic, and generational fissures. The "green hell" of the war proved to be a hothouse for the growth of Bolivian radicalism. Many of the cadres of the next decades' most active political movements served in the Chaco; many were brought together in resistance to what they saw as an absurd and squalid war. In the harsh light of defeat, radical ideas acquired a new and urgent appeal.

Two currents converged to prepare the way for the Bolivian Trotskyist movement. One grouping of exiled "defeatists" was represented by Aguirre Gainsborg, the young Marxist intellectual whose apprenticeship in Trotskyism took place among Chilean Oppositionists who would soon break from the international movement. The other was led by the charismatic Marof, whose home brew of indigenist, Marxist, and nationalist ingredients was pitched with the slogan "Land to the Indian, mines to the state." Their merger would establish an idiosyncratic, specifically Bolivian Trotskyist movement in 1935.

Return to an Early Grave

The Bolivian Trotskyist organization was the first of the new parties formed in the wake of the Chaco War, predating both the Revolutionary Nationalist Movement (MNR) and the Party of the Revolutionary Left (PIR). The Trotskyists' Partido Obrero Revolucionario (POR; Revolutionary Workers Party) was founded in 1935 at a congress of exiled revolutionaries in Córdoba, Argentina. To understand the future course of Bolivian radicalism, it is important to examine the conditions in which the POR was formed and the basic concepts underlying its strategy.

In 1934, Aguirre's Izquierda Boliviana, which had changed its name to Agrupación Comunista Boliviana (ACB), formed a "united front"—more precisely, a bloc aiming at organizational fusion—with Marof's Grupo Tupac Amaru (GTA). A subsequent report to the international Trotskyist movement stated that the GTA, starting with "a few communist intellectuals and workers," had been joined by "various comrades who were obliged to desert from the front and managed to reach [Argentina], almost all of them under prosecution by Military Tribunals." At the time of its alliance with the ACB, Marof's group had grown to include "fifty members in Argentina and a hundred among Bolivian prisoners in Asunción," the Paraguayan capital.[1]

The "united front" was announced at the end of Marof's *La tragedia del altiplano*. Circulated in late 1934, a joint manifesto of the two groups stated: "The universities are closed. . . . The working class has been torn from the gloomy darkness of factories, workshops and mines, to find itself caught in the gears of the military machine and sent to fight the proletarians of Paraguay. . . . Our impoverished peasants, the Indians, were transported . . . to defend rights they do not know or have. . . . The war has devoured armies of adolescents." Only the workers, "led by their class party" and allied with the peasants, could defeat the "feudal-bourgeoisie in its military or civilian forms." However, the document states: "Tupac Amaru and Izquierda Bolivi-ana, embryos of the party of the working class, address themselves to the army, publicly declaring that they are in agreement with progressive militarism put in the service of . . . the working people, that is, genuine democracy: the socialist revolution."[2] The appeal to "progressive" military officers—members of the commanding stratum of what Lenin and Trotsky called the core of the bourgeois state—was a sign of the times in a country turned upside down by the war. Young officers would soon rebel against the old regime and declare a semi-corporatist "military socialism," disorienting the founders of Bolivian Trotskyism.

Commenting on the manifesto, Aguirre stated that Marof's group and his own "have the same viewpoint [on] strictly national issues," but the GTA's position was not so clear "from the international standpoint." Aguirre's organization "has publicized its adherence to the platform of the Fourth International"; Marof and Keswar had not. "What are our comrades of the GTA waiting for?" he asked. "Will we align ourselves with the inter-national revolution or with socialism 'in one country'?" In any case, "Our comrades are ready to prepare a Conference of the two groups to unify and form a party. FORWARD! But above all let us begin the discussion."

However, Aguirre's document ends with a ten-point program out of kil-ter with his appeal for alignment with international Trotskyism. Beginning with "Immediate peace" and "Democratization of the army," it is purely national in scope and does not go beyond the bounds of capitalism. It calls for "a Constituent Assembly with representation of soldiers, workers, Indi-ans and university students"; nationalization of oil and mines, distribution of lands; abolition of tribute; inviolability of Indian communities' lands, and restoration of those taken from them; and protection of small-scale property. Absent are prior calls to "destroy" the existing army and establish a workers' and peasants' government.[3]

A report on the origins of the POR (likely written by Aguirre) noted: "When the war broke out, the reaction completely swept away Bolivia's communist groupings (a Communist Party never existed)." Radicals were "imprisoned, executed by military tribunals or confined in isolated regions, reduced to nothingness." Revolutionary agitation was carried out at "the personal initiative of some comrades mobilized with the troops"; those who "played an active role, albeit one of desperate resistance," would later help found the new party. The GTA's manifesto "began to circulate among the troops, reaching front-line fortifications," and the group started recruiting deserters. "Without knowing of the GTA's existence, our comrades who fled from prison or internal exile, or were expelled from Bolivia," reached

Peru and Chile. Some joined the official Communist Party "but were soon expelled for 'putting forward the Trotskyist platform on the struggle against the war'" and formed a group with "the transitory name 'Izquierda Boliviana.'" Once the war entered its second year, the GTA and IB contacted each other, "working out a programmatically based united front" and publishing declarations "which entered Bolivia, above all at the front, and reached militants held prisoner in Paraguay."[4]

While it is difficult to measure the impact of this agitation, we know it intersected growing disaffection at home. In the war's second year, an Indian lawyer later recalled, radical workers and students held a quiet May Day meeting in the Sucre cemetery, away from the eyes of the police. The students "had painted big portraits of Lenin and Trotsky and held them side by side." Among them was a group of "*muchachas* who sometimes gave out bread to soldiers marching to the front, wrapping it in revolutionary pamphlets that wound up being read there, even by some Paraguayan troops."[5]

In June 1935, Eduardo Arze recalled, Aguirre Gainsborg traveled to Córdoba to "reach an agreement with [Marof's] people in Argentina." As "we waited for news," Arze was not idle, experiencing yet another raid by the Chilean police, and spending many a day in Izquierda Comunista leader Zapata's office in the Chilean parliament, "discussing how to overthrow capitalism and establish socialism."[6]

In Córdoba, Aguirre, Marof, Keswar, and others held a merger congress, founding the Partido Obrero Revolucionario (Revolutionary Workers Party). Its goal: to lead a socialist revolution in Bolivia. When Aguirre returned, Arze remembered, "he brought back a seal of the POR, with the image of a condor." Always ready to poke fun, one comrade said "it looks more like a carrier pigeon."[7] The new party used the condor seal on the letter it sent Trotsky announcing that the "Bolivian section" of the International Communist League (ICL), "embryo of our future Fourth International," had been formed "amidst the sacrifices and terrible experience of the Chaco war." Although "the 'objective' conditions for our development in Bolivia are favorable," the new party was "still not strong," it stated, and "increasingly needs active incorporation into the ICL." The POR would make "every effort to fulfill our duties toward our international organization," and asked the ICL leadership to give "the greatest attention to our problems."[8]

The accompanying report states that the "groupings which formed the basis for the new and first communist party of Bolivia (the POR)" had to rely on their own forces. Having "fulfilled their duty," they now required international assistance. It asked that the Argentine and Chilean ICL sections each send a member to "reinforce" the Central Committee of the POR, given the Chaco War's "significance for Latin America" and the movement's opportunities in Bolivia, where the situation "is highly favorable to a revolutionary crisis." This would help "overcome our localistic communism" and prepare a "class front" against the danger of intervention. The final section notes that "a broad discussion resulted in unanimous approval" of theses on the international situation, Bolivian politics, the struggle against the war, the agrarian question, separatism in Bolivia's eastern region, the character of the revolution and immediate tasks, and statutes of the POR.

The congress elected Marof general secretary, with a Central Committee composed of Aguirre ("Maximiliano Fernández"), Arze ("J. Delgado"), Valencia ("Ivan Keswar"), Marof himself ("Vicente Flores"), and three others known to us only as Altajiri, Chumacero, and Justiniano. The report is signed by Fernández, Delgado, and Justiniano "for the Central Committee," but not by Marof.[9]

There is no record of any answer. Bolivia was, after all, a remote, isolated, and little-known part of the world. For its part, the international movement faced a deadly campaign of persecution, Trotsky's expulsion from one country after another, and a terrible paucity of human and material resources. Yet the apparent lack of response to the Bolivians' request for international assistance could only accentuate the isolation of the new party, which would prove tragically vulnerable in the coming period.

The POR's foundation "was of major importance in the history of the Bolivian left," Klein notes; the first radical party to emerge from the war, it became "part of the vanguard of the revolutionary movement." An adversary admitted that "the Trotskyist current had the merit of being the first to organize as a Party."[10] In 1935, however, its political identity was confused. With fragile links to the international Marxist heritage Aguirre wanted to espouse, its politics were often closer to the radical-nationalist populism then emerging in several Latin American countries.

Guillermo Lora, who later became a central party leader, admits the POR was "organized hastily in response to the social upheaval" and did not "sufficiently overcome" differences between the Aguirre and Marof groups. In early writings Lora described the party founded in Córdoba as "a centrist group, antiwar above all, vegetating in isolation from the masses." (In the Trotskyist lexicon, "centrism" means vacillating between revolutionary and reformist politics.) The 1935 congress brought "organizational, not political" fusion, with "theory provided by the Grupo Tupac Amaru" of the "adventurer" Marof. The party was conceived as "a united front of various tendencies against . . . imperialism and the feudal-bourgeois governments," an idea espoused by Haya de la Torre's nationalist APRA in Peru. For his part, Marof later declared that the POR was not "founded to last forever." Motivated by "the consequences of the war," it was "only a party for the given moment."[11]

In 1935, there was little real clarity about the party's international affiliations. Describing the newly founded POR to a fellow radical, Keswar wrote that it "is a communist party, but does not belong to the official or Stalinist movement," without mentioning its request to join Trotsky's movement for the Fourth International. An Argentine Trotskyist noted that at the time, one of Marof's closest collaborators was "Costa . . . a confirmed Stalinist" who opposed the POR affiliating to Trotsky's ICL. In the report on its founding congress, the POR noted that "Paraguayan Stalinist leader Oscar Creydt" and a "Bolivian Stalinist who lives in La Plata" attended as "fraternal delegates." Against the chauvinism fanned by the war, Creydt's presence might have symbolized unity with persecuted Paraguayan leftists. Yet after Trotsky gained refuge in Mexico, Creydt attacked him and his Latin American cothinkers as agents of "provocation and espionage" for the Gestapo and the FBI. Trotsky called Creydt's smears "moral preparation" for the first attempt to assassinate him in Coyoacán.[12]

The party's actual political program was also unclear. In June 1935, the journal *América Libre* was established in Córdoba, with Marof as editor. In an article titled "The First Mass Party in Bolivia," Keswar wrote that the POR's founding theses addressed "all Bolivia's problems," but "Land to the tiller and mines to the state are the postulates for immediate practical action, posing defense of the nation's personality."[13] He was not alone in posing an immediate ("minimum") program in essentially nationalist terms similar to those used by the "statist" reform movements taking shape elsewhere on the continent.

Who would give land to the tiller, or would the peasants take it themselves? Were the mines to go to the existing ("bourgeois") state, or to a new ("workers'") state? Questions like this would acquire flesh and blood when revolution broke out on the altiplano. The ten-point program of the Marof-Aguirre "united front" was slightly expanded in a statement the POR published early in 1936. The call for a Constituent Assembly was now the first point; although it demanded "expropriation of latifundia by the peasants," the program did not address the issue of the state apparatus nor call for the establishment of a workers' and peasants' government.[14] Problematic as well was the party's description of the ruling class as a "feudal-bourgeoisie," which communicated disdain but did little to clarify the nature of Bolivian society. Akin to Stalinist theories of "anti-feudal" revolution, it helped set the stage for an alliance with nationalist sectors looking to modernize capitalism, against more retrograde ("feudal") groups in the nation's elite.

Marof and the POR

Aguirre hoped the POR would become a revolutionary vanguard like the Bolsheviks in the days Lenin and Trotsky led the Russian Revolution. Marof had other ideas. These varied in time and place, but throughout the next period his writings projected the image of a group identified with a caudillo (himself), a minimum program centered on nationalizing the mines, and a vocabulary similar to that of national-populist movements that came to the fore in the years preceding World War II.

"Our basic slogan is 'create,' rather than copying schemas or tactics," declared Marof's *América Libre*. In Latin America, "Our national anthems, fiery with freedom and glory, are comical when . . . the iron hand of foreign monopoly capital has seized us by the throat." "Stuck-up government officials" "display the rings in their noses, dancing in 'independence' parades, while most public figures . . . betray the vital interests of the people." In his next book, *Habla un condenado a muerte* (Words of a Man Condemned to Death)—a characteristic blend of political tract and self-promoting travelogue—a declaration by the Committee for the Return of Tristán Marof proclaimed: "Marof, 'undesirable and pernicious' for dictatorial governments, is also the first soldier and orienter of the Partido Obrero Revolucionario (POR), a left grouping that in the near future will play the most important role that any political party has played in Bolivia." Curiously, Marof admitted that although he suffered persecution, the government did not actually condemn him to death.[15]

The book's political viewpoint is similarly contradictory. In a typically Marofian adjectival flurry, he describes the POR as "a party of impassioned, virile and honorable militants." Ex-president Saavedra was now talking of a "'home-grown [Bolivian] socialism'," but, like capitalism, socialism is "a world phenomenon," and proposals for a "'popular front' would yoke us to Saavedra," an oligarchic caudillo. It would be wrong to "remain in the anti-feudal and anti-imperialist stage," as mere anti-imperialism does not mean "covering the entire curve" or that "the revolution's basic problems have been resolutely faced." Instead, "only the socialist revolution, headed by its proletarian vanguard, can go through to the end." Still, "full-blown socialism" could not be established "at one stroke," but Bolivia could take a "first socialist step" through "nationalization of the mines and oil, possession of the land by those that work it, socialization of certain industries," with political power "naturally in the hands of the workers and peasants, represented by their socialist vanguard."[16]

Painting swathes of rhetorical color, Marof remained unclear about this "first step." The Trotskyist conception of permanent revolution was far from claiming that "full-blown socialism" could be established "at one stroke." It held that the survival of a proletarian regime would require expropriating the entire ruling class and extending revolution—particularly to the dominant capitalist countries—to lay the basis for a classless society of material abundance. National isolation was one source of the POR's political weakness. Yet Marof proudly wrote that while "living the most terrible lives," its activists "hold congresses, publish manifestos and newspapers," with the "passion of victory and destiny embedded in [their] soul," doing it all "without the aid of any international body."[17]

The long-term effects of programmatic confusion emerge with Marof's appeals to Bolivian nationalism and patriotic army officers. A socialist movement would have great prospects in this "landlocked, mountainous country which can be defended with certain advantages," he wrote. The Bolivian people "can give itself the government it chooses and fight arms in hand for its integrity and wealth." This would "not be a war like the one in the Chaco, but an eminently national war." At a gathering where friends sang Bolivian folk songs, a sympathizer played an Andean stringed instrument:

> You have to hear this man play the *charango*: he is the archetype of those combative *chicheños* [local men] who often mounted their steeds in civil conflicts, following a caudillo and dying for a chimerical freedom. But the socialist idea has reached even the mind of this man in his multicolored poncho. He, in all simplicity, believes it necessary to fight the rich, because the rich are allied with foreign companies and are not Bolivians. He understands nothing of theory, but has heard it said that in Russia, some formidable men named Lenin and Trotzky fought for the people and destroyed the rich, founding a new society. While the *chicheño* plays his charango . . . in his enthusiasm and excitement he cries out: ¡Viva Bolivia Libre! ¡*Viva la revolución socialista*![18]

Beyond the paternalistic tone, it is symptomatic that Marof approvingly cites the viewpoint of the charango player (whether real or a product of artistic license matters little): the rich "are not Bolivian." Populism characteristically identifies anti-imperialism with xenophobia. Within a few years, this would be a central theme of the MNR's "revolutionary nationalism."

Marof's book describes discussions with young army officers assigned to guard him when the Argentine authorities sent him back to Bolivia, where he was briefly detained before being deported once again. Speaking with a certain Lieutenant Villarroel, he "gave a long explanation of imperialism," which meant "the fatherland does not belong to Bolivians." He told another, Lieutenant Aillón, that "as a POR manifesto states, socialism in its first stage is precisely the nationalization of our sources of production, banks, railways, oil; socialization of the countryside and of the companies that suction off our wealth and labor; liberation of the Indian." Still, "Lt. Aillón, like many young officers, wants to know if socialism is against the army." Marof's response: "We are not against the army which nourishes itself from the people and subordinates itself to the party of the people, which carries out the national defense of our riches, of all the goods possessed by a united society living in solidarity." But "we are implacable enemies" of "finance capital . . . which comes to this continent not to build but to destroy," and of "the army which is at the service of imperialist companies and domestic millionaires. We consider that army traitorous and anti-Bolivian." While "we place ourselves on the international plane," socialism "does not exclude the defense of nationality."[19]

The idea that the army could change its "anti-Bolivian" nature and put itself at the service of "the people" would be taken up by the young officers who seized power after the Chaco War, then by Gualberto Villarroel (apparently the very man who had guarded Marof) when he took over during World War II. It has continued to influence the Bolivian left through the present, notably in Lora's call to "Bolivianize the armed forces" and some labor leaders' appeals for "patriotic officers" to seize power during the mass upheaval of 2005.

Marof also relates a conversation with a Bolivian general named Quintanilla: "I told him, you need to be a Bolivian general and not a Yankee general. You will be a Bolivian general if you carry out the expulsion of Standard Oil."[20] Soon, a new junta would do just that; another would do likewise with Gulf Oil. Each mine massacre showed that such measures did not change the army's nature. In a very different spirit, Trotsky wrote at the outbreak of the Spanish Civil War in July 1936: "The officers' corps represents the guard of capital. . . . At the approach of the proletarian revolution [it] becomes the executioner of the proletariat." It must be "dissolved, broken, crushed in its entirety"; the army must be "replaced by the people's militia, that is, the democratic organization of the armed workers and peasants," which is "incompatible with the domination of exploiters big and small."[21]

We may sum up this first phase of Bolivian Trotskyism as follows. Merging vigorous currents of radical thought, the party formed in 1935 generated concepts and slogans that would resonate for decades. The POR proclaimed Bolivia's indigenous heritage and the central role of the mining proletariat. It argued that national liberation and social emancipation were incompatible with the political and social system that led to the Chaco debacle. At the same time, at its birth the POR already displayed significant contradictions. Was its appeal to Bolivian nationalism or Marxist internationalism? Did it seek to replace the existing state apparatus in a proletarian-led revolution or win part of the nation's elite to a statist reform of capitalism? Was it a section of world Trotskyism or a Bolivia-centric group? These dilemmas would haunt the POR's founders in the tumultuous years that followed as the party experienced the first in a series of political and organizational crises.

The POR "Disappears from the Scene"

Far from the glorious victory envisaged by Bolivia's rulers, the Chaco War became a humiliating defeat that opened the floodgates of social discontent and spelled the end of the old way of ruling. When a ceasefire was signed in June 1935, the old order awaited the *coup de grace*. Yet the longed-for end to the bloodshed caused the POR to suffer a collapse so complete that it had to be "refounded" three years later. Despite *América Libre*'s claim that it was "Bolivia's first mass party," the exile group had no base within the country. A little over a year after its founding congress, "Max Fernández" (Aguirre) wrote that the POR "was composed EXCLUSIVELY of the Bolivian Marxists exiled during the war, as their country was closed off by the wall of repression necessary for maintaining the Chaco carnage." Himself included, "no more than three or four" cadres "succeeded in returning individually to Bolivia," where they "encountered the reality of a proletariat disorganized and intimidated by the war and its consequences."[22] For the time being, Marof remained in exile.

The Aguirre/Marof "confederation" of exile groups had always lacked "a united cadre and coherent ideology." Now, its militants were excruciatingly vulnerable to the brusque changes of the postwar period. Looking back, a party leader later observed: "The 'old' POR, born in a situation caused by the war . . . , did not survive it; the party played no role in the postwar period, marked by accentuated class struggle. The POR disappeared from the scene."[23] In September 1935, Alipio Valencia ("Comrade Keswar") recalled, "José Aguirre G. returned from Chile with the mission of establishing the POR in Bolivia." Instead, he "abandoned [this] work for the time being" and joined a nationalist student circle. Participants I interviewed shared this assessment. The POR "did not exist" after the war, said Eduardo Arze. "When I came back" to Bolivia in early 1937, after three years studying in Chile, "nobody was speaking in the name of the POR," agreed Oscar Barrientos.[24]

Repression played its part. The army arrested Aguirre and Keswar as soon as they came home (both were released at the insistence of labor leader Waldo Alvarez); and Luis Peñaloza, another POR founder, was imprisoned as an army deserter. A year after the war's end, Peñaloza described the situation: "The censorship imposed by the war has continued," as the bourgeoisie attempted to "keep it going as long as possible, so [Bolivians] will be unaware of the world's judgment on the Chaco war." The damage done by chauvinism, together with "the relative youth of the labor movement," its poverty, and the lack of a "large-scale workers' press," made it difficult for "the masses' disaffection [to] crystallize into genuine socialist action."[25]

Leaving the POR behind when he returned from exile did not mean Aguirre ceased to have an impact on Bolivian politics. Soon, he was playing a prominent role in the La Paz labor federation, becoming a close ally of its leader Alvarez. He would make his mark most deeply as the mentor of the "Beta Gama" group, a circle of young Bolivians who would later lead the country's nationalist movement, among them future presidents, cabinet ministers, and ambassadors. Far from his exile dream of founding a Bolivian brand of Bolshevism, he helped cohere the national-populist milieu that would reap political benefit from the Chaco disaster. As Arze explained, "to have some kind of activity, Aguirre started organizing would-be aristocratic middle-class youth, called Beta Gama . . . young guys from the club set." Barrientos concurred: "Beta Gama consisted of intellectuals from the upper middle class, *señoritos*, people who met in clubs."[26]

When Aguirre joined, the group changed its name from Acción Nacionalista Beta Gama to Acción Socialista Beta Gama (ASBG). This was a sign of the times: the desire for change led "everybody in the postwar period to call themselves 'socialists.'"[27] Confusion abounded regarding terms like "socialism," "nationalism," even "national socialism," and some were attracted to the idea (posited by Mexico's Vasconcelos, Peru's Haya de la Torre, and others) of an Ibero-American "race" with a special destiny. Trying to change their spots, Saavedra's Republicans renamed themselves Republican Socialists. Amidst this ferment, Beta Gama joined other small groups in a complicated dance of negotiations, alliances, and splits. One of the most important was led by young activists who left the Nationalist Party of former president Hernando Siles to form a new "Socialist Party."

What is most remarkable about Beta Gama is the cast of characters, a virtual Who's Who of future MNR leaders. One, sometimes listed as general secretary, was ex-president Siles's son, Hernán Siles Zuazo, who would become the MNR's *Sub Jefe* (No. 2 man) and two-time President of the Republic (1956–60, 1982–85). Also sitting with Aguirre on the group's executive committee were Julio Zuazo Cuenca (cabinet member under Villarroel), Víctor Andrade (foreign minister under the MNR), Luis Iturralde (a key MNR diplomat), and others. Walter Guevara, who later headed the MNR right wing and briefly served as president (1979), was another member of the group, which Lora admits gives "the impression of an MNR cell, though at the time, nobody dreamed of establishing the MNR." Indeed Aguirre's adherence to Beta Gama prefigured some Trotskyist leaders' decision to join the MNR after the 1952 Revolution.[28]

The human continuity between Beta Gama and the future MNR was not a coincidence. Under Aguirre's leadership, the group became a progenitor of Bolivia's own brand of populism. The "socialism" it propounded was a left-wing nationalism based on an amalgamation of social classes. Written by Aguirre, Beta Gama's program declared: "The socialist state will be built on the basis of the people, the middle class, proletariat, peasantry and the small proprietors interested in their liberation from the yoke of imperialism as well as feudalism." "Beta Gama" may have stood for Bolivia Grande, reflecting the territorial revanchism prevalent since the Pacific War. "As an immediate step toward establishment of the Socialist State, ASBG will seek the national organization and defense of its [sic] conquests, reinforcing the principles of 'Nation' and 'Unity.'" As "a doctrine," the program declared, socialism "belongs historically to the proletariat, but in practice, in today's Bolivia, the initiative belongs to the young intellectual middle class."[29]

Having convinced *El Diario* to give him a regular column, Aguirre addressed a wide range of issues, from supporting indigenous ayllus against landlords to opposing proposals for a "corporatist" political system. The column served him as a platform to call for a "Unification Congress of the left" to establish an all-inclusive Socialist Party. With two other Beta Gama leaders, Aguirre announced that "the Revolutionary Socialist Cell (formerly Nationalist Youth), Beta Gama and Bolivian Socialist Party . . . have discussed the basis for a LEFT UNITED FRONT" and a "youth congress" to consider "establishing a new political party and program, leading to the fusion of all existing socialist groups." Another article reported a unity pact between Ricardo Anaya's Left Group and Beta Gama. Though Saavedra's Republican Socialists were excluded from these unity negotiations, in April 1936 they too were invited to join a "proletarian united front" to demand a wage increase and confiscation of Standard Oil.[30]

Although dizzying, the carousel of splits and mergers is important. In addition to Aguirre, Siles Zuazo, and other Beta Gama members, key players included Anaya (future spokesman of the pro-Moscow PIR), Augusto Céspedes and Carlos Montenegro (ex-Nationalist Party members who became key MNR ideologues), Alvarez (soon to be the first "worker minister"), and many others with crucial roles in the nation's history. The post-Chaco left was grouping around a political outlook that would lay the basis for the "statist" project soon taken up by disaffected officers and sectors of the nation's elite.

From exile, Tristán Marof called on "all socialists, from one end of the country to the other, to maintain unity, erasing differences" and "allying with similar groups." A "principal role," he proclaimed, would be played by "wholesome officers who want to see Bolivia free, without chains." Nor was Aguirre reticent in appealing to nationalism; he called for "complete nationalization of foreign capital (mines, oil, transport, credit)" while "defending capital in favor of Bolivia," "national capital . . . the nationalist stage of socialism." When he and Siles Zuazo joined union leader Alvarez in a "Left Socialist Bloc," they announced that it "has never and does not now obey any foreign inspiration."[31]

Aguirre's enemies were unconvinced, warning against "disruptive Trotskyism" and "the concept of Permanent Revolution and Proletarian Revolution in Bolivia," as one La Paz paper put it. Another used the exiled Russian Bolshevik to spice up an article on performers who had arrived in La Paz, exclaiming: "Gypsies! The word is a strange exorcism, a kabbalistic invocation of distant wisdom from all the roads of the world"; they were brothers to "wandering geniuses" like "Knut Hamsun and Trotsky, who embrace the ambulant priesthood, crossing all horizons like sparrows."[32] Yet in Aguirre's writings, Trotskyism and the POR *brillaron por su ausencia*— were conspicuous by their absence.

Marof's prediction that young officers would play "a principal role" came on the eve of a major shift in Bolivian politics. In early 1936, the political order was about to crumble. Those occupying the Palacio Quemado had little claim to legitimacy: Vice President Tejada Sorzano had simply pushed Salamanca out and seized the presidency himself. The old parties were discredited by the Chaco fiasco; workers and the urban poor were increasingly assertive; thousands of Indian conscripts returned to find the old conditions of servitude intact. Demobilized soldiers were forming associations of every description, many of a radical hue. In Sucre, the *Ex-Combatiente* proclaimed: "We are living at a politically decisive moment. . . . The mass of ex-soldiers was dragged to the trenches all together, enslaved to the interests of the Rosca. . . . We belong with the disinherited classes and must have a socialist ideology. . . . Ex-combatants: either we unite, or we will fall once again into the insatiable jaws of capitalism."[33]

The tipping point came in May 1936 when graphic workers sparked a general strike demanding a 100 percent wage increase for all. Strikers patrolled La Paz, virtually controlling the nation's capital. On May 17, a military coup was carried out by colonels David Toro and Germán Busch, allied with Saavedra's Republican Socialists and the Nationalist Party dissidents who had formed a new "socialist" movement. On May 20, Toro was named head of a "socialist military junta." Oscar Barrientos recalls: "The red flag was raised over the La Paz city hall."[34]

Seeking to control social unrest, the junta moved to incorporate labor directly into the government. Toro created a Ministry of Labor and appointed Waldo Alvarez—the graphic workers' leader who was Aguirre's comrade in the Left Socialist Bloc—to head it. As one La Paz daily proclaimed: "This Is the First Time a South American Government Has Given a Worker a Cabinet Post." Toro also set up a "State Socialist Party" and (with support from the new Labor Minister) declared its intention to establish what he called "corporatist unionism": obligatory membership in unions that would be an "arm" of the state, "for its defense and under its tutelage and control."[35] Though Toro did not remain in power long enough to push this project through, he decreed a labor code, minimum wage, and restrictions on commercial profits.

As "the first project for populist government," observes Bolivian historian Mario Miranda, Toro's regime drew on a "revolution of aspirations" to unite politicized officers, urban reformers, technicians, and bureaucrats from the mining industry. Elements from ex-president Siles's "frustrated nationalist party" took the lead in Toro's "State Socialist" party, particularly Carlos Montenegro, who later played a central role in founding Bolivia's "populist party par excellence, the MNR."[36] Toro's short-lived government made its mark on history by confiscating Standard Oil's Bolivian properties in 1937. Preceding Mexico's famous oil nationalization by a year, the measure reflected the increasing awareness that conflicts between the world powers were giving Latin American governments new margins for maneuver.[37]

In July 1937, Toro was overthrown by his former colleague Busch, backed, many believed, by the tin baron Patiño. Advised by Víctor Paz Estenssoro and other young nationalists, Busch called a convention to decree "protection" of Indian communities, "limits" to the exercise of private property, and other populist measures. Nonetheless, "the oligarchy's power remained intact." In 1938, Busch declared himself dictator, but soon found himself at a dead end. Without mass support and increasingly alienating the elite with his demagogic posturing, he shot himself in August 1939. As "military socialism" gave way to a more traditional military regime under generals Quintanilla and Peñaranda, the "suicidal dictator" entered the pantheon of failed nationalist strongmen, icons for the future Movimiento Nacionalista Revolucionario.[38]

Aguirre, Marof, and "Military Socialism"

A central goal of the Toro/Busch "military socialist" regime was to subordinate dissident sectors to a renovated political structure. Marxists had long considered the incorporation of labor leaders into "bourgeois" cabinets a particularly dangerous form of class collaboration, the "socialist ministerialism" excoriated by Lenin and denounced anew by Trotsky and his cothinkers when Communist parties joined governments of the Popular Front. Like the rest of the Bolivian left, however, the founders of Bolivian Trotskyism were unable to resist the regime's initial popularity.

When Waldo Alvarez became Minister of Labor, he surrounded himself with an "advisory committee" of young leftist intellectuals. Future PIR leaders Anaya and José Antonio Arze were named technical and juridical adviser, respectively. Aguirre received the more prestigious post of Undersecretary to Alvarez, later joining the Ministry of Industry and Commerce. In May 1936, Aguirre was the first signatory to a Left Socialist Bloc statement "supporting and declaring our confidence" in Alvarez, the bloc's general secretary. It vowed to "provide him with all our cooperation" as he "occupies the Ministry of Labor . . . the workers' first conquest in the State," while "recogniz[ing] in the present political regime one of the means that can most directly serve the proletariat's conquests and demands."[39]

The honeymoon was short. In June Saavedra's Republican Socialists warned that "The Entire Country Must Be On Guard Against Communism," launching a furious red-baiting campaign. Despite Alvarez's support to Toro's obligatory unionization plan, in August 1936 a number of labor bodies rejected "fascist-style syndicalization." In response, the press launched attacks on the Labor Minister and his supporters in the local FOT labor federation. The nationalist daily *La Calle* wielded Aguirre's past as a bludgeon: "Trotzkyites" were trying to turn the Labor Ministry into an Alvarez "clique," while "Trotzkyite Loud-Mouths Bring Anarchy to the FOT." "Will We Be Governed by Deserters?" the newspaper asked. Another called for an "iron fist" to "purge the country" of the "red extremism" of "adherents of the Third and Fourth Internationals."[40]

Though Aguirre and his friends had strayed far from the international movement, attacks on Trotskyism reached a fever pitch. *La Calle* printed almost daily broadsides against communists "breast-fed by Moscow or oriented by the Fourth International," the "traitorous action of the long-distance *pongos* (vassals) of Trotsky, the biggest felon toward the workers' cause," "ultra-reds on the Trotskyite payroll," "the Judaic ego-worship of Leon Trotsky," the "nefarious Trotsky cell, whose leaders in Moscow have been shot as traitors, disloyal elements and deserters," the "Trotskyite Plan" for a "Trotskyite revolution in which nobody would work," and the "utopian formula of a 'permanent revolution' outside time and space."[41]

The drumbeat prepared the way for a new round of repression: "The Government Will Energetically Repress Communist Activities," the press reported in September 1936. When Toro issued a decree against communism, many leftists were arrested and deported. "Worker Minister" Alvarez remained in the government for two more months. Having made the labor leadership responsible for the military regime, his usefulness came to an end, and his resignation was accepted in December.[42]

Exiled again to Chile, Aguirre wrote self-critically that "our comrades" had made undue "compromises and concessions" (see figure 2.1). Specifically, "entry into the apparatus of the bourgeois state" was "COLLABO-RATIONISM!" and led workers to "serve the bourgeoisie." When "posturing became uncomfortable for the military . . . communists were banned and persecuted" while the "worker minister remained in power side by side with Colonel Toro." The POR's founders should have maintained the party "implacably . . . as the vanguard of the proletariat." The task now was to "reorganize the POR in Bolivia, leave the (Toroist) Socialist Party, fully accept the role of vanguard, and return to confidence in the proletariat."[43]

In a letter to friends in Bolivia, Aguirre called for "removing the blindfold from the workers' eyes, beginning by removing our own blindfold." Participation in government posts had "become" (he did not specify when) "liquidation of any revolutionary theory and practice" and "our authority to call for independent struggle by the proletariat." Joining the Socialist Party—which proved to be "no more than the Toroist Party"—put "a tombstone over our theory and our prestige with the workers." Back in Bolivia, however, Alvarez and Eduardo Arze helped form an ephemeral Workers Party which issued a statement supporting the new military president, Busch, "insofar as the present government continues its socialist work."[44]

And what of the POR's erstwhile leader Marof? His expulsion from Argentina and brief internment in Bolivia led to protests by the La Paz Socialist Party and FOT, together with furious polemics for and against him

La última fotografía de José Aguirre Gainsborg

Figure 2.1 "The last photo of José Aguirre Gainsborg" (center), *La Calle*. (Courtesy of Biblioteca y Archivo Histórico del Congreso)

in the daily press. In a letter to a left-nationalist paper, Marof stressed, "I am a defender of Bolivian interests and I want the best for my fatherland."[45]

This apparently entailed some rather Byzantine machinations. A Russian researcher in now-public Comintern archives writes that in March 1936, ex-Nationalist Party "socialists" asked Marof to join their alliance with Toro and Busch, who were preparing their coup. However, Toro considered mine nationalization impossible without assuring a foreign market. Since "the USSR could be an alternative to Western markets," they proposed to send Marof and Keswar to sound out the Soviet leaders. Marof contacted the Argentine Communist Party, saying he was interested in establishing a pro-Soviet party in Bolivia. Concerned to counteract "Trotskyites" like

Aguirre, the Argentines passed the suggestion along to the Comintern, which accepted on condition that Marof and Keswar publicly renounce Trotskyism and declare their solidarity with Soviet policy, specifically the Popular Front. However, "events moved faster than the mails and Moscow's decision-making process: Marof was unable to maintain contact with the coup plotters, and the Comintern lost interest."[46]

Marof finally returned to Bolivia in September 1937 and had a cordial meeting with now-President Busch, who "became my friend and confided in me," he later reminisced. Eduardo Arze recalled people saying Marof could have "a lot of influence" on the young president. The following year Marof published a new pamphlet, appealing to the military's "socialist government" to "tip over to the side of the people, fulfill its historic mission, and lay the foundations for Bolivia to cease being a semicolony." He proclaimed: "only if the army is united with the suffering people will it be able to achieve in practice the ideal of triumphant socialism. We are speaking of an integral, Bolivian army . . . emerging from the guts of the people . . . to build the foundation for a sovereign Bolivia independent of foreigners and finance capital." Socialism "would be the most solid bulwark of our territorial integrity."[47] The former defeatist now saw himself as an adviser to the military nationalist junta.

What Was to Be Done?

In early October 1938, Marof and other activists met in La Paz with Aguirre, who had managed to return from exile. Accounts differ as to whether the gathering was convoked as a "conference" of the POR or, as Arze claimed, a discussion on founding a new socialist party.

According to Arze, the meeting was held in his home. Marof presented a document stating that Aguirre had joined up with "petty-bourgeois intellectuals, sons of the feudal-bourgeoisie, who chattered endlessly about socialism without the slightest conviction or knowledge of Bolivian reality, out of sheer dilettantism and to get posts in the Toro administration. Comrade Aguirre wasted his time. His failure was foreseeable, and . . . the whole Beta Gama group took a rightward path." Now, Arze recalled, "Marof said, 'we need a party with freedom of movement . . . to meet people, bring them together, gain their sympathy.'" Socialism should be adapted to "the almost nonexistent . . . theoretical level" of the Bolivian masses, who "react with the heart, not the brain," he declared in good caudillo style.[48]

As for Aguirre, Arze recalled his being "brilliant but abstract." He called for "building the party only with pure, qualified people," called the regime a "military-police government" with which revolutionaries could not compromise, and became angry during the debate. "It turned into an argument between Aguirre Gainsborg on one side and myself, his friend for many years, on the other. . . . He wanted something that was going nowhere, certainly not toward forming a party." Eventually Aguirre gave in, saying, "One of Comrade Marof's characteristics has always been to present the facts objectively. I withdraw my proposal." No votes were taken, but participants agreed to hold another meeting.[49]

Marof later claimed that Aguirre accepted his view that the POR had been formed only "for the given moment" of the Chaco War, and that "we agreed to change the POR's name . . . in order to participate in the elections." In an article published just after Aguirre's death, former POR member Luis Peñaloza presented a different picture: Aguirre, who had "distanced himself" from Marof, "refused to participate in any event seeking to proclaim socialist parties he considered spurious," rejecting "political opportunism" presented "in the name of tactics." "Just a few days ago," Aguirre had expressed this "in a political thesis that determined his isolation."[50]

In early November 1938, Marof called on "all leftist sectors to join" *en bloc* in a Gran Partido Socialista. Previous efforts, he declared, had been hampered by "the low level of the proletarian masses, demagogy and infantile extremism." Other former POR members who signed the appeal included Eduardo Arze and Alipio Valencia.[51] Eventually adopting the name Partido Socialista Obrero de Bolivia (PSOB; Socialist Workers Party of Bolivia), the new group gained influence in the labor movement, won parliamentary seats, and published a newspaper called *La Batalla*. Marof would eventually specialize in attacks on what he called the "Nazi MNR," winding up as an adviser to right-wing presidents Enrique Hertzog (1947–49) and Mamerto Urriolagoitia (1949–51).

The demise of the "first" POR—the party established in 1935—was symbolized by a bizarre milestone in the history of Bolivian radicalism: the sudden, tragic, and absurd death of José Aguirre Gainsborg (see figure 2.2). Days after the October 1938 meeting with Marof, he went to a La Paz amusement park with some friends. Climbing aboard a Ferris wheel, he removed the safety bar "in a show of sang-froid." He fell, injuring a child and young woman on the ground. His skull broken, Aguirre died two hours later.[52]

Shaken by the premature loss of one of Bolivian radicalism's most talented figures, La Paz university students, the Cochabamba labor federation, and other groups declared mourning for Aguirre. Numerous obituaries appeared in the daily press. Even *La Calle* declared that "Aguirre Gainsborg's

Figure 2.2 Poster commemorating Aguirre, 1953. (Courtesy of Bibliothèque de Documentation Internationale Contemporaine)

Death Is a Major Blow to Bolivian Socialism," printing a photo of Aguirre and two friends, their hats at jaunty angles, "moments before leaving for Chile the last time [Aguirre] was exiled" (figure 2.1, referenced above). Others noted that Aguirre left "the narrow confines of our milieu . . . for the heady breezes of the open world," and that "He held more than one high place in official circles. Easily, through his own unquestionable merits, he could have gained a seat in parliament or even headed a ministry. But he preferred to fight from below rather than traffic in his ideals."[53]

Many who had worked with Aguirre reacted with shock, even anger. "What a stupid death for such a brilliant man!" exclaimed Díaz Machicao. "His soul drunk with red banners, the revolutionary . . . died liked a little boy," one obituary commented. "Faced with the revolutionary commotion of the world, the new men should not die like that, but on the barricades," protested another friend, recalling his admiration for "the unforgettable Comrade Aguirre Gainsborg," who "gave up the white bread of the social class he renounced" for exile and prison, those "great universities for revolutionaries."[54]

In addition to Luis Peñaloza, another future leader of the MNR eulogized Aguirre. Addressing his departed comrade from Beta Gama and the Left Socialist Bloc, Hernán Siles Zuazo declaimed in a funeral oration: "Brother José, older brother in ideals, guide for the spirit . . . , you disdained the golden calf of power and fought, giving everything while asking nothing." For "our lost generation, it will be difficult if not impossible to fill your post and follow the path you began to mark out."[55]

Siles soon became the number two leader of the MNR. As Vice President, then President of Bolivia, he would be the nemesis of radical miners and a determined opponent of Trotskyism. Although short on content and long on pathos, Siles's 1938 funeral speech shows how intertwined the roots of the MNR were with those of Bolivian Trotskyism.

Trotsky and the Warisata Indian School

A photo of Aguirre not long before his death shows him visiting the Aymara town of Warisata, where Elizardo Pérez—a former member of his Izquierda Boliviana—had established Bolivia's first indigenist school (see figure 2.3).[56] It symbolizes another aspect of Bolivian Trotskyism's interpenetration with the ideals of Indian emancipation central to the radical tradition. Sometimes called the ayllu school, Warisata pioneered a "liberationist" model of Indian education in Latin America. On one of its walls, the Andean earth deity Pachamama appeared in bas-relief, holding a hammer and sickle. Pérez hired leftists like Eduardo Arze and Alipio Valencia to work with him. One of Warisata's most dedicated teachers and publicists was the young artist Carlos Salazar, who later founded his own Trotskyist group and whose brother Jorge became a top leader of the POR.

In 1940, Arze and Valencia joined Pérez in Mexico to attend the first Inter-American Indigenist Congress. The two seized the opportunity to visit Trotsky in the fortified house where he was living in Coyoacán. Signatories to the POR's 1935 letter to Trotsky, they would be the only Bolivian

Figure 2.3 Carlos Salazar (left) and Ana Pérez at Warisata. Behind them, Pachamama, an earth deity, holds a hammer and sickle. (From Salazar Mostajo, *Gesta;* courtesy of Cecilia Salazar de la Torre)

Figure 2.4 Trotsky (center) in Coyoacán with Alipio Valencia and Eduardo Arze. (From Salazar Mostajo, *Gesta;* courtesy of Cecilia Salazar de la Torre)

revolutionaries ever to meet the "Old Man." (See figure 2.4.) Decades later, Arze remembered being "captivated by the human feeling of Trotsky," who talked with them about "the importance of a party," the political situation in the United States, "social psychology," and Elizardo Pérez's work in the field of Indian education.[57] Trotsky was so interested in the Warisata school that he asked to meet with Pérez himself, but this plan was disrupted when the Mexican painter Siqueiros led the first assassination attempt against Trotsky in May. Three months later, another assassin completed Stalin's assignment.

The Warisata school eventually succumbed to government hostility, but its example spread to other parts of Latin America. Describing it as Bolivia's "greatest revolutionary experience in the field of education," Salazar notes that it helped lay the groundwork for the indigenous mobilizations of the 1950s.[58] The town of Warisata renewed its reputation as a seedbed of Aymara rebellion during the Gas War of 2003.

Old political structures proved unable to contain the social tensions unleashed by the Chaco War. Young officers stepped into the breach in the name of "military socialism," an early version of Latin American populist regimes. Seeking to subordinate the labor movement to a renovated nationalist state, the "military socialist" project was counterposed to the program of a socialist revolution led by the working class. Yet contradictions in the outlook of early Bolivian Trotskyism left it vulnerable to the young officers' initial popularity. The program of permanent revolution called for working-class political independence from all "bourgeois" governments, but Bolivian Trotskyism's founders were drawn into supporting the nationalist regime.

When labor leader Waldo Alvarez became Bolivia's first "worker minister," and his adviser Aguirre backed him, they set a fateful precedent for the Bolivian left. Aguirre later criticized the course he and others had adopted. Yet he was unable to counteract the decision by Tristán Marof, the movement's other central founder, to launch an ideologically diffuse "socialist" party based on the caudillo's personal prestige. The shattering of the POR had a macabre echo in Aguirre's death.

The pieces would be picked up again and reassembled in the city of Cochabamba. As we will see, the POR that young intellectuals "refounded" there was not a linear continuation of the first attempt. The party sought to articulate revolutionary positions on key issues of national life; it won over energetic and talented activists; it undertook a vigorous turn to the working class and established a following in the mining proletariat. Nonetheless, a pattern had been established. Popular enthusiasm for nationalist strongmen would repeatedly disorient Bolivian Trotskyists, leaving them ill prepared when disillusionment set in and the nationalists' fortunes ebbed. In the years that followed the party's "refoundation," it developed ways and means of political activity that would mark it for decades thereafter. Central to its course was the alliance it formed with miners' leader Juan Lechín and the labor wing of a new nationalist movement.

Under the Sign of Pulacayo

The "first POR" met an early demise, its founders veering sharply from the path they marked in 1935. The individual most closely linked to Trotskyism, José Aguirre Gainsborg, was dead. If the story had ended there, Bolivian history would have been markedly different. Instead, the movement revived, reorganized, and by the middle of World War II was growing in urban centers and mining regions, grabbing headlines and winning ground from "Stalinist" rivals.

Oscar Barrientos was a participant in the last meetings between Aguirre and Marof. Two months after Aguirre fell to his death, Barrientos called a meeting in his home town of Cochabamba. "I said it was necessary to establish the POR [and] won over three, four or five people," all university students. With these "young guys . . . I refounded the POR" in December 1938. Under the pseudonyms Varriosky—a Russified version of his surname—and Tomás Warqui, he became the tiny group's "General Secretary."[1]

Starting over almost from scratch, its political reference point was a collection of brief, schematic theses from the "refoundation" congress. The first states that in colonies and "semicolonies" (independent in name yet dominated by imperialism), the "law of combined evolution" turned local ruling classes into "feudal-bourgeoisies." The "Latin semicolonies [of] Indoamerica," bound ever closer to Yankee imperialism, were no exception. However, imperialism itself had "prepared the objective and subjective conditions of proletarian revolution throughout the world." The coming world war would "unleash the world proletarian revolution," which "will begin in the colonies and semicolonies." The war would bring "a momentary economic boom for [Bolivia's] feudal-bourgeoisie, since imperialism needs our raw materials for its war effort," but "also bring, as an immediate consequence, the social revolution."

Trotsky's young admirers garbled his concept of permanent revolution. Where he argued that the proletariat of "backward" countries might be first to seize power, they proclaimed it would inevitably begin there. Trotsky argued that the Fourth International must resolve the "crisis of proletarian leadership" (the subjective factor, in the movement's lexicon) and foresaw that war would eventually bring new social upheavals. The refounded POR claimed capitalism had *already* prepared the "subjective factor" and that the war would immediately "unleash" revolution.

Other theses state that Bolivia will have "a *revolution of a combined type,*" bringing together workers' insurrection and peasant uprising, given "the Indian's pressing need to destroy the yoke" of landlord domination. This process would be "led by the proletariat," yet genuine socialism could not be built in one country alone; revolution must be "consummated" on the world stage, laying the basis for an international socialist society. The last texts stress that "our party is completely opposed to those of the bourgeoisie—it is their antithesis," and lay out a detailed plan for the cells, local, regional, and central committees the POR would form.[2] This, however, remained music of the future. For the next years the POR consisted of Barrientos's circle of friends in Cochabamba, which began calling itself the Central Committee—a committee of the whole, evidently, since the party had no other members.

After the old leaders "bowed down to the government," Guillermo Lora wrote, the POR was refounded "amidst the general indifference of a proletariat that had been deceived and the pious disdain of 'socialist' celebrities, [and] openly presented itself as Trotskyist." Nonetheless, it was far from clear what this implied. At first, reported a veteran Cochabamba Trotskyist, the group "operated inside four walls, closed in, with few militants." The "Central Committee" was little more than a club of friends, playing at "conspiratorial" measures while opening its meetings to any sympathizer who happened to show up. A small typewritten review was issued, then a journal called *Pauta* (Guide), whose few copies were distributed to "initiates" rather than the public at large. As for Barrientos, Lora said he was an "overgrown kid" who one day arrived breathlessly to announce: "I've solved the food problem! We'll raise rabbits!"[3]

Incongruously situated as Ambassador to Mexico in 1992, Argentine ex-Trotskyist Jorge Abelardo Ramos recalled his visit to Cochabamba forty-five years earlier. Aguirre Gainsborg's old POR had been "very lax, loose, incipient, a bit like the 1930s Trotskyists in Buenos Aires, from the prehistory of Trotskyism." For his part, Warqui was "a total bohemian" who lived in "a kind of wooden mill next to a lake in Cochabamba," with a huge library. When activists decided to replace him, "it wasn't hard to get Warqui out of the leadership of the POR. What was hard was to get him away from the lake. . . . Temperamentally, he was not a party militant. He was a guy who thought, read, discoursed and drank coffee."[4]

Yet almost immediately after its refoundation, the POR could claim a real achievement: the Bolivian University Student Federation's approval of a radical Program of Principles written by Ernesto Ayala Mercado, soon to be one of the best-known leaders of the party. Lora describes Ayala as "a remarkable orator" who was also "a mixture of dandy, revolutionary intellectual, bohemian and Don Juan." The program emphasized that students' struggles could not be carried out "in isolation from the class struggle," linking them with those of Bolivian workers and "the exploited classes of the world." It denounced racism, emphasizing that "historical and natural sciences teach that there are no superior or inferior races," and demanded that "social and production relations in the countryside" be transformed to resolve the "agrarian/Indian question." The student federation would "take part in any work tending toward the seizure of power by the workers." As "Bolivia's fate is linked to the triumph of the world socialist cause," it called for a "Confederation of Socialist Republics of Latin America."[5]

The program's approval was a coup for the POR, but the party did not win many recruits on the campuses, soon dominated by the pro-Stalin Partido de la Izquierda Revolucionaria (founded in July 1940). Nonetheless, it gained some members from leftist groupings in Potosí and Oruro. Through Ayala, the Trotskyists met Agar Peñaranda, one of the first women in the POR and eventually one of the most influential as head of its Sucre regional committee.[6]

Oscar Barrientos recalled another early effort to break out of isolation. After the POR's refoundation, some older sympathizers warned: "'You have to avoid becoming a sect.' So I said . . . we're going to [try to] be a mass party." He talked to "some important people in Cochabamba," "representatives of the most famous intellectuals in Bolivia," and told them: "Elections are coming up. As well-known figures, we want you to be candidates of the POR." The campaign was publicized with large-print posters, but the instant "mass party" fell flat when the candidates received a low number of votes.[7] The POR did not become a functioning national organization until an influx of new members and new methods gave rise to a new leadership in the 1940s (see figure 3.1).

International Relations

In their 1935 letter to Trotsky, the founders of the original POR referred to it as "a new section of the International Communist League, embryo

Figure 3.1 POR leaders in 1947. From left, Jorge Salazar, Ernesto Ayala, Guillermo Lora, and Oscar Barrientos. (Courtesy of Emma Bolshia Bravo Cladera)

of our future Fourth International." Connections were tenuous at best, as shown by the paucity of references to the Bolivian group in public and internal publications of the international movement. In early 1938, preparations to found the Fourth International (FI) accelerated. At a meeting of the movement's All American Pacific Bureau, U.S. Trotskyist Max Shachtman called for overcoming "the terrible tradition" of "talking about our Internationalism" but doing little "consistent work . . . in the International movement . . . especially with [regard to] the Latin American countries." Reports were made on several countries, but Bolivia was not mentioned.[8]

The International Secretariat noted that "no link has yet been established . . . with the comrades of several Latin American countries (Bolivia, Panama, Ecuador, Peru, Costa Rica, etc.)." When the FI held its founding conference in September of that year, a report on organizations affiliated or in contact with the International referred to a "Bolshevik-Leninist Group" in Bolivia, without details. The following month, Bolivia did not appear on a list of 37 FI sections.[9]

In its 1938 theses, the refounded POR stated that it was "subject to the fundamental principles of *democratic centralism* of the FI" but was "not yet a national section," as this required reaching "a higher plane of organic development and political influence." Some communication began with the Socialist Workers Party of the United States, which sent its weekly, *The Militant,* but contact became more difficult when World War II broke out. In May 1940, the FI held an "emergency conference" to deal with issues posed by the onset of war. This time, a report on Latin America did discuss the POR, stating:

> From the beginning it was politically a confused organization. As a result . . . [it] went through a series of organizational crises. One of its leading elements, Tristan Marof, a typical petty-bourgeois radical, who uses socialistic phraseology, betrayed and deserted the movement. . . . He is constantly attempting to form a new socialist party. He collaborated with the semi-fascist [sic] dictatorship of Busch, thereby discrediting our movement in Bolivia. . . . [To understand] the crisis that our Bolivian section went through, it is necessary to bear in mind that Tristan Marof is a person with a revolutionary past, and consequently is popular among certain sections of the anti-imperialist forces.

As for the "militants who remained loyal to revolutionary socialism," they "are trying to reorganize their forces under the banner of the Partido Obrero Revolucionario":

> Not very long ago they addressed an official communication asking for admittance to the ranks of the Fourth International. From the documents elaborated in the form of theses . . . we find that in general they are of a revolutionary character, although incomplete in many respects. Quite naturally we must take into consideration that our movement not only in Bolivia, but also in most of the other Latin American countries, is in process not only of organizational but of political formation.[10]

While accurately noting the POR's legacy of political confusion, the FI does not seem to have followed up with real efforts to overcome it.

The party began to be called the Bolivian section of the FI, but it remains unclear when and how this relationship was formalized. As for the POR's leadership at the time, Lora described it as so lackadaisical that when it received a report from the FI on Trotsky's August 1940 assassination, it let two months pass before copying it for distribution in Bolivia.[11]

At the beginning of the war, exiled German FI members had a group in Bolivia. The POR also corresponded with the feuding factions of Argentine Trotskyism, especially the one led by the idiosyncratic "Quebracho" (Liborio Justo). Quebracho became famous when he yelled "Death to Imperialism" at Franklin D. Roosevelt during FDR's state visit to Argentina's president, General Agustín Justo, who just happened to be his father. Quebracho tried hard to establish a following in Bolivia, with little success. More influential were some Brazilian exiles, notably Fúlvio Abramo, who walked more than 450 miles to reach Santa Cruz, as there was no room in the oxcart bearing three of his comrades. Abramo later recalled discussions with an activist who "had been in La Paz with Tristán Marof and José Aguirre Gainsborg," as well as the student Wálter Asbun, whose connections with a rich relative provided some financial support for the movement. Abramo was able to remain until 1946, when Gualberto Villarroel's nationalist regime expelled him from the country.[12]

A "Very Emphatic Fellow"

The early 1940s saw the rise of a new and dynamic figure in Bolivian Trotskyism who would be central to its successes and failures for the next six decades: Guillermo Lora Escóbar. The future POR leader was born in Uncía in 1922. His father, a liberal-minded small entrepreneur with agricultural and mining interests, became a very junior partner of the Patiño company. His mother was a woman from the countryside, described as a *señora de pollera* (lady who wore traditional multilayered skirts).[13]

Guillermo's schooling took him from Oruro to the San Calixto high school in La Paz, where a professor lent him leftist books "and I became a Marxist," opting to devote himself to politics rather than literature, which "always interested me." Continuing his studies at the Colegio Nacional Ayacucho, he was elected president of the student center, editing a paper that the administration burned in the school's patio after it criticized several teachers. After obligatory military service in Cochabamba, he enrolled in the city's law school. When his professor Ricardo Anaya, a leader of the newly formed PIR, asked him to join the pro-Stalin party, Lora refused. In contrast, Trotsky's *Literature and Revolution* won him over. Carlos Bayá, a young student familiar with Warqui's POR circle, put him in contact with the movement, apparently in 1941.[14]

Warqui (Oscar Barrientos) described meeting "a kid who had just done his military service and was studying law here. . . . He used to come to our meetings and sit there listening, without uttering a peep. After a year, he decided to go to the altiplano . . . and gave quite a push to the POR in La Paz." In contrast to the laid-back Warqui, Jorge Abelardo Ramos called Lora "a very emphatic fellow" who "wanted to get things done."[15]

Lora's name is a household word in Bolivia. A strikingly large proportion of intellectual and political figures were associated with him at some point in their careers. As this author has witnessed more than once, he could not walk down the street without being stopped by La Paz literati, comrades, ex-comrades, trade unionists, and TV camera crews. His Aymara features are instantly recognizable in innumerable Bolivian historical documentaries. He was one of the nation's most prolific and broadest-ranging authors. Beginning in 1942 with articles on the PIR, the second anniversary of Trotsky's assassination, and the need to "Defend the Soviet Union" against Hitler's invasion, his *Obras* (Works) number well over sixty volumes.

Lora described himself as "a taciturn being" with "intense pride as well as a certain disdainful attitude toward other people, most simple comforts, everything superfluous and social obligations." Often called "El Fiero," meaning both the fierce one and a person with pockmarks, he has inspired great loyalty among followers, punctuated by bitter disputes. While almost unanimously recognizing his talent and enormous energy, critics (including many former associates) are often scathing. Oscar Barrientos described him as "an order-giver," whose "temper, boss-like manner [and] terrible pride" meant that "many people . . . did not want power [in the organization] to be in Guillermo Lora's hands."[16]

After moving to La Paz, Lora organized a POR cell that made a splash in early 1942, plastering the city with posters against imperialism and the Rosca. "Fourth International Cell Discovered," the press reported, after a police investigation led to "the minor Ramallo, secondary student at a night school . . . who was found pasting the posters up on Illampu Street." In the apartment of Ramallo's history professor, Guillermo Lora, police found "abundant extremist literature and the addresses of the [party's] leaders in this city." Several were soon arrested.[17]

"Aborted Conspiracy to Establish Trotskyist Regime in Bolivia," blared one paper; "Fourth International Attempted to Overthrow Government," trumpeted another. Breathlessly, the press claimed the cell had thirty members; it was led by Lora, who used the name Puka Tankara, "wrote the manifestos . . . and gave the main instructions"; another of the "subversive elements" employed the equally indigenous-sounding pseudonym Quilco Tuculunqui, and a third was called Cachete (Cheek). The "red propaganda" was part of a "vast revolutionary plan," declared the deputy chief of police, and the posters were made "by some artist": Miguel Alandia Pantoja, the Chaco War veteran who served as the cell's treasurer. Lora was not captured, but three Bolivians and a "supposed Argentine anthropologist" were. In addition to the Central Committee in Cochabamba, the POR had groups "in La Paz, Oruro, Potosí, Sucre, Pulacayo and other places," and received foreign correspondence. Its purpose: "to overthrow the current government and establish a new order of things."[18]

Some columnists saw a lighter side. Under the headline "We've Been Saved from the Fourth International, Only to Fall into the Hands of the Gestapo," *La Calle* sarcastically remarked that "the Fourth-ist danger has been exorcised, since 'Cachete' and his four friends have been arrested and cannot 'overthrow' the government," going on to mock *La Razón* for claiming Gestapo agents were active in La Paz. Yet the story still had legs: "POR Members Visited Our Editors," a Cochabamba daily reported. A delegation headed by Ernesto Ayala had come in to say the POR did not receive money from anyone, "has nothing in common with the PIR, Maroff [sic] or the traditional parties," and would welcome the trial threatened by the government (which declared it "outside the law"), as a way to get out the real story. However, a judge freed the imprisoned *poristas* (POR members) and dismissed the charges.[19]

POR versus PIR

Lora drew the lesson that a more professional form of party organization was required. For the time being, it was not feasible to remain in La Paz. He wound up at the Siglo XX mine in Llallagua, "where I began to form a small group [of workers] who considered me their friend, since I helped them with various things," although he did not take up their suggestion to get a job there as a white-collar employee. Indeed, he "became a miners' representative without ever working as a miner." The Llallagua-Uncía region was a crucial area for revolutionary activity: employing 12,000 workers, its mines were less isolated than many others, being near to Oruro and its major railway lines.[20]

As World War II heightened miners' economic importance, it deepened their discontent. Tin was so crucial to the Allied war effort that the

U.S. Senate Armed Services Subcommittee insisted that Bolivian tin prices be frozen for the duration. These "democratic prices," as they were called, were far below those on the open market. As a result, "Bolivia's contribution to the war effort from 1941 to 1945 was ten times greater than U.S. aid to all of Latin America throughout that decade." Mine companies were "reaping a bonanza from the insatiable Allied demand," while miners "suffered overcrowding, inflation and intensified labour discipline," notes Laurence Whitehead. The situation called for "a campaign for labour militancy." However, in line with Soviet policy, the Stalinist PIR "felt it must do nothing that would detract from the war effort" and "restrained its fire against the mining companies." Its theoretical position helped justify this attitude: in the process of "bourgeois-democratic transformation," the PIR declared, "the native bourgeoisie, progressive capitalism, marches toward an alliance with the proletariat, toward . . . national unity."[21]

Although the PIR was the largest left-wing party, it had already found it difficult to "penetrate into the mines and factories, because it did not have a revolutionary program emphasizing the importance of the proletariat, the working class," recalls an Oruro activist recruited to Trotskyism during this period.[22] Now, the PIR's open support to U.S.-allied tin barons alienated miners who were being worked to death by these same employers, jailed by their "Rosca" spokesmen when protests broke out, and attacked with arms supplied by their U.S. patrons. Meanwhile, politicians who had scorned the PIR now found it useful to have this ostensibly Marxist party share responsibility for maintaining labor peace. It would not be long before a PIR Minister of Labor ordered troops to occupy the mines and repress militant strikers.

The POR decided the time was ripe for a vigorous political offensive. In 1942, a prominent pro-Stalin spokesman visited the country: the Mexican lawyer Vicente Lombardo Toledano, whose Latin American Workers Federation called on workers to maintain "anti-fascist unity" with the United States. Recalling that Lombardo had been a "director of the attacks against Leon Trotsky" in Mexico, a POR leaflet warned that his "mission is to get mine workers to continue giving their lungs to Wall Street."[23] Taking a page from the Moscow Trials, PIR leaders branded the POR "Nazi-Trotskyites," accompanying this with violent attempts to silence their critics. They found themselves increasingly vulnerable to the epithet the POR hurled back: "Rosco-Stalinists."

In the mining city of Oruro, the POR established a small group that met in the home of Lora's former classmate Alberto Aguilar. One of the most active members was Fernando Bravo James, a Chaco veteran and schoolteacher who worked for a time in the mines. The POR won a significant victory when it recruited Leticia Fajardo, one of the city's most prominent leftists. At eighteen, Fajardo became a local celebrity after carrying the red banner in a march inaugurating a leftist conference. Right-wingers attacked, firing at the marchers, but she continued to carry the red flag. Fajardo joined the PIR's youth group, then the PIR itself. In 1944, when she was twenty-five, she published a letter of resignation: the PIR had "betrayed the historic interests of the proletariat," putting itself "in the unconditional service of the feudal-bourgeoisie," she wrote. After analyzing the programs of the different parties, she had "reached the conclusion that the only one that fights for the socialist revolution and expresses the real needs of the proletariat" was the POR.[24]

Fajardo became a lawyer and public defender, an organizer of factory workers—many of them women—and, after joining the POR, adviser to unionists at the San José mine, bakers, and other labor groups. She was also active in POR work among indigenous peasants, as the party organized a number of rural unions in the Oruro region during World War II despite heavy repression in the countryside. Fajardo was one of those blamed for a local Indian uprising in which landowners had their throats cut. During the crackdown of the late 1940s, she moved temporarily to Argentina, where she married Adolfo Perelman, a left activist who became an adviser to Lechín and friend to the group of Trotskyists who eventually entered the MNR.[25]

A former comrade remembers Fajardo as "a real teacher to me, with a great library" of socialist classics that he devoured as an adolescent gravitating to the POR during World War II. "She was in her mid-twenties then, extremely friendly, with a down-to-earth manner even though she was a philosophy teacher as well as a lawyer." Active in political and union work for many years, Fajardo authored a volume of poetry about the working people of the altiplano, with a cover illustration by Miguel Alandia.[26]

The POR expanded to new areas, still recruiting by the handful. A party leader seeking to emphasize postwar growth claimed that as late as 1945 it had only seventeen real members. In Sucre, Hugo González Moscoso was won over by his secondary school teacher, Ernesto Ayala. Four other students joined them in founding a Regional Committee of the POR. On the first anniversary of Trotsky's assassination, "we organized a commemoration" that was broadcast on the radio. The local archdiocese newspaper "came out with the headline 'Fourth International in Sucre,' basically calling for us to be wiped out. That was how my membership in the Fourth International

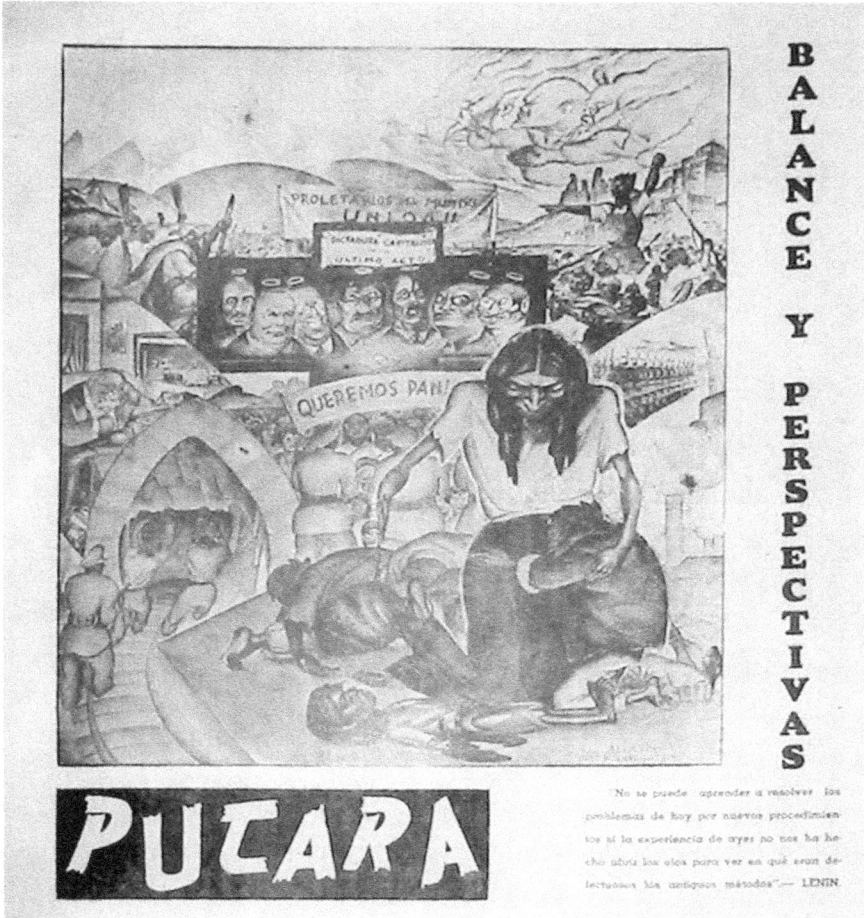

Figure 3.2 *Pucara* (1945) cover by Miguel Alandia Pantoja. (Courtesy of Emma Bolshia Bravo Cladera)

began." The Sucre committee had good relations with a semi-autonomous grouping in Potosí called the Centro Obrero Revolucionario, led by Ismael Pérez and future Trotskyist senator Lucio Mendívil, which eventually fused with the POR.[27]

The Potosí committee published the first issue of *Lucha Obrera* (Workers' Struggle). The POR had experimented with a political-cultural journal called *Pucara* ("fortress" in Quechua; see figure 3.2), but *Lucha Obrera* became its central publication after production was moved to La Paz

Figure 3.3 From its first issues *Lucha Obrera* featured striking graphics. (Courtesy of Emma Bolshia Bravo Cladera)

(see figure 3.3). However, González noted, the paper was initially so focused on miners' issues that a packet was returned from Tarija, an agricultural region in Bolivia's south, with a note saying there were no miners there.[28]

The Catavi Massacre

In late 1942, a major strike broke out at Patiño's mines in Catavi, one of a series of labor conflicts in the Oruro and Potosí regions. The outbreak was inconvenient for Anglo-American interests: after Japan occupied British Malaya the previous year, half the tin for the Allied war effort came from Bolivia. The government, then headed by General Enrique Peñaranda, sent troops to crush the strike, massacring workers and imprisoning dozens of union activists. One of the regiments was commanded by Major Gualberto Villarroel, who would soon seize power.[29]

Women played a crucial role in the Catavi conflict. Miners' wives were outraged by the closing of the company stores (*pulperías*) they depended on to feed their families. When the army shot down an elderly woman named

Figure 3.4 Detail of Miguel Alandia Pantoja mural depicting Uncía and Catavi massacres. (Courtesy of Cecilia Salazar de la Torre)

María Barzola, she became a symbol of the suffering and determination of miners' communities. Occurring "at a moment when the mine workers were experiencing a process of historical transition in their class consciousness," the Catavi Massacre became "a landmark in the formative stage of their class identity"[30] (see figure 3.4).

Many decades later, a long-time activist from Oruro remembered the impact it had on him:

> I was 15 at the time. Our parents used to send my brother and me to sell clothes and other merchandise to the miners. We were there on December 21, 1942. We saw the mobilization, when the workers came down from the company offices in Catavi. They were shouting for a wage increase and chanting "Long live the miners! Viva Bolivia!" There were explosions, the sound of machine-guns, rifles. We had to gather up the things we were selling.
>
> The shots were flying everywhere, but we were curious. With a certain amount of audacity, we made it to the plaza in Llallagua where the cadavers, the people whose bodies had been destroyed by machine-gun fire, were being taken. It was a scene out of Dante, there was so much blood, screams, pain. The miners didn't have guns or even dynamite, but the soldiers were very well armed. They just opened fire on the mass of people. There were men, women, many mothers with their children, because mothers take their children to demonstrations, since there is no one to look after them. We saw all the bodies gathered together at the kiosk in the plaza of Llallagua. We had to leave because the shooting didn't stop. . . .
>
> This event made me devote myself to politics, because of my indignation at the massacre, the way the defenseless people were shot down, not knowing what to do when faced with machine guns.

Back in Oruro, an older schoolmate put him in contact with the POR, where he met leaders like Fernando Bravo, Leticia Fajardo, Alberto Aguilar, and Humberto Salamanca. His first task was to distribute leaflets denouncing the massacre. He decided to do it in the middle of the night, leaving them under people's doors. When he was ordered down to the police station for questioning, a sympathetic journalist told him: "Say nothing, and always remember, there's nothing worse than a stool pigeon."[31]

The POR called for a general strike to support the embattled miners, who "have made a modest demand: that they be permitted to live as human beings." Lora advised union delegates during the strike and suffered the first in his long list of arrests when police caught him with the stencil of a strike support manifesto. In the United States, the Socialist Workers Party's *Militant* wrote that the U.S. ambassador had "joined the Bolivian government and capitalists in smearing [mine] strikers as Nazi saboteurs." After shooting down the Catavi strikers, the "butcher Peñaranda visited the United States, was feasted by Roosevelt at the White House, and hailed by the capitalist press as a champion of democracy and a firm ally."[32]

It was Víctor Paz Estenssoro, however, who became famous for denouncing the government's handling of the strike, using his Chamber of Deputies seat for a fiery interpellation (parliamentary question) on the Catavi affair. The episode raised his profile as *Jefe* of the MNR, officially founded only months before by *La Calle* journalists, ex-functionaries of the Toro and Busch regimes, and several former Beta Gama members.

The MNR was far from being a party of the left. In its early years, it displayed the marked influence of the Axis powers. *La Calle* had long been obsessively anti-Semitic: a favorite theme was the ethnic background of tin baron Mauricio Hochschild, whose newspaper *La Razón* it sneeringly called "the Jewish daily." The MNR's founding program was full of diatribes against "the maneuvers of Judaism," socialism ("an argument for helping foreigners meddle" in the nation's affairs), internationalism, and the "universalist ideology of a working class that is only now being born in our country." In quasi-indigenist language it proclaimed, "We carry in our blood the heritage of the children of the Sun," but promised only to "study the Indian agrarian question on a scientific basis," so that the "adequate organization" of agriculture could produce "the greatest yield." It called for nationalizing public services but not the mines. Paz Estenssoro had, in fact, served as a lawyer for the Patiño company.[33]

Although its denunciation of the Catavi Massacre got union activists' attention, the early MNR was a markedly urban, middle-class party with few links to labor and fewer still to the peasantry, seeking "national unity" rather than class struggle. Nonetheless, its leaders understood that to become a nationwide political force it needed to gain support among the working classes and include "pro-labor" themes in its discourse. The MNR hit the big time not by organizing from below but from the top down. The opportunity came when it joined the government of Major Gualberto Villarroel, who seized power in December 1943 in what U.S. Trotskyists called "a typical South American coup d'etat by a military clique of young officers."[34]

Villarroel was backed by the military lodge Razón de Patria (Radepa, loosely Cause of the Fatherland) in alliance with the MNR, which got three cabinet seats. Paz, known as a talented technocrat, was named finance minister. In its nationalist outlook, but not its resources (given Bolivia's extreme poverty), the new regime was similar to that of Juan Perón and the other Argentine officers who took power that same year. Once in office, the MNR found it wise to modify its language. It was not, in fact, a fascist movement; its Axis sympathies reflected the frustrated "anti-imperialism" of elite sectors whose "career open to talent" was blocked by the Rosca, closely identified with Anglo-American interests. Disencumbering itself of pro-Axis baggage became a priority after Villarroel, under U.S. pressure, temporarily ousted the MNR from the government.

"I am not an enemy of the rich, but I am more a friend of the poor," reads the plaque to Villarroel outside the Palacio Quemado. His government launched some labor reforms and gained popularity in the mines by backing formation of the nationwide Miners Federation (FSTMB) in June 1944. Vowing to respect private property and support the Allied war effort, he sought to control grassroots organizations as much as possible, cracked down on left- and right-wing opponents, and attacked universities where opposition groups were active.

Bolivian Trotskyists found it difficult to arrive at a clear analysis of the new regime. Shortly after Villarroel took over, the POR warned that with this coup by "*criollo* Nazis," the "MNR will impose savage oppression." The Oruro branch formed a "Proletarian Committee to Fight Nazi-Fascism."[35] Hugo González later explained:

> The party had a contradictory position. . . . Under the influence of Allied propaganda and the characteristics of the Radepa lodge, there was a tendency to say that Radepa was a fascist group, and this was extended to the Villarroel government. However, this was not a firm characterization. . . . There had not been any investigation or nationwide discussion about this in the party. What led the party to make this characterization was the systematic repression carried out during the Villarroel-Radepa government . . . In Sucre, I was arrested with the leadership, made up of teachers and students, and shipped off to the Coati penal island.[36]

In Oruro, the young POR member Enrique Ferrante was accused of undermining labor support to the regime, arrested, and subjected to severe torture and simulated executions. With the aid of Fernando Bravo and others, he escaped to Argentina, establishing close bonds with Trotskyist activists there before returning to Bolivia and taking up a leadership role in the party's Sucre Regional Committee.[37]

While wary of further repression, the party began to modify its characterization after Villarroel convened a national Indian Congress in 1945 and vowed to attack the *pongueaje* system of rural labor obligations. (The promise remained a dead letter but was widely seen as indicative of progressive intentions.) When the PIR and Rosca parties formed the "Anti-Fascist Democratic Front" (FDA) against him, the POR "rejected this . . . and worked against both the oligarchy and Villarroel."[38]

A POR leaflet denounced "the 'Rosca' which has been forced into opposition and solemnly intones phrases about 'democratic liberties'" despite its record of repression, as well as the Villarroel government, which enforced "suppression of union independence and pitiless oppression of the national majority, while obeying the desires of Washington (that is, capitalism, which lives off Bolivian workers' lungs)." Instead of joining "either of these bourgeois gangs," workers should form a "Proletarian United Front . . . to break the chains of private property and its MNR government." Another flier denounced "class collaboration and national unity loudly preached by MNR demagogues, the opposition Rosca," and PIR "servants of Yankee imperialism." The PIR was especially vulnerable: its leader José Antonio Arze asked the United States to send troops to overthrow Villarroel, saying this "would not be an old-styled imperialist intervention" but an example of the "cooperation which the democratic forces of South America desperately seek."[39]

The POR did not have a unified response when Villarroel was overthrown in a popular uprising encouraged by the right but fueled by widespread anger at his repressive actions and inability to meet basic needs of the urban population. In one of the most famous images in Bolivian history, Villarroel was seized by a crowd—including market women said to have stabbed him with the long pins from their ponchos—and hanged from a lamppost in front of the presidential palace.[40] The "antifascist" FDA used tripartite committees of teachers, students, and laborers to mobilize protest, then set up a government of Rosca parties and the PIR. Because the overthrow of Villarroel on July 21, 1946, marked the beginning of a new and painful period of Rosca reaction, "who did what when" would be a highly charged question.

Due to a "lack of political homogeneity," Lora writes, POR groups in different cities had distinct, sometimes counterposed, positions. In Cochabamba, leading party member Carlos Cossío represented university students on the local Tripartite Committee, a long-time militant recalled, and was "the first to come out on the balcony of the municipal building and speak in its name the day after Villarroel was hanged." In Oruro the party remained neutral, influenced by miners who sympathized with Villarroel. In La Paz, party members took part in the rising, under the leadership of young economist and novelist Jorge Salazar Mostajo, then the POR's Secretary General. A "Left University Front" participated in the overthrow, issuing a manifesto signed by a Leading Committee that included the POR's Edwin Möller. Möller recalled that in La Paz, "We participated actively, militarily. We even took over Radio Nueva América and called for creating the tripartite committee of workers, students and teachers, against the reactionary tendency that called for turning power over to the little old men of the Supreme Court."[41]

A "worker POR member" from La Paz wrote that the PIR lied by "claim[ing] the POR was not present in the struggle against Nazi-fascism": POR members were "on the barricades, arms in hand, leading the people's action," unlike the "revolutionaries of July 22," office-seekers who arrived the day after to pick up the spoils. It was they who "warned of the danger that the bourgeoisie and its servants would take advantage of the uprising." Two weeks after Villarroel's fall, an "emergency" POR gathering hailed "the revolutionary ascent and sharpening class struggle," while vowing to "heighten workers' distrust of the [new] government" and "attack the FDA and the bourgeois slogan of National Unity." While denouncing the FDA as the "United Front of the Bourgeoisie," it called for the tripartite committees to "oversee and check" (*controlar*) the government's actions.[42]

Villarroel's fall also gave rise to discussions within the international Trotskyist movement. A Mexican Trotskyist newspaper, later echoed by the American Socialist Workers Party (SWP), denounced the United States for backing the overthrow of Villarroel. To justify this, "Yankee imperialism . . . characterized [his government] as Nazi-fascist." The SWP's theoretical journal stated that despite the masses' heroism, the Rosca-PIR alliance reaped the uprising's benefits. The article, written in Bolivia, warned of possible clashes between anti-Villarroel workers in the cities and pro-Villarroel workers in the mines. In a book emphasizing the plebeian nature of the July 1946 revolt, an Argentine leftist quoted Trotskyist painter Miguel Alandia, who emphasized the POR's opposition to the new regime, declaring: "Only on the basis of a revolution that spreads through Latin America and is supported by the North American working class can our revolution in Bolivia develop positively, in a socialist sense."[43]

To the Mines

The POR held an important conference in 1946, attended by forty delegates from La Paz, Oruro, Cochabamba, Sucre, and Santa Cruz. The Cuban Trotskyist press enthusiastically reported the event, which showed that the POR was "growing stronger, in the midst of major strike struggles," and that the "formation of a genuine proletarian vanguard is proceeding."[44] The gathering was "the point of departure for acting as a national party," undertaking "a turn to the proletariat," Hugo González remembered; it was a refreshing contrast to the previous gathering, a "failure" attended by less than a dozen delegates. The party center moved "from the provincial, university

Figure 3.5 Trotsky commemoration rally in Oruro, August 1946. Leticia Fajardo and Fernando Bravo stand in front of the banner; Guillermo Lora is directly beneath them. (Courtesy of Emma Bolshia Bravo Cladera)

city of Cochabamba, where our leadership had been vegetating, to the number one industrial center, La Paz." Some workers from a glass factory attended, and the POR also began to carry out work in a bottling plant and several textile factories. Above all, it launched "a heavy turn toward work in the mines."[45]

This made Oruro even more important. In August 1946, the city's main daily reported the local POR's well-attended commemoration of Trotsky's assassination, part of a "campaign to recruit new members." Comrades in New York were thrilled: *The Militant* described presentations by Leticia Fajardo and two other women militants, as well as Lora and Fernando Bravo, revolutionary poetry, and the singing of the "Internationale" and the "Workers' Marseillaise."[46] A photo of the rally shows a group of women around a smiling Fajardo, who proudly raises her fist in front of a banner reading "VIVA TROTSKY" (see figure 3.5).

That Lora's father lived near Oruro was helpful as the young activist worked to strengthen links with mine unionists. Some were rank-and-file miners; a peasant radical remembers one friend: "This guy was a leader, kind of a Trotskyist, but he never got anywhere near a school. He learned to read as a worker, and Guillermo Lora taught him." The most important contact, however, was Juan Lechín. The tall, handsome, and gregarious son of a Lebanese merchant, he had been a white-collar mine employee, gained popularity on the company's soccer team, and held a minor municipal post in Catavi. Lora states that the POR started meeting with him in early 1945, when he was already the "unquestioned" leader of the FSTMB.[47]

Lechín would later claim that "Lora was selfish and wouldn't lend his copies of pamphlets by Trotsky, even though we lived together for six months." Lora says Lechín was briefly a secret member of the POR (while also belonging to the MNR), but Lechín insisted he never joined the Trotskyist party. After Villarroel's fall, the press identified Lechín as one of the main spokesmen for the MNR; a typical article warned: "Propaganda Circulating in Favor of Paz Estenssoro-Lechín." As Lora admits, Lechín "was clearly working as the vanguard of the nationalists within the labor movement, even in his moments of greatest radicalism." Noting that Lechín and his lieutenant Mario Torres "calibrated their speeches to the masses' moods," he cites a POR report describing the FSTMB leaders making "Villarroel-ist propaganda" since they wanted to "get immediate support" from miners.[48]

The crucial contradiction was that POR leaders were the main advisers to MNR member Lechín. By all accounts (including his own), Lora was the most important—writing speeches, documents, and resolutions for the labor leader—but Hugo González noted that "the entire [POR] leadership in La Paz and above all in Oruro" acted as advisers to Lechín, who "played a role filled with ambiguities." Lora's younger sister Gloria remembers that "Guillermo was Lechín's teacher. When we lived in Llallagua, [Lechín] always used to come looking for him. So did Mario Torres and a lot of the other union leaders." Years later, Lechín was part of the MNR government, "so one of the times Guillermo got arrested, I went to complain. Right to his face, I told Lechín: 'You've forgotten how you always used to come looking for my brother.' 'No, no,' he said, 'it's not like that at all.'"[49]

Lora's description of preparations for Lechín to address a labor gathering in early 1946 illustrates how the POR conceived of the relationship. "The speech had been carefully worked out by the POR leadership. . . . In short, it was the POR program in trade-union language." For Lechín, "whatever his personal, caudillo ambitions," it meant "making a leap into the void" because the text criticized both the Rosca and the MNR, which was "his party." Thus "it was necessary that he play his role well, and he was put through some real training. He rode to Siglo XX in a railway car, sitting with the POR's general secretary. . . . It was a long trip, and he kept going back to the speech, reading it over again and again." For a whole period, "Lechín continued reading the speeches written by the leadership of the POR."[50]

Bismarck is reputed to have said that every alliance consists of a horse and a rider. The young POR militants believed they were in the saddle.

Lechín's relations with the POR grew closer in a period when he was relatively "isolated and forced to operate on his own," observes political scientist James Malloy. "It was not the style of the MNR bourgeois elite to spend any considerable time in mining camps, or any non-urban place for that matter," but "the MNR needed labor might" and used Lechín to gain influence. Given his relations with the Trotskyists, and its eventual reliance on mine worker support, the MNR was "rooted in an alliance (often an uneasy one) with the POR." For its part, the POR hoped to push the MNR in a "more radical direction."[51]

The POR helped give Lechín a more revolutionary image, with the nationalist party accruing most of the political benefit. While presenting their own viewpoint in articles and manifestos, Bolivian Trotskyists were becoming a radical appendage to *lechinismo* in the labor movement, while Lechín guarded the MNR's left flank. Despite the Trotskyists' "campaign against petty-bourgeois nationalism," Lora writes, "for a whole period there was a tacit front between activists of the POR and the MNR." "Everything" the POR did in this period "led objectively to the numerical, but not political [sic], strengthening of the MNR." This bred "the intricate confusion . . . in workers' brains between the goals, methods, organizational nature, and so forth, of the MNR and the POR."[52]

In their self-concept and vocabulary, POR activists were fighting for Trotsky's program of permanent revolution. In practice, rather than winning political independence of the working class, they built up the MNR's labor wing. The young POR's signal political triumph, about to occur at Pulacayo, simultaneously displayed a signal political weakness, the alliance with Lechín (see figure 3.6).

It is no exaggeration to say that in 1946 the Trotskyists burst upon the labor scene. At the FSTMB's Third Congress in March of that year, they scored a major coup. In a letter to the Fourth International, a party leader claimed: "Our POR comrades turned this congress into a Trotskyist demonstration and a repudiation of the government regime." At the beginning of the miners' gathering, *La Razón* reported: "The revelation of the congress [is] Guillermo Lora, delegate of the Unemployed Workers Union." At the inaugural gathering, Lora "stood out for his oratorical gifts, though he proved to be inspired by Trotzkyite politics . . . attacking private property, the imperialist powers, and governments that organize massacres." Of all the delegates, Lora "gained the most applause, proposing the formation of a proletarian united front and condemning the alliance of left and liberal parties." After Lechín criticized the regime "indirectly," and recording secretary Nelson Capellino did so directly, the Labor Ministry's

Figure 3.6 Juan Lechín (center, gray hair) at COB meeting, ca. early 1970s. First from left, seated: Marcelo Quiroga; fourth from left (partly obscured): Guillermo Lora. (Courtesy of Cesar Escóbar)

inspector general, attending as the government's representative, left the hall.[53]

"Third Miners' Congress Begins with Violent Discussion on Credentials," the press reported the following day. The Labor Ministry's spokesman intervened to challenge Lora's credentials, saying he had "incrusted himself in the Federation in order to take it along the path of the Fourth International." Lora replied that he "would a thousand times rather be a red internationalist than a fascist." Newspapers competed for angles: "The Unemployed Miners Union Wants the Trotskyist Partido Obrero Revolucionario in Its Leadership—Miners' Congress Begins," one headline announced. Another gleefully claimed, "Lora, Leader of the Fourth International, Was Fired as a Do-Nothing in February" from a job as legal adviser in a branch of the Agriculture Ministry. The Minister of Labor issued a communiqué denouncing the "POR membership" of FSTMB recording secretary Capellino, adding: "Mr. Guillermo Lora has no legal standing" at the event, "since the Union of Unemployed Workers he claims to belong to does not exist."[54]

In his POR-written speech, Lechín denounced "class collaboration" and called for the destruction of capitalism. Resolutions appealed to workers to take "the path of class struggle, without any sectors of the bourgeoisie," calling for a collective contract, strike funds, a labor confederation independent of political parties, and "a workers' bloc to fight against capitalism." The gathering also adopted demands drawn from the Fourth International's "Transitional Program" (although this was not stated), including creation of workers' defense groups, a "sliding scale of wages" (to compensate for inflation), and a "sliding scale of hours" (to shorten the workweek at no loss in pay and provide more jobs).[55]

In late September 1946, the POR held its own Fifth Conference, attended by delegates from La Paz, Oruro, Cochabamba, Potosí, and Sucre. The gathering was chaired by Escóbar (Lora), who lost to Miguel Núñez in the election of a new general secretary after he was criticized for breaking "democratic centralism" by taking "precipitate" disciplinary action against a party member. The conference decided to publish a manifesto and strengthen the party by forming "workers' cells," but "not to print membership cards." In its effort to aid the formation of peasant unions, it would encourage them to affiliate with the FSTMB.

With national elections on the horizon, the conference voted to "fight the activities of the Tripartite Committee, since it is . . . a reactionary organization," and to withhold support from any presidential candidate presented by the PIR. There was "a wide discussion of the possibility that the party might win seats" in Congress, and the majority voted to seek the POR's "legalization" in order to run "with our own slates, and together with those of the miners." Since "we will be running in agreement with the miners, the Oruro party committee must keep in permanent contact with FSTMB leaders."[56]

The Thesis of Pulacayo

A Web site promoting tourism in Bolivia notes that visitors to its spectacular salt flats may pass through Pulacayo, "a significant town in Bolivian social history, for here the famous Tesis [sic] of Pulacayo was formulated."[57] (Its other attraction is a train once robbed by Butch Cassidy and the Sundance Kid.) The renowned Pulacayo "Thesis"—a credo of revolutionary radicalism adopted by the miners' union in late 1946—continues to be a reference point for social movements.[58] Its approval by Bolivia's most important labor organization is a landmark of Latin American Trotskyism.

In November 1946, the FSTMB was scheduled to hold a new congress in the mining town of Pulacayo. In preparation, the POR wrote a document outlining the Federation's "central tasks," consisting of a series of points or "theses"; the text became known interchangeably as the Thesis (singular) or Theses (plural) of Pulacayo. Guillermo Lora later claimed miners "dictated" it to him, but he clearly drafted it, with input from other POR leaders. Fernando Bravo's wife remembered being the one who typed it up, and Hugo González said: "The party gave the Thesis of Pulacayo to the Llallagua miners so they could present it."[59]

The miners' congress was chaired by the secretary-general of the Pulacayo union, Julio Bardales. A Chaco veteran and acquaintance of Tristán Marof, he considered himself a moderate leftist and later commanded armed miners on the MNR side in the 1949 civil war. Interviewed in an old age home, Bardales recalled that "el Fierito Guillermo Lora"—with whom he was imprisoned on four different occasions—became influential in the Miners Federation by "going around advising small and medium-sized unions." He remembers that Lora's Thesis was voted quickly, with little debate, at the end of the congress after Lechín and his lieutenant, "el Loco Mario Torres," were already gone: "'Having seen the theses written by compañero Guillermo Lora, those in favor,' people yelled yes—approved."[60]

Their decision was a national sensation. The Thesis was published in full by the daily press.[61] A section entitled "transitional demands" repeated the slogan of a "sliding scale" of wages and hours, calling for workers' control of the mines, "armed pickets" or "armed worker cadres," and formation of a national labor federation. The authorities and press were most alarmed by the overtly political standpoint of the document, which proclaimed: "We must not make any bloc or compromise with the bourgeoisie" and counterposed a "proletarian united front" to "the fronts which petty-bourgeois reformists are constantly proposing." The union decided to run candidates in workers' districts, seeking to send a "Miners Parliamentary Bloc" to both chambers of congress and "convert parliament into a revolutionary tribune." While "our representatives will be a minority" in opposition to the government, "they will unmask the maneuvers of the bourgeoisie from within the chambers themselves."

Denouncing support to "any government that is not our own, that is, of the working class," the Thesis put forward a clear and unequivocal position:

"Worker" ministers do not change the structure of bourgeois governments. So long as the state defends capitalist society, "worker" ministers become vulgar pimps for the bourgeoisie. The worker who exchanges his post of struggle in the revolutionary ranks for a bourgeois cabinet portfolio goes over to the ranks of traitors. The bourgeoisie invents "worker" ministers the better to deceive the workers. . . .

The FSTMB will never join bourgeois governments, because that would mean the most open betrayal of the exploited masses, forgetting that our line is the revolutionary line of the class struggle.[62]

When they made this statement in 1946, the authors of the Thesis knew how badly things had gone ten years before, when labor leader Waldo Alvarez joined Toro's government. One can only imagine what they might have said if someone had suggested that they would support Lechín and Torres as "worker ministers" in an MNR government. That is precisely what happened during the 1952 Revolution, but those events were six years in the future.

A crucial section of the Thesis analyzes the "type of revolution to be carried out" in Bolivia. It has been a commonplace in the Trotskyist movement to state that its "inspiration" was "the Marxist conception of Permanent Revolution."[63] It begins by stating: "The proletariat, even in Bolivia, is the revolutionary class *par excellence*." Amidst "the amalgam of the most diverse stages of economic development," capitalist exploitation predominates. The miners "are the most advanced and combative sector of the country's proletariat," which was becoming "one of the most radical" in the world due to its "extreme youth and incomparable vigor," its lack of "parliamentary or class-collaborationist traditions," and the "extreme belligerence" of the country's class conflicts.

The document refers to a "bourgeois-democratic revolution" that would be led by the working class rather than "'progressive' sectors of the bourgeoisie." However, the Thesis states confusingly, "those who claim we propose an immediate socialist revolution in Bolivia are liars," since "we know quite well that objective conditions for this do not exist." Instead, "we state clearly that the revolution will be bourgeois-democratic in its objectives and only an episode of the proletarian revolution because of the social class that will lead it." The concept of a bourgeois-democratic revolution under proletarian leadership differed significantly from Trotsky's theory that the "tasks" historically associated with bourgeois revolutions would be carried out by the working class in a proletarian socialist revolution, supported by the poor peasants.[64]

Linking Bolivia's workers to the international proletariat, as they sought to destroy "an international force: imperialism," the Thesis declared solidarity with North American workers, even stating (perhaps because of the postwar strike wave there) that "the U.S. is a powder keg which a single spark can set off." Nonetheless, its discussion of revolution in Bolivia is essentially circumscribed to the national terrain. This is another contrast with Trotsky's permanent revolution theory, which stressed the need to spread revolution, above all to the dominant capitalist countries, because a workers' state isolated in a poor country would succumb.

The Thesis vows "war to the death against reformist collaborationism" and, implicitly attacking the PIR, denounces "'leftists' hired out to Yankee imperialism." Yet it does not mention any party by name, including the MNR. Given that Lechín, Torres, and other union leaders were MNR members, it would clearly have been an embarrassment to do so. Nor does it pose the need for a revolutionary party of the working class.

Some writers have pointed to the "revolutionary syndicalist" outlook of many union activists. One maintains that "the Thesis of Pulacayo tended to accentuate the anarcho-syndicalist components [of labor ideology] and center political action in the union: this would be the basis for the positions taken by the FSTMB in the April 1952 days that led to the national revolution begun that year."[65] However, FSTMB leaders were not "non-party" men. When *el compañero* Lechín" would visit Potosí in the late 1940s and "talk about the Thesis of Pulacayo," retired miner Julio García recalls, "the workers were confused as to whether he was a Movimientista or a Trotskyist. . . . The workers confused the POR with the MNR." Ideological confusion was so widespread, Lora admits, that "at a certain point" the "man in the street could not see the difference between the POR and the MNR."[66] This was innate in the situation: the POR wrote the Thesis for union leaders who wove a strand of revolutionary discourse into their appeal while backing a decidedly non-proletarian, outspokenly anti-socialist party: the MNR.

There can be little doubt that the Thesis both reflected and further stimulated Bolivian miners' militancy and class consciousness. They might die young after giving their lungs to the mine, despised as "ignorant" Indians—but the Thesis said they would become masters of their fate. The Thesis proclaimed they would lead all Bolivia to a different future. The Thesis meant this and more to miners driven time and again to radical revolt. The fateful contradiction, played out in the ensuing years, was the role its authors played in entangling this combativity with illusions in the nationalist party.

Reactions

Approved at the miners' congress, "the Tesis de Pulacayo became the official ideology of the FSTMB," and provoked strong reactions across the political spectrum. A spokesman for the extreme right later lamented that it was "one of the most widely discussed and influential documents in Bolivia's political life." Enrique Hertzog, who became Bolivia's president in March 1947, attacked it as "an insult to good sense and a crime against the social order," whose authors deserved to be "placed outside the law." Two years later, his Minister of Labor told parliament: "The Thesis of Pulacayo . . . has been a political weapon to attack the government." The Republican Socialists denounced "the conglomerate of false, apostate leaders and pharisaical traffickers," whose "extreme doctrines and ideology, under Trotzkyite guise" served to "twist and denature" workers' legitimate aspirations "since the . . . Miners' Congress at Pulacayo."[67]

PIR leader José Antonio Arze said members of his party fought to "unmask the demagogic maneuvers of the professional agitators of Trotzkyite affiliation" at the Pulacayo congress. A clerical paper thought it prudent to remind readers that "Communism, Whether PIRist or Trotskyist, Is the Antithesis of Catholicism." Meanwhile, "Anti-Thesis of Pulacayo" was the nickname given to a manifesto by Walter Guevara, theoretician of the MNR's right wing. Decades later, supporters of popular front president Hernán Siles Zuazo, then chief of the "MNR-Left," blamed social unrest on the Pulacayo "Thesis of Disaster."[68]

As the FSTMB prepared for its 1947 congress at Colquiri, a progovernment newspaper urged miners to abandon "the false inspiration of 'the permanent revolution.'" Another warned against "professional agitators" who were "inciting rebellion, provoking illegal strikes and angrily, insistently preaching the 'dictatorship of the Proletariat,'" whereas miners' real problem was the "organic decadence that results from alcoholism" and "turns into hereditary diseases, that cause the race to degenerate."[69]

Officials expressed alarm when they visited mine camps. "POR Agents Provoke Hostility to Congressmen," the press complained. Labor Minister and PIR member Alfredo Mendizábal warned: "The Trotzkyite POR operates with impunity, with erroneous doctrines aimed at sowing anarchy in the mine camps and penetrating the countryside to subvert the peasant masses." At the union congress, he told the assembled miners: "The Government of National Unity expects the greatest effort from you and all Bolivians, in order to carry out, victoriously, the bourgeois-democratic revolution."[70]

However, Lechín told the conference that "our wisest move was declaring at Pulacayo that Miners Federation leaders will never be part of any bourgeois government," never "become bourgeois ministers instead of occupying the magnificent post of revolutionaries." The "Thesis of Pulacayo has

[been] a source of guidance in moments of difficulty," as "we have become conscious revolutionaries" oriented by "the hope of proletarian revolution." Moreover, "only those who seek to liquidate the FSTMB would try to destroy the Thesis of Pulacayo." The Thesis should be widely circulated: "Comrade slaves of the mines, have the valor to speak your truth, the truth of all the oppressed." POR member Miguel Alandia greeted the delegates in the name of the Central Obrera Nacional, the labor federation the POR was trying to establish. President Hertzog reacted ominously: "We must put an end to agitation in the mines," especially since the Colquiri gathering "ratified the criminal theses of the Pulacayo Congress, simply repeating the vulgar anarchism that has no place in our country."[71]

Bolivian Trotskyists viewed the Thesis as their most important achievement. "At Pulacayo, the workers showed they have acquired a full consciousness of their historic mission," a POR manifesto declared. The document's revolutionary conclusions "are valid not only for the mining proletariat in particular, but the Bolivian proletariat in general." Lora later wrote that "as it expresses the proletariat's strategic objectives, [it] is perennial, so long as capitalism is not buried." Even his opponents within the movement would celebrate it for decades to come: in the 1960s, the POR group led by Hugo González had a special song about the Thesis.[72]

The international Trotskyist movement greeted the Thesis of Pulacayo as an important step forward, but there were some critics. After a group of Latin American Trotskyists visited Bolivia in September 1947, they observed: "The 'Thesis of Pulacayo,' a particular expression of our transitional program, came out not as a document of the party [i.e., the POR] but as a program of the Miners Federation. This hesitation to act directly as Trotskyists, constantly shielding oneself behind the trade-union organization, is a proof of political weakness," which they compared to Cuban Trotskyists' earlier practice of publishing key documents "under the signature of the Havana Labor Federation" when they were influential in that body. The report criticized the "lack of emphasis our comrades place on differentiating the POR" from the FSTMB, particularly since key union leaders were "originally Movimientistas" (in reality, they still were). This helped reactionaries portray the Trotskyists "as agents of the MNR."[73]

Writing shortly after the 1952 Revolution, French Trotskyist Pierre Broué put forward a different critique: while it "formulated tasks whose realization posed the question of power," the Pulacayo Thesis "never took up the question of preparing for the seizure of power." If the Bolivian masses were "preparing for the decisive battle . . . their leadership was not prepared for the breadth of the coming struggles."[74]

Six Years of Rosca Repression

The Pulacayo Thesis stated that when tin barons attacked miners' basic interests, workers should occupy the mines. FSTMB leader Torres warned that the employers were threatening to close the important San José mine in Oruro. However, the promised occupation did not occur: "frightened by the tasks they faced, union leaders capitulated without a fight," giving in "at the decisive moment and entering negotiations with the government," Broué wrote. "The working class lost the initiative." Seeing that it was "retreating, disoriented by the failures of its leadership," the Rosca took the offensive to launch "a period of bitter defeats."[75]

This period of reaction, from late 1946 to 1952, has entered Bolivian history as the *sexenio rosquero*—six years of Rosca rule. Filled with repression, the purging of radical workers, MNR conspiracies for a "putsch," and the disintegration of the political order, it set the stage for the April 1952 Revolution. Zavaleta calls the sexenio a "prolonged civil war" in which "the weapons were those of the miners, the dead were miners, the large-scale operations of resistance were carried out by the miners, and the practical and military leadership were those of the miners."[76] Its most important episodes were the January 1947 massacre of miners in Potosí; President Hertzog's imposition of a state of siege; mass firings at Patiño Mines in December 1947; the 1949 massacre at Catavi-Siglo XX; persecution of FSTMB and POR leaders; a "civil war" launched by the MNR; finally, the 1951 elections, which the MNR won but the government refused to respect.

The sexenio drove the last nails into the coffin of the Stalinist PIR. Having "tasted power under the temporary post-Villarroel government," notes Klein, the PIR refused to give it up when "the most reactionary wing of the traditional parties" won the 1947 elections, "determined to destroy the FSTMB and all radicalism in the labor movement." When this hard-line regime "used the PIR ministers to direct the attacks on the workers," the PIR was "destroyed as the representative party of the left."[77]

The PIR's disgrace brought new opportunities for the POR, which extended its influence to new sectors while intensifying work among the miners. A party report claimed that by early 1947 the POR led nine factory unions in La Paz and three in Oruro. It was also involved in union organizing among white-collar government employees, including at the Central Bank. POR Central Committee member Edwin Möller, who had learned trade unionism among miners at Milluni, organized the Government Workers Union in 1946 and helped lead a strike of this sector the following year. He was one of seventy-five activists fired and tried for subversion as a result.[78]

The opening shots of the sexenio rosquero were fired in the city that had, for centuries, symbolized the wealth and misery of Bolivia's mines: Potosí. For the miners' movement and the Bolivian Trotskyists, the events of January 1947 marked a new period. The clash occurred when miners joined a wave of labor protests against the Supreme Court's decision that a new retirement law could not be applied retroactively. Arrests of labor leaders and some local MNR members heightened discontent. As the miners used the materials of their trade to make their point, "Eighty thousand dynamite blasts exploded on Wednesday the 29th," reported the daily press. Appealing to fear of the Indian masses, authorities denounced the miners as "savages."[79]

Large numbers of demonstrators were shot down in the streets of Potosí. This was another in the long list of mine massacres, but with an important political difference: it was the PIR Minister of Labor who ordered troops into the mines; the Potosí mayor and police chief were also PIR members. The pro-government press branded the miners subversives. One headline blared: "The Potosí Movement Was Organized by Political Agents of the MNR and POR." PIR supporters claimed the miners had "attacked" the city "to the cry of 'Long live the POR,' 'Long live the MNR,' 'Glory to Villarroel,' etc." They congratulated themselves for having "defeated, in Potosí, the miners' Villarroelism (Lechinism), a sword of Damocles hanging over Bolivian Democracy."[80]

In a communiqué protesting the massacre, the POR's Central Committee called on the workers to "strengthen their cadres in order to respond to the organized violence of the bourgeoisie," denouncing the PIR, which, "to better carry out its role as servant of the big mining firms, has taken on the task of massacring workers." Another, "The Truth about the Potosí Events," criticized the MNR for spreading inflammatory rumors, while stating that the PIR "hates the miners, who know it is a lackey of the Rosca." The PIR had seized "the opportunity for a cowardly massacre of its defenseless enemies," while falsely claiming "that the POR agitated the miners, as an excuse to kill off the revolutionary vanguard." Evidently fearing further reprisals, the Cochabamba branch maintained: "For now, the POR limits itself to asking [the authorities] to abide by social legislation. It does not want to agitate or subvert public order." An extensively documented POR pamphlet later accused PIR authorities of "massacring more than 300 workers in Potosí."[81]

The next months brought escalating accusations that the POR and MNR were united in a subversive conspiracy. A Republican manifesto said the POR was the product of "an abortion from the MNR," denounced the "ingratitude and treason" of "fake representatives of the mine workers' will," like Lora, Capellino, and Torres, and reminded readers of the "the Arab (Turkish) origin" of the "notorious Juan Lechín." Under the headline "POR: Mask for the MNR," the house organ of Marof's Socialist Workers Party of Bolivia (PSOB) said Lora's party "acts not under its own steam but spurred by the urgent needs of the MNR." Responding to such attacks, the POR stressed that it "fights and will continue to fight against the MNR."[82] Both public and internal documents show that throughout this period, party leaders believed they were combating the MNR and all other "bourgeois and petty-bourgeois parties." At times, they still went so far as to call the MNR "fascist." Nonetheless, their bloc with its labor wing deepened.

Under the headline "The POR Does Not Know Whether to Unmask Lechín or to Wait for the Miners Themselves to Grow Disillusioned with Him," a right-wing paper published an analysis of the party's dilemma. Cynical but perceptive, it sheds light on this formative period. "Public opinion" believed "the mine workers were marching toward a socialist revolution," it noted, as their "revolutionary phraseology" provoked "the fear of Bolivia's big bourgeoisie." Indeed, "many thought the submissive Indian of the altiplano, once dragged into the mineshafts, was experiencing a tremendous delirium in favor of Lenin and Trotzky," particularly since Lechín "became a friend of Guillermo Lora, the raging Trotzkyite who was his first advisor." Yet the real "relations of Lechín with the Fourth International group called POR" consisted of Lechín using Trotskyists to help him become "the miners' *caudillo*," although, in reality, he was far from pursuing socialist objectives. This had "made them the instrument of Lechín rather than making him an instrument of the POR." Thus, "either the POR will unmask Lechín, attacking him for his unbridled spending of proletarian money, his hidden deals, his insincerity, his possible collaboration with Hertzog, whom the POR rejects," or Lechín "will get tired of them."[83]

"Unmasking" Lechín was not the path the POR took. In April 1947, for example, under editor Lora, the party press published the tribute "Lechín According to a Miner from Chocaya." The miners "are ready to give our lives" for the union leader, it stated; the more the Rosca intrigued against him, "the more gigantic J. Lechín grows" as "he represents the cause of the exploited." The piece ends: "Comrade Lechín, leader of the mine workers, *salud!*" and appears next to a speech by newly elected Senator Lechín.[84]

The Miners Parliamentary Bloc

In the elections of 1947, two pro-Rosca coalitions presented presidential candidates; the MNR was effectively banned from running its own,

Paz Estenssoro. Enrique Hertzog won, although his total—less than 45,000 votes—underscored how tiny the electorate was at the time.

In line with the call of the Pulacayo Thesis for a "miners parliamentary bloc," the FSTMB ran a slate of seventeen candidates in mining districts.[85] Under the name "Frente Único Proletario," it included Lechín, Torres, and other union leaders, together with several POR spokesmen. The POR announced that it was "collaborating with the Mine Workers Federation of Bolivia in the parliamentary elections . . . and authorized some of its members to join the Proletarian United Front slate." The objective was not to "gain paradise through parliament" but to "denounce, from within parliament itself, the Rosca's plots and the reformists' servility." In a letter to the International Secretariat of the Fourth International, a party leader claimed that "8 of the candidates are POR militants and 9 are miners who, though not *poristas*, are pro-POR."[86]

The campaign was the talk of the mining towns. Grover Alejandro remembers that as a child in Potosí he saw graffiti during the elections warning, "Guillermo Lora: Atheist." Potosí POR spokesman Lucio Mendívil—a former Beta Gama member and "great guy," according to Lora—was elected to the Senate together with Lechín. Eight of the others won seats in the Chamber of Deputies, including POR members Lora and Aníbal Vargas (representing districts in Potosí), Jesús Aspiazu (La Paz), and Humberto Salamanca (Oruro). Lora was assigned to coordinate this Miners Parliamentary Bloc (BMP in accordance with its Spanish initials).[87]

Together with Sri Lanka, and Vietnam before World War II, Bolivia was one of the few places where Trotskyists spoke from the parliamentary tribune. Reading the official Record (*Redactores*) and reports in the daily press, one is struck by the brilliant panache of Lora's speeches and the plodding pedantry of some of the Bloc's other members. Its interventions in Congress ranged from impassioned expositions of Marxist theory to promoting elementary labor legislation and registering votes on pork-barrel projects proposed by other congressmen.

Sometimes the young radicals were clearly having fun. "We're agitators," two BMP members told a local prosecutor when questioned about "agitating the miner masses" in San José. The official's effort to strip them of parliamentary immunity failed, as did the attempt to unseat Lechín on the accusation of "instigating" an Indian revolt in Ayopaya involving "sedition, organized attacks, arson and other crimes."[88]

The BMP—a virtually unstudied chapter in Bolivian history—drew controversy from its first moments in Congress. Delegate (congressman) Lora proclaimed: "The miners are acting under an ideological program, a defined objective, the banner of the Congress of Pulacayo." The Bloc "has stated that if the bourgeois Parliament does not defend the miners' interests, they will move toward revolution and renovation, and will have no problem in abandoning the bourgeois Parliament," he added. Yet even some supporters felt he went too far when he wrote critically of the hanged president Villarroel. "We elected Guillermo and now we're going to hang *him*," a group of armed Llallagua miners told an Argentine visitor.[89]

What is most fundamental about the BMP is the political dynamic it embodied. In late 1947, Lora complained of some Bloc members' "opportunism," insisting: "We oppose the BMP being identified, openly or not, with the MNR." In a subsequent "balance sheet," he observed that the BMP's "head in the Chamber of Deputies was Lora, but he was surrounded by elements belonging to different parties," so some were "controlled" by the MNR or even the Republicans. He seems not to have questioned the basic concept of an electoral, programmatic alliance with labor leaders affiliated to the MNR. One of his first parliamentary interventions was to defend Mario Torres against PIR spokesmen who attacked him for "having been one of the most active members of the MNR." Noting that "Torrez [sic] is not a Trotskyist, while he was proud to be one," Lora said the FSTMB spokesman "had undoubtedly been a member of the MNR," but "at least apparently, from his objective expressions, has rectified his conduct," adding that he could not personally "guarantee this change, [as he] could not scrutinize Mr. Torrez's conscience." Pro-government Senator Pedro Zilvetti rejoined that the POR and MNR had "political relations," noting that "in the miners' districts where the Miners Bloc got support," ballots were cast for Paz Estenssoro.[90]

Abroad, comrades in Mexico hailed "Bolivian Trotskyists' Triumph in Elections." Rallying support among unionists for a sliding scale of wages and hours in the United States, *The Militant* was glad to report: "Bolivia Deputy Introduced Bill on Sliding Scale."[91] Among the most extensive reports were those of a Uruguayan paper which headlined "Great POR Victory" and "Latin American Proletariat Sends 9 Revolutionary Representatives to the Bolivian Parliament."[92] However, the group of Latin American Trotskyists who wrote critically of the Pulacayo Thesis, after their September 1947 visit, also criticized "the way election propaganda was carried out," with a series of "limitations completely alien to the methods of a Marxist party." In particular, "the Bolivian comrades did not present their candidates under the banner of the POR, but within the so-called Miners Bloc, which was supposed to be the political expression of the national Mine Workers Federation." As a result, their "electoral activity was basically dominated by a trade-unionist approach."[93]

A Peruvian representative to the POR's national conference reported that the POR had been "incapable of . . . delimiting the party's boundaries" in its relations with FSTMB leaders. By convincing them to sign radical statements, including the Thesis of Pulacayo, "our comrades got the impression that they were running the show." Moreover, "our comrades' activity in the Miners Parliamentary Bloc calls for strong criticism." Although they gave the impression that it was "a homogeneous bloc," half the union leaders in it "have maintained or still maintain relations with the MNR." By "writing his speeches and leaflets," the party was helping to create "the Lechín myth," while the bloc's "'unity' has prevented the POR from appearing with its own physiognomy in parliament."[94]

The BMP also caused friction inside the POR, eventually leading to a bitter factional struggle. Hugo González later called it a bloc between the POR and "a labor wing of the MNR," confirming that the public viewed it that way at the time. The bloc "did not arise through a rank-and-file discussion but one among the top leaders," he said. "I remember one night I stayed in Oruro and participated in a meeting of mine union leaders with Lechín and the *poristas*. . . . It was really cold, so somebody brought a bottle of *pisco* brandy and we had a drink as the meeting began. Lechín was at the podium. . . . He says, '*Compañeros*, the situation is thus and such, so we need to run in the elections in alliance with the *poristas*. We're going to fight the Rosca,' etc., etc. And all the leaders say, 'Yes, we agree.' And that was it." As for the POR's own spokesmen, what they did in parliament "was not discussed or planned" by the party, as "everyone did what they wanted." This continued despite resolutions seeking to assert control over POR members in the BMP and guarantee its "political independence with regard to all other parties and unions."[95]

Some of the rancor involved Lora's parliamentary salary, an issue that almost led to his expulsion from the POR, according to González. Lora allegedly argued against turning the money over to the party because he was in parliament as a representative of the miners, but he eventually said he would give it to his own faction. "Accusations and counter-accusations" included some of a personal nature—including "amorous piracy"! Lora later recalled "the impression that an incredible civil war was going on within the POR's ranks." Citing conflicts over organizational issues, the POR asked the Fourth International to explain proper norms for factional struggle. More fundamental issues of policy were addressed by those who argued that the party was subordinating its political line to its work in the unions or that the Bloc blurred the line between the POR and the MNR, with one internal critic noting that "in the mine centers we are so easily confused with the MNR that people believe the two parties are synonymous."[96]

After the press reported frictions within the BMP in late 1947, the POR's La Paz committee published a special leaflet reproducing an interview with Lora and Lechín. Bloc members in the Chamber of Deputies operated "under my leadership," Lora said, "strictly adher[ing] to the political resolutions of mine union congresses and the fundamental lines of the Thesis of Pulacayo." Senator Lechín called the idea of a split in the BMP "a gross slander," as "the Bloc continues to fight with all its forces" in the interest of all workers.[97]

Though still small, the POR continued to register growth, although González said the leadership never knew exactly how many members there were. Abelardo Ramos thought that when he visited in 1947, the POR "might have had 100 or 150 members throughout the country," including "a lot of young people," but "due to the particularities of Bolivian society, there was an echo to everything they said, in the press, on the radio," so the party's influence far outweighed its numbers. The following year, a document on the FI's upcoming World Congress said the POR had a "maximum" of two hundred members. Curiously, a U.S. government intelligence report claimed the combined membership of the FI's Bolivian and Chilean sections "is estimated to be between 5,000–6,000."[98]

The small party's big role in union politics came under intense scrutiny in the period following the Potosí massacre and the election of a new hard-line government. "Trotskyists In Bolivia Face Hertzog Terror," warned *The Militant* in July 1947, and Mexican comrades reported: "Bolivia's Rosca-PIR Government Attacks the Masses." Authorities heightened police persecution of the POR, banning *Lucha Obrera* and destroying some members' homes in Oruro as the government accused the BMP of preparing "a seditious revolt" there. Attacks on the POR accompanied the jailing of union leaders, a push to take firearms of various descriptions away from local mine unions, and the Patiño company's drive to break the union at Catavi. When President Hertzog authorized Patiño Mines to fire all its workers at Llallagua, Catavi, and Siglo XX, miners and bank employees launched a major strike. However, the POR informed the SWP in a letter about the crackdown, the workers were defeated after Hertzog imposed a state of siege.[99]

Lora used his parliamentary seat to denounce the wave of repression and formally challenge the state of siege, but in 1948 the government demanded "reorganization" of the unions, the press campaigned against extremist "demagogy," and a PIR spokesman sought a "criminal trial" against Lora for allegedly slandering him when he was Minister of Labor. As the FSTMB prepared a new gathering, "The President Said, 'Whole Country

Watching Deliberations of Miners' Congress,'" with Hertzog warning that the nation was "tired of seeing these deliberations serve as a platform for agitators." The press demanded that miners "reexamine" the Pulacayo Thesis crafted by "political agents for exotic international theories encrusted in some of the country's labor organizations." Reports on the union congress zeroed in on "the Bolivian Section of the Fourth International, which in accordance with the slogans of the permanent revolution formulated by Leon Trotzky, seeks and prefers illegality and violence in the struggle for social improvements." Forced to publish "clandestine" editions—featuring Miguel Alandia's powerful graphics—*Lucha Obrera* denounced Hertzog's "unending assault on hard-won conquests" of the labor movement and the wave of "inhuman repression" against peasants who had protested abuses by *gamonales* (landowners) in several rural regions. "The pain of the indigenous population is the indelible stigma of the Hertzog Government," it charged in March 1948.[100]

The climate grew grimmer still after Hertzog called new elections the following year. When the MNR received the second highest number of votes, Hertzog turned power over to his vice president, Mamerto Urriolagoitia, popularly known as "The Goat" because of his trademark goatee. Faced with mounting repression, the POR launched a campaign to form a "political front" against the government. "POSSIBLE ALLIANCE OF TOTALITARIANS," the front page of a pro-government daily reported, providing lengthy extracts from a POR leader's letter to the MNR *and* the PIR. The letter called for an alliance based on a "platform of struggle," including "defense and broadening of democratic rights," separation of church and state, "equality of rights for men and women," universal suffrage for men and women over eighteen, "including illiterate workers and peasants," strengthening labor organizations, and unionizing peasants and public employees. The PIR quickly said such an alliance was out of the question "because just like their Trotzkyite counterparts all over the world, the POR has been and still is an ally of Nazi-fascism."[101]

Undeterred, the POR's Central Committee approved a lengthy resolution on the need for "an *anti-imperialist united front* program" to "mobilize the proletariat and . . . put the question of political power on the table." The document called the MNR "a displaced, adventurist bureaucracy that wants to take power at any cost," having "already demonstrated its prostration before foreign imperialism," adding "the MNR's slogan is: Never frighten the State Department!" As for the PIR, it served only its leaders' ambitions and the policies of "the Stalinist bureaucracy." Nonetheless, "we must oblige the MNR and PIR to take clear and responsible positions in defense of the people and against imperialism," forming a front with the POR as well as the miners, factory workers, and other labor sectors. "The slogan of an ANTI-IMPERIALIST FRONT with the 'national' bourgeoisie (MNR) and Stalinists (PIR) does not mean we have changed our political line," the CC stressed. The slogan "is justified by the native bourgeoisie's position against imperialism (a bourgeois, small-minded and inconsistent fight against imperialism) and the 'left turn' Stalinism has undertaken on a world scale" due to Cold War tensions.

In addition to the democratic demands already proposed for a "plat-form of struggle," the resolution added slogans for nationalization of banks, mining, and other industries, and of the land—"to benefit the slaves of the countryside"—as well as a workers' and peasants' government. The MNR and PIR would doubtless reject these, so the POR might have to accept a "reformist" program for the alliance, while "not losing its own physiognomy within the front." The document also admonished the POR's own local committees to improve functioning and "perfect our methods of under-ground work." A subsequent manifesto "insisted on" the POR's "call on unions, the PIR and MNR" to form the front.[102]

In effect this was a move to extend the POR's alliance with the labor wing of the MNR to embrace the nationalist party as a whole. This involved bending the concept of a "united front," which for Trotsky had meant a revolutionary party carrying out limited, specific *action* together with other forces, such as a protest, strike, or even "military defense" against a reaction-ary threat. (Trotsky's followers had, for example, fought on the Republican side against Franco in the Spanish Civil War.) What the united front did not mean, he insisted, was a political bloc or common program, let alone one involving bourgeois parties. The POR's fear that such a political bloc would endanger "its own physiognomy" would prove increasingly justified.

Civil War

Urriolagoitia launched a new crackdown in May 1949, announcing: "The government has documents proving that a general strike is being pre-pared throughout the country." The "revolutionary plan" was particularly dangerous as it included preparations for "an Indian uprising." The Interior Ministry pointed the finger at Lechín, Mario Torres, and other MNR mem-bers, together with "Guillermo Lora, who operates in the Catavi-Llallagua union to . . . execute the shadowy plans of communism that hide behind the POR, most widely known through the famous 'Thesis of Pulacayo.'"[103]

The government moved to arrest FSTMB and POR leaders at Siglo XX. When miners received the news that their leaders had been taken to prison,

Figure 3.7 June 1949, President Urriolagoitia takes on "union agitators." The severed tentacle at the top right is labeled "POR." (Courtesy of Biblioteca y Archivo Histórico del Congreso)

they stopped work, seized the barracks of the Carabineros (elite police force), and took hostages, among them North American managers and technicians. Government troops attacked, massacring hundreds of miners (estimates range from 200 to 2,000); three hostages lost their lives. "LECHÍN, LORA AND TORRES INSTIGATED THE MINERS," blared a banner headline in *El Diario*, accompanied by a cartoon showing the president chopping a tentacle marked "POR"[104] off an octopus called "Union Agitators" (see figure 3.7). The government stripped parliamentary immunity from Miners Bloc members, as well as from Hernán Siles Zuazo and other MNR leaders, and sent them into exile, announcing a "state of siege throughout the Republic" so the populace would not be "at the mercy of irresponsible, fanatical hordes led and armed by the MNR and POR." A show trial was staged against miners' leaders accused of the deaths of the Siglo XX hostages. Sentenced to die, they were freed years later after the uprising of April 1952.[105]

Set off by a downturn in the price of tin, spiraling inflation escalated mass discontent. In early August 1949, President Urriolagoitia addressed the nation, warning that the actions of "the miner agitators Lechín, Lora, Torres and others" had led to "frequent illegal strikes, creating an anarchic ferment of violence among the working classes." Although they had been deported, danger continued, as the "Nazi-fascist" MNR, "arm-in-arm with the Trotskyites of the POR, is encouraging the conspiracy of the extremist left." Urriolagoitia's Minister of Labor told parliament, "the Thesis of Pulacayo . . . from the juridical, penal standpoint, is a crime" and was being used as "a political weapon to attack the government." As "the crime of sedition is clearly defined," it was necessary to enforce the law.[106]

At the end of August, the MNR launched a coup. When military sectors failed to support it, the nationalists were forced to rely on their own clandestine fighting groups, a serious setback as they had always sought to ally with a wing of the armed forces. Insurgents were quickly defeated in La Paz but managed to seize some provincial cities. During the ensuing struggle known as the Civil War of 1949, the MNR established headquarters in the city of Santa Cruz. Fearing that the social order could be torn apart by class conflict, it was reluctant to distribute arms to the population but finally decided to mobilize some labor and middle-class sectors. Miners, some of whom had received military training during the Chaco War, played an important role in the fighting.

Pulacayo union leader Julio Bardales remembers receiving instructions "from Lechín, by *chasqui* (messenger), to guard the area." Some hotheads said, "Look, we have the keys to the *pulpería* (mine store), let's take a bunch of dynamite and blow up the rail tracks," but Bardales refused. He was named head of a "Revolutionary Junta" that resolved to "officially turn over command of this district to the leadership of the [Mine] Workers Union, so they may exercise the powers corresponding to the functions inherent in the union body of this mining district." Grover Alejandro, son of a miner in Potosí, remembers the workers "going down to the city and seizing the police station" when the civil war began, suffering "savage persecution" when the army counterattacked. Another retired miner and former POR member from Potosí says workers captured rifles and "scored big victories, but the ammunition ran out." Some hid in the caverns of the Pailaviri mine, inside the Cerro Rico.[107]

It is unclear whether the POR knew what was afoot before the MNR—a highly conspiratorial organization at the time—launched its rising. "When defeat appeared inevitable," Lora later wrote, the MNR grew desperate, and some local groups "invited the POR to join them" in the fighting. In Sucre,

POR activist Enrique Ferrante organized an anti-Rosca protest, but, Eduardo Mendizábal recalls, "we couldn't participate in the fighting because there were so few of us." Local POR leader Agar Peñaranda greeted the MNR's attack on the Rosca, an obituary states, but "opposed the POR membership taking up arms with desperate groups that never appealed to the masses' direct action," seeking only to "take over the bourgeois state machine."[108]

In some areas, party militants did join the combat. In Potosí, POR members joined the local Revolutionary Junta, which coordinated armed actions; the poristas "seized Radio Internacional and called on the workers to take up arms." A Llallagua POR member fought as part of the Green Arrow miners' group. In Tupiza, Edwin Möller participated in a POR plan to organize a miners' militia and "seize buildings, the police station, all that."[109]

Hugo González was with Möller. On the radio, they got the news of POR members joining the fighting in Potosí. Because of a railway strike, Möller and González decided to walk the ninety-five miles to Atocha, hoping to mobilize the miners there. When they finally arrived, the area was occupied by the army. "It was a small-scale attempt to join the war. We fell prisoner and then escaped" with the help of two soldiers. The government issued an order for Möller and González to be shot.

They soon discovered that the party leadership (then headed by Guillermo Guerrero and Víctor Villegas) "opposed our intervention," considering it "an adventure compromising to the party's stability," and "didn't even want to meet and protect us." Reaching Oruro, they were aided by Fernando Bravo, and subsequently made it to La Paz, where they "basically forced the leadership to reincorporate us into party activity and approve what we did."[110] (See figure 3.8.)

Government tactics sought to make future rebels think twice. "Mine workers who fell prisoner in Santa Cruz, Camiri and Incahuasi were put on military planes and flown toward Oruro, where they were tossed from the air into Lake Poopó." Mine and peasant union organizer Enrique Encinas recalls that "the working class died like flies." Truckloads of captured miners were taken to another lake called Tranco "and pushed into it while they were still alive, their hands tied behind their backs with wire . . . and weighted down with stones."[111]

After two months of bloody clashes, the rebels were driven out of the areas they had managed to seize. Their last redoubt was the remote zone near Ñancahuazú in southeastern Bolivia where Che Guevara would perish two decades later.[112] Government forces won, but theirs was a Pyrrhic victory. Although the MNR suffered heavy losses, its reputation rose as the party of resistance to the Rosca.

Figure 3.8 POR leaders, late 1940s. From left: Fernando Bravo, Enrique Ferrante(?), Hugo González, Miguel Alandia, Ismael Pérez, and an unidentified member. (Courtesy of Emma Bolshia Bravo Cladera)

POR members were able to score two small moral victories. In mid-September 1949, the press reported "The Surprising Appearance of the Agitator Guillermo Lora in the Chamber of Deputies." Despite being banished to Chile, Lora had somehow made it back to La Paz, calmly walked into parliament, and taken a seat. After all, the miners had elected him. When a reporter asked him how he had managed to do this, he replied it was a "professional secret." Parliamentary authorities then escorted him to the Uruguayan legation, and he left the country once again. Several months later, when President Urriolagoitia inaugurated a national teachers' congress in Sucre, Cochabamba delegate Ernesto Ayala took the floor to subject him to "every kind of mockery and scorn, until the entire audience erupted in uncontainable laughter." The president, "red with fury, had to leave in a hurry, followed by his aristocratic coterie."[113]

Möller and González devoted themselves to building the Union of Industrial and Commercial Workers in La Paz, which became an important base for the party. They also helped establish a Coordinating Committee with factory workers and other unionists, including followers of the MNR, the PIR, and the Bolivian Communist Party (PCB) that dissident PIR youth members had just formed. The Interior Ministry warned of the "subversive and antipatriotic activities" of this committee, "composed entirely of Stalinist and Trotskyist members."[114] With Möller as "secretary of agitation," it launched a general strike on May 18, 1950, against the catastrophic fall in workers' purchasing power caused by an 80 percent devaluation of the Bolivian currency.

The Fourth International's press service reported that mine, factory, railway, bank, and other workers joined the strike. The government declared a state of siege and brought strikers before military tribunals. When police and army troops fired on a demonstration, workers built barricades in the streets. On the second day of the strike, seven army regiments surrounded the Villa Victoria textile workers' neighborhood in La Paz, which airplanes then strafed and bombed while artillery shelled it from bases in El Alto. "These *barrios* were completely destroyed. Where workers' houses stood before, today there are only ruins. The casualties among the workers were enormous. It has not been possible to find out how many died." Together with Möller and González, captured POR members included bank and railway union leaders.[115]

The POR tried to organize military resistance, distributing dynamite and old rifles, even an aged machine gun. The strike committee's membership had to be renewed four times due to arrests, until the entire party leadership fell prisoner. They were sent to the island of Coati in Lake Titicaca, where severe beatings were administered to González and Villegas. After a hunger strike by two hundred prisoners, the *poristas* were exiled to Chile, where González had to spend eleven months in the hospital.

In the aftermath of the strike, *La Razón* serialized an internal POR circular that government forces had found in Cochabamba. Reporting the lead-up to the strike, it noted that in addition to the Coordinating Committee, a Four-Party Committee was set up by the POR, MNR, PCB, and PIR. The latter three parties had shown little interest in a common platform, however, although the POR made some progress in "conversations with the MNR's left wing" in La Paz.[116]

On the basis of information from "comrades Mendizábal and Arancibia," the circular also discussed a crisis in the POR's Sucre organization. "Comrade Mata" (Enrique Ferrante) had taken it upon himself to "reorganize" the branch. If important political differences underlay this unauthorized measure, "they should be discussed and made known throughout the Party" by means of an internal bulletin. At the end of June, the POR was shaken by the news that Ferrante had killed himself and his girlfriend, Salwa Sauma Karam. Her parents, prominent Arab merchants, opposed her marrying a revolutionary. Ever since a Brazilian comrade won him to Trotskyism in his native Santa Cruz, Ferrante had been one of the party's most promising young activists. In Sucre, he was befriended by Agar Peñaranda. "When Ferrante attended an international Trotskyist conference in Buenos Aires, we helped him, even giving him clothes for his trip," Mendizábal remembers. "Then he came back, and this thing with Salwa happened right away." His funeral procession was joined by crowds of oil and railway workers, artisans, students, and teachers. "I have never seen a bigger or more emotional burial, because everybody [in Sucre] went, even though they didn't share our ideas," Mendizábal recalls.[117]

The POR and the Fourth International

The FI's reports on repression in Bolivia reflected world Trotskyism's heightened interest in the isolated Andean country, as well as efforts to strengthen communications and organizational ties in the wake of World War II. Annihilation of most of the International's experienced cadres during the war was a factor in the political crises of 1951–53, when the FI split between supporters and opponents of its new central leader, the Greek Cypriot Michel Raptis ("Pablo"). The war had also accentuated the POR's isolation.

In 1946 and 1947, leaders of the POR and the North American SWP corresponded on the need for closer collaboration, in line with the Trotskyist movement's internationalist principles. One POR letter in English stated, "we . . . ardently desire to give an international orientation to our movement, we want to overcome our isolation in the discussion and in the solution of our most burning political and organizational problems," and requested "discussion material of our movement, of its tendencies, on the question of the Soviet Union, etc." In late 1946, the FI's International Secretariat (I.S.), newly reconstituted in Paris, wrote that "no direct news" was arriving from Bolivia. Matters began to improve in late 1947 when the Bolivians established direct communication with the Secretariat, and Trotskyists from Argentina, Chile, and Peru attended a POR conference. However, the POR did not participate in the Second Congress of the FI, held in 1948. González recalls a Uruguayan Trotskyist bringing the documents during a visit to Bolivia. Yet Lora observes that the POR "continued to live on the margins of the International's life." The "party as such never intervened" in discussions regarding other sections, "nor did it send its political opinions to the International Secretariat." The I.S. did not promote genuine international discussion of the POR's political line; its correspondence simply referred to "accomplished facts."[118]

In late 1948, the FI established a provisional Buró Latinoamericano (BLA; Latin American Bureau) in Montevideo. Attending its plenum in December of that year, "Mata" (Ferrante) was criticized for refusing to report on the internal crisis that tensions between Lora and other leaders had caused in the POR. In a letter to the Bolivian party, the BLA complained that "you have already been asked to send all the documents relating to your activities since [the party's] foundation," made suggestions for overcoming the crisis, and stressed that the disputes "must be known and discussed by the various Latin American sections, the Latin American Bureau and the I.S." The BLA also wrote Lora personally about his "openly undisciplined attitude," which "could lead to a split in the party."[119]

A further link with the international movement was provided by journalist and SWP cadre Sherry Mangan, a former member of the "Harvard poets" circle who had carried out delicate and dangerous tasks for the International in Europe during World War II, as well as in Latin America. Mangan traveled to Bolivia and stayed for two years, as he "desperately desired to put into a novel 'the heroic and to date ever defeated struggles of the Bolivian tin-miners.'" The title would be *Catavi*, or *Mountain of Death*, and characters included Lechín and Lora, whom Mangan visited in prison. Yet Mangan's wife became gravely ill, eventually dying in Cochabamba, and the book was never published. Although Mangan did not play a significant role in the POR's internal life, he helped arrange trips abroad for party leaders, including Lora, who paid "heartfelt tribute to the North American revolutionary and friend" after Mangan died in 1961.[120]

In August 1951, for the first time the POR sent a representative to a world gathering of the FI: the Third World Congress. Hugo González was chosen, traveling from exile in Chile through Argentina to Paris. At the congress, he gave a report on Bolivia and spoke to Michel Pablo and another I.S. leader, Pierre Frank, proposing that Lora go to Paris to work with the International. They agreed. Lora, who had been discovered trying to return to Bolivia, was being held in the Panóptico prison along with the miners condemned for the death of the Siglo XX hostages. The World Congress elected him part of an honorary presidium of "comrades imprisoned in Bolivia, China, Greece and Vietnam."[121]

Lora was eventually released from prison, only to be exiled once again. González recalls the difficulties of contacts in this period: he and Lora met at the Oruro train station when the two men returned clandestinely to Bolivia. Lora's stay was brief: he was on his way to Europe. González was beginning a tour of the POR's regional committees, to inform them of the World Congress decisions and help reorganize party structures disrupted by repression. The tour was interrupted by the April 1952 uprising, which began the National Revolution. Lora recalled that when he made it to Paris, he "liked the Indochinese comrades" he met there but found the FI leaders decidedly unimpressive. Just for fun he told them: "We Bolivian Indians are known to eat people."[122]

The World Congress sparked an internal conflict that would soon split the Trotskyist movement into two hostile camps: the majority, loyal to the I.S. of Pablo, Frank, and Ernest Mandel; and an "International Committee" (IC) centered on the SWP, the British and Swiss groups, and the majority of the French section. The BLA would align with Pablo, to whom its leader, the Argentine "J. Posadas" (Homero Cristalli)—a flamboyant autodidact known for singing tangos at international conferences—was fiercely loyal. The IC had fewer adherents in Latin America, mainly veteran Chilean Trotskyists and the Argentine faction led by "Nahuel Moreno" (Hugo Bressano). Given the remoteness of Bolivia's POR, it would be some time before the I.S. and IC would compete for its loyalties.

The split reflected Pablo's belief that since the end of the war, the FI had "entered a period essentially different from any we have known in the past," in which capitalism's crises and the approach of a Third World War would overcome "subjective" obstacles—what Trotsky called the crisis of revolutionary leadership—and push the masses' current leaders inexorably in a revolutionary direction.[123] His opponents accused him of charting a course toward "liquidation" of the FI itself. In Latin America, "Pabloism" entailed increasing adaptation to nationalist organizations dominant in much of the region.

Pablo's I.S. insisted that the POR function in a purposeful and disciplined manner. A World Congress resolution observed that the Bolivian section had shown "organizational looseness" and a "lack of political clarity regarding goals and tactics," and had "not delimited itself sufficiently from other political currents, which exploit the mass movement."[124] Simultaneously, Pablo and his cothinkers included Bolivia in their increasingly explicit theoretical justifications for adapting to these very currents.

In a report to the Congress, Pablo said "the anti-imperialist and anticapitalist mass movement frequently takes confused forms, under petty-bourgeois leadership like the APRA in Peru and the MNR in Bolivia, or even bourgeois leadership like Vargas in Brazil and Perón in Argentina." The term *petty*-bourgeois was no semantic slip: it implied that the MNR had an intermediate, malleable nature. A Latin American delegate underlined the new concept that these nationalist currents had an "anti-imperialist and anti-capitalist character," while the "Resolution on Latin America" said the POR should seek to "influence the left wing of the MNR, which rests on . . . the workers' milieu," and "put forward, on specific occasions, a tactic of anti-imperialist united front with this organization (MNR) on the basis of a concrete program which will include, and make even more precise, the demands contained in the Pulacayo Thesis of 1946."[125]

In calling for a programmatic front with the MNR, the international leadership had more in mind than episodic joint actions, coordinated defense, or military blocs against government repression. Taking a further, fateful step, it called for a *government* of the MNR, or even a POR-MNR coalition. The resolution stated:

> In the event of a mass mobilization promoted or mainly favored by the MNR, our Bolivian section will support it with all its forces and intervene energetically to advance it as much as possible, even carrying it through to the seizure of power by the MNR, on the basis of the progressive program of the anti-imperialist united front.
>
> If, on the contrary, it becomes evident in the course of these mobilizations that our Bolivian section has as much influence as the MNR over the revolutionary masses, it will launch the slogan of forming a Workers' and Peasants' Government *constituted by both organizations*, with the above-mentioned program and supported by Committees of workers, peasants and revolutionary elements of the urban petty bourgeoisie.[126]

These were not abstruse exercises in doctrine but questions of policy with far-reaching consequences for Bolivian radicalism, as Pablo systematized the adaptation to the MNR that the POR had practiced since its alliance with Lechín began. By explicitly taking this policy a giant step further, proposing that the POR support the MNR taking power, the programmatic groundwork was laid for backing the regime that took over in April 1952. This was a far cry from Trotsky's "permanent revolution," which demanded opposition to any bourgeois or "petty-bourgeois" regime. (See Appendix.)

Until Pablo, the FI had maintained that ongoing blocs with nationalist parties would tie the laboring masses to class enemies, obstruct effective struggle against imperialism, and prepare the way for defeat. The MNR's leaders were not only scions of Bolivia's elite, they had already participated in regimes (Toro, Busch, Villarroel) that sought to subordinate the masses to what Marxists called the bourgeois state. Although French Trotskyists opposed Pablo's "liquidationist" positions in Europe, no voices were raised against the Third Congress guidelines for Bolivia. If these conceptions had been challenged before the outbreak of revolution on the altiplano, the future of Bolivian Trotskyism might have been very different.

The MNR Wins the Elections

In the year before the outbreak of the National Revolution, the POR made repeated attempts to establish an "anti-imperialist united front." Efforts to form a front met with "considerable success in the trade-union field," Lora observes, but the "political panorama preceding the April 1952 revolution" was conditioned by the failure of the ephemeral Four-Party pact to "transform itself into an anti-imperialist front," which "accentuated the POR's isolation" and internal tensions.[127] Hugo González says that after the MNR's exile leadership managed to reestablish structures within the country, it concluded that it had no need for the Four-Party pact.

Instead, the MNR planned a new *pronunciamiento* (coup attempt) with a sector of the army. As "camouflage," it ran candidates in the general elections of May 1951.[128] Popular discontent led to a landslide victory for MNR candidates Paz Estenssoro and Siles Zuazo. In response, President Mamerto Urriolagoitia carried out a "self-coup," popularly dubbed the *Mamertazo*, turning power over to a junta headed by General Hugo Ballivián.

This latest military dictatorship was unable to overcome mass disaffection, further inflamed by acute shortages of basic articles of consumption due to a dispute with the United States over the price of tin. For eight months, no tin was shipped to the United States. "To Bolivia," the *New York Times* noted, "the lack of outlet for one-half of the one product on which its entire economy is based has proved well-nigh disastrous," depressing the "already low standard of living of its people." When Ballivián attempted to "divert public attention to Bolivia's old territorial dispute with Chile," this had little effect.[129] Soon, Siles Zuazo won over cabinet member Antonio Seleme, head of the elite *Carabineros* police force, to the coup conspiracy.

The POR's policy on the 1951 presidential race remains unclear. A number of scholars claim it backed the MNR. Lora is equivocal; Möller recalled the party telling members to cast a blank vote for president and vice president; González said it was so disorganized by repression that it lacked a clear line, although some may have voted for the Paz-Siles slate.[130]

Just before the April 1952 uprising, an internal POR circular reported that "in accordance with the [World Congress] thesis on Latin America," a party leadership plenum had "adopted the tactic of the FUA" (anti-imperialist united front). "Do not lose sight for a minute," it admonished, "that *we are not guided by the objective* of splitting or *breaking up the MNR* at this point, with some sectors of its members leaving and drawing closer to us. On the contrary, what we are seeking is to penetrate its working-class circles, arm them theoretically, and have them evolve toward the left *together, in their totality*. When this process has matured, we will study anew what to do." In an "Open Letter to the Unions and the MNR" published on April 1, the POR "calls once again on the MNR to define itself": was it in the "camp" of the "working-class masses," or the "front of the oligarchy"? According to the declaration, the "will of the masses expressed in the May 1951 elections" required formation of "an MNR government." An MNR historian later wrote that with this call, "Lora's POR was tailing the MNR in April 1952."[131]

The six years of Rosca repression had fortified the MNR's reputation among many working- and middle-class sectors, while solidifying the POR's alliance with its labor wing. The relationship had its ups and downs, but after each separation the Bolivian Trotskyists would take their place again by Lechín's side.

In an interview immediately after the April 1952 uprising, Guillermo Lora—still in Paris—summed things up. "In recent months," the POR had "undertaken a broad political campaign," appealing "to all mass parties, among them the MNR, to organize a common front in the struggle against imperialism."

Echoing the "Open Letter," he said the first of the "central slogans put forward by our party" was "restoration of the constitution of the country through the formation of an MNR government which obtained a majority in the 1951 election." While criticizing the government Paz had just established, Lora added that "far from succumbing to the hysteria of a struggle against the MNR, whom the pro-imperialists have baptized as 'fascists,'" the POR was "marching with the masses to make the April 9th movement the prelude of the triumph of the workers' and peasants' government."[132]

With the "National Revolution" of 1952, Bolivia's working people would be confronted with the reality of the MNR in power. For the party that staked its hopes on permanent revolution, this would prove a decisive test.

4

Trotskyism and the *Revolución Nacional*

Bolivia's National Revolution was one of the most dramatic events of Latin America's twentieth century. A mass upheaval that transformed the nation's political landscape, it demolished the old regime's governmental apparatus, carried out extensive land reform, nationalized the largest tin companies, and enfranchised the indigenous majority. Only the Mexican Revolution had been of comparable scope, although, as Alan Knight notes, "Mexico produced no equivalent of the insurgent Trotskyist miners of the 'red fortress' of Catavi or the maximalist Tesis de Pulacayo."[1] The Bolivian Trotskyists were on the barricades of the April insurrection and helped lead the revolution's powerful new labor organizations.

Exceptionally broad and deep, the Bolivian Revolution wound up highlighting the *incapacity* of the nationalist/populist regime to carry out a thorough-going social transformation. It did not emancipate the country from foreign domination, lift it from its position as the second poorest in the hemisphere, resolve the question of land tenure, create integrated economic development, or ensure effective democratic rights for the indigenous masses. In the vocabulary of Trotsky's permanent revolution, these "bourgeois-democratic tasks" remained unresolved.

After twelve years of "National Revolution," the MNR was overthrown by the very army it had reestablished, leaving Bolivia's population mired in poverty and illiteracy and still dependent on a single export product (tin) whose market was controlled by the United States and Britain. The average miner continued to live less than forty years. The indigenous peasantry had received the suffrage and, in some areas, part of the land, but continued to suffer racism and exclusion from real political power.

When the MNR took over in 1952, anti-imperialism was its watchword. Yet in the polarized climate of the Cold War, it was careful not to overstep the bounds laid down by Washington. As a Brazilian historian noted, the erstwhile anti-imperialists "merited the blessings and aid of the U.S. government," the guardian of "capitalist order . . . [and] main partner in mine exploitation." Ensuring that destruction of the old regime did not produce a full-fledged social overturn, the MNR assuaged Washington's long-standing fear that Bolivia, located in the very "heart of South America," might ignite a regional upheaval. "Our Revolution Is Not Social but National, Said the Chief of State," Víctor Paz Estenssoro, in a declaration reported by the main pro-government daily.[2]

To understand the fate of the Bolivian Revolution, it is essential to grasp the role of the "MNR Left." The MNR's top leaders had little initial appeal to workers and peasants. These former lawyers and journalists sought to channel and control the plebeian radicalism of a hungry, mobilized, laboring population. To do so, they needed help from leaders with real roots among the masses, above all the charismatic miners' leader Juan Lechín. Astutely, Paz gave them cabinet seats. To cover his own left flank, Lechín drew assistance from the POR. Bolivian Trotskyists faced enormous revolutionary opportunities, but tied as they were to Lechín's coattails, they reinforced illusions in the new ruling party. Having ridden the mass upheaval to power, the MNR would stifle the passionately voiced revolutionary aspirations of Bolivia's poor.

The Days of April

The uprising of April ninth was not supposed to be a revolution. Hugo González, who participated in the fighting, noted that the MNR did not, initially, call on the masses to mobilize. "They did not want commitments to the masses; they wanted to come to power without involving them."[3] Instead, MNR leaders planned a coup d'état in concert with General Seleme of the Carabineros, as well as the fascistic Falange Socialista Boliviana (FSB). Organized in cells, the MNR's own trusted members would back them.

MNR leaders were experienced putschists, and they laid their plans with professional élan. Yet the FSB backed out, and insurgents encountered unexpected resistance from loyal military units. When mass sectors joined the fighting, *The Militant* reported, "Seleme, horrified at this turn, quickly deserted and fled."[4] Hernán Siles, son of a former president and top MNR leader on the spot, tried to convince the high command to accept a joint army/MNR government. The army refused. MNR leaders seemed ready to give up the attempt.

However, in the face of the army's advance on La Paz, the civilian population waged street battles that rapidly became an all-out insurrection. This does not mean accepting what former POR militant Gonzalo Trigoso criticizes as a widespread "myth of spontaneity." Accounts by members of the MNR underground apparatus show considerable military and technical preparation. What is clear is that mass participation by workers and the urban poor, after the MNR/army conspiracy began to come apart, put a distinctive social and political stamp on events. "Regardless of the MNR's original vision of the process," writes one political scientist, "in April 1952 the country was in the hands, not of the MNR's military coplotters, but of hastily cobbled together militias of workers, party activists, townspeople, and miners. Armed and radicalized, these people demanded more than another coup or rebellion—they wanted a revolution."[5]

Factory workers like those of the main La Paz glass works played a major part in the fighting. Armed with Chaco-era rifles, dynamite, home-made bombs, or nothing but wooden sticks, the miners of Milluni entered the fray. Those of Oruro followed suit. In Potosí, Grover Alejandro recalls, "My father said, 'as a miner I can't just stand by while this is going on,' so he got his old Mauser [rifle] from the Chaco and went to fight." Enrique Encinas, a miner, peasant leader, and Trotskyist sympathizer, insists: "They want you to believe it was Dr. Paz who made the revolution, but it wasn't him; it was the work of the working class." The revolution "was a popular insurrection, *pues.*"[6]

Seizure of the military arsenal in the capital's Ayacucho plaza brought civilian rebels ammunition and some modern weapons. Cochabamba's main paper reported: "Groups of miners appeared in El Alto . . . and took two train cars full of munitions. Civilians and miners came down to the capital, taking the Army troops by surprise, forcing them to retreat in disorder or surrender to the revolutionaries. The action was decisive. . . . Two hours later, with two cannons they had captured from the Army, the victorious civilians from El Alto entered the Plaza Murillo," outside the presidential palace.[7]

The standing army fell to pieces. "To consolidate the revolution we destroyed the army," says Encinas after describing three days of bitter fighting. Demoralized remnants took refuge in their barracks; militias of miners and factory workers became the only effective armed force. The new regime was worried that "more than 10,000 rifles and machine guns still were in the hands of the Popular Militia, the main force of the revolt," reported the

New York Times.[8] With the Rosca's repressive apparatus shattered, the key to power was control of the workers' militias—fundamentally a *political*, not institutional, question.

Juan Lechín was thus the linchpin of MNR control. Widely popular among the working class, he was the central leader of the April rising. It was Lechín, heading throngs of armed workers, who "took" the Palacio Quemado. He knocked on the door and demanded to be let in, but the old government had fled. Finding himself in charge of the presidential palace, he simply turned it over to Siles. Encinas recalls: "We went [to the palace] and *compañero* Lechín told us, 'We've taken over the government, Siles Zuazo is in there now, you guys go rest.'"[9] Siles declared that MNR "Jefe" Paz Estenssoro—already familiar with the Palacio Quemado—would soon fly in from exile to take charge as president, with himself as vice president and a cabinet including Lechín and two other "worker ministers."

Under Lechín's leadership, a powerful new labor federation formed a week after the uprising: the Central Obrera Boliviana (COB; Bolivian Labor Federation), exercising what was officially called "co-government" with the MNR, both a recognition of the COB's power and a means of co-opting it. Encinas points to the contradiction: "*El Juan Lechín* was now the top leader of the working class and on the other side he was also Minister of Mines and Petroleum, named by Paz Estenssoro," so he "couldn't work well on behalf of the working class."[10]

In the first years, the COB's authority went far beyond the normal reach of a trade union body. A seeming infinitude of social sectors affiliated; to this day, "*cholita*" market women march through La Paz chanting "*¡Viva la Central Obrera Boliviana!*" In the period after April 1952, peasants, street vendors, and other "nonproletarian" sectors relied on the COB to resolve problems that would, elsewhere, have been the province of government functionaries. In the countryside, COB-linked unions were often the highest community authority.

Workers' militias and the COB's exceptional weight meant there were "elements of dual power in Bolivia," as *The Militant* explained: "This is a scientific term used by Marxism to describe a situation that often occurs in genuinely popular revolutions, where a government of so-called 'moderate' character is raised to power by revolutionary masses; an uneasy period follows, where neither the government nor the masses have full power; this must be followed eventually by the government subduing the masses, disarming them and bringing them under control, or by the masses altogether losing patience with the government, setting out to replace it with a new one pledged to carry out their radical demands." Argentine Trotskyists published a special journal on the Bolivian events, emphasizing: "This is the central, distinctive feature of Bolivia's revolutionary process: the people in arms facing a government that lacks the attributes of a normal bourgeois government, that is, the backing of military forces that can effectively be directed against the masses"[11] (see figure 4.1).

MNR representatives hastened to reassure the United States. The uprising was still in progress when Siles Zuazo told the foreign press that the revolt "is completely democratic, without any connection with international communism." Bolivia's international agreements "will be respected," he vowed, and the MNR would begin an era of "pacification." From Buenos Aires, Paz said the rising was "a revolutionary return to legality." His party was "completely anti-Communist," a "national party" that had "not only tin workers in our ranks" but members of other classes. Its plans were "not anti-capitalist." Under the headline "High Bolivian Sets Anti-Marxist Aim," the *New York Times* reported: "The present Bolivian Government is the last bulwark against communism in this country, Vice President Hernán Siles Zuazo declared." He "forcefully indicated the Government's intentions to keep the groups of the extreme Left under close control."[12]

Two years before, Paz had condemned the call for nationalizing the mines as "an extremist provocation."[13] After the April insurrection, the labor movement demanded immediate nationalization: the old slogan "mines to the state," going back to the origins of Bolivian Trotskyism, was the order of the day. Given the threat that workers could directly seize major mines, Paz sought to assuage U.S. fears while ceding to mass pressure, naming a commission to study the issue for six months. In October 1952, "tin barons" Patiño, Aramayo, and Hochschild had their properties nationalized under the aegis of a state company, the Corporación Minera Boliviana (Comibol). "Co-government" was extended to the mines through an institutionalized "workers' control" integrating labor leaders into Comibol management.

"*Compañeros*, at this very moment the death certificate of the mine owners' Rosca is being signed," a POR member told the crowd of workers who gathered in Cochabamba to celebrate the measure. The local labor federation had chosen him, its Secretary of Relations, to give the speech, and "I will always remember using that phrase," he said half a century later. Yet as James Malloy observes, the decree "represented a transaction: tin was nationalized, but it was clear that this was not a socialist measure." Only the three large firms were taken over; medium-sized and small mining properties were unaffected. "The principle of private property was not attacked."[14] The government paid the tin barons over US$22 million in compensation, despite the wishes of radical sectors of the mass movement. Bolivia's tin remained

Figure 4.1 Civilians in arms, 1952 Revolution. Top: Standing behind barricade (Courtesy of Museo de la Revolución). Bottom: Standing in line with rifles. (Courtesy of Feliciano Muruchi Poma)

subject to the monopolies that dominated the international metal market. The MNR turned down the Soviets' offer to build a tin smelter for Bolivia, which did not have one, while opening the door to foreign oil companies.

A significant early measure was the decree of universal suffrage (July 1952), which ended the Spanish literacy requirement previously used to exclude the indigenous majority. After peasants in key agricultural regions began seizing landlords' estates, agrarian reform was decreed in August 1953. The MNR sought to pacify the countryside and create a layer of small proprietors as a bulwark against radical miners and urban workers.

Bolivia "between Wall Street and Trotsky"

The eruption of armed Indian miners, laborers, and peasants onto the political stage of a desperately poor country in the heart of Latin America was in itself a profoundly radical event. The question now posed by the revolution was: How far will they go? Will they be content with a partial, compensated mine nationalization under the watchful eye of Wall Street and Washington; fiscal policies subject to IMF approval; wealth and privilege remaining in the hands of those elite members not directly associated with the old Rosca? In the months after April 1952, this remained very much an open question.

Le Monde's prestigious Latin America correspondent, Marcel Niedergang, summed it up in a front-page headline: "The Bolivian Revolution between Wall Street and Trotsky."[15] Writing about the "powerful POR," he opined that "the Bolivian Trotskyists have a remarkable leader, Guillermo Lora," and "may be the only people in Bolivia who know exactly what they want." They "have had considerable influence in the latest union congresses,"[16] he added. Beyond this, the renowned French journalist aimed to make a fundamental point. With the title "Between Wall Street and Trotsky," he posed the question of which road the revolution would follow: a controlled "modernization" that preserved private property, in alliance with the United States, or a thorough-going social upheaval, a "permanent" revolution to uproot the power of the ruling classes and extend revolt beyond Bolivia's borders?

In adamant disavowal of the more radical option, the MNR government repeatedly and explicitly denounced Trotskyism while espousing "multi-class unity." Drawn from intellectual sectors of the Bolivian elite and upwardly mobile members of the middle class, the MNR leaders sought to represent and strengthen a modernizing sector of the bourgeoisie—to substitute themselves for it when necessary. Víctor Paz Estenssoro was now

El Jefe de la Revolución Nacional, with the "V" of his first name converted into a symbol of the revolution. As the MNR's leaders pursued the old dream of *Bolivia Grande*, they conformed to the populist pattern of arguing for "a harmonious vision of society in which all conflicts should dissolve themselves in favor of the grandeur of the Nation."[17]

In a programmatic speech to the MNR's 1953 convention, Paz declared that "the national bourgeoisie has opened its eyes" to see that "its interests lie with the National Revolution, because the hard currency previously taken away by Patiño, Aramayo and Hochschild will now remain at the country's disposal to buy machinery . . . and other production goods." The "national" entrepreneurs would use this to "establish industries in line with the industrial promotion policy," and "will also benefit from agrarian reform," which would "create a market for large consumer industries." He warned against "left parties not identified with the national interest," reiterating that the MNR was "revolutionary but not communist"; indeed, the National Revolution was "the only means of combating communism."[18]

In proclaiming his party's anticommunist *bona fides*, Paz did no more than tell the truth. From its inception, the MNR proclaimed its antipathy to Marxist socialism. However, to provide "scientific" backing to its multiclass ideology, it borrowed Stalinist ideas, particularly the "bloc of four classes" and "two-stage" concepts that emerged from Comintern policy in China. In his 1953 convention speech, Paz borrowed from Mao Zedong to underline his point that the revolution's "convergence of interests . . . even includes the bourgeoisie." The flag of the new People's Republic of China had one large star and four small ones, Paz noted, "representing the four social classes that are fighting for China's liberation: proletariat, peasantry, middle class and bourgeoisie." As a "vanguard party" of the "people," the MNR should represent all classes, rejecting "seductive proposals . . . unrealizable in the present historical stage" and "sectarian" attitudes that would "push" the bourgeoisie into the arms of reaction. "Worker minister" Ñuflo Chávez said MNR doctrine applied "general principles of scientific socialism" to "our historical reality," creating "the theory of the National Revolution, [which is] antifeudal and anti-imperialist, eminently revolutionary and democratic."[19]

The MNR regime took remarkable pains to combat Trotskyism. In September 1953, President Paz declared that if a "Trotskyist government" came to power, it would not survive because "Bolivia is a country that depends on foreign nations."[20] Of the large number of publications devoted to denouncing the permanent revolution, one of the most striking is "Nationalism and the Demagogic and Pro-Imperialist Action of Trotzkyism," a pamphlet by MNR theorist Juan Fellman Velarde. With heavy sarcasm it attacks "the 'permanent' clash of Trotzkyism with reality," its attempt to "push the Bolivian working class into fighting windmills" and to "sabotage the Bolivian proletariat's unity with other social classes that have an interest in liquidating imperialism and feudalism."[21] As the revolution neared its first anniversary, the government mouthpiece *La Nación* stated: "The internationalist politics of Trotzkyism, dragged by the hair into our midst, is no more than an infantile and reactionary adventure, since it seeks to implant a Bolshevik-type dictatorship in our *Patria*—a workers' and peasants' government—in complete ignorance of the economic stage the country is living through."[22]

The MNR did not rely on the arms of criticism alone. It fought to subordinate labor and peasant organizations as much as possible to the government, co-opting leaders and bureaucratizing structures. At the same time, it pushed to reestablish a reliable armed force to safeguard the social order and do away with elements of "dual power." Early on, it established a widely feared political police called Control Político, as well as shock brigades, among them women's groups called "Barzolas" after the heroine of the Catavi Massacre.

In opposing the "Trotsky" option, did the MNR embrace "Wall Street"? Increasingly, it did. Using U.S. money and advisers, it eventually succeeded in reestablishing the standing army, with a decree cosigned by Lechín. After Siles succeeded Paz as president, the government decided that mass mobilization had waned enough for it to launch a full-scale attack on labor through stabilization plans proposed by U.S. experts and the IMF. By 1958, Bolivia was so dependent on Washington's assistance that one-third of its budget was paid directly with U.S. funds. Government supporters, including peasants who had benefited from agrarian reform, were sent to smash a miners' strike at San José in 1959, and an MNR *comando* massacred dissident miners at Huanuni. By late 1964, "Paz was obliged to rely on constant police action to keep control."[23]

A nationalist government unable to maintain control over the masses, whose disappointment with failed promises generated constant disorder, became a liability for Bolivia's elite as well as the U.S. State Department. The "revolutionary nationalists" were overthrown in 1964 by a U.S.-trained "revolutionary" air force general, beginning a new cycle of extreme repression.

Role and Policy of the Bolivian Trotskyists

When the "revolutionary" government railed against Trotskyism, it was not indulging paranoid delusions. The POR occupied strategic positions in the labor movement and, soon enough, sectors of the peasantry. Highly visible and vocal, Bolivian Trotskyists were the most forceful advocates of the revolution going "all the way" to a socialist expropriation of the entire capitalist and landlord class.

However, the policy of the Partido Obrero Revolucionario was not the intransigent opposition to bourgeois-nationalist regimes demanded by the doctrine of permanent revolution. Nor did it maintain the watchwords of the Pulacayo Thesis, opposing the entry of "worker ministers" into a capitalist government. Instead, the POR combined leftist criticism of the regime with support, especially to Lechín and the other worker ministers, seeking to push and pressure the government to fulfill the aspirations of the masses. The recently formed Bolivian Communist Party (PCB), with its explicit theory of a progressive bourgeoisie, was well to the right of the POR and less conflicted when it came to backing the nationalists. Yet given its history as a seedbed of radical ideas, the POR's equivocal attitude influenced large numbers of activists, seeming to mark the leftmost limits of radical politics.

In the revolution's early years, the masses tended to accept the MNR's self-image as the voice of "the people." The laboring poor fervently hoped the new government would meet their daily needs and broader aspirations for national and social emancipation. In its own way, the POR both reflected and reinforced the illusion that the MNR would do this, even if it meant breaking from the capitalist framework.

The axis of Bolivian Trotskyists' politics was their orientation to Lechín's MNR Left, which headed the COB labor federation while participating in Paz Estenssoro's cabinet. That the MNR could not govern without the support of the COB was a reality daily embodied in "cogovernment." The POR had played an important role in the COB's foundation and was prominent in the labor federation's leadership. When the government announced that the tin barons would be compensated for nationalized mines, the POR succeeded in having the COB protest this decision. Meanwhile, the POR returned to its role as author of the radical theses and speeches that Lechín, Torres, and others needed for mobilizing as well as controlling the masses.

The POR's adaptation to the government's left wing paved the way for a deep-going crisis in the party, the absorption of many of its leaders by the MNR, and the frustration of its hope to lead a deeper radicalization of the revolutionary process. Tensions over its attitude to the MNR in power led to a devastating split of the POR three years after the Revolution.

On the Barricades

When the April ninth uprising broke out, the POR was still reeling from the repression of 1949–50. Revolution broke out before the party could carry through reorganization allowing effective, centralized functioning on a nationwide scale. One of its most talented leaders, Guillermo Lora, was in Europe. An internal report, written weeks later, stated that "our party was present in the events"; it "tried to establish a concrete goal for the masses' armed struggle, and published a declaration" inspired by the FI's resolution on Latin America. Lora later wrote that the party was unable to gain full advantage from its prior work because its members "intervened in an isolated way," rather than as a united organization, in the April days.[24]

Nonetheless, in La Paz, Oruro, and elsewhere, POR militants played significant roles on the barricades, as well as in the Comando Obrero (Workers Command), made up of miners and factory and construction workers, that played a central part in defeating the army. Edwin Möller recalled that "in the Comando Obrero, headed by Lechín, our representative was the painter Miguel Alandia Pantoja, with whom I was closely linked. I was active during the three days of fighting . . . together with one of the party's national leaders [Víctor Villegas], fighting against the cadets. . . . When all seemed lost, the miners of Milluni came in behind the army and liquidated it, and things turned in our favor." An eyewitness wrote that "the Army forces, having surrendered, were marched through the city under the guard of revolutionary militias headed by the 'Comando Obrero.'"[25]

Hugo González said that when it seemed the MNR coup was being defeated, Siles declared it had failed and bid the insurgents farewell. "But the masses, filled with hatred, rage and desperation, took to the streets." Then, "Lechín took the correct step of going to the factories. The masses came out. We went to the factories too." The head of the Carabineros fled, but "nobody told his troops, so a lot of the fighting was done together with them." González continued:

> We participated in the attack on the arsenal in the Plaza Antofagasta, which is now the [La Paz] bus station, and we got mortars there. We were on the barricades that cut off the army as it went up toward Laikacota [a hill strategically dominating the capital]. . . . We used a mortar to clear out the positions the army took on Laikacota. . . . Alandia Pantoja, Villegas and I were on the Yungas barricade. We suggested that the mortar be taken to [a higher position where it could fire on] the Military College, as well as the regime's key regiment. Lechín

showed up and vetoed us, saying they shouldn't be destroyed. . . . He
was the leader then, he had authority.

Lechín took a huge mass of people and a Bolivian flag, and marched
to the Government Palace. He knocked on the door, to get them to
open up. . . . [Laughs.] That's how the Government Palace was taken:
they opened it up. They turned the palace over, and the people inside
surrendered.

The president had fled. In Oruro, "we intervened in the fighting between
the miners and the army through the party's Regional Committee. . . .
Comrade Fernando Bravo was there, fighting in the battles at Papel Pampa
with our miners, who came from Huanuni and Catavi."[26]

A former member, who had witnessed the Catavi Massacre as a teenager in 1942, recalls the fighting in Oruro, strategic center of the mining
industry, during the April days. Despite rumors of an imminent rising, the
party had made no concrete preparations. When fighting broke out, he met
up with Bravo and other comrades, and everyone agreed they should take
part. "The POR participated, not in an organized way but spontaneously."
They were there when mine union leader Mario Torres addressed a crowd
of insurgents, "saying we had to consolidate the revolution that was winning in La Paz and make sure the government couldn't mobilize units from
further south." Since the Carabineros were giving out some arms, "I got a
light machine gun, with its ammunition belt and everything. I'd done my
stint of obligatory military service and was familiar with this weapon." The
insurgents marched to the Second Army Division, which they took after
firing a few shots. Smashing through the door with a truck, they seized
weapons inside. From there they proceeded to the main objective, the barracks of the Camacho Regiment.

An officer, Blacutt, claimed he would convince the regiment to surrender peacefully. Headed by a large number of women, the crowd marched to
the entrance of the barracks, and Blacutt went inside. It was a trap:

> After several minutes the soldiers started firing on the crowd. It was
> an ambush and it turned into a massacre. This was a mistake by the
> officers, because the miners and factory workers went up into the hills
> near the barracks and dug in there. The San José mine is up there, it
> was the miners' natural habitat, and they used the guns they had got-
> ten and rained intense fire down on the Camacho Regiment.
>
> President Urriolagoitia and the Rosca decided to mobilize troops
> from the south, but the miners, together with MNR members, mobi-
> lized to the south of the city, taking up positions in the cemetery and
> people's houses. The soldiers tried to come up through sandy areas

without trees or cover, so they were picked off. They were defeated and had to surrender. The miners took them prisoner. People were angry because of the massacre, so the soldiers were paraded through the streets of Oruro in a kind of march of disgrace, flanked by miners on both sides.[27]

Another POR activist who joined the fighting in Oruro was Modesto Sejas, a militant of Quechua peasant origin who joined the party in 1947 together with a group of secondary school students in Cochabamba. On April 9, 1952, Sejas took a bus from La Paz to Oruro. "I arrived at 3 p.m. in the midst of the fighting. . . . I made contact with the Regional Committee and started working with Fernando Bravo. . . . We devoted ourselves to leading [combat], going from one place to another to reinforce the struggle, to organize. . . . The slogan was to overthrow the Rosca." During the insurrection in La Paz, Sejas said, the workers told Lechín to take power, but he refused.[28]

In Potosí, the Trotskyist miner Julio García was one of the thousands attending a meeting in the central plaza when news of the fighting reached the city. Union leader Nicolás Bernal reminded the workers of their battles in 1947 and 1949. "He was up on the platform and he said, 'Compañeros . . . who will take political power in Potosí?' There was a general cry, a roaring sound: '¡Los mineros!'" The workers felt "the leader of the revolution will be the working class." Bernal told them, "we have to form commissions to get the cachorros [sticks] of dynamite ready." A POR miner spoke, supporting what Bernal had said. "We went down Bustillo and Chayanta streets, and saw nobody on the streets, because the miners were coming down, firing their dynamite charges . . . yelling 'Down with the Rosca, down with the regime of tyranny.' And we had a few old Mauser rifles."

Marching to the central army barracks, they encountered virtually no resistance. The miners' leaders said, "Compañeros, we are not going to kill anybody here, because the soldiers are the sons of the Condoris, the Mamanis" and other Indian names, "in other words, of workers and peasants." The soldiers surrendered. Bernal asked them, "'Where are the officers?' But the officers had all run away." Taking weapons, the miners went to capture City Hall and other key buildings. "It was then that some Movimientista figures appeared, middle-class people, engineers, lawyers. They said, 'We applaud the miners,' and embraced some of the workers. 'We have just constituted the Revolutionary Political Command,' they said. They put themselves in charge and divided up the mayoralty and other posts among themselves." After the miners took the risks, García says, "it was a big error" to let the MNR spokesmen take over the city.[29]

Critical Support to the New Regime

"The masses believed this was their government, they believed the MNR was going to make the revolution," Hugo González said. "And even our own comrades"—at least "a sector" of them—"believed this too."[30] The party's political line reflected these illusions.

One week after the uprising, the Cochabamba press published a communiqué from the local POR. "From the first moments . . . the POR participated at the grassroots level," it stated. "Many of our worker comrades fell in the terrifying massacres that occurred in La Paz, Oruro and the mining centers." The declaration called for "immediate organization of Workers' and Peasants' Councils" and "distributing arms to the workers," because "the rifle on the worker's shoulder is the only guarantee of his conquests and his only defense against those who organize massacres." At the same time, it said "the Anti-Imperialist United Front has occurred *de facto*, in the joint struggle against the oligarchy's power." As the task at hand was "to present a united bloc against the imperialist feudal-bourgeoisie," the POR "does not seek to divide the ranks of the MNR; instead it wants the masses to consolidate their victory over the Rosca," proposing a "platform of the Anti-Imperialist United Front . . . for joint struggle by the Partido Obrero Revolucionario and the *compañeros* of the Movimiento Nacionalista Revolucionario." This included "immediate constitutionalization of the country by turning power over to Paz Estenssoro," a general amnesty, abolition of pongueaje (compulsory labor in the countryside), an across-the-board wage increase, "independence of the union movement," and other planks.[31]

In the internal report circulated after the uprising, the POR wrote: "We should not begin a frontal attack on the MNR, but simply demand that the MNR respect and fulfill the will and aspirations of the masses. . . . Our position toward the government is summed up as follows: Support and defense of the government against the Rosca and imperialism. We support every progressive measure it takes, without renouncing criticism of its vacillations. But this criticism must not be confused with an anti-MNR phobia."[32] Consciously or not, this echoed the 1917 call to "support the Provisional Government insofar as it struggles against reaction" that Stalin and some other Bolsheviks adopted after the February Revolution in Russia. Trotsky often repeated Lenin's bitter attack on that position.[33] Interviewed in Paris, Guillermo Lora was asked, "Is our party in the vanguard of [the] struggle?" He answered: "Yes, and it supports the left wing faction of the new cabinet. It should be said that we alone are capable of defending every progressive measure through the mobilization of the masses." The party was "far from succumbing to the hysteria of a struggle against the MNR." *Lucha Obrera* wrote approvingly that while seeking to "maintain its class political independence," the newly formed labor federation "supports the government . . . to the degree that it fulfills its promised program," and "has two worker ministers in the petty-bourgeois cabinet, but completely controlled . . . by the COB."[34]

Over the next months, the POR expressed the hope that mass pressure could make Lechín's left wing predominant in the government, and that this would lead to the *transformation* of the existing regime into a "workers' and peasants' government." In October 1952, a party conference defined the POR's position as follows:

> 1) Support to the Government against attacks from imperialism and the Rosca; 2) Support to any progressive measures it decrees, while indicating their scope and limitations. This support will not be merely formal, but real and active, which means fighting in the unions, universities and countryside and workers' mass mobilizations so that, through the measures imposed by their power, they will gain consciousness of the need for their own government. 3) In the struggle between the two wings of the MNR, the POR supports the left, made up of workers, peasants and impoverished middle-class elements, showing this left that its future depends on the understanding and ideological clarity it achieves. . . . The POR will support the MNR left . . . in every attempt to deepen the revolution and fulfill the working-class program, as well as its complete control of the government, displacing the right wing.

Indeed, the MNR was "in transition" toward a revolutionary, proletarian policy, the POR press declared. Almost a year later, *Lucha Obrera* editor Villegas said "my party is calling on the left wing [of the MNR] to work to transform the present government into a worker-peasant government."[35]

This was a perspective for a pressure group, not an independent party fighting to break sectors of the mass movement away from the MNR in order to prepare a struggle for power. During a decisive period in the reshaping of the Bolivian state after April 1952, the POR repeatedly presented itself as just that: a group with ideas and proposals for pressuring the ruling party to do what ought to be done. The Pablo leadership of the FI reinforced this; in late 1952 the I.S. wrote that "the way the POR . . . has acted up to now is generally correct," approving its effort to avoid "isolat[ing] itself from the ranks of the left wing of the MNR," and "the critical support granted the MNR government, accompanied by direct revolutionary activity among the masses, for the purpose of exercising and reinforcing their pressure" and independent mass organizations. The SWP also referred to the POR's "critical support" to the government.[36] Although Lora later denied that this was his party's line, its drive to "transform" the government through support to "worker ministers" was reiterated countless times.

Trotskyists in the COB

Trotskyist influence in the Central Obrera Boliviana was so marked that the right wing of the MNR coined a new pejorative: *trotscobitas*, a play on words combining "Trotskyist" and "COB-ist." The London *Economist* wrote that the COB's "real managers were the Trotskyites," who "used it to put pressure on the government." The conservative journal exaggerated when it claimed the POR, "one of the world's few important Trotskyite parties," had been no more than an "appendage" of the MNR, "in particular of its labour wing, headed by Sr Juan Lechín, now Minister of Mines," but accurately noted that the "Trotskyites' great value to him has been that they could write impressive programmes for his union."[37]

Bolivia's conservative press was less restrained, railing against the role of these "extremists" in the labor movement. *Los Tiempos* (Cochabamba) charged that the COB "was born on April 9th under the paternity of Guillermo Lora," adding: "the POR's influence within the unions was so visible that the public . . . soon grew accustomed to the POR's slogans: Nationalization of mines without compensation, liquidation of the bourgeois army, armed peasant militias, collectivization of the land, etc., etc." The COB's affiliates in each department (province), called CODs, were organized "due to the clandestine work of the Trotskyist militants, many of whom . . . joined the MNR to 'orient' the ranks," it complained.[38]

An important figure in the foundation of the COB was the renowned Trotskyist painter Miguel Alandia Pantoja, who had been involved in the party's agitation for a Central Obrera Nacional in the period before the Revolution. Edwin Möller said Alandia served as "coordinator" in the COB's foundation and invited him to the 17 April 1952 meeting at the graphic workers' hall where it was set up. Alandia was also the first director of the COB's newspaper, *Rebelión*. The *New York Times* expressed dismay that the paper hailed Iran's oil nationalization, "voiced solidarity with the Korean, Indo-Chinese, Egyptian and Moroccan 'warriors for independence,'" and declared: "We, together with all the workers of the world, will continue the revolutionary struggle until the final victory."[39]

Alandia embodied the contradictions of the POR's position. Born in Catavi in 1914, deeply influenced by the miners' suffering and struggles, he was sent to fight in the Chaco, fell prisoner, then escaped from Paraguay. Drawn to the "indigenist school" of painting, he began producing images of the war, later becoming a close friend of Guillermo Lora in the period when Lora embraced Trotskyism. A member of the La Paz "cell," he ran on the Miners Parliamentary Bloc slate in 1947 and was prominent in street fighting during the April 1952 uprising. Yet Alandia also became a good friend of President Paz and Vice President Siles, and exercised enormous influence on Juan Lechín. When huge murals were commissioned to represent the Revolution in the halls of government, Alandia was given the job and handsomely paid for his striking images of miners, peasants, the Indian rebel Tupac Katari, and other themes (see figure 4.2). For a brief period, he served as Head of the Culture Department of the Ministry of Education.[40]

Noting that Alandia "is a tireless revolutionary in the social and artistic fields," La Nación proclaimed that Alandia's mural in the Government Palace "will continue to make the National Revolution's ideas a reality and transmit them to future generations."[41] The parallel with the Mexican "revolutionary" regime's employment of left-wing muralists like Diego Rivera was striking. After visiting Bolivia, Rivera referred to Alandia's "very important mural in the Government Palace," which shows "there is now a movement of monumental collectivist art in our continent."[42]

Alandia was not the only POR member prominent in the COB. José Zegada was the COB's recording secretary. Others occupied additional posts, though they did not, in general, meet as a "fraction" to coordinate policy and tactics. Edwin Möller recalled, "I was the most prominent Trotskyist leader on the executive board," serving as Secretary of Organization; the Economist wrote that he "skilfully led" the POR's forces in the COB. Möller also continued to lead the union of commercial workers, whose newspaper Emancipación addressed disputes in the COB, "agrarian revolution," education reform, and many other issues. In January 1953, after a failed coup attempt by right-wingers, La Nación reported that Möller was one of the main union speakers at a "monster rally in support of the government," paraphrasing him as saying "the huge turnout gives an idea of how much support there is for the government of the National Revolution."[43] Outside the capital, POR members were influential in the regional CODs, particularly those of Santa Cruz and Cochabamba.

Relations with Lechín reached a new peak of intensity as the POR's old role of "advising [him] came back in '52," in González's words. While standing "side by side with Paz" in the government, Lora writes, Lechín "returned to Trotskyist postures, adapting to the masses' radicalization, and surrounded himself with POR militants, reciting . . . speeches that they

Figure 4.2 Section of Miguel Alandia Pantoja mural, *Monument to the Revolution*. (Courtesy of Cecilia Salazar de la Torre)

wrote." González gave details: "I wrote speeches" for Lechín in 1952 and 1953, "and so did Comrade [Jorge] Salazar, a member of the POR leadership who was . . . Lechín's secretary. Inside the government palace, Möller wrote speeches for Mario Torres, and we would go listen to them [in the plaza] down below." The MNR astutely used Lechín's leftist credentials. A pamphlet on Movimientista heroes referred to the "great historical magnitude of his work . . . as a revolutionary of the left, based on Marxist doctrinal orientation," adding: "From the Thesis of Pulacayo to the Nationalization of the Mines, his clear trajectory shows the firmness of his convictions."[44]

Leftist associations were useful when the government needed to present a radical face to mass sectors demanding fundamental social changes. Paz Estenssoro met with Lora in early 1953, although an internal POR report said the interview, while "cordial in tone," consisted of "the two interlocutors sounding each other out, without any further importance." At almost the same time, attacks on the POR signaled the government's drive to restrain mass radicalism: Trotskyists were targeted by resolutions demanding their expulsion from the COB, and La Nación called them "a grave danger to the Bolivian proletariat" and an "unconscious instrument of imperialism and the Rosca." The regime forbade print shops from publishing the POR's Lucha Obrera; members selling it in mine and factory districts were arrested. It soon became common for POR sales "brigades" to face MNR "commandos" swooping down to beat them up and hand them over to the Control Político secret police.[45]

"All Power to the Left" (of the MNR)

The Thesis of Pulacayo had vowed that miners' leaders would "never join bourgeois governments, because that would mean the most open betrayal of the exploited masses." The "bourgeoisie invents 'worker' ministers the better to deceive the workers," it declared. However, a history of the COB notes that its very first resolution was to "ratify" Juan Lechín and Germán Butrón as ministers of Mines and Labor, respectively, "with the approval of the workers of the entire country." During this period, according to Lora, the COB "did not take a single step without previously consulting [the Trotskyists] for their opinion." There is no indication that POR spokesmen in the COB opposed Lechín and Butrón joining the cabinet. Instead, they presented this as a conquest of the labor movement, with Lora declaring in May 1952 that "the textile workers decided to impose their conditions on the right wing of the MNR; they obliged it to accept working class elements in the new cabinet who constitute its left faction." He later wrote that "at the POR's suggestion, the COB voted that its decisions were binding on the 'worker ministers,'" and the federation required them to inform it fully of government affairs.[46]

"Complete control of the state by the left wing of the MNR" became a leitmotif of the party's propaganda. When the demand for a "Workers' Majority in the government" caused some concern within the FI's International Secretariat, the Bolivian party defended the slogan.[47] In September 1952, the POR held its Ninth Conference, whose proceedings—prominently reported in *La Nación*—were translated into Aymara and Quechua, given the significant presence of indigenous peasant delegates. The gathering ratified the line of supporting the MNR's "progressive measures," and the government's left wing in particular. A report to the FI stressed the idea that the "MNR's working-class ranks" should defeat the MNR's right wing and take control of the government, as well as POR proposals "to the MNR's left factions to form an alliance on the basis of a minimum program."[48]

The POR sent a message to the MNR's national convention in early 1953, arguing that "to fulfill its historic mission," the convention should be "the scene of reaction's defeat." If the ruling party's "left wing succeeds in imposing itself and acquires a proletarian physiognomy, the POR is ready to collaborate with it and even fuse our cadres." This "new party organization would need to reflect itself in governmental forms, which could only be those of a worker-peasant government."[49]

The Trotskyists were sometimes stern in critiques of "worker ministers" to whom they offered guidance, denouncing them for the COB's increasing bureaucratization, for approving the government's decision to reestablish the standing army, and other "anti-worker" measures. Insistently, however, and particularly at moments of national crisis, the POR called for these same ministers to take control. Rather than intransigent opposition to a bourgeois government, the POR proposed that the transformation of Bolivian society be undertaken by the government's labor wing, or even by Paz himself.

In June 1953, pro-Rosca groupings and the Falange launched a series of coup attempts. When Paz responded by rhetorically threatening big business owners if they "attempt to place obstacles in the path of the National Revolution," *Lucha Obrera* headlined "Radicalization of Víctor Paz Estenssoro," claiming: "THE PRESIDENT, REVISING ALL OF HIS PAST POLITICAL STANCE, POINTED OUT ANTI-CAPITALIST OBJECTIVES FOR THE REVOLUTION, NOT JUST ANTI-IMPERIALIST AND ANTI-FEUDAL ONES. This language could very well be called Trotskyist. It is unfortunate that [his] attitude is only the result of a nervous crisis created by the frustrated plot—the tone of his speech is that of a threat rather than an organic political conception." The POR paper suggested what it called a "political solution": "The only left-wing way out of the situation . . . was to impose the complete domination of the [MNR] left in the Cabinet." It presented a series of radical demands (union militias, sliding scale of wages, workers' control), ending: "All this struggle must center on the slogan 'Total control of the state by the left wing of the MNR.'" "All power to the 'Left'!" another issue headlined.[50]

Reporting on the president's failure to fulfill the appeal "that the Cabinet be controlled by the [MNR] left," *Lucha Obrera* then came out with a "Program for the Left Wing of the MNR." "To us revolutionaries," the POR paper lamented, "the President's conduct seems mistaken." While "it is true that a Chief of State has responsibilities, they are to the people above all," so he "has all the more reason to abide by the popular will and respond to the workers' aspirations, organizing a Cabinet made up exclusively of men from the left wing of his Party." POR members in the COB had proposed that "the names of the Ministers be considered together with [a] program." Thus, "the COB's candidates will join the Cabinet with a program and their actions will be supervised by the working class. The COB's pronouncement is an improvement in its relations with the Executive and will allow the workers to have better control over the Ministers who emerge from their class."[51]

Boasting that the MNR Left "has only been able to count on orientation from us," *Lucha Obrera* hailed the "correct position on the ministerial issue" the COB then took, for "grouping the 'leftists' together on the basis of a slate presented to the President of the Republic." Thus "people who join ministries as workers' representatives will not be doing so simply as personal collaboration by particular leaders" but on the basis of the "program specially approved by the COB." The labor federation had called for "putting more workers into the government, as well as complete control of the government by the MNR left."[52]

In early 1954, the POR issued a leaflet supporting a member of the MNR Left against a representative of its right wing during the MNR's internal elections to its La Paz Departmental Command. The leaflet criticized the Lechinistas for "going from one conciliation to another," thereby "putting the revolution in danger," and making the "grave error" of choosing a candidate "with a shady past . . . known for clerical leanings, a fanatical anticommunist" who expressed "disdain for the worker-peasant masses." Nonetheless, "the POR calls on the ranks of the MNR to support the Revolutionary Nationalist Popular Front slate, to prevent a defeat for the left and establish the basis to push the revolution forward."[53]

In her travelogue of post-Revolution Bolivia, the German-Ecuadoran journalist Lilo Linke provides an anecdote showing the impact these concepts had among members of the POR's rank and file. In La Paz, Linke asked a friendly young Trotskyist named María Julia if she thought "the MNR will betray the revolution." "Not at all," she replied. "They can't, even if they wanted to. The masses are on the march: nothing and nobody can stop them. Not only that, but I'm told that the leaders of the MNR have gotten close to our party. This proves that what they need is a definite political orientation, which we can give them."[54] (See figure 4.3.)

In 1954, the government again stepped up repression against the Trotskyists, launching large-scale arrests of POR miners, peasants, and union leaders; establishing blacklists; and escalating the crackdown on *Lucha Obrera*. "In this dirty task, the 'worker ministers' bear the greatest responsibility," Lora wrote in a Mexican Trotskyist journal.[55] Yet the POR itself had helped build these leaders' reputation among the worker and peasant masses.

Peasant Upheaval in Cochabamba

One of the revolution's achievements was a significant agrarian reform, which also eliminated the system of personal service to landlords known as *pongueaje*. The MNR's original program did not propose any overturn in land tenure, only to "study" how to attain higher productivity through "adequate organization" of agriculture.[56] Nor did the new government call for "land to the tiller," let alone agrarian cooperatives or collectives. The reform was finally proclaimed sixteen months after the uprising, largely in response to a wave of land takeovers by armed peasants. The epicenter of this mobilization was the village of Ucureña in the Cochabamba Valley, Bolivia's breadbasket. Ucureña was the center of Bolivian Trotskyists' work among the peasantry. The rapid extension of this work, and the political conflicts it generated, constitute a fascinating, overlooked aspect of Latin American radical history.

Bolivia had a long history of rural unrest, but the peasantry played almost no role in the April 1952 insurrection, which occurred in urban centers. The destruction of the army opened the way for popular mobilization, unleashed by the insurrection, to spread gradually to the countryside. In some areas, including Cochabamba, this process was facilitated by the presence of politicized ex-miners in local communities. Localized protests began in late 1952, reaching a level of intensity that made "civil war . . . a menacing possibility," a North American anthropologist noted.

Figure 4.3 Visitors to the *Monument to the Revolution*, under Miguel Alandia Pantoja's "Education and the Class Struggle." (Photo by author)

The government was "forced to act," signing the agrarian reform decree "in the Indian village of Ucureña under the watchful eyes of fifty thousand *campesinos*." It aimed for a gradual and limited redistribution, curbing direct action by peasants who went beyond the limits of government control. Implementation varied greatly between regions, but many of the country's latifundia were left untouched, with only 28.5 percent affected in the first two years. In Cochabamba the figure was only 16 percent.[57]

What would be done from "above" and from "below" was a burning question with far-reaching implications. The POR's response reflected the contradictions of its outlook. When Paz announced that a working group would be formed to prepare an agrarian reform law, the POR responded: "We know that in creating the agrarian reform commission, the government seeks to strangle the movement of the peasant masses." Nonetheless, "given this commission's deliberative nature and the fact that it is beyond the state's political control," the party would be willing to participate if invited. It went on to demand "nationalization of the land without compensation, to be turned over to the peasant organizations," linking this to its political strategy by reiterating that "the POR will work to achieve the evolution of the left sector of the current government toward the worker-peasant government" in order to achieve this task. Reflecting its prominence in the mass movement, the POR *was* invited, sending Ernesto Ayala to participate in the commission alongside a long-time PRI agrarian expert and government representatives, almost all of whom, according to MNR historian Luis Antezana, were "'left' *hacendados*" (landowners).[58]

In the commission's debates, Möller recalled, the POR argued to "maintain the unity of the [Indian] communities, convert them into cooperatives . . . without forcing things, and expropriate all the latifundia, whether they were productive or unproductive." The position of Peasant Affairs Minister Ñuflo Chávez, a leader of the MNR Left, was similar to that of the Stalinist Urquidi: "respecting the productive latifundia, dissolving the communities and turning the land over to the peasants" individually. In a "thesis" presented to the COB, Möller spoke of "agrarian revolution" but depicted this as something the government would promote, "taking as the starting point what the masses have already done" through direct action. "The objective of government policy toward the countryside cannot be the initiation of a long capitalist cycle," he wrote, "but a transition to higher social forms." The state "should allow and aid organization of a National Peasant Confederation, so as to establish the revolutionary worker-peasant alliance."[59]

The POR press gave heavy coverage to the situation in the countryside, denouncing abuses by the gamonales (landlords) and publicizing land seizures. One article reported the takeover of a hacienda in the province of Charcas, where "whipping was a daily practice, together with the right of the first night, expropriation of cows and sheep, [and] murder." The peasants "carried out the agrarian revolution in their area" and "hoped the 'revolutionary' government would at least congratulate them for taking this step." However, "to achieve their complete liberation they must trust only in their own organized forces." Another reported that "numerous POR peasant cells" had "sent denunciations to *Lucha Obrera* reporting that many *gamonales* are dividing up their estates and pressuring the Indians to buy them." This should be prevented through land occupations "by the union organization itself."[60]

One month before the agrarian reform decree, *Lucha Obrera* stated that the POR "has been the only political party that takes account of the deepest tendencies motivating the peasant movement," turning them into "programmatic formulations and slogans" while educating "peasant fighters who are playing a vanguard role." Because of this, August 2, when the decree would be signed, "will be a day of victory for the peasant masses and also . . . for the Partido Obrero Revolucionario." After its promulgation, however, the party complained that the decree was "designed to pacify the countryside in order to carry out a bourgeois-type reform." However, "the Executive, with the ceremony in Ucureña and the parallel peasant mobilization, has given an even greater push to the exploited rural population's combativity, practically unleashing the peasant avalanche."[61]

The POR and Peasant Radicalism

During the months leading up to the agrarian reform decree, officials expressed acute concern over the Trotskyists' role in rural areas around Sucre, Lake Titicaca, and other regions. The strongest focus was on Cochabamba, where peasant mobilizations moved from local strikes to the formation of armed groups to seize estates, and landlords formed armed detachments under their own command. Under headlines like "Rural Agitation by Trotskyist Elements Denounced," *La Nación* warned of attempts to create a "climate of subversion."[62] Struggles within the Cochabamba peasant movement reflected differing local priorities (in some areas land, in others water), personal rivalries, conflicts between villages, the degree of Church influence, and other factors. The clearest line of division was between pro-government leaders and a radical current based on direct action by the peasants themselves. The radical tendency, centered in Ucureña and other parts of Cochabamba's Valle Alto (Upper Valley), was headed by POR members and some MNR activists who followed their lead.

The clash was summed up in counterposed slogans, as one peasant leader, an ex-miner and former POR member, recalled: "The *poristas* wanted to take over all the peasant federations. Among them were the peasant *porista* Encarnación Colque, Orlando Capriles, Emilio Pérez and Modesto Sejas. Their slogan was the Agrarian Revolution, and the government's slogan was Agrarian Reform. We saw that with Agrarian Reform, we would have had to obey all the legalistic laws. What was needed was to take over the estates!"[63]

The names of these and other Trotskyist peasant leaders were featured in a torrent of articles in *Los Tiempos*, the conservative Catholic daily that spoke for Cochabamba *gamonales*. Blaring headlines reflected the scope of mobilization together with landlords' class and racial fears: "Coup in Peasant Federation, POR Militants Oust Leadership" (4 January), "Indians' Violence Causes Alarm . . ." (22 January), "Trotskyist Leaders Ousted . . ." (27 January), "Police Arrest Peasant Agitators" (31 January), "Hundreds of Armed and Hostile Indians Demand Leaders' Freedom in Ucureña" (1 February), which "has fallen into the hands of the POR" (5 February), "Sivingani Peasants Follow Orders of Ucureña Leaders, Not Authorities" (21 April), "Indian Agitation Harms Agrarian Reform Commission's Work" (25 April), "Hundreds of Indians Sow Panic in Tarata" (12 May), "Peasants Continue to Seize Haciendas' Arms" (13 May).

Political turmoil within the Cochabamba Peasant Workers Union Federation was reflected in *Los Tiempos'* coverage. After the POR-led radical faction ousted pro-government leaders, they retaliated by proclaiming the expulsion of "extremists." On January thirtieth the police arrested POR militants and other protest "chiefs" (including MNR member José Rojas) on the charge of "stirring up peasant areas by preaching demagogy." What happened next was described by SWP spokesman Bert Cochrane in a Detroit lecture on "The Revolution in Bolivia": "When peasants in the fields got word that their leaders had been arrested, they downed tools immediately and marched from all sides on [the city of] Cochabamba, armed with clubs, hunting rifles, iron bars, and even improvised arms hastily devised by using stems filled with powder, which are exploded by setting a match to them." A thousand Ucureña peasants occupied the city center. Local authorities tried to drown out speeches by Modesto Sejas and Emilio Chacón by honking car horns. An MNR leader gave an anticommunist speech, police fired tear gas, and armed members of a group calling itself Vanguardia del MNR helped drive out the protesting Indians.[64]

Rojas and another leader were taken to La Paz, where the president himself met with them, "promis[ing] to support Rojas in his desire to be the main leader in Cochabamba, on condition that Rojas would support the MNR and not the 'communists of the POR'." Calling for stern measures, Peasant Affairs Coordinator Víctor Zannier was quoted in a *Los Tiempos* headline: "The *Poristas* Are Responsible for the Indian Uprisings." The *New York Times* reported: "According to a memorandum submitted by the Cochabamba police chief to the Minister of Government, the outbreaks have been caused by increased activity of agitators for the Partido Obrero Revolutionary [sic]. . . . These organizers . . . have been telling the Indian farmers that they are the only group that will accomplish a distribution of land." Although the article claimed the agitators were "under the orders of Edwin Möller, an important member of Minister of Mines Juan Lechín's Central Workers of Bolivia," in reality the Cochabamba POR militants acted largely on their own.[65]

For its part, the Bolivian Communist Party told an Argentine journalist that "the Trotskyists are the worst enemies of things going the way they should, they're extremists who have a lot of support, above all in Cochabamba, and indirectly influence the left wing of the MNR." The "dangerous leftism" of their peasant agitation would "provoke serious problems if they're not made to toe the line."[66]

The COB leadership alternated between protesting repression of the peasant radicals and denouncing their "attitude of provocation and rebelliousness" aimed at "creating problems for the government." Peasant Affairs minister and MNR Left spokesman Chávez wrote Paz to complain of peasant unions that followed "POR slogans" and to report that he had ordered the detention of several peasant leaders, "especially Manuel Cruz Vallejos" of the POR. In Ucureña, "POR leader Modesto Sejas is the main author of this anti-Government agitation, so I have ordered that he be arrested." Chávez summed up: "Since agitation in the countryside is directed by the Partido Obrero Revolucionario and there will be no peace while this party's leaders continue to enjoy not only rights but privileges, I insist on the need to exile all the POR's leaders and members, who number no more than five hundred throughout the country." If "overall measures against the POR" are not taken, "I will be forced to resign from the Post with which your Presidency has honored me."[67]

The minister's demand to exile POR members was not fulfilled (nor did he resign), but repression was stepped up. Armed MNR groups organized in rural areas in June and July 1953 were sometimes used against the POR. Apparently hired by local *gamonales*, gunmen (some armed with machine guns) assassinated Manuel Cruz Vallejos, the Sacabamba POR peasant leader Chávez had denounced. Hired guns also killed seventeen-year-old peasant leader and POR supporter Alberto Herbas in Pojo. A POR call for international solidarity stated that the killers of Herbas were "later torn to pieces by the infuriated peasant masses."[68]

"We Led All the Land Takeovers"

The turbulence in Cochabamba was vividly recalled by Modesto Sejas, born in 1927 to landless peasants in the village of Totora who spoke only Quechua at home. During high school in 1946–47, he and a small group of Jewish students in Cochabamba formed a short-lived group called Youth Social Studies Vanguard, some of whose members joined the POR. In January 1947, he gave a speech at a Cochabamba labor meeting defending the Potosí miners massacred by the PIR. Members of the PIR were present, and "physically kicked me out." Cochabamba POR leader Carlos Bayón took him home and cleaned him up. Shortly thereafter Sejas joined the party, which had around thirty members in the city, including students, peasants, mechanics, painters, and some other workers.

After participating in the April 1952 uprising, Sejas devoted himself to peasant organizing in the Cochabamba region, explaining that pro-government peasant leaders "will not make the agrarian revolution, but only some reforms which will not be what we need." Agitation was mainly carried out in Quechua. When COB leaders came to a Cochabamba peasant federation meeting in January 1953, "we argued with Lechín for two days, and we defeated him. We argued for the agrarian revolution and he argued for agrarian reform, the MNR's position." For POR peasants in Cochabamba, the agrarian revolution meant this:

> Socialization of the land . . . so *gamonales'* estates would pass directly into the hands of the unions as collective or cooperative property. . . . [The MNR], advised by the U.S. State Department, wanted to divide up the land—a counterrevolution on the agrarian question.
>
> We led all the land takeovers. . . . We explained that the property will not be divided up, we will run the haciendas, we will grow, we will industrialize, we will bring in machines, we will irrigate—we will do all these things through a collective administration, that of the unions. [The peasants] understood just fine. . . . This was the only organization which took over the lands entirely.

In contrast, haciendas remained intact in Sucre, parts of La Paz Department, Santa Cruz, and several other areas. POR and peasant federation activists organized armed defense groups and militias. Peasants "would rather sell their plows than go without weapons," Sejas said, adding that the Barrientos military dictatorship later changed the caliber of army rifles to make it harder to get ammunition.

When POR supporters were arrested in January 1953, the peasant union took over the city of Cochabamba. Released from jail, POR spokesman Encarnación Colque made a speech in Quechua. Speaking for "the agrarian revolution, the worker-peasant militias," "against the MNR government" and its proposal to reestablish the army," Colque said: 'Compañeros, why do we need an army that will massacre workers and peasants? We are going to organize another kind of army, one that will defend the interests of the workers and peasants, an army of overalls and ojotas,'" the distinctive sandals worn by many Bolivian peasants.

In this period, Sejas noted, "our organization grew so much that the POR became a mass party in Cochabamba." It opened two headquarters in the city of Cochabamba and one in Ucureña, each guarded by armed members. "Every night we suffered attacks by the thugs of the gamonales and the MNR." Although the "great POR leader" Cruz Vallejos and "the top POR leader in Pojo," Herbas, were murdered, and many others imprisoned, "for two years [the police] were unable to capture me. I had a very good group, organized and armed. . . . I was arrested in La Paz, when I went to the [POR's Eleventh] Conference." After his arrest he was severely tortured. Once released, he spent the years until 1962 underground and in exile. Interviewed at the age of sixty-five, Sejas maintained his revolutionary outlook and had returned to active participation in the Trotskyist movement.[69]

Guillermo Lora recalled opposing the enrollment of "too many" peasants in the Cochabamba POR. The peasants claimed to be revolutionaries, he said, but were being "tricky" since all they wanted was to get some land. "The POR has discovered something that Lenin, Trotsky and the Bolsheviks did not know," he claimed, "and that is that the peasant is really a small proprietor."[70]

In 1953, however, the POR's Central Committee worried that peasant mobilization in Cochabamba was too radical, ran contrary to a nationwide downturn in labor activism, and was out of line with national party positions. An internal circular warned: "The MNR bureaucracy is determined to satisfy the imperialists' desires and has found a pretext in the Party's mistaken actions," among them "the 'localist' direction of the work on the agrarian question." While citing "differences among our comrades" there (some considered the peasant agitation too militant), it declared that "Cochabamba has acted outside the bounds of any control, outside the line of the Party, unaware of the most basic disciplinary norms," adding: "It is necessary to put an end to the sporadic and isolated uprisings that only weaken our forces."[71]

A special resolution on the Cochabamba Regional Committee warned against "sectarian, adventurist deviations incompatible with the Party's strategy," declaring that "the Cochabamba peasant movement is disproportionately advanced in relation to the rest of the country and in relation to the workers' movement as such." An isolated rising and land occupations in Cochabamba "would be a genuine adventure whose negative results for the overall mass movement and the Party's future would be incalculable," allowing "reaction to retake the offensive" and "unleash bloody repression against the peasants, [who would be] deprived of effective support from the workers and peasants of the rest of the country." Thus "it is urgently necessary to explain these dangers to the peasant masses and make them understand that the slogan 'Occupy the land,' while still correct, cannot be carried out under present conditions, and the moment of its application must be determined by the Party's CC when conditions have matured sufficiently on a nation-wide scale."[72]

These warnings involved more than simple tactical caution. The CC's nationwide strategy sought to deepen the POR's alliance with the MNR Left, which was violently hostile to the "uncontrolled" peasant mobilizations in Cochabamba. Counseling patience to Cochabamba activists, the POR leadership was preparing to participate in the government's agrarian reform commission and would later write of the "victory" gained with the August 1953 agrarian decree. It was a Marxist axiom that to gain lasting victory, peasant risings—usually "localist" due to the nature of rural life—must help to fuel a nationwide, proletarian-led revolution. It was equally axiomatic that this required a revolutionary leadership committed to bringing workers' power to bear in defense of embattled peasants. The idea that it was not possible to seize the land was clearly false: that was precisely what the peasants were doing in Cochabamba. The POR leaders' message resembled what Stalin told Chinese Communists in 1925–27: curb peasants' land seizures because they threaten the party's bloc with the nationalist Guomindang.

That the POR's orientation toward the MNR lay behind these disputes is clear in a letter to the FI's International Secretariat, stating that in Cochabamba, "two factions are confronting each other" in the party, "one rightist [i.e., more moderate than the official party line], the other ultra-leftist." The group veering to the right had an "erroneous interpretation" of party resolutions, "above all an overestimation of the possibilities of the government," expressing "positions that capitulate to the MNR." In reaction, "the other faction upheld ultra-leftist positions that pose . . . the danger of an immediate break of the Party from the masses who still believe in the MNR," and of "pushing our comrades into adventures in the mobilization of the peasants." The CC had "put an end to all these mistakes" and a "reunified" Cochabamba committee now "follows its directives."[73]

Yet differences not only continued but deepened. The tone of local Trotskyist agitation comes through in a leaflet published on the Revolution's second anniversary by the POR's Ucureña Local Committee. Denouncing the government for indemnifying the tin barons and acting as "middleman selling small lots to the peasants," it told them: "Defend the lands that have been occupied, unto death if necessary. . . . Reject the government's agents and bureaucrats, pay not one cent for the occupied lands, take not one step backwards. On the contrary, agitate the masses toward the organized occupation of the haciendas where this has not been done." A "genuinely peasant, honest and revolutionary leadership" must be "completely independent of the government," which is "capitalist in nature, as proven by its openly rightist policies," it declared, ending with these words: "The peasants and workers have nothing in common with this government, because *our* government will be the Worker-Peasant Government. Through the POR, we fight to establish that government."[74]

Ideas were weapons, and the Ucureña comrades needed them to be sharp. Insisting that workers and peasants had *nothing* in common with the *capitalist* (not merely "petty-bourgeois") MNR regime, the Quechua "ultra-leftists" were putting forward a view diametrically opposed to that of the national POR leadership.

Factional Explosion

The conflicts over Cochabamba prefigured the factional strife that would tear the POR apart in 1954–55. Facile observers routinely wax ironic about leftist infighting, but the issues behind Bolivian Trotskyism's factional explosion were real, acute, and intimately linked to the revolution's future. In the broadest sense, the conflict expressed the contradiction between the party's formal adherence to Trotsky's permanent revolution and its practice of seeking to pressure the regime to the left. Could the "revolutionary" government be pressured into a radical break with the U.S.-dominated framework of Latin American capitalism? Could the MNR really be transformed into an instrument of the laboring poor? If so, why maintain an independent Trotskyist party? If not, what conclusions needed to be drawn about the party's strategy and slogans? Were Trotskyist leaders guiding Lechín's MNR Left toward socialism, or were the Lechinistas co-opting the Trotskyists?

The POR's factional polarization was related to the 1951–53 split between followers and opponents of Michel Pablo, which divided the Fourth International, but it did not reproduce the lines of that split. Personal and organizational frictions added fuel to the fire. To further complicate matters, the "official stories" of the two factions—and the ways the events entered Bolivian political history and that of the FI itself—diverge significantly from evidence provided by documents of the time and interviews with participants.

Given the prominence of Guillermo Lora, Edwin Möller, Ernesto Ayala, Hugo González, Fernando Bravo, and other POR leaders in Bolivian public life, the party's blowup is a familiar topic among labor and left activists, intellectuals, historians, political scientists, journalists, and commentators. Conventional wisdom holds that the POR divided between "Pabloists" and "anti-Pabloists," with the former joining the MNR. What really happened is very different. Internationally, Pablo and his followers did advocate "entrism" into many Communist, social-democratic, and labor parties, and some nationalist movements. In Bolivia, however, the grouping most closely associated with Pablo did not wind up joining the MNR. Instead, it was the great majority of the faction led by Lora and Möller (who sought to avoid identification with either the Pablo or anti-Pablo camps in the FI) that carried out "entrism" in the ruling party.

Rather than a bilateral fight, the internal struggle involved: (1) the Fracción Proletaria Internacionalista (FPI; Proletarian Internationalist Faction) of González and Bravo; (2) the Fracción Obrera Leninista (FOL; Leninist Workers Faction) of Lora and Möller, which subdivided into (a) a large grouping that "entered" the MNR and (b) Lora (eventually joined by a handful of others), who encouraged some form of entrism in the MNR but broke with Möller at the last moment; (3) a grouping around Warqui (Oscar Barrientos) in Cochabamba, which was loosely linked to the FOL and supported the entrists; and (4) a separate group in Cochabamba, led by POR peasant activists and a Swiss immigrant, which opposed both the FPI and the FOL, rejected entrism, and charged that the entire national leadership of the POR was capitulating to a bourgeois regime. This last group, whose existence has been a virtual secret of Bolivian Trotskyism, evolved from the Cochabamba "ultra-leftists" denounced by the Central Committee.

In June 1953, the POR held its Tenth Conference, approving extensive "theses" written by Lora. After the gathering, according to Lora, controversy broke out on the document's characterization that the mass movement was passing through a period of "downturn," and that the POR's task was to formulate slogans allowing it to win over the masses rather than orient to an immediate struggle for power. More fundamental was the way the theses characterized the government: while defending "the bourgeoisie's interests," it was "petty-bourgeois" (i.e., of an intermediate class character), "constantly shifting between the imperialist pole and the proletarian extreme."[75]

The document went beyond calling for the defeat of right-wing military attacks on the government. Despite the traditional Trotskyist distinction between "military defense" against rightist threats and impermissible "political support" of a nonproletarian regime, it put forward a species of overall, "critical" support to the ruling party. Its guiding slogan was to "demand that the government fulfill the postulates of the revolution."[76] This formalized the strategy of pressuring the regime. Rather than counterposing itself to the widespread idea that the MNR had the laboring masses' interests at heart, the POR would base its policy on that illusion.

The theses laid out the idea that the Lechinistas, although confused, vacillating, and capitulatory, could be pressured to defeat the MNR right and take over the government. The MNR Left's predominance would "profoundly modify the nature of the MNR and allow it to draw quite close to the POR." This could even mean "a possible coalition government of the POR and MNR which would be a form of realizing the 'Worker-Peasant Government' formula and, in turn, constitute the stage of transition toward the dictatorship of the proletariat." Appended was a brief text with slogans for defeating the rightist coup attempt of late June 1953, ending: "This entire struggle must revolve around the slogan 'Complete control of the state by the left wing of the MNR.'"[77]

Lora later stated that the part on the MNR Left was "inspired . . . by a talk with Lechín that Escóbar [Lora] had right after he returned from Europe," in which "Escóbar told the labor leader that if he really followed a revolutionary line, he should go ahead and displace Paz from power, but [Lechín] said this was not possible, because the MNR President identified with the left's positions."[78]

Hugo González was elected General Secretary at the POR's Tenth Conference. Soon, he recalled, "troubles began in La Paz" with Möller and Lora. They started acting "over the head of the party, and this was reflected in the COB," where Möller was still Organization Secretary and both Lora and González were delegates. "The differences began to appear in public. . . . They would speak in the party's name without consulting the rest of the leadership." The basic difference, he said, was that Möller and Lora were pushing hard for a "united front with the MNR," whereas other POR leaders had a perspective of "independent work."[79]

Pablo's I.S. considered the Tenth Conference document confused and too soft on the MNR. In January 1954, it urged the POR to adopt a "reorientation": continuing to call on the MNR Left to break from the right and adopt a revolutionary policy, the party should more aggressively seek to influence mass sectors that were becoming disillusioned in the MNR by means of the call for a Constituent Assembly and "a systematic, vigorous campaign for the *workers' and peasants' government*."[80]

Lora claims that the I.S. and Latin American Bureau (BLA) used a combination of pressure and flattery to win over "unconditional" supporters. He and Möller were placed in a "minority . . . defending the totality of the line approved in the historic [Tenth] congress" of the party. When factions were formed, the Lora-Möller FOL defended this line, while the FPI sought to "replace it with the conceptions of the I.S.," advocating "pushing the masses to power." In contrast, he and Möller "believed the tactic of the left front, a version of the anti-imperialist front with a basically Trotskyist program, could lift the party out of its isolation." This front would be "a long-term political bloc," not "circumstantial accords." With Möller, he began "soundings" on the possibility of the MNR Left and POR forming this alliance, while citing precedents like the Miners Parliamentary Bloc, the Four-Party Pact of 1950, and the POR 1951 appeal for a front with the MNR.[81]

In March 1954, the Political Bureau (PB) criticized Lora and Möller for disciplinary infractions like issuing their own press releases and leaflets and "establish[ing] relations, on their own account and without PB control, with various people and groups, seeking to carry forward their policy of a Left Front." By April 1954, when the POR convened its Eleventh Conference, the FPI and FOL factions had been formally established. The González-Bravo FPI accused Lora and Möller of a capitulatory attitude toward the MNR; Lora notes they did not question the concept of an anti-imperialist front, only its applicability at that time. Coordinating closely with the FPI, Pablo's I.S. charged that Lora's campaign for "the unity of all left parties in an Anti-imperialist United Front would mean the absence of a struggle against the MNR and practically abandoning the campaign for the workers' and peasants' government."[82]

The conference established a "parity" leadership, with two general secretaries—González and Lora—and a CC and Political Bureau made up of equal numbers from the FPI and FOL. The unity effort soon failed, with each side blocking the other's initiatives. Conflict increased when the FOL discovered a letter from Pablo recommending a firm hand against Lora's "opportunist and capitulatory conceptions" and claiming it was "very possible" that he had been urged by the North American SWP—which spearheaded the anti-Pablo International Committee (IC)—to "split the Bolivian section." Lora replied that his faction "does not even have any correspondence with the SWP." He "refused to believe" that the I.S. and its Bolivian supporters would "fight us in such a harsh and dirty way on the basis of guesswork or gossip." The Central Committee had previously voted to "defend the International" against the IC, condemning the SWP's "desertion from the revolutionary camp."[83] However, Lora now proposed that the POR seek the unity of world Trotskyism without supporting Pablo's I.S. or Cannon's IC. Although his faction did not align with the SWP, his claim not to have corresponded with it was false.[84]

In May 1954, Lora, together with González and another FPI member, attended the "Fourth World Congress" convened by Pablo's I.S. Lora states that he and Pablo then drafted a document "which halfway recognized the downturn and advised drawing closer to the MNR ranks to win them over."[85] Despite this attempt at a rapprochement, by mid-1954 the Bolivian POR was essentially split.

The situation alarmed Sucre POR leader Agar Peñaranda. Head librarian at the local university and daughter of a famous writer, her *tertulias* (social gatherings) were frequented by musicians, artists and writers. Eduardo Mendizábal describes Peñaranda as "extremely intelligent . . . a person who studied languages and taught philosophy, and the one 'guilty' of recruiting me to the POR." Known in the party as Marcel, she authored texts on Marxist philosophy and the history of Bolivian women. Marcel was a member of Lora's FOL. However, she asked that it "abstain from issuing public communications, since this means committing the same error for which the [González] faction has been criticized: taking the factional struggle outside the party." Moreover, the FOL "does not have a uniform political line."[86]

Meanwhile, Warqui (Oscar Barrientos) wrote a long analysis, observing that the FOL's positions favored entrism in the MNR, which he supported, while criticizing the party's younger leaders for a series of character flaws and errors in judgment. Lora had "written good material" on the heavy-handedness of the González faction, but "for the last seven years he [Lora] played the role of absolute Monarch (*el partido soy yo*)"—I am the party, a play on Louis XIV's phrase *l'État, c'est moi*. As for the "parity" Political Bureau, it "never held meetings."[87]

In October 1954, the Bolivian left was stunned by the news that virtually all POR leaders associated with Lora had joined the MNR in a ceremony at the National Palace. Many were important union officials, and the move took place on the eve of the First Congress of the COB. A major blow to the Trotskyist movement, the event entered the country's political lexicon as *el entrismo en el MNR*: "entrism" into the MNR. Lora did not join his comrades-in-arms when they became MNR "entrists." An activist who lived through the events and asked to remain anonymous told me, "Lora was the chief of the entrist faction without being an entrist. . . . After all of those people [went] into the MNR, he came out with his own paper, *Masas*, all alone."

Official party accounts and public memoirs have provided a range of contradictory versions over the years, but the documentary record provides a different picture, in which Lora emerges as a sorcerer's apprentice, unleashing a process he could not control. The call for an "anti-imperialist front" to draw closer to the MNR ranks, insistently proposed by the Lora-Möller faction, was the direct precursor of entrism. History would clash with exigencies of party prestige, as entrism in the government party (directly counterposed to the concepts of Trotsky's permanent revolution) became almost a synonym for careerist abandonment of principle.[88]

Lora's *Collected Works* reprints a 1953 pamphlet, "Bolivia and the Revolution of National Liberation," noting that it appeared "under the signature of Juan Duin, pseudonym of G. Lora," and "served to organize a Trotskyist faction inside the ruling MNR," but this "work did not prosper because those in charge were bribed by the MNR leadership." Late in 1954, Lora reported that his wing of the POR had decided to break with the FPI and "put a party fraction inside the MNR left." He subsequently stated that Möller had written him "suggesting the possibility of carrying out an entrist maneuver into the MNR." Lora "responded that in general and in principle, this could not be ruled out," but concrete political circumstances would determine whether it would be opportune, and in what form. In any case, "entrism by the POR's leaders could not be accepted."[89]

Be that as it may, in October 1954 Lora wrote: "Our tactic must be to penetrate, starting now, into the MNR ranks, in order to show in deeds our capacity and seriousness as revolutionary leaders." The same month he wrote the SWP that he had returned from the World Congress when a conference of the FOL was under way "and almost all the decisions had already been made." It "was resolved 1) To break with the other faction, that is, split the Party; 2) To break with the I.S. and declare ourselves neutral on the issue of the International. These two points were adopted against my will, since I believe they were not convenient for our long-range plans. . . . 3) It was decided to place a P. [party] fraction into the MNR left, to carry out our own work. The tactic is highly dangerous but may produce surprising results; 4) A considerable fraction is being prepared for the COB congress."[90]

In late 1954 a Chilean Trotskyist reported that the "Serrano [González] faction makes the accusation . . . that entrism is nothing but the opportunism of comrade Möller, whose passage to the MNR has been in preparation for a long time." Regarding "comrade Lora, who appeared as the faction's caudillo when the [POR's] split occurred and partial entrism was agreed upon, he broke from Möller and withdrew from the faction." Möller later recalled: "I said, the correct tactic here is entrism into the MNR. Lora thought this thesis was correct, but not with the leading people." Möller considered this absurd because only if POR leaders joined could they "form a new party with the MNR left." Möller "won the vote by 12 against two." Lora characterized this as a betrayal, "and the next day he expelled me in the name of the POR."[91]

The FPI denounced their ex-comrades for joining the MNR, blaming Lora as well as Möller. Years later, Hugo González vividly recalled the entrists swearing loyalty to the MNR. They made "the sign of the cross before a crucifix, in the presence of Paz Estenssoro." All the while, Lora "paced nervously in front of the palace." FPI members watched from the street, "burning with anger," saying "the general ordered in his troops, but remains in the rearguard."[92]

Möller played a central role at the Congress of the COB, serving on the event's four-man Organizing Committee with fellow entrist José Zegada, as well as Miguel Alandia, then the labor federation's Press and Propaganda Secretary. Möller told the assembled delegates that he had joined the MNR after realizing that "the aspirations I have fought for over the course of many years have been crystallized by *compañero* President Víctor Paz Estenssoro with the nationalization of the mines, agrarian reform," and other measures. FPI reports to the I.S. denounced the Möller group's conduct, charging them with openly anticommunist behavior. While isolated, FPI spokesmen were able to speak on several points.[93] The entrists continued using Trotsky-flavored vocabulary for a short period but were soon absorbed entirely by the MNR Left. Many would later help Lechín form his ill-fated MNR splinter group, the Revolutionary Party of the National Left (PRIN).

Unearthing the Cochabamba Opposition

Two main factions of the POR emerged from the party's central leadership and shared common conceptions on the nature of the MNR (viewing it as a petty-bourgeois party whose labor/left wing could be transformed by pressure). They gave rise to the two largest Trotskyist organizations of subsequent decades, one led by Lora, the other by González.

Yet buried beneath the charges and countercharges of these main players is an unknown part of Bolivian left history. Absent from "official" stories is a separate grouping, based among leaders of the party's explosive peasant work in Cochabamba. Before it was silenced by government repression, this faction vociferously rejected the conceptions guiding both wings of the party's national leadership. Word of its existence emerged in an interview with Modesto Sejas, who had been a member of the faction and was unable to hold back tears when describing what happened to it. Years passed before documents unearthed from dusty archives fully confirmed Sejas's account. By then the aging Quechua Trotskyist had died in a Cochabamba street, run over by a heedless motorist.

Sejas said the Cochabamba faction was led by a talented activist who used the pseudonym López, came originally from Switzerland, and maintained contact with a cadre there who had joined the movement while Trotsky was still alive. (The Swiss FI section was one of four that founded the anti-Pablo IC.) The Cochabamba faction, which included a "group of women," was called the Fracción Leninista and considered itself "more orthodox" than the others, opposing Pabloism and condemning the idea of entering the MNR or pressuring the ruling party to change its nature.

López, Sejas, and their cothinkers did not succeed in extending the faction beyond Cochabamba. They held a clandestine meeting for this purpose, but when they went to the POR's Eleventh Conference bearing their documents, they were arrested. For this reason, the conference was held without their attendance. During the raids, police seized a duplicating machine in the house of POR militant Alfonsina Paredes, an important literary figure in La Paz. They gave it back after a phone call from Edwin Möller. However, the Swiss militant and his wife, also a faction member, were deported to Uruguay and later returned to Europe. The repression dispersed the faction, with some of its Bolivian members taking refuge in other countries.[94]

In a letter to Michel Pablo defending himself against the accusation of "Cannonism," Lora mentioned a conference of the POR's Cochabamba Regional Committee, referring to a "Swiss militant, known for carrying out a systematic campaign against the International Secretariat." Warqui wrote to the I.S. with his own view of the factional lineup, referring to "the 'Swiss comrades,' who with their enormous ignorance and tactlessness, heated our boiling cauldron even further."[95]

The Quechua/Swiss Leninist Faction is long forgotten, but its writings provide an alternative, critical view of the National Revolution and Bolivian Trotskyists' policy. To hear their voice, it is necessary to unearth their documents from piles of old papers in a basement vault of Bolivia's Congress, and from old boxes tied with faded green string at a library outside Paris. They include "theses," open letters to the party membership, correspondence, and leaflets. Some are signed by "Juan López" alone, others by the Swiss comrade together with Zenón Claure (Sejas), José Rodríguez, and others; one is signed "Manuel Cruz Vallejos Cell," after the assassinated POR peasant leader.

As Sejas had recalled, one of their central points was to insist that the MNR was "the party of the national bourgeoisie." One document noted that Trotsky had emphasized, against Stalin, that the Chinese nationalist party was bourgeois, and "the MNR is the 'Kuomintang' of Bolivia!" As for the government, it was not "transitory" or "petty-bourgeois," but an expression of the "dictatorship of the bourgeoisie" which revolutionaries must oppose.[96]

The POR had allowed the MNR to pull the wool over its eyes when it took limited measures under mass pressure. "Shouting 'Down with Yankee imperialism!' the [MNR] took the first hidden steps to come to an arrangement with the imperialists," López wrote. "Shouting 'Down with the Rosca and the *latifundistas*,' the bourgeoisie nationalized the mines with compensation, that is, paid for them," and "did not even consider touching the lands of the *latifundistas*." Nonetheless, "the masses continued on the road of the proletarian revolution, as the peasant movement, including the Cochabamba peasant federation, shows us in particular," while the POR was highly influential in the national and regional labor federations, "gain[ing] ground everywhere, if it acted as a revolutionary workers party."

Yet the POR's influence was undermined by its "illusory and opportunist policy toward the 'left wing' [of the MNR], which sowed illusions among the masses." Far from fulfilling the POR's hopes, the MNR Left had proven to be "a lackey of the bourgeoisie and traitor to the working class and poor peasants." Instead of hoping it would embrace a revolutionary program, "we have to get the masses off the capitalist bandwagon to which both the 'right wing' and the 'left wing' have tied them." The policy adopted by the POR's Tenth Conference deepened the errors, helping the MNR "apply the brakes to the masses" and bureaucratize the unions, while the party's position on the worker ministers, "whom the government needed and still needs to hold back the masses," was "absolutely irresponsible and close to betrayal." "When 'worker' ministers, even in the form of delegates from the

COB, enter a bourgeois government, a government which is not of the proletariat, they serve only to deceive the masses, they pass over to the ranks of betrayal, as the Thesis of Pulacayo quite rightly says." The government had "repaid" the party by "directing its fire against the POR," striking "one blow after another, imprisoning and persecuting *porista* militants and revolutionary workers and peasants."[97]

The faction mocked the Cochabamba Regional Committee's proposal to conduct "surveys" of the party membership, calling it the latest example of how "the customs, manner and thinking" of the party's CC, PB, and Regional Committees "no longer have anything to do with democratic centralism nor with the proletarian democracy that should prevail in a Bolshevik party." The POR was "completely disorganized"; regional committees were self-appointed; even the PB did not function since "each of the 'big shots' wants to be in charge and do whatever he likes." Members knew two groupings had arisen in the national leadership, but not what they were or "who stands for what." Word was going around "that Lora and Möller took the party seal to sign a national left front, but with whom?" Members were in the dark, and "nobody wants to tell us."

In underlined phrases, the document reiterated that the MNR was "a bourgeois party that succeeded in politically exploiting and fooling the workers and poor peasants for its own interests." Instead of telling the truth to the masses, "as bitter as it may be," *Lucha Obrera* "calls Lechín the Bolivian workers' leader, continuing to spread illusions in Lechín and Co. instead of unmasking these betrayers." The broadside ends with a "Survey of the Leadership by the Membership," posing a long series of questions including "Who is the top leadership of the POR?" "Who should elect the Regional Committees?" "Can the party's official line be criticized internally after a congress?" and many others.[98]

Subsequent documents denounced Lora's pamphlet for the MNR's national congress as "publicly making propaganda for the MNR and discrediting the POR," as well as *Lucha Obrera's* advice to Lechín and headlines like "On Guard, *Compañero* Lechín" and "Lechín Betrayed by the Right." As POR leaders' opportunism had brought the party "to the brink of disappearance," the Cochabamba group declared its complete opposition to both national factions, support to the International Committee against "Pabloism," and the need for all party members to study the issues behind the split in the International.[99]

Documentation also supports Sejas's account of what happened to the Cochabamba group. In mid-1954, the González faction reported: "Comrade Claure [Sejas], freed after his detention in La Paz during the [party's]

Eleventh Conference, is obliged to live in hiding in Cochabamba, as an order has been issued for his arrest. As for Comrade López, who . . . was detained with Claure in La Paz, he had to leave the country because he is a foreigner."[100]

International Debates

The mass insurrection of April 1952, the formation of workers' militias, nationalization of the tin mines, peasant land seizures, and enfranchisement of the indigenous majority drew the attention of left activists around the world (see figure 4.4). For members and supporters of the Fourth International, the events were exciting and, in a sense, personal: their small, marginalized organization was big news on the distant altiplano.

The tradition of Trotskyist internationalism, together with public meetings and reports, encouraged them to view the Bolivian section's struggles as their own. Although they came to know more about Bolivia than most college professors, the intricacies of Trotskyism in this exotic land remained daunting. Nonetheless, the positions of the Bolivian POR caused controversy in a number of Trotskyist parties. The following are some of the highlights.

Ongoing coverage of the Bolivian section's activities, and frequent appeals for solidarity against government repression, appeared in the International Secretariat's *Quatrième Internationale*, the SWP's *The Militant*, and the French section's *La Vérité*, which were widely read in other FI sections. Internal bulletins provided more information, as well as directives and opinions from the international leadership. On a few occasions, these bulletins contained impassioned debates on the POR's positions.

Within the SWP, a minority faction led by Dennis Vern and Sam Ryan waged a solitary campaign of criticism. The "Vern-Ryan tendency" considered itself the most consistent opponent of Pabloism, with a distinctive analysis of events in the Soviet bloc. Ryan devoted sustained attention to Bolivia. Two months after the April 1952 uprising, he strongly questioned the positions Lora expressed in the lengthy interview *La Vérité* and *The Militant* published after the insurrection. Ryan disapproved of the POR's characterizations of and critical support to the MNR, insisting that workers be warned that this bourgeois party was their enemy. While criticizing POR support to leaders of the MNR Left, Ryan considered it correct to call on them to break from the bourgeoisie and form a workers' and peasants' government. He asked the SWP leadership to help the POR correct its tactics. Ryan followed up the next year, complaining that the SWP leadership had never answered his June 1952 critique and comparing the POR's line to

Figure 4.4 Miners' militia: Alandia's cover for *Estaño*, magazine of the government-owned mining company, 1962. (Courtesy of Biblioteca y Archivo Histórico del Congreso)

that of Mensheviks in the Russian Revolution and Stalinists in the Chinese upheaval of 1925–27.

He returned to the attack the following year. Although the *International Committee Bulletin* referred in passing to Pablo's "liquidationist" tactics being applied to the Bolivian MNR, Peronism in Argentina, and other movements, the SWP leadership had still not answered him. He denounced the POR's call on Paz to appoint a cabinet drawn from the MNR Left, yet weakened his critique by proposing that the party call on the Lechinistas to present their own candidates in elections, then give them critical support under the slogan "the left to power." As for the SWP, it had not fulfilled its responsibility to devote more attention to revolutionary strategy in Latin America.[101]

Ryan's documents are virtually unknown among Bolivian Trotskyists. The SWP sent the first one to the POR with a letter saying it did not represent the opinion of the party, which lacked sufficient information for a real discussion of his points. The SWP had confidence in the POR and the I.S., it continued; if something were amiss, the International would intervene. Nonetheless, if anyone in the POR wished to respond to Ryan, the SWP would be glad to publish this reply.[102]

No such answer was forthcoming. The attitude the SWP leadership expressed—agnosticism combined with passive confidence in the international leadership (that is, Pablo and his closest associates)—is another aspect of Bolivian Trotskyism's tragedy. The Vern-Ryan tendency wound up joining former Trotskyist Max Shachtman's Independent Socialist League, which, eager for ammunition against the FI, published reports—sometimes perceptive, often tendentious—from a correspondent critical of the POR.

A more extensive discussion was carried out by the Nahuel Moreno tendency in Argentina, which seems to have been the sponsor of an eye-catching public bulletin called *Revolución en Bolivia*. At the same time as they waged a virulent, often obscure polemical war against other Argentine Trotskyists and dissidents in their own ranks, in May 1952 the "Morenoites" put forward these slogans: "Demand that Paz Estenssoro's government be formed with worker ministers elected and controlled by the Miners Federation and the new Central Obrera" and "Demand of your worker ministers the loyal and rapid fulfillment of the resolutions approved by the FSTMB." The "two wings within the MNR," they averred, "presently express the interests of the proletariat and the bourgeoisie."[103]

In 1953 (when they began their own "entrism" into the Peronist movement), they decided these concepts were erroneous, launching what would long remain their characteristic slogan for Bolivia—"All Power to the COB!"—while admonishing the POR: "Our influence should not be achieved because we are scribes and stenographers for Lechín . . . & Co., who let us write a great program but stop us from carrying it out."[104]

A heated polemic broke out after José Valdez, a member of the Moreno group who lived in Chile and visited Bolivia, critiqued the POR's Tenth Conference theses, opposing the slogan "Complete Control of the State by the MNR Left Wing" and warning: "The proletariat should not be given illusions about the possibilities of radicalization of some sector of the MNR." Instead, he wrote in late 1953, "the immediate objective is to unmask the MNR as a whole, especially its representatives in the COB."

The following year, Valdez accused the leaders of the POR and FI of "open capitulation to the bourgeois government of Paz Estenssoro." The slogan of "critical support" to it provided a "portrait of the Menshevism prevailing in the I.S., the BLA, and the Bolivian POR's CC." Further, he had come to the conclusion that the slogan "All Power to the COB" had "lost validity" when "I realized that the COB, bureaucratized and controlled by the MNR, did not represent the aspirations of the working classes." Crucially, the POR should "stop, once and for all, thinking about entrism into the MNR's 'left wing.'" Enraged, Moreno defended his slogan (adding that it could be phrased as "All the Ministries for the COB Leadership"), while accusing Valdez of "theoretical and interpretive formalism," abstentionism, opportunism, "professorial fetishism," petty-bourgeois attitudes, and contact with elements alien to the party.[105]

Urging the POR comrades to call a conference of Latin American revolutionaries "to discuss a program of action on a continental scale," Valdez aimed his most impassioned criticism at what he saw as their national narrowness. Referring to the ram's horn (*pututu*) traditionally used to signal alarm or convoke assemblies, he wrote: "They seem content for the Indian's war cry—which he launches with his *pututu*—to remain in isolation. They seem to want to enclose it in their valleys, and carry out the revolution there. They seem to want to play the *pututu* for themselves alone. We daresay that if the *pututu* does not sound again, for all the exploited of this continent, the Bolivian Revolution will be one of the most painful experiences of the world proletariat."[106]

Bolivian Trotskyism was intimately involved in both *pena y gloria*, the pain and the glory, of the Bolivian Revolution, one of the highest points *and* most painful experiences of labor radicalism in the Western Hemisphere. The old Rosca regime was defeated; the old slogan of "Land to the Indian, mines to the state" had acquired flesh and blood. Trotskyists were crucial in shaping the COB union federation, with its armed militias and national power unique in the Western Hemisphere; they led peasant land seizures that shaped agrarian relations for decades; their message was proclaimed in persecuted opposition papers and huge public murals.

Yet the revolution they helped prepare did not become "permanent." Instead, they saw it halted halfway, blocked, frustrated in its advance toward genuine social and national emancipation. The mine workers smashed the old state, but their leaders gave power to Paz Estenssoro. Erstwhile denouncers of dollar diplomacy turned to the White House, circumscribing the revolution within Cold War bounds, rebuilding an apparatus to repress the masses whose courage and sacrifice had toppled the old order.

The POR's history of "anti-imperialist fronts" with the MNR, mediated by the latter's labor wing, began long before the revolution. After the uprising of April 1952 and the formation of the MNR regime, the contradictions between this collaboration and the party's social revolutionary goals could no longer be contained. Bolivian Trotskyism emerged from the National Revolution profoundly divided, but this crisis did not lead to an overhaul of its outlook and political practice. Instead, it would continue to look to the nationalist labor leadership in each of the upheavals that marked Bolivian history over the following decades.

Cold War Calculus

As Bolivia's revolution institutionalized, the ruling MNR took one step after another to the right, often in response to prodding from Washington. A leading leftist intellectual summed up the process: "One thing led to another. . . . In 1953 the government was willing to grant certain concessions in exchange for U.S. aid, but would have thought it madness to accept a plan like the one" the IMF pushed through in 1957, when "the monetary stabilization plan was imposed. A little later came the reorganization of the army. North American advisers were accepted into key administrative organizations," and foreign investment was encouraged in the oil industry. Next came the use of force against the workers as a precondition for gaining credits for the mines. "One concession led to the next in a sequence that made it impossible to tell the seriousness of each new step. . . . The revolution did not crumble from a single blow, it fell bit by bit, piece by piece." By the time the military overthrew the MNR in 1964, this was "a shot fired into a corpse."[1]

The Cold War was a key factor. Tin prices were driven to record highs by the Korean War, together with upheavals in tin-producing lands like Indonesia and Malaya. When that war ended in mid-1953, the metal's price fell drastically, causing serious fiscal problems for Bolivia. It was simultaneously demonstrated that Third World nationalist regimes moving too far to the left risked harsh retaliation from the White House. One month after the Korean War armistice, Prime Minister Mossadegh was overthrown in Iran. Another U.S.-backed coup soon ousted Guatemala's left-nationalist Arbenz regime. A state visit by Arbenz's vice president, who expressed solidarity with the Bolivian Revolution, did not sit well with Washington, where Secretary of State John Foster Dulles voiced concern about Bolivia's "orientation." Writing on "The Lessons of Guatemala," Bolivian Trotskyists drew a parallel to their own country: "if the revolution is not extended and combined with the struggle against capitalism, for workers' and peasants' power, it will succumb."[2]

An explicit Cold War calculus guided U.S. policy-makers' decisions on Bolivia. Their demand that former owners be compensated for nationalized tin mines was met with alacrity by the MNR, which ostentatiously increased dependence on U.S. aid in mid-1953. At the same time, U.S. embassy officials worried that the MNR "lacks a strong military or police force with which to preserve order in the face of a deteriorating economic situation." As "the longer the tin problem remains unsolved, the Government will be less able to resist the Communist attempts to undermine it," it was "urgent" to "firm up [U.S.] policy toward Bolivia" and "seize the initiative in offering the financial and other aids that may be necessary to keep this tinder box, which might set off a chain reaction in Latin America, from striking fire." After a tour of Latin America, President Eisenhower's brother wrote that emergency economic aid had been of "fundamental importance in easing the critical situation and preventing Bolivia's rapid descent into economic chaos with consequences that could have been favorable only to the Communists."[3]

Another factor in the MNR's right turn was its determination to rein in the labor movement, which many officials considered too powerful and prominent in the nation's political life. A central concern was the power of the tin miners, with their unions, militias, and multilingual *radios mineras* (miners' radio stations), and their tradition of struggle and hard-edged proletarian pride. The government decided to launch an open clash with labor, over U.S.-backed plans for what is today called *structural adjustment*. Winning the showdown and basking in White House approval, the MNR moved to fully reestablish the standing army and clamp down hard on plebeian radicalism. Things were going to change, insisted the ruling party: no longer would the regime be vulnerable to the popular militias set up in the revolution or the class passions it had unleashed.

Trotskyism in the Late 1950s

The MNR's decision to attack the labor unions, whose support had been crucial during the Revolution's initial phase, confronted Bolivian Trotskyists with dangers and opportunities. The dangers were clear: as vocal critics of the regime and partisans of the labor movement, they knew they would be on the receiving end of government repression. At times this meant seizure of party publications, beatings, or relatively brief detentions at the hands of MNR *comandos*.[4] On other occasions militants were subjected to formal arrest, imprisonment, "confinement" in remote areas, or exile. The opportunities arose from increasing disaffection with a regime whose popularity had once seemed unlimited. As the labor-identified current with the hardest line toward the MNR, the movement stood to gain if elements of the working class broke with the regime.

Yet Bolivian Trotskyism now took shape as two separate and counterposed parties, each calling itself Partido Obrero Revolucionario. One became known as the POR-Lora (or POR-Masas); the other as the POR-González (or POR-Lucha Obrera). More informally, they came to be known as *los fieros y los largos*: followers of "El Fiero" Lora versus those of Hugo González, nicknamed "El Largo" (the long, tall one) because of his height.

Guillermo Lora devoted the second half of the 1950s to building an organization virtually from scratch. This began when he founded his own newspaper, *Masas* (Masses). As a recent retrospective noted, "whether as a journal, weekly, daily or conspiratorial pamphlet, despite repression and hostility from the governments of the day . . . *Masas* has survived for five turbulent decades" since its first issue appeared in October 1954.[5] While winning a readership and reputation for the paper, Lora carried out the "primitive accumulation" of cadres in labor and intellectual milieux. In addition to Miguel Alandia, Agar Peñaranda, and a handful of other party veterans, Guillermo's younger brother César Lora and half-brother Filemón Escóbar joined the group. Both went to work in the mines, becoming popular union leaders at Catavi-Siglo XX, which Escóbar dubbed "the Bolivian Petrograd." Later joined by Isaac Camacho, they won over Cirilo Jiménez and other important union activists.

Escóbar's memoirs report that he was won to Trotskyism by Catavi "Workers' Control" representative Sinforoso Cabrera, who had been a POR supporter. "When we first went into the mines" at Siglo XX-Catavi, "there were no POR members there." Recruitment was facilitated by Escóbar's job: his department "went through all the *rajos* and *parajes*" (work sites) collecting ore samples, so he was able to get to know miners from all the other sections. Interviewed years later in Bolivia's parliament (where he had become an "indigenist" spokesman), Escóbar said poristas shared power in the Siglo XX union with PCB members Irineo Pimentel and Federico Escóbar (no relation), often running joint POR-PCB slates. This alliance did not break up until the period when Che Guevara came to Bolivia.[6]

Younger Lora half-brothers Miguel and Andrés also signed up. Miguel moved from the countryside to go to high school at Siglo XX, joining a POR-sponsored youth group of miners' sons and daughters called the

Figure 5.1 Young Trotskyists at POR-Masas congress, Siglo XX, early 1960s. (Courtesy of Cesar Escóbar)

Maxim Gorky Cultural Center. This "parallel group," established around 1958, organized sports activities, amateur theater, sex education classes, and literature discussions, as well as biweekly classes on Marxist texts taught by César, Filemón ("Filipo"), and other cadres. The Gorky Center also had branches in La Paz, Cochabamba, and Potosí. Won over by Filipo in this period, Dionicio Coca remembers that at Siglo XX "the party cell was a school for us. We read literature, and not just political literature. That's where I learned the Greek classics, like the *Iliad*."[7]

Andrés Lora lived in Llallagua and helped his mother, a cook, by carrying food to the miners. He began listening to Trotskyist workers talking politics on their lunch breaks. "Sometimes they said, 'Hey kid, get out of here,' but sometimes they'd send me for cigarettes and I could hang around," especially during political education classes (see figure 5.1). In 1959, at the age of thirteen, he joined the Juventud Porista (POR Youth) and became its *responsable* (leader). Later, he too went to work in the mines.[8]

While Guillermo Lora had to begin anew, the POR of Hugo González began its separate existence with a more solid base. It continued to produce a larger and more elaborate paper, *Lucha Obrera*, a stream of pamphlets, and other publications. These included special bulletins in unions where the party was active, such as the FSTMB and the teachers' union, where

Fernando Bravo and his wife Elsa Cladera (a sympathizer) were prominent activists.[9]

Their party devoted significant attention to work among women. "Toward Women's Liberation" (1959) was the first pamphlet published by the POR-LO's *Lucha Minera*. Another bulletin stressed "woman's importance in the revolutionary struggle, whether she is a worker or a housewife." Women from the mine camps should attend union meetings "and every national miners' gathering," and housewives' committees "should be organized and linked to the union organizations," on the national as well as local scale. "Siglo XX and Catavi must send housewives' delegates to the next mine union plenary," it insisted.[10]

The González group also made advances among peasants, notably in Achacachi (near Warisata), where the peasant movement adopted a program it proposed. In the late 1950s, peasant delegations from Chuquisaca and Oruro attended a gathering of its mine worker members, and the POR-LO held a special conference in Ucureña, attended by "thirty peasant comrades," to discuss agrarian issues and "the worker-peasant alliance." This meeting also resolved to promote "special organizations of peasant youth and women" within the rural unions and Ucureña Peasant Federation, "to bring them into the struggle and address their specific problems."[11]

The POR-LO recruited an energetic union leader from a match factory, Alejandro Carvajal, who was soon brought into its Political Bureau. Carvajal lost the ability to speak when a police gas grenade struck his head during a factory workers' protest, but he trained himself to speak again, albeit with difficulty, and remained an active Trotskyist until he died, destitute but unbroken, in July 2007. Over his decades in the POR-LO, he had many differences with its central leader, about whom he joked, "González is like Mount Illimani," the snowy peak that dominates La Paz: "tall, cold and silent."

Carvajal reported that in 1959 the group had "perhaps more than 300" members, with a Central Committee of twenty-nine, "the majority of whom were workers, mainly miners." Others included factory, construction, sanitation, and social security workers. A prominent member was flour-mill workers' leader Eulogio Sánchez, whose newspaper ran stories about the anti-Stalinist revolt in Hungary, "the Arab Revolution," and a front-page article on the Little Rock crisis in the United States, comparing it to "Ku Klux Klan-type" racism against indigenous people in Bolivia.[12]

The POR-LO's mine worker cells in Siglo XX, Catavi, and Llallagua grew to a total of eighty to ninety members. Among them were the Vásquez brothers, Cardenio and Elio, and their cousin Felipe. Elio remembers the

POR split coming as a surprise to him and other Trotskyist supporters in the Catavi region, who "almost got demoralized" but decided to push ahead with revolutionary work. Felipe worked at Huanuni, one of the most politicized mines. When he joined the POR-LO in 1960, after a period as a sympathizer, it had a significant presence there, with more members than the Communist Party. One reason he chose the González group was its "connection to the Fourth International" and his view that it was "somewhat broader and more democratic" than the other POR, which failed to gain adherents at Huanuni. Besides, he said laughing, "Lora thinks he's Trotsky."[13]

César Lora, nicknamed *El Chinito* because of the shape of his eyes, soon became a beloved figure to both wings of Bolivian Trotskyism and thousands of militant miners (see figure 5.2). He worked *interior mina* (inside the mine) as a *perforista* (driller), one of the hardest and most prestigious jobs. Unlike Isaac Camacho, "who was very elegant," César was somewhat *tosco* (rough) in his manner, his brother Miguel recalls, but *muy dadivo* (very generous). If he saw a peasant who needed clothes or shoes, he would take out all his money and give it to him. Andrés Lora recalls that César "had a very special kind of language, the workers would listen to him." *Masas* supporter Angel Capari agrees. "He explained things . . . in simple terms, sometimes in Quechua. This was important, because many miners could not read or write."

Remembering César as an "ideal revolutionary" of "innate" political talent, Dionicio Coca has a different memory: during spells in the countryside, "César liked to read Miguel Cervantes' *Don Quixote*. Sometimes he talked to us in a Cervantine type of Spanish, and we didn't always get it." Pastor Peláez was won to the *Masas* group after meeting César in 1954. "He was very important for the workers' movement," says the retired miner.

Across the factional divide, POR-LO members said César often helped their group. Carvajal even claimed César belonged to *both* PORs, participating in the LO wing's Catavi cell. Elio Vásquez remembers César as "a real autodidact," with deep roots in the countryside: while working as a *huacani* (cattle merchant) for Comibol before going into the mines, he was a peasant leader and joined land seizures in Norte Potosí.[14] For innumerable miners, within and outside the Trotskyist ranks, one of the worst memories of ensuing decades was the day César Lora was taken away from them forever.

In 1956, the POR-LO launched Bolivia's first Trotskyist presidential campaign, running González for president and Bravo for vice president. It saw the campaign as an important way to promote its ideas and affirm its right to participate in national politics. However, a special election-day issue of *Lucha Obrera* added an appeal for workers to vote for COB leaders

Figure 5.2 César Lora. (Courtesy of Víctor Montoya)

who were on the MNR slate.[15] The MNR remained strong enough to win the election hands down, with Paz Estenssoro's second in command, Hernán Siles, gaining the presidency. POR-LO candidates received less than 2,500 votes.

The two Trotskyist "parties" competed fiercely for name recognition, disputing which was the authentic POR. Asked to explain the basic difference, Elio Vásquez says: "We were part of an international organization. Trotskyism is internationalist, the class struggle is international," but "Lora's group was nationalist, it only existed in Bolivia, so its objectives were small, and it knew nothing of the outside world." Highlighting its status as the "Bolivian section of the FI," the POR-LO was affiliated to the International Secretariat (later United Secretariat) of Michel Pablo, Ernest Mandel, and Livio Maitan. Lora's organization denounced them as "Pabloists, characterized by revising Trotskyism and drawing closer to Stalinist positions."[16]

Declassified U.S. government documents show intelligence operatives filing numerous reports on activities of Bolivian Trotskyists, particularly the González group (apparently because of its enthusiasm for Castro's Cuba), from translations of resolutions to reports on internal meetings, conferences, and Marxist education classes. Despite their effort to remain well informed, agents' dispatches include many factual errors, such as identifying one of the most famous Stalinist mine unionists as a Trotskyist and claiming "no ideological difference" existed between Guillermo Lora and Hugo "Gonzales."[17]

A CIA manual on the Fourth International sniffed that *Masas* was "a badly mimeographed monthly which is distributed clandestinely in about 1000 copies," claiming Lora's wing had "about 800 active members" a decade after the POR split, with "some strength among the tin miners." The González group, with "about 300 members," published "about 1500 copies" of the bimonthly *Lucha Obrera*. The POR-Masas would probably have been pleased by the membership estimate but discomfited by the claim that the LO group, "although the smaller, seems to be the most active one, with a following among the revolutionarily most vital miners."[18]

Battle over "Stabilization"

In late 1956, a showdown began between the miners and the government under newly installed President Siles, then a leader of the MNR's right wing, who put himself forward as the most intransigent opponent of labor radicalism. *Masas* observed that "you don't have to be clairvoyant" to know what "Siles's rightist government" was aiming for. It would try to "annihilate" workers' gains and provide "every guarantee to finance capital to exploit the country."[19]

Faced with skyrocketing inflation, and believing this would lessen opposition to anti-union measures, the government established a Stabilization Commission backed by the International Monetary Fund. Its de facto head was the flamboyant George Jackson Eder of International Telephone and Telegraph (later notorious for its role in the overthrow of Salvador Allende), who controlled its composition and decisions. The commission designed an austerity program, promptly dubbed the Eder Plan, demanding a 40 percent reduction in government spending, removal of price controls, and a wage freeze after one year. Instead of *Plan Estabilizador*, radical workers called it the *Plan Estrangulador*: the strangulation plan. Eder later wrote that it meant "the repudiation, at least tacitly, of virtually everything that the Revolutionary Government has done over the previous four years." "The stabilization measures are the spear point of imperialist oppression aimed at [Bolivia's] revolution," Guillermo Lora declared during a speech in Oruro.[20]

One of the most explosive measures was to end subsidies to the company stores called *pulperías* at mines and other enterprises. "Though the situation has been untenable for the workers in Bolivia for a long period already," an FI bulletin observed, "the fact that there were fixed prices in the commissaries for the miners helped this . . . group of workers at least to remain alive." In Quechisla and elsewhere, "miners and their wives seized the 'pulpería' and turned it over to the trade union for management." In Catavi, Huanuni, and San José, "the women took the initiative in similar actions."[21]

The Eder Plan severely strained relations between Siles and his vice president, Ñuflo Chávez of the MNR Left, while bringing "cogovernment" with the COB to the breaking point. Lechín distanced himself from the plan after protests and strikes at San José, Siglo XX, and other areas. Labor agitation had to end, Siles insisted. In the face of opposition, he went on a hunger strike, the *New York Times* reported, "as a final means of persuading the Leftist elements in the Central Workers Federation not to start any strikes." The president did not limit himself to Gandhian gestures, demanding that congress grant him extraordinary powers and sending armed MNR squads to attack labor strongholds. When Siglo XX miners launched their own hunger strike against his policies, Siles said they should "blow up."[22]

The conflict dominated the COB's Second Congress in June 1957. After Siles spoke to defend the austerity plan, delegates debated three counterposed theses. The railway union argued for avoiding conflict with the government. In contrast, Fernando Bravo presented a document (which the press called "the Trotskyist-inspired miners' thesis") calling for the COB to break with cogovernment and launch a head-on struggle against austerity. In a dramatic floor debate—ranging from economic theory to the Suez crisis and the situation in the Soviet bloc since Stalin's death—Ernesto Ayala and Edwin Möller faced off against their former comrades, presenting the COB executive's more moderate thesis. Leading a powerful sector of delegates (among them Leticia Fajardo) and backed by Lechín, the ex-POR "entrists" carried the day.[23]

Nonetheless, the COB congress voted to call a general strike, which Siles promptly denounced as the work of "Trotskyist leaders." After massive government pressure caused many unions to back down, the COB leadership called the strike off. Yet, the POR-LO argued, the source of Siles's strength was precisely the "capitulatory spirit" and "lack of an independent perspective" of union leaders bound to cogovernment, while the Communist Party (PCB) had openly opposed the strike.[24]

Siles followed through by encouraging government-loyal labor leaders to form a "Bloque Restructurador" pledged to "restructure" the COB. The aim, warned the POR-Masas, was "using divisionism and terror to destroy workers' growing opposition to MNR leaders' plans." According to the government, POR-LO miners wrote, "the *workers' and peasants' militias* should not exist, only the massacring Army; the *miners' radio stations* should not exist, because they are 'clandestine,'" the remnants of "workers' control" should be abolished and unions banned from "discussing national and political issues . . . limiting themselves to 'pure trade unionism.'"[25] The Restructuring Bloc was supported by the Ministry of Interior and MNR *comandos* who carried out armed incursions into mining camps, clashing with union militias.

The crisis further radicalized important sectors of the Miners Federation, centered on the Siglo XX mine complex. In December 1957, an FSTMB congress approved theses written jointly by the PCB and POR-Masas and presented by the Siglo XX delegation, calling for opposition to the Eder Plan, "political independence" of the union movement "from all government tutelage and interference," and strengthening the militias. This was a major defeat for the pro-Siles delegates' campaign to "Support the Stabilization Plan and the *Compañero Presidente*." The masses had "gone beyond the petty-bourgeois party" (MNR), César Lora declared; now "the only way out is to forge our own government."[26] Siles retaliated by dispersing the FSTMB's next national congress.

By mid-1958, the Bloque Restructurador was in serious trouble, with the defection of construction, railway, and peasant unions. In Catavi, a miners' assembly "declared null and void the reactionary decrees" of the president, putting "all the union's armed militias in a state of emergency against provocations by . . . government-created goon squads." Catavi was now "liberated territory." Early the next year a wave of unrest swept the country. "Bolivians Cling to Ideals of 1952, but Most Are Disenchanted with Results of Revolt as Anniversary Nears," headlined the *New York Times*. "The Bolivian Revolution approaches its seventh anniversary . . . in a state of crisis," it observed.[27]

With an elected strike committee chaired by César Lora, the miners' walkout blocked attempts to dismantle price subsidies in the pulperías. The mobilization emboldened factory workers and others to rebel against the Bloque Restructurador, which soon fell apart. As unrest spread in the countryside, MNR peasant leader José Rojas was replaced by an army general as Minister of Peasant Affairs. "In Ucureña," noted a BLA report, "a peasant asked the general in Quechua why he was named to this post, since he is an army officer, in other words an enemy of the peasants."[28]

Radicals' growing influence in the mine union dismayed nationalist spokesmen, who feared the situation was spinning out of control. In the United States, Bolivia's unrest grabbed more headlines: "Tin Strike Perils U.S. Aid to Bolivia—Armed Miners Insist upon Price Subsidy as World Fund Demands Its End"; "10,000 Tin Miners Strike in Bolivia—Government Orders Stores to Withhold Price Rise as Result of Protest." *Time* denounced a rally by a "noisy, violence-bent band of Trotskyites, Communists and left-wing rabble-rousers" chanting "Down with imperialism!" "Led by Trotskyite Boss Víctor Villegas, 200 men stormed police guarding the [U.S.] embassy," it complained. *Life* joined the chorus: "A Danger to Stability, Armed and Angry Miners," it headlined over a full-page photo of "a militant miner" holding "homemade dynamite grenades stockpiled at union headquarters in Catavi."[29]

Early the next year, right-wing unionists were defeated by a POR-Lechinista bloc in the union elections at the Huanuni mine, where POR members held the post of general secretary at various points in the late 1950s.[30] When the defeated pro-Siles slate killed several workers and refused to turn over the union hall, a battle ensued. "It all exploded spontaneously, and the leftists asked for help from Siglo XX," remembered Huanuni miner Felipe Vásquez. Three *porista* workers died in the fighting. César Lora, "defying the women of Huanuni," prevented them from lynching a pro-Siles gunman when he surrendered. After these events, Dunkerley notes, "yellow [pro-government] unions would reappear in Bolivia's mines and factories but never again would they attract popular support."[31]

Figure 5.3 Trotskyists at mine union congress, early 1960s. From left: in leather jacket, white shirt, Isaac Camacho; white jacket, Flavio Ayaviri; leather jacket, Guillermo Lora; behind him, with cigarette, Filemón Escóbar. Far right in checked cap, César Lora. (Courtesy of Cesar Escóbar)

President Siles attacked the POR by name no less than nine times in his address to the MNR's convention in early February 1960. "For years, systematically and, it is only fair to note, with noteworthy organizational ability," he stated, the POR and PCB had "gradually displaced leaders from the MNR and built a federation of feuds in Catavi, Llallagua and Siglo XX." This "powerful PORista Communist axis" sought to carry out "a plan carefully designed by extremists, especially Guillermo Lora," so government supporters were forced to take action against them.[32] (See figure 5.3.)

Late in Siles's presidency, *La Nación* published a three-part article denouncing Lora's influence on a plenary of the FSTMB leadership. Red-baiting is rarely a high literary genre, but the sardonic vignettes were penned with brio by René Zavaleta, an accomplished intellectual who later moved to the left. Describing Lora's call for a strike against layoffs and in defense of price-controlled rice, meat, bread, and sugar for miners, Zavaleta wrote:

> Guillermo Lora . . . aspires to be, and sometimes is, the happy owner of a *porista* dictatorship over the mining proletariat. . . . He is famous, in more than one circle, for his Bohemian slouch, crowned by a wavy mane, and for his mimeograph machines. . . .
>
> Delight in a success foretold led Lora to publish, in *Masas* (28 November), everything that would be decided at the miners' plenary on the following day (the 29th). . . .
>
> At two o'clock on Monday, the deliberations began. Three hours later, a strike was called. Lora's slogans were approved unanimously, with no argument.[33]

National elections were held in 1960: MNR candidate Paz Estenssoro returned to power, while the figurehead post of vice president was occupied by Lechín, whose attempts to gain approval from the United States (which still saw him as a radical labor agitator) included a state visit to Taiwan. Due to his personal ambition, Zavaleta wrote, Lechín "began by echoing [Trotsky's] Transitional Program and wound up traveling to Formosa [Taiwan] to exchange greetings and pleasantries" with anticommunist dictator Chiang Kai-shek.[34] Still, after helping reelect Paz, Lechín was publicly marginalized from the regime.

The PCB discredited itself in radical circles when it proclaimed that the MNR slate, allegedly a bulwark against reaction, was also "its" slate in the 1960 presidential elections. Bolivian Trotskyism gained little credit when the elections led to a squalid confrontation between the two PORs. When the González group presented candidates, Lora appealed to the National Electoral Court to recognize his organization as the real POR and "cancel the registration" of the "usurpers" of the party's name, who were "nothing but docile instruments of the international sect called Pabloism," which is "totally alien to the interests of the Bolivian revolution." The POR-LO responded furiously with an "Open Letter to the Ranks of the 'Masas' Group," stating that Lora had asked the court to "punish our Party for belonging to the Fourth International." It urged Lora's followers to break with him, as this was the final straw.[35]

In a long submission to the Electoral Court, later published as a pamphlet, POR-LO leaders argued: "The Lora family . . . which acts with pretensions of being a political party," has "no real or legal existence," and was already denied registration in 1956 and 1958. Mockingly, they described its leadership as "Guillermo Lora, Alfonsina Paredes (a member only when she is romantically involved with him) and Miguel Alandia Pantoja (more painter than revolutionary militant)." They reviewed Lora's political record, notably "pushing his faction toward entry into the MNR"—a "simple sell-out" to the government party—and declared: "Yes, we are internationalists, because we are Trotskyists, revolutionary Marxists."[36]

Paz Estenssoro returned to the Palacio Quemado amidst the fracturing of the MNR's populist class alliance. At the hemispheric level, he faced the challenges posed by the Cuban Revolution. After a brief period of friendly advice to Castro, the MNR distanced itself when Cuba defied Washington and aligned with the Soviet bloc. Paz admired John F. Kennedy, visited him in the White House, and became a stalwart of the Alliance for Progress that Kennedy launched to counteract the influence of Cuba's revolution. In 1964, Bolivia cut diplomatic relations with the rebellious isle. Escalation of the Vietnam War, under Kennedy and his successor Johnson, caused tin prices to rise, benefiting the Bolivian regime.

Not long after Kennedy's election in 1960, Paz personally ordered a financial aid package for Bolivia "within a matter of hours" after a request from Press Secretary Pierre Salinger. Arthur Schlesinger Jr., one of the new president's closest advisers, argued that if Latin America's "possessing classes make [a] middle-class revolution impossible, they will make a 'workers-and-peasants' revolution inevitable."[37]

U.S. aid to Bolivia shot up by more than 600 percent from 1960 to 1964. A hefty portion went to the military, which tripled in size from 1958 to 1964 and increased its budget share from 6.8 percent in 1958 to 16.8 percent in 1964. As the national security doctrine consolidated, Kenneth Lehman observes, "Bolivia became a laboratory to test ideas regarding the new role Latin American militaries might play" in shoring up the region and preventing more Cuba-type setbacks. In 1963, Bolivia had "more graduates from the U.S. Army Special Warfare School at Fort Bragg than any other nation in the hemisphere."[38]

Eventually, entire graduating classes from Bolivia's military academy would be sent to the U.S. Army's School of the Americas (SOA), formally inaugurated that year. (SOA graduate Hugo Banzer, one of Bolivia's most prominent dictators, was inducted into the school's Hall of Fame in 1988.) An officer who attended the military academy in the 1970s said training exercises featured attacks on COB headquarters and invasion of the radical peasant village of Achacachi. After graduating, he was sent to the SOA, where he learned "how to torture" prisoners, together with the axiom that "a dead subversive was better than a prisoner."[39]

Soon after returning to office, Paz launched the "Triangular Plan," co-sponsored by the United States, West Germany, and the Inter-American

Development Bank. The program called for laying off more than 20 percent of Comibol's employees and closing several mines. Underscoring his loyalty to Washington, Paz turned down Nikita Khrushchev's offer to help Bolivia (at extremely favorable terms) build its own tin smelter. In December 1960, the USSR sent a parliamentary delegation to promote the offer. Comibol's official magazine dryly reported their visit to "the important mining centers of Catavi, Llallagua and Siglo XX (where they were cordially received)."[40]

In reality, their reception was spectacular. Trotskyist leaders at Siglo XX mobilized their forces to greet the delegation. If Paz refused the Soviet offer, they said, the miners would "accept it with revolutionary enthusiasm." POR-Masas members stayed up the night before making little red flags with the symbol of Trotsky's Fourth International (the hammer, sickle, and 4). These were distributed to miners coming off the night shift, who stuck them in the slots of their helmets usually occupied by small electric lights. The party also made red banners and flags with slogans "supporting the Russia of Lenin and Trotsky, to distinguish ourselves from the Moscow bureaucracy." PCB supporters reacted angrily. Before the eyes of the astonished Soviet delegates, "an all-out battle" broke out between Stalinists and Trotskyists, Filemón Escóbar recalled. Laughing, he described *Life* magazine's report on the incident: "They said Bolivian miners are illiterate and don't even know that Trotsky died a long time ago."[41]

Bolivian Trotskyism and the Cuban Revolution

While the MNR used hostility to Cuba to demonstrate fealty to Washington, the Bolivian left saw defense of the Cuban Revolution as a banner of struggle against imperialism. Both sections of the Trotskyist movement greeted and defended the Cuban Revolution, but they did this in different ways.

Hugo González's POR-Lucha Obrera not only defended the revolution but politically supported the *Fidelista* leadership. The POR-LO took this position despite the Castro regime's adoption of key aspects of the outlook, practices, and structure of what Trotskyists had traditionally called the "Stalinist bureaucracy" of the USSR. Reservations regarding the Cuban leaders diminished when followers of J. Posadas, more critical toward Castro, split from the POR-LO.

Differences among the Bolivians also reflected the debates gripping the Latin American left with regard to the guerrilla warfare strategy. In his 1963 manual on the subject, Che Guevara wrote that the Cuban experience had made "three basic contributions to the mechanics of revolutionary movements in the Americas": "popular forces can win a war against the army"; the "insurrectionary *foco*" (guerrilla nucleus) can create the conditions for revolution; and "in the underdeveloped Americas, the basic terrain of armed struggle must be the countryside."[42] Venezuelan Communists and other proponents of electoral leftism found themselves on the receiving end of sharp polemics from Fidel Castro.

One of the most controversial aspects of these debates was the conclusion, formulated by Régis Debray, that Latin American radicals could "do without a vanguard Marxist-Leninist party of the working class" during the guerrilla phase of a revolution, as the guerrilla army itself "will be the nucleus of the party." Debray attacked Bolivian Trotskyists for organizing workers' self-defense instead of a guerrilla *foco*, and—echoing the vocabulary of mainstream Communist parties—branded Trotskyism as "pure and simple provocation."[43]

Debray had previously called Bolivia the one Latin American country "where the revolution might take the classical Bolshevik form."[44] In fact, Trotskyists' traditional view was that the proletariat, leading the poor peasants, would carry out a "classical" insurrection as the basis for a new state power. Under the impact of the Cuban Revolution, the idea that revolutionary strategy should now include guerrilla warfare became part of the basis for the "reunification" negotiated by followers of Pablo and Mandel with some of the Trotskyist groupings that had split from them. The result, in 1963, was the formation of the "United Secretariat of the Fourth International" (USec), of which González's POR-LO was the Bolivian section.

The González group embraced the strategy of guerrilla warfare modeled on the Cuban example. Indeed, this became increasingly central to its public identity and self-image, as reflected in its publications, union activities, and peasant work. Citing Bolivia as "an example of the influence of the Cuban Revolution" in late 1960, Pablo's *Fourth International* magazine hailed "the Peasants' Union of Omasuyos on the Bolivian altiplano" for its message of solidarity with Cuba, which was printed in *Lucha Obrera*. In 1961, a party leaflet proclaimed: "We workers want to follow Cuba's example, so [the government] persecutes us and tries to isolate us from the Cuban revolution." After the Bay of Pigs invasion, a women's group in which González supporters were active protested "the criminal invasion victimizing Cuba, the only free territory of the Americas." A POR-LO leaflet called for "a general strike on the day Cuba is invaded or the MNR government breaks relations."[45]

Together with "The Trotskyist Marseillaise" and other tunes, a PORLO songbook includes "To Cuba," the revolutionary island that "flourishes gloriously right under Uncle Sam's nose." Another, "El Guerrillero," proclaims: "I come from the *socavones* (mineshafts), together with the peasants, to defend the revolution . . . Long live Workers' Cuba, death to the invasion!" The group later boasted: "Since 1965 our party . . . defined itself in favor of the guerrilla line, siding with Che Guevara," since "guerrilla warfare . . . has become the dividing line separating real revolutionaries" from "charlatans."[46]

Guillermo Lora's POR-Masas also greeted the social revolution in Cuba and the island's spectacular break with U.S. dominance of the hemisphere. "Because the Cuban revolution is ours, because it is our heartfelt desire that it survive, we have defended it from the first moment," it proclaimed. However, "we do this as Marxist fighters, not lackeys." This meant criticizing the "errors committed by Castro's regime" and the "Stalinization" of its leadership. When Castro proclaimed that Cuba was a socialist country, Lora wrote: "This is an impressive revolution." However, "the Cuban proletariat is facing the historic task of putting itself at the head of the revolution and setting up its own government."[47]

"The Break with Cuba Is the Most Rotten Act of the MNR," declared a *Masas* headline. "The best way to defend the Cuban revolution," the paper insisted, "is not to become an all-expenses-paid tourist, but achieving the victory of the proletariat in our country." Then "the worker-peasant government will avenge [the MNR's] outrage against Cuba." Lora visited the island in the mid-1960s and met with Castro, whom he saw as "enthusiastic, talking endlessly about things like raising pigs, but completely ignorant about Marxism."[48] The POR-Masas also warned against Khrushchev's reliance on "peaceful coexistence" mediated through the United Nations.

In later years, Lora denounced the *foco* strategy in unequivocal terms as an example of petty-bourgeois politics and "ultra-left adventurism."[49] In the 1960s, however, his writings on the subject were less consistent. At times, his party mooted participation in a guerrilla front. In 1963, he criticized Guevara's *Guerrilla Warfare* for "extreme schematism," as it presented "a set of recipes its author claims must be applied to all countries." It was "absurd to convert the Cuban experience into a recipe" for all Latin America. Although Venezuela's guerrilla movement struck Lora as promising, "and we hope guerrillas will spread and become stronger," it would be "out of place at this time to have guerrillas in Bolivia." Moreover, Guevara was wrong to "assume the guerrilla *foco* can create the revolutionary party."[50]

The Cuba question was also taken up by Carlos Salazar, leader of the small Liga Socialista Revolucionaria. In 1960, he wrote that "theoreticians of the bourgeois democratic revolution" were incapable of understanding how a country like Cuba could adopt measures "that fall within the framework of socialist tasks." The "case of Cuba is a proof of the permanent revolution," he observed, while warning that due to its "programmatic and doctrinal weakness," Castro's regime had embraced "the Stalinist bureaucracy." The "interesting nature of Castro's measures," Salazar stressed, "should not make us lose sight of the main problem, having to do with the revolution's limitations: its national character, which carries with it, like a cancer, an element of imperialist restoration. In the final analysis, this will determine the revolution's future, proving that only an international socialist revolution can achieve definitive victory."[51]

In 1962, a new group was formed in Bolivia when followers of J. Posadas, head of the Buró Latinoamericano (BLA), split from the González POR. The BLA had, until that point, been an arm of Michel Pablo's I.S., but Posadas had grown disenchanted, having taken to extremes some of Pablo's more adventuresome concepts. Pablo had posited that a "war-revolution" would issue from an East/West confrontation; Posadas concluded that the USSR should launch a first strike so communism could rise from the ashes of war. Alejandro Carvajal recalled Posadas charging comrades "afraid of nuclear war" with being "cowards," not revolutionaries. One former Bolivian *posadista* recalls that Posadas's speculations about UFOs led other groups to "call us the 'extraterrestrials'." Despite its leader's theories, the grouping was a significant political current in several parts of Latin America, likely including the majority of the region's Trotskyists in the early 1960s.[52]

The Bolivian POR-LO addressed a letter to Fidel Castro protesting "repressive measures . . . against the Cuban Trotskyists," widely respected working-class activists who were aligned with the BLA.[53] After a visit to Latin America, I.S. member Livio Maitan wrote that the majority of the POR-LO's leadership originally sided with Posadas and was undergoing a serious internal crisis. The BLA sent four representatives to try to win the Bolivians over, while Pablo warned against Posadas's "irresponsible, odious and ridiculous gossip" and "extreme political confusion." In the end, only a minority followed Posadas. U.S. operatives filed a "Field Information Report" noting that members "who sympathize with the Latin American Bureau of the International Trotskyist movement met in Huanuni on 8 and 9 December 1962 and expelled the leaders of the POR," including González. The party's "majority . . . will continue to support González," it noted, but "followers of the BLA will split" to form their own group.[54]

This new group called itself the POR-Trotskista (POR-T) and was led by Cochabamba-born Amadeo Vargas, one of the Bolivian movement's most

Figure 5.4 POR-Lucha Obrera outing, ca. 1961. Standing men, from left: César Lora or Jorge Velarde, unidentified, Félix Romero (tailor), flour workers' leader Eulogio Sánchez, unidentified, Fernando Bravo (teacher), Comibol worker Elio Vásquez, factory union leader Alejandro Carvajal, unidentified, Hugo González, Félix Mirabal, Huanuni miner Florentino Calustro, Ismael Pérez, Encarnación Colque (?), Huanuni miner Cardenio Vásquez (overalls). Seated, second from left, Huanuni miner Felipe Vásquez. (Courtesy of Emma Bolshia Bravo Cladera)

energetic cadres. The POR-T had little influence in the labor movement but vigorously circulated its paper, *Voz Proletaria*, and attracted some prominent intellectuals. Emma Bolshia Bravo remembers the split as personally painful and politically difficult for POR-LO members who had worked closely with Amadeo Vargas and other Posadas followers (see figure 5.4). The POR-LO received a further blow that year with the sudden death of Bravo's father, Fernando Bravo, who had been second only to González in the leadership. The FSTMB called his death an "irreparable loss." A La Paz elementary school is named for him today.[55]

A New Cycle of Military Rule

1964 marked a turning point for Latin America. In March, a junta fulsomely backed by the United States took power in Brazil, anchoring a new model of hard-line dictatorships. In Bolivia, discontent with the Paz regime escalated, with many now calling him El Mono (The Monkey), alleging a certain simian quality, instead of El Jefe de la Revolución Nacional. When the government announced new cuts in the Comibol workforce, a long and bitter miners' strike ensued in which César Lora again played a leading role. Paz responded by jailing prominent union activists.

Alejandro Carvajal recalled that mine worker members of the MNR took to publicly burning their party cards.[56] Popular revulsion against the MNR reached the point that Lechín quit and formed his own Revolutionary Party of the National Left (PRIN), which included many former Trotsky-ist entrists such as Möller. The MNR right wing also withdrew, forming a separate Authentic Revolutionary Party (PRA).

As his 1960–64 term neared its end, Paz declared he would seek reelection, over the opposition of Siles Zuazo and a segment of the MNR. Siles, accompanied by Lechín, went on a new hunger strike "in a last-ditch attempt to block the re-election." Unsurprisingly, their stomach pangs did not deter *El Jefe*. More significant was Paz Estenssoro's choice of running mate: General René Barrientos, a flamboyant air force officer known as "the Pentagon's man," as noted by *Masas*, which had warned for some time that "The Pro-Imperialist Army Is Becoming Master of the Country." Bar-rientos was copilot of the plane that brought Paz back home from exile after the April 1952 revolt. As a rising star among MNR military men, he led a Washington-financed "Civic Action" plan, then trained in the United States, where he was befriended by Air Force General Curtis Le May, later known for his call to bomb Vietnam "into the Stone Age." *Time* lauded Bar-rientos as the "Steve Canyon of the Andes," referring to the pilot hero of a he-man comic strip.[57]

The election was marred by repeated clashes between goon squads hired by different sectors of the MNR. Paz forces relied partly on "the famous Barzolas," a newsmagazine noted: plebeian women hired to fight with metal pipes, knives, and other weapons, often "an irreplaceable shock brigade" for the MNR leadership. Despite cries of election fraud, Paz won his coveted reelection in 1964, but Barrientos's ascent showed a shift of power toward the "Army party" of military men eager to rescue the nation from growing disorder. As Paz repeatedly told Mine Minister René Zavaleta, "I am the last civilian president."[58]

As the country became a pressure cooker of mobilizations and counter-protests, a tragic marriage of convenience brought together almost all the political forces disenchanted with Paz. Guided by Siles, it included follow-ers of Lechín (historic leader of the MNR Left), Walter Guevara (historic leader of the MNR right wing), the ultra-rightist Falange, and remnants of the old Stalinist PIR. Behind the scenes, U.S. Air Force attaché "Fox" culti-vated Barrientos as the up-and-coming strongman.

"¡Abajo la bota militar!"

The Barrientos coup came immediately after a pitched battle between army troops, including U.S.-trained "Rangers," and armed miners. After Barrientos became vice president, the threat of repression led César Lora and Isaac Camacho to buy a small stock of weapons for the Trotskyist miners of Siglo XX. A U.S. journal quoted "the Trotskyites' 'Secretary General for the Unemployed'" at the mine: "We Trotskyites formed a cooperative of *jucos*"—the Quechua word for owls, used for those who take ore at night—"which sold stolen tin ore back to the company. We used the profits to buy arms." The La Paz newsweekly *Vistazo* reported: "In Siglo XX, the Trotsky-ists' organization and armaments were very impressive: duly equipped, they would form up, about a hundred divided into pickets of ten, with a machine gun, rifles and dynamite."[59]

At the end of October 1964, a pitched battle occurred after miners' radio stations broadcast the rumor of an army attack on workers in Oruro. POR and PCB union leaders from Siglo XX and Catavi mobilized trucks and buses full of miners to go to their defense. César Lora's younger brother Andrés was fourteen at the time. He recalls, "I went in one of the Trotskyist trucks and we were ambushed, it was terrible." Many comrades were killed or wounded.[60]

POR-LO militant Elio Vásquez participated in the ensuing "Battle of Sora-Sora":

> The army attacked at dawn when we were on the road to Oruro. First went a truck of people from the *Masas* group, with some others too. The army started machine-gunning them from just above Sora-Sora. They fired back, many were wounded, including one of our com-rades. They got under the truck to protect themselves. A bus going to Sucre passed by and they commandeered it to take the wounded to Huanuni.
>
> The next day we came in 15 or 20 trucks from Siglo XX and Ca-tavi, going toward Oruro. The *soldaditos* (soldiers) saw us, because the miners came down the *pampa* throwing their *dinamitas*, and the soldiers started running away to the hills. We chased them through the hills, and they were throwing their weapons away to run faster.

As they approached Oruro, the road was choked with dust clouds. Dusk was falling, visibility getting worse by the minute, and "the army had just taken the big hill in Oruro." Then "they started firing down at us. So César Lora said '*Compañeros*, it's too late, they have defeated us here, they've already taken the hill and in a few minutes it will be dark and a lot of us will get killed, we had better fall back.' That's what we decided to do, in our assembly there, so the buses turned around." Filemón Escóbar, who commanded one of the miners' detachments, believes "we committed a grave error when we did not take Oruro, it was an error to fall back." The Trotskyists' role in the combat reinforced their authority among the miners. In contrast, workers taunted PCB leaders as cowards, saying they took refuge in an ambulance.[61]

In the turmoil surrounding Paz Estenssoro's reelection, many workers and students, fed up with the MNR, hoped it would be thrown out and replaced by a leftist regime. Alejandro Carvajal said detailed plans were made for an uprising, with the participation of the POR-LO, other radical groups, and the Lechinistas; but Lechín tipped off Barrientos. On November 4, 1964, Barrientos carried out what Escóbar calls "a counterrevolutionary coup with popular trimmings, thanks to Lechín," whose PRIN joined the "People's Revolutionary Committee" that initially supported the coup. The González group published a pamphlet arguing that the junta had "usurped the people's victory," having "defrauded the masses" after the defeat of their "main enemy," the Paz regime.[62]

An ominous turning point for Bolivia, the Barrientos putsch marked the beginning of a new cycle of military rule that would last until 1982. U.S. support was enthusiastic and munificent. The State Department had long viewed a strong Bolivian army as "insurance" in the event of "political chaos" caused by the "collapse of, or an unfavorable reorientation of the MNR regime." The CIA contributed more than $1 million for the coup, writing that the agency's goal was to "encourage a stable government favorably inclined toward the United States" and support the general's "plans to pacify the country." Barrientos, whom one rival described as having dropped straight from a tree into the presidential Cadillac, became a symbol of Latin American "*gorila*" (military) dictators allied with Johnson's White House. When Johnson met the new strongman, national security adviser Walt Rostow handed him the CIA file, saying: "This is to explain why General Barrientos may say thank you when you have lunch with him."[63] At first, COB leaders held on to the illusion that they might "cogovern" with this administration, as they had with previous ones. An incident that captured the popular imagination symbolized their disorientation: after Barrientos occupied the Palacio Quemado, Lechín went to ask him to appoint some "worker ministers." Barrientos booted him out and Lechín, running away from the palace, lost one of his shoes.[64]

COB leaders' attitude put the POR-Masas in a bind. The party had warned that Lechín was "eagerly seeking an alliance with the right-wing parties," and a POR congress in February 1964 stressed rejection of "adventurist coups and provocations." Still, the party was unable to abandon hope in the man it had made so many blocs of its own with: "in the hypothetical case that Lechín turned to the left to the point of joining a revolutionary front, the POR would support this," it declared, adding: "we call on all the revolutionary parties, those that say they represent the working class, the Lechinistas, to form a revolutionary front of the left, making it possible to mobilize the masses toward their own government." The resolution also pointedly stated: "In the army not all are generals, much less agents of imperialism and counterrevolution. Let us not forget the young officers, the non-coms and soldiers intimately linked to the masses and vulnerable to revolutionary propaganda. We hope these elements will become the backbone of the revolutionary struggles of the future."[65]

When Barrientos took over, the POR-Masas proclaimed: "¡Abajo el mamertazo!" in an allusion to the 1949 takeover by despised Vice President Mamerto Urriolagoitia. A Vistazo headline read: "We Miners Do Not Support the Government Junta, Says César Lora, Siglo XX Worker and Member of the Miners Federation."[66]

Purges and "deregistrations" of labor organizations followed. An operative for the American Institute for Free Labor Development reported which unions were still "pro-communist"—mine and factory workers' federations in particular—and which were "anti-communist." The teachers' federation "was led by communists for many years but pro-democrats took it over in April, 1963, thanks to help from the AIFLD labor center in La Paz." Unions would have to "apply for re-recognition with the Labor Ministry," and ad hoc labor committees "will be desconocidos (not recognized officially)." This would be accomplished through junta decrees that were "delivered to me at the airport in La Paz minutes before my departure." Meanwhile, "the communist controlled National Workers Central (COB) will be desconocida when it applies for re-recognition with the Labor Ministry. COMMENT: This will be the first real confrontation the Junta has had with the communists and Juan Lechín Oquendo."[67]

Barrientos's number two was General Alfredo Ovando. A conspicuous role in repression was played by Interior Minister Antonio Arguedas, a former PCB member who joined Barrientos's "Popular Christian Movement." Taking advantage of Barrientos's fluency in Quechua, the junta proclaimed a "Military-Peasant Pact" as he toured the countryside presenting the military as benefactors, even protectors against a "communist threat" to take what little property peasants had gained from agrarian reform.

The most effective base for insurgency in Bolivia was the tin mines. One of Barrientos's first steps was to demand that the miners give up their arms. *Vistazo* asked, "Is It Possible? Surrender of Arms," quoting the general's statement "regarding the arms the people have had in their power since April 9, 1952": "I demand that you have faith in the Armed Forces and turn your weapons over to them."[68]

His demands were echoed on Wall Street: "Until they were closed," the *Wall Street Journal* noted, "the miners' radio stations throughout the country could effectively mobilize workers for strikes and violent uprisings within a few hours," using the workers' militias. The *Journal* accused mine worker "Trotskyites" of organizing "wholesale robbery of the best tin ore" to purchase even "heavier weapons," reporting that after a battle, "a 50-calibre machine gun was unearthed in the front yard of a Trotskyite leader" in Catavi. When key unions made a pact in defense of their right to organize, the government summarily deported Lechín. "Predictably," remarked the stock brokers' house organ, "miners struck," but "the junta sent troops and planes" to suppress them. "Barrientos then declared a state of emergency at the mines, abolished the miners' unions and drastically cut their wages, removed union leaders' immunity from discharge and sent many of them into jail or hiding."[69] Bolivia's Trotskyist movement was hit hard by the repression. Not content with imprisoning and banishing leaders and activists, the junta destroyed five of Miguel Alandia's murals in La Paz.

The Death of César Lora

In May 1965, on behalf of the Mine Federation's executive committee, César Lora denounced the "sinister plans of the *gorilas*," whose junta was "really led by U.S. agents, although those playing the role of puppets are Generals Barrientos and Ovando." Fighting "not merely for the interests of our own sector" but for "the elementary rights of human beings," the miners would show that "the military boot must not and cannot crush the Bolivian people." When labor organizations were banned, he took up the task of organizing clandestine unions.[70]

"Some other union leaders left for Argentina," Angel Capari recalls, "but we *poristas* decided we should go underground. So César Lora, the federation's Secretary of Labor Conflicts, and Isaac Camacho, who was a section delegate, these two comrades went into clandestinity. . . . Those that could, we maintained contact with the workers, to orient them on how to defend themselves against Barrientos." Andrés Lora remembers: "The POR's slogan was not to abandon the workers. You had to print the leaflets, do the work at midnight, the worker cadres had to arrive early to leave the leaflets with the workers' timecards."

Andrés was particularly close to his older brother. When César came to stay at their father's house to recuperate from a mine accident, he and Andrés slept in the same bed. "They put platinum in his foot, and he'd ask me to warm it up for him." When the army "raided the mine districts after the coup, with the slogan of killing the leaders," Andrés told César he wanted to go underground with him. César said, "No, stay in school and keep studying." That was the last time Andrés saw him alive.[71]

Guillermo Lora saw the inside of uncountable prison cells and suffered innumerable exiles and banishments. He could be charming and cultivated, but few would have called him a soft man. Yet what he recalled with tears in his eyes was this: "You know, my younger brother, the one they killed, he was not only an activist but a very good writer too. We collected his writings and published them as a special pamphlet." Miguel Lora noted that César wrote about technical aspects of mining in addition to union struggles.[72]

Angel Capari was one of the POR members chosen to go to La Paz with a document written by César and Isaac to present the miners' demands to the junta. "The government threw us out, saying we were the Trotskyists who go around bothering the government and the workers." Pastor Peláez, who was in the same delegation, says "as soon as we came back, the next morning we were fired." He was blacklisted from the mine. "Instead of our time cards," Capari remembers, "they had orders from Barrientos to fire us all. Many were exiled to inhospitable regions, but others of us were not arrested because we were underground."

"Then the telegram arrived saying that César Lora had been assassinated on the road near San Pedro," Capari continues. "He was killed by a bullet in his forehead." The murder, with a .38 revolver, occurred on July 29, 1965. Four decades later, none of those interviewed could hide the pain and sorrow it caused; the impact on the miners' movement as a whole was deep and long-lasting. "Because of the persecution in Llallagua, I couldn't live there. I had to leave through Norte Potosí," remembers Peláez. "My uncle heard about it on the radio, that they had killed *el César*. There was nothing I could do then but cry," he says, his voice breaking. Like many others, he named his son after his murdered friend.

The government refused to release the body. The POR-Masas discussed the idea of physically "rescuing" the cadaver, but in the face of insistent demands from the family and mine workers, the authorities finally allowed it to be brought back home. His Quechua accent more marked now, Angel Capari relates that "we went to get the body of César Lora from San Pedro." Then "we buried him in Siglo XX, because he was a leader of the Miners Federation. All of Siglo XX was there, and the peasants came too, because of his relation with them. Maybe 100,000 people in all." A bust of him stands there now.[73]

A recording made during the funeral march lists contingents of miners, *palliris* (women who extract tin from rocks in the slag heaps outside the mines), and workers from other industries. One banner read "Glory to César Lora, Defender of the Miners—Down with the Organizers of Massacres against the Workers!" Dynamite explosions and the pututu horn accompany reports in Spanish and Quechua, impassioned speeches, and workers chanting: "Glory to Lora," "Death to Hunger and Poverty," "Long Live the Siglo XX Union," "Down with the Agents of Yankee Imperialism," "*¡Abajo la bota militar!*"[74]

Andrés Lora remembers: "From the Plaza del Minero to the cemetery, six or seven kilometers, all filled with people accompanying the body. These things made a big impact on our lives. The workers wrote songs in homage to César, and they would go to the *chicherías* and sing them openly, with the army right there."[75] His granddaughter sings them today. The most famous is the "Huayño de César Lora": *Los mineros lloran sangre por la muerte de un obrero / Ese ha sido César Lora, asesinado en San Pedro.* "The miners cry blood for the death of a worker / César Lora, murdered in San Pedro," the lyrics relate, adding the traditional chorus: "For the miner there is no justice, no pardon / Shameless capitalists try to crush him."

For Bolivian miners, collective memory has been key to survival and mobilization. In one of his short stories, René Poppe, a Bolivian literary figure closely acquainted with Trotskyism, writes of a desperate wildcat strike inside an unnamed mine. "The older workers told of similar events they had lived through," asking: "What was it that *el César Lora* said?" They "needed the memory of their departed leaders. The words were heavy with evocation. Every worker, telling his part of the memory, would help carve their almost physical presence. It was as if they had never been murdered; as if they were there again, in every *paraje*, agitating, discussing."[76]

César Lora was not the only POR-Masas leader assassinated that year. In May, graphic worker Julio César Aguilar led a strike in Cochabamba. Two months later, he was seized by police and killed.

New Battles and Experiments in Unity

The battles that began with the suppression of the miners' strike broke out again in September 1965. *Newsweek* reported: "It was Saturday evening and in the bleak Andean village of Llallagua the bars were crowded with tin miners relaxing after their week's work. Suddenly, the wife of Isaac Camacho, a Trotskyite labor leader, rushed into one of the bars shouting: 'The police have taken my husband!' Within minutes, every saloon in Llallagua emptied and the tin miners of Bolivia, armed with guns and dynamite, again went on the rampage. For three furious days the miners attacked barracks, radio stations and other public buildings."[77] The junta declared a state of siege and sent more troops.

POR-LO militant Elio Vásquez was present at the "Siglo XX Massacre" of September 1965 and remembers it differently. Returning from visits to underground groups in Quechisla, Huanuni, and Colquiri, he had just gotten home when soldiers banged on the door. "I could see their boots through the part below." He and others were taken out, "and *pucha*, we saw the army deployed all down the streets." They took them to the Miraflores barracks.

Back in Siglo XX, under the leadership of Isaac Camacho and Filemón Escóbar, the clandestine union functioned literally underground, inside the mineshafts. Isaac came out of the mine on a Saturday and was seized by the army together with other workers. When a delegation went to ask after them, its members were seized as well. "So the workers called a general assembly, but the army came and started shooting them, *tatatata*, and silenced the siren that was sounding the alarm. The workers went to the mine to get dynamite and attacked the police station to try to free Isaac and the others."

That night "we heard jeeps arrive" at the barracks. The soldiers took out Isaac, Cirilo Jiménez, and other leaders. In Siglo XX, miners took up positions in the hills. The army asked for reinforcements. "So then the planes arrived, and the fighting went on for two nights and three days." A group of high school students "went out to chant 'Down with the Government, Free the Prisoners!' and an airplane started strafing them." Vásquez estimates approximately eighty workers were killed and two hundred wounded. The activists were shipped off to the jungles of the Beni. A "Christmas amnesty" freed them, for the time being.[78]

Under the impact of Barrientos's repression, Bolivian Trotskyists carried out two different experiments in "unity." An opposition bloc called People's Democratic Council (CODEP) was formed in late 1965, with a manifesto "Against Fascism, For Social Justice," signed by Guillermo Lora for the POR-Masas, a sector of the MNR, the Maoist party, and several smaller left groups, and Lidia Gueiler of Lechín's PRIN (then married to Edwin Möller, she later became Bolivia's only female president). Lora subsequently recognized that CODEP was "very similar to the effort to establish a popular front."[79]

The CODEP sent a delegation to the Tricontinental Congress sponsored by the Cuban leadership in January 1966, but its delegates were not admitted because the organizers said the official Communist Party (PCB) was the only legitimate representative of Bolivian workers and peasants. (This was the party that Fidelistas throughout the continent later accused of betraying Che Guevara's guerrilla war.) Lora "remember[ed] with some bitterness how we were excluded and kept almost as prisoners during the . . . Conference, and later, Fidel's violent, unjust attack on us," which Lora attributed "partly to the influence of Régis Debray."[80]

In March 1966, the POR-Masas and POR-LO announced that they had achieved "a triumph for the Bolivian masses" by joining forces "as a result of the maturity and experience achieved over the past years." Naming a national secretariat composed of Guillermo Lora and Hugo González, the united party decided to publish *Masas* as its topical newspaper, *Lucha Obrera* as a theoretical journal, and not to affiliate with any international tendency. The united POR called for "fighting by every means against the Military Junta which has inaugurated a fascist regime aimed at physically destroying trade-union, political and student organizations."[81]

In a letter to Livio Maitan, a top POR-LO leader said the "parity" leadership was a concession to the Lora group, but unification helped attract new members. Cadres from both tendencies had worked together well in a campaign to protest Barrientos through "posters, leaflets, wall murals, etc." The POR-LO wing was "mainly made up of workers, in factories, the railways and flourmills," while Lora's wing "has more people in the university than we do, but we have more secondary students."[82] The experiment was short-lived, giving way to a new separation. Each side accused the other of culpability for the mésalliance's breakdown, but differences went deeper, notably on guerrilla warfare.

Pulacayo or Ñancabuazú?

For many people in the United States and Europe, what Bolivia brings to mind is Che Guevara, who died there in the attempt to make it his base for a regionwide guerrilla struggle. At the tactical level, the decision to establish operations in the Ñancahuazú region was particularly miscon-ceived. Not only was the terrain unsuitable, but the local peasantry was markedly conservative, having received significant parcels of land from the government.

A more fundamental problem was Guevara's *foco* theory itself. Present-ing revolution as the project of a small group of heroes in the mountains, it overlooked the actual class struggle in Bolivia. Although Che had admired Bolivian miners since his 1953 visit, his National Liberation Army (ELN) essentially asked the most self-sacrificing militants to give up *being* miners. "Do not listen any more to the false apostles of mass struggle," warned an ELN communiqué "To the Miners of Bolivia." In Latin America, the struggle "must be developed by a small mobile vanguard, the guerrillas," who "await you with open arms and invite you" to join the ELN.[83]

In practice, Che's strategy relegated tens of thousands of militant min-ers to the role of sideline supporters. Yet repeatedly, both before and after Che's Bolivian tragedy, wide sectors of the country's impoverished popula-tion grouped themselves around the miners when the time came for head-on conflicts with the regime. Thus it is symptomatic that Guevarism's pub-licist Debray called the Bolivian proletariat "a class deluded as to its own political importance and with an overweening self-confidence."[84]

Guevara's conflicts with the pro-Moscow Communist Party have been widely described, as have his criticisms of the Soviet leadership, which he viewed as conservative and fearful of Third World revolution. For their part, the Soviets—and many of their Latin American followers—viewed Guevara as a loose cannon suspiciously well-disposed toward Maoist China, perhaps even infected with "Trotskyite" heresy.

In late 1966, Interior Minister Arguedas singled out POR members at the Huanuni mine for a criminal trial. As the army and U.S. special forces zeroed in on Guevara's *foco* the following year, Arguedas declared: "All political leaders who have supported the guerrillas will be arrested." *Radios mineras* would be stopped from broadcasting any and all "subversive programs." Both the *Masas* and *Lucha Obrera* PORs were banned, together with pro-Moscow and pro-Beijing Communists. Filemón Escóbar, Gui-llermo Lora, his brother Miguel, Alejandro Carvajal, and others were sent into internal exile in remote tropical towns. Maoist leader Jorge Echazú recalls being held in a prison camp with Escóbar and many other Trotsky-ists. Despite his hostility to their views, he said they and the rest of the prisoners maintained unity against the camp authorities.[85]

The two main wings of Bolivian Trotskyism continued to diverge on guerrilla warfare. The POR of Hugo González was enthusiastic. Several members made trips to Cuba, among them Comibol worker Elio Vásquez, who got a scholarship to study there. Long before Guevara reached Bolivia, U.S. intelligence reports warned of "guerrilla warfare planning" by "the Lucha Obrera sector of the Bolivian Trotskyist party."[86]

However, neither POR was involved in Guevara's *foco*. Only after his death, when surviving followers sought to continue the guerrilla struggle, did some Bolivian Trotskyists become involved in those efforts, as the González group argued that the fight for socialism "can only be undertaken . . . by guerrilla warfare in the countryside, the mines, and the cities" in a 1968 "Report from the Bolivian Underground." "Forward with the Thought of Che Guevara!" a later leaflet proclaimed, defending "our comrade Felipe Vásquez," an "active miners' leader from Huanuni accused of being a guerrilla combatant."[87]

As for the POR-Masas, years later Siglo XX miner Dionicio Coca summarized its position: "The POR had an analysis of the *foco* strategy. Che was not with the masses . . . and was also geographically isolated. It was tragic for such great fighters to be abandoned. We of the POR thought this guerrilla movement basically amounted to an adventure" rather than an effective means of struggle. At the time, the position of Lora's group was less definitive. In April 1967, in a resolution declaring solidarity with the guerrilla movement, "irrespective of its strength or weakness, its virtues or defects," the POR-Masas called guerrilla warfare "nothing less than the people's method of struggle against the sell-out, anti-popular military dictatorship."[88]

Three months later, Lora criticized the concept that the *foco* was the "preeminent method" of struggle and "the party of today," which Debray had argued in his best-selling *Revolution in the Revolution?* However, "we greatly appreciate the effort to keep an armed *foco* going, since this can contribute to the outbreak of insurrection." Referring to the Organization of Latin American Solidarity, formed in line with Guevara's call to create "two, three, many Vietnams," Lora wrote that OLAS could become a "single Latin American command of revolutionary forces," if it "overcomes its current sectarianism and opens its doors to all leftist tendencies." For Bolivia to be "converted into a real Vietnam," however, the "guerrilla *focos* must be removed from their isolation" and "rooted in the mass movement."[89]

This was far from the intransigent critique the POR-Masas later advanced. In a mid-1967 interview, Lora vowed "completely limitless aid and support," including sending "men as well" to join the guerrilla forces. Meanwhile, he called again for "a left front that would include the Marxist parties, the PRIN and the MNR." The youth groups of these parties (with the exception of the pro-Moscow PCB) had already formed an "anti-imperialist front" the previous year.[90]

La Masacre de San Juan

The period's most horrific episode of repression began to take shape in early June when Barrientos decreed a state of siege "due to communist subversion." He raged against the workers of Huanuni, who had declared the mines "liberated territory." This was a "traitorous declaration" by "agents of red imperialism," he said. A planned miners' protest in Oruro brought further denunciations.[91]

Several participants described what happened next. Angel Capari remembers: "We prepared a plenary meeting of miners at Siglo XX, to demand that wages lost to inflation and cuts be restored," and fired workers rehired. "The miners' assemblies also decided we should send one or two *mitas* (day's pay) to send medicines" to the guerrillas. This was "simply out of free instinct (*libre instinto*), not because we had any political accord with Che Guevara, despite what the Stalinists tried to say." The decision was supported by miners from both wings of the Trotskyist movement.

The miners' plenary was scheduled to begin on June 24, the fiesta of San Juan: St. John's Night, coinciding with the late-June Andean winter solstice celebrated since pre-Columbian days. "We didn't know the government had prepared a massacre," Capari says. Traditionally, "on that night we make the *ch'alla* (offering) and *fogatas* (bonfires). The miners come out with their charangos, their guitars, everything they can, to dance and have a drink." He continues:

> Around 3 or 4 in the morning there were shots, but people said, "No, it's nothing, just bottle rockets." Also, the miners always use dynamite, even for parties. But the siren sounded. A lot of people were confused and thought that meant to go to work, since the siren usually sounds at 5 o'clock to wake you up. They went to the *bocamina* (mine entrance) with their *guardatojos* (helmets) and work clothes. They were caught there when the army started massacring them. *Al guardatojo que veían, lo metían bala para matar.* (Every helmet the soldiers could see, they filled with bullets to kill the miners.) When dawn came, everyone saw they were completely surrounded by the army, with many people killed. One woman had the fetus ripped out of her by bazooka fire.

"My wife woke up, there was shooting," remembers Pastor Peláez. "We couldn't do anything; Siglo XX and Llallagua were totally surrounded. My aunt worked as a servant at the barracks, and an officer told a *soldadito* to kill one of the miners, but the soldier didn't want to, because he was a miner's son. So the lieutenant killed the soldier right there."[92]

"After a violent clash, the Army occupied Catavi and Siglo XX," reported the press. "Law and order will be maintained at all cost," proclaimed Barrientos. Arguedas warned that "extremists" were still "inciting violence" and vowed to use "all the government's resources for the immediate capture" of the "main agitators, who are Trotskyists, such as Isaac Camacho" and others.[93]

Capari remembers the political struggle the miners waged "after the massacre, when we had to bury the dead."

> The army said, "One by one." But we gave the slogan to the *compañeros mineros*: "All together, we will take all our dead to the cemetery." And so we gathered, with the siren sounding, and the army could do nothing.
>
> It was there, in the cemetery, that Isaac Camacho appeared, to lead and to speak and to denounce what had happened. He had been in hiding. He said we had to denounce to the world this unspeakable massacre, that Barrientos had given the order to kill the miners.
>
> This is how we buried them. Then Isaac immediately went back below ground, nobody knew where he went. But a short time later they caught him in a house in Llallagua. They took him away, tied up and bleeding, toward La Paz, and they "disappeared" him. We have never been able to find his body. Many more of us fell victim to repression then as well.[94]

The figure of Isaac Camacho joined that of César Lora in the memory and culture of Bolivian Trotskyism: Miguel Alandia's powerful portrait of the two labor martyrs became the movement's best-known graphic image (see figure 5.5). The POR-Masas published a pamphlet reproducing Alandia's depiction of César's body, as well as several of his murals, together with the poem *"Muera el general"* (Death to the General) and French journalist Yannick Aubron's lyrical "Fiesta and Revolution."

In October 1967, the manhunt against guerrillas and their sympathizers reached fever pitch with the capture and summary execution of Che Guevara. Braving the crackdown, Guillermo Lora was interviewed in the press expressing "my sincere homage to Che Guevara and the other guerrilla fighters who have been killed." At the same time, he reiterated his "disagreements with Guevara," particularly the view that guerrilla war was now "the only valid method of struggle." The guerrilla *foco* "does not, by itself, resolve all the problems posed by the revolution." Guerrilla fighters

PARTIDO OBRERO REVOLUCIONARIO

ASAMBLEA POPULAR
ORGANO DE POSTE OBRERO

HOMENAJE

CÉSAR LORA - ISAAC CAMACHO - J. AGUILAR
MARTIRES DE LA CLASE OBRERA

**Los Màrtires Poristas
Hacen Posible la
Victoria de la Revolución**

Viva el Gobierno
Obrero-Campesino !!

Figure 5.5 POR-Masas poster commemorating César Lora and Isaac Camacho. (Courtesy of Bibliothèque de Documentation Internationale Contemporaine)

would be "unlikely to survive their isolation" unless they merged with the mass movement and "really become the armed fraction of the people in revolt."[95]

Years later, former POR-Masas cadre Daniel Campos recalled a long stretch at San Pedro prison in a cell next to former PCB leader Mario Monje. Monje had met with Guevara in Ñancahuazú, only to turn his back on the *foco* and threaten to expel PCB members who remained with the guerrillas, making his name a synonym for betrayal among Che's sympathizers around the world. In San Pedro, he was the only prisoner to receive the daily papers, which arrived at 7 a.m. He would pass them over to Campos. "We never had any polemical discussions," Campos remembered. "There was just one time when Monje said, 'Why should we have agreed to [Guevara] leading the guerrilla struggle, especially if we didn't even agree with the guerrilla strategy?'"[96]

Che's ELN revived when Inti and Coco Peredo called on his followers to return to combat. The González group—which changed the name of its newspaper to *Combate*—was determined to participate actively and link itself with the Guevarists. In 1969, a supporter of "the militant vanguard represented by the ELN and POR" wrote: "The strategies of these two organizations have moved closer and closer together during the past year."[97]

A bleak picture of the results emerges from an internal report to the SWP. Unlike the ELN, "the POR, after it adopted the line of guerrilla warfare, did not carry it out in practice." There was "some confusion" among POR-Combate members "over the exact differences" with the ELN, which had "the official endorsement of the Cuban leadership." Pursuing the guerrilla strategy, "the POR has brought into the party persons who do not consider themselves Trotskyists and are not in political agreement with the party's program." The POR "suffered the repression aimed at the guerrilla movement" but did not gain the fame the ELN achieved through its actions. "All except two of the POR comrades who visited Cuba quit . . . and joined the ELN." In fact, "the POR lost members to the ELN continuously."[98] If the idea was to be Guevarists, it seemed logical enough to join the official Guevarist group.

González's followers had to endure the taunts of Lora's POR, which said their "combat" amounted only to a failed "expropriation" of a gas station. Worse, the POR-Masas began to call González a "suspicious" element. Years later, Hugo González insisted that whatever errors the POR-Combate had made in the 1960s and early 1970s, it would have been "absurd" to "stand aside" from the young radicals who tried to continue Che's struggle in Bolivia.[99]

1967 was a year of bitter losses. The year 1968 brought new hope to Bolivian Trotskyists. A May Day leaflet by the Union of Bolivian Women, in which Trotskyists were active, saluted "the workers of Bolivia, especially the women who work in mines, fields, factories, offices, schools and workshops." "Only by liberating the people can women be liberated," it stressed, calling on workers to remember "all the martyrs of labor," from Chicago's Haymarket to "Catavi, Milluni . . . Villa Victoria and so many battlefields all over the world." If "imperialism is an international business," the struggle against capitalism drew strength from international solidarity.[100]

The new year brought the Tet Offensive's stinging setback to Johnson's war against revolution in Vietnam. Trotskyists' clandestine publications covered Indochina, the May-June upheaval in France, student protests and repression in Mexico, and Soviet intervention in Czechoslovakia, which they condemned as new evidence of Stalinism's bankruptcy. In Bolivia, the high level of repression continued to stifle mass movements. Still, teachers went on strike in October, and factory workers struck against the state of siege. Late that year important peasant sectors broke from pro-Barrientos organizations that had been an important prop for the military regime.

The 1960s brought an end to the National Revolution period. Bolivian Trotskyists were not surprised when mass discontent undermined the MNR. They saw this as confirmation of their view that the nationalists, committed to capitalism, could not resolve the nation's deepest problems. Trotskyists were deeply involved in the tumultuous struggles that ensued, but the MNR's decline did not lead to the workers' and peasants' government they advocated. Instead, the MNR's own military men, backed by a U.S. administration preoccupied with counterinsurgency in the wake of the Cuban Revolution, opened a new cycle of military rule. In its offensive against labor, the junta aimed deadly blows against the Trotskyists, weakening but not destroying their ability to organize. The dragnet against Guevara's guerrillas brought new mine massacres and new forms of worker resistance, in which Trotskyists played a central role. Yet divisions among them deepened. For its part, the COB leadership lost prestige through its short-lived alliance with Barrientos and weak role in post-coup resistance. When the political situation opened up at the end of the decade, old alliances would be renewed.

"The First Soviet of the Americas"

The Bolivian left, labor, and student movements breathed a collective sigh of relief in April 1969 when President Barrientos died in a helicopter crash. "Filipo" Escóbar remembers the news being greeted with "a real party," punctuated by dynamite. "After five years, labor militants emerged from clandestinity. In the mineshafts, workers again showed that defiant gaze that seemed to say to the oppressors: Your time will come, you sons of bitches."[1]

The ensuing period brought a new swing to the left in Bolivian politics, with intensified labor and student radicalism and the eventual reawakening of peasant activism. The chameleon of Bolivian nationalism changed shades again, taking on the olive-green coloration of a new populist military regime, only to give way to a new and brutal right-wing junta. Political patterns formed in the 1952 period reemerged as the Trotskyist movement generated ideological and political alliances with the central leadership of Bolivian labor.

A New Period of Polarization

The death of Barrientos set off a power struggle with far-reaching consequences. His vice president took office, only to be ousted in September 1969 by General Alfredo Ovando. Influenced by the nationalist military "revolution" that had begun in Peru the previous year, Ovando shifted government discourse leftward. At the same time, officers who played central roles in tracking down Che Guevara's guerrillas remained prominent in the military hierarchy.

Ovando brought left-leaning civilian intellectuals into his cabinet, most importantly Marcelo Quiroga Santa Cruz as Oil and Mining Minister. Proclaiming the need to "assure the nation's sovereignty on the basis of its sources of production," it proposed to nationalize Gulf Oil, recalling measures taken by the "military socialists" of the 1930s. On October 17, army units seized Gulf Oil properties. Ovando signed a nationalization decree but announced the company would be compensated, provoking demonstrations and protest statements from labor and leftist sectors.

The Lechinista leadership of the COB emerged from illegality and called on "workers, peasants, professionals, clergymen and forward-looking officers" to establish an "anti-imperialist united front."[2] In late 1969, the La Paz departmental labor federation (COD) held its first conference since the Barrientos coup. Key demands included rehiring miners fired for union activity, Lechín's return from exile, and expulsion from Bolivia of the Inter-American Regional Labor Organization (ORIT), notorious for its close ties to U.S. intelligence agencies. Activists, including *porista* mine workers, fought to reopen union halls closed after the 1964 coup.

In January 1970, as controversy continued over the terms of Gulf's nationalization, General Juan José Torres, the new armed forces commander, gave a speech at the La Paz university (UMSA). In the absence of a bourgeoisie or proletariat strong enough to "defend the country from imperialist exploitation," he declared, this task fell to the armed forces, which would need to take "social measures, participating in the civilian advance of nationalism, with the exclusion of the international right and left." Revolutionary nationalism, he later avowed, was "the only way to stop communism."[3]

Guillermo Lora's POR declared that the Gulf nationalization, "despite its limitations and bourgeois modality, is positive but insufficient . . . opening the door for the masses, politically led by the proletariat and certainly not the military government, to actually expel imperialism and carry out national liberation, which will lead to posing socialist tasks." Lora denounced the POR-Combate for claiming the measure was a response to an "imminent popular insurrection" and calling for a "great mass front" under the leadership of the ELN, a group Lora now called an expression of middle-class students' "desperation."[4]

Ovando's nationalization received unqualified support from the journalists' union and its new, widely read newspaper, *Prensa*, which was backed by Oil Minister Quiroga. The union's new president was Andrés Soliz Rada (later Evo Morales's first Energy Minister), theoretician of the Grupo Octubre. Octubre's roots went back to the 1940s, when some

Argentine Trotskyists argued that their Bolivian comrades should be more supportive of nationalist leaders. Octubre saw Ovando as leading a "left wing" of the military, and its "theses" were passed by a national congress of newspaper workers. The "Posadista" POR-T, believing that nationalist regimes were swept along in an unstoppable dynamic of revolution, also supported government measures, arguing that "nationalism had to be understood, you couldn't just say nothing was going on," as a former member put it.[5]

In March 1970, Trotskyists played a central role in forging a new generation of activists when students launched the "University Revolution" at Bolivia's foremost institution of higher education, UMSA in La Paz. The protest were led by a "troika" of a Maoist and two Trotskyists, one of whom was Alfonso Velarde, today the head of UMSA's Physics Department and one of the POR's most effective spokesmen. Velarde said the University Revolution reflected "a strong political consciousness among students, who identified with struggles like those carried out by the miners." Students in each faculty *"desconocieron* [threw out] the deans and administration, and created a Revolutionary Student Committee which took control of the university." Each department sent delegates, who chose the troika. They also threw out professors who had collaborated with the Barrientos dictatorship.[6] The first administrator to be ousted was Law School Dean Alipio Valencia, who as "Comrade Keswar" had been a founder of the POR thirty-five years earlier.

The University Revolution led to the formation of the POR-Masas youth group, URUS. The letters stood for Revolutionary Union of Socialist University Students but had a special resonance: the Urus were one of the altiplano's principal indigenous peoples at the time of the Spanish Conquest. URUS became one of the most active student organizations at UMSA and university campuses in Cochabamba, Sucre, and elsewhere. Many of Bolivia's most prominent intellectuals passed through its ranks.

The new political situation also made it possible for the FSTMB to hold a congress at Siglo XX, seeking to recapture ground lost since the Barrientos coup. Scoring a victory before the congress when the local union at Siglo XX adopted their theses, Lora's followers formed a new bloc with the Communist Party (PCB). The opposing bloc centered on Lechín's PRIN, the Maoist PCML, and the Revolutionary Christian Democratic Party (PDCR, a new guerrilla-influenced group). A commission was formed to work out a document on FSTMB strategy, combining slices from the PCB's thesis with parts from the POR-inspired Siglo XX text. In addition to Lechín, the FSTMB elected its own leadership troika: one independent, PCB spokesman Simón Reyes, and the POR-Masas's "Filipo" Escóbar, now the Trotskyist movement's most prominent labor leader. For its part, the POR-Combate called on the congress to "rebuild armed miners' detachments and valiantly declare fighting solidarity with those who, through guerrilla warfare, are fighting for Bolivia's national and social liberation."[7]

Labor and student radicalization generated a reaction within the business community and the military. The newly formed Bolivian Private Enterprise Confederation (CEPB) opposed the Gulf nationalization, as did civic leaders in Santa Cruz, the eastern department (province) that had received an 11 percent royalty on Gulf revenues.[8] Responding to pressure, Ovando made a right turn in March 1970, firing Oil Minister Quiroga and relieving Torres of his command due to the tone of his speeches.

Political polarization sharpened in May when the COB held its Fourth Congress, chaired by Lechín. Activists considered the gathering an ideological watershed because it adopted a new programmatic text known as the "Socialist Theses of the COB." A product of the bloc between Lora's POR and the pro-Moscow PCB, it was an odd mélange of concepts derived from Trotsky's permanent revolution and the Stalinist theory of two-stage revolution. Point four stated: "To reach socialism it is necessary, beforehand, to unite all revolutionary and anti-imperialist forces. . . . The anti-imperialist popular front is the alliance of workers, peasants and the urban masses . . . within [which] all social and political currents converge that are pushing for a basic change in Bolivia's situation. . . . The expulsion of imperialism and the solution of the remaining national and democratic tasks will make the socialist revolution possible."[9] Prefiguring Bolivian Trotskyists' dilemmas in the ensuing period, an unmistakable intention poked out from the theses' verbiage: accommodate activists eager to reassert labor's power, but leave room for alliances with nationalist forces in a new version of the COB's outlook during the National Revolution.

In July 1970, having gained significant support among students, the ELN attempted to establish a new *foco*. Approximately seventy-five ELN members headed to Teoponte, near La Paz, where they blew up a gold-panning plant. Among them were Paz Estenssoro's nephew Néstor Paz Zamora (whose brother Jaime became president in 1989) and folk singer Benjo Cruz, who said he had "exchanged my guitar for a rifle."[10] The army wiped out all but half a dozen of the would-be guerrillas in September, dealing another devastating defeat to the Guevarist strategy hailed by the POR-Combate, among others. Student demonstrations rocked La Paz in protest against the young idealists' massacre.

Torres Comes to Power

In October tensions within the armed forces exploded in a round of coups and countercoups. Hard-line officers, the right wing of the MNR, and the Falange backed a power bid by General Rogelio Miranda. Ovando's son-in-law Hugo Banzer, a strident anti-communist, joined the conspiracy. Ovando refused to relinquish his post, but on October 6 power was turned over to a military triumvirate. That evening, General J. J. Torres, backed by Major Rubén Sánchez, proclaimed that he would take power. Lechín's PRIN, the PCB, a sector of the MNR, and Lora's POR issued a "Pronunciamiento of the People's Parties" calling for a "popular anti-imperialist government."[11]

What tipped the balance in Torres's favor was the general strike launched on October 7. "There were huge demonstrations supporting Torres," remembers POR-Masas activist Alfonso Márquez, "but the POR said Torres serves the bourgeoisie. We were able to turn this movement into an organization where the workers would discuss the fate of the country: the Comando Político [Political Command], which later convoked the People's Assembly."[12] The Comando, in which Guillermo Lora was a central figure, had been established by the COB, its constituent unions, left parties, and a section of the MNR shortly before Torres took over.

Torres invited the Comando Político to name a third of his cabinet, a proposal then pushed up to half the seats. The offer was hotly debated within the Comando, with the PCB and others urging that it be accepted. Lora, in a maneuver drawn from the POR's approach to worker ministers of the past, urged the Comando to set conditions: for example, it should be able to recall the ministers and appoint "political commissars" to accompany them. When the Comando agreed, the government withdrew the offer.[13]

While Torres sought labor support as one pillar for his regime, another was the "institutionality" of the armed forces. Torres appointed General Luis Reque Terán—a leader of the CIA-supervised counterinsurgency against Che Guevara—as overall commander of the armed forces, promised that officers involved in recent coup attempts would be assigned posts "in accordance with their rank," and proclaimed: "We have succeeded in maintaining the unity of the Armed Forces." "Tomorrow," POR-Combate supporters warned, "this same Bolivian army, trained in the anti-insurrection and anti-guerrilla school, will attack the workers, whether Torres or someone else is in power."[14]

Expressing a different conception of the relation between the army and the working class, the Comando Político presented a list of demands signed by many of the key figures from 1952, together with the labor leadership who had emerged in the 1960s: COB head Lechín; FSTMB leaders Víctor López, Simón Reyes, and Filemón Escóbar; Hernán Siles and Ñuflo Chávez for a sector of the MNR; Edwin Möller for Lechín's PRIN; PCB and Maoist leaders; Lora for the POR-Masas; even ex-comrade Keswar for the bar association. This "Mandate of the Popular Forces" included amnesty for political prisoners, restoring workers' wages, and respecting university autonomy. The eighth point called for "workers' and people's militias to defend, together with the patriotic Armed Forces, the rights and interests of the Nation." Another Comando statement referred to "our militant support to the government of General Torres" against "fascist forces."[15]

Once in office, Torres carried out a balancing act between social sectors whose antagonisms were breaking out after years of rightist rule. In his first public appearance as president, he was booed by leftist workers who demanded he swear loyalty to the people. Seeking support from the miners, he restored their pay to 1965 levels and toured the mines, where "euphoria" greeted his "noble gesture," according to Comibol's magazine. Filemón Escóbar, now FSTMB treasurer, explained the decree to union assemblies at Catavi and Siglo XX. In a separate Siglo XX event, Torres paid homage to the victims of the Night of San Juan massacre, promising that "they will be the last martyrs." Climbing Potosi's Cerro Rico, he "made a solemn oath to defend the nation's patrimony, freedom [and] the well-being of the working class of the mines." The "imperative of the hour," Comibol stressed, was now "responsible and disciplined labor."[16]

Despite his vow that there would be no more martyred workers, Torres left Hugo Banzer in charge of the Military College. On January 11, 1971, Banzer attempted a new military coup. In response, miners struck and marched on La Paz. "Armed with Mauser rifles and dynamite, the miners entered the city," writes Escóbar. "The *guardatojo* (miner's helmet), gumboots, rifle and dynamite symbolized the only real opposition" to the coup. Workers rallied in the Plaza Murillo outside the presidential palace, demanding "Arms, arms to smash the military fascists! They asked that the whole military high command be purged. The walls resounded with chants of *Workers to power!*"[17]

Throughout the following period, the demand would be repeated. Julio García, a POR-Masas member who had worked closely with César Lora, was general secretary of the Potosí miners' union and leader of the region's labor federation (COD). He remembers a subsequent march to the presidential palace in 1971: "It was a huge demonstration. People were asking for weapons. They chanted, '*Arms, arms, give us arms!*'" Instead, Torres insisted, the people must have confidence in the army; it would defend them. In March, another putsch broke out in Santa Cruz. Arrested for his involvement, Falange leader Mario Gutiérrez was, like Banzer before him, set free.[18]

At the university, young people continued to pour through the breaches that had opened in the old structures of repression. Edgardo Herbas was a UMSA student won to URUS in the University Revolution. Under his leadership, students took over the offices of the U.S.-sponsored Centro Boliviano Americano. The symbolic but high-profile blow against North American influence was an unforgettable experience for young Trotskyists.[19]

As the Lora POR's youth arm, URUS echoed the party's call for the workers to take power and its polemics against the PCB and others for giving "critical support" to the government, a position Masas denounced as "Menshevism." Nonetheless, Lora believed "nationalists in epaulettes" could sometimes be allies of the working class. "At that time," he later noted, "the idea was widespread—and shared even by us Marxists—that the military group running the government would distribute arms, seeing that only by supporting themselves on the masses and giving them adequate fire-power would they be able, at least, to neutralize the right wing of the military."[20]

Hugo González's POR was more categorical. A month after Torres took power, it warned: "Only opportunists desperately eager to sell out could put the label 'revolutionary' on the acrobatics the military caste engages in, precisely to head off the advance of real revolution. However progressive or liberal the bourgeois army may appear at certain times, it is strictly the antithesis of revolution." The POR-Combate insisted that "the revolutionary process . . . has its fullest expression in armed struggle and guerrilla warfare," calling Lora's rejection of this strategy a symptom of illusions in an ephemeral bourgeois democracy. The González group's position was shared by USec leaders like Livio Maitan, who declared: "at the present time the International will be built around Bolivia," through a "breakthrough" based on guerrilla warfare.[21]

May Day 1971 manifested the continuing radicalization of many labor and student sectors (see figure 6.1). When Torres and government officials sought to lead off the march, Masas reported, some contingents ostentatiously separated themselves from them. Posters of César Lora and Isaac Camacho were prominent, together with "enormous portraits of Leon Trotsky."[22] In late May, student groups organized an "anti-imperialist week." As demands grew for action against U.S. agencies, Torres said he would expel the Peace Corps, fueling disquiet on the right, already up in arms against the left, which it called the Zafra Roja (Red Harvest).

Figure 6.1 May Day, 1971. POR-Masas contingent. (Courtesy of Biblioteca y Archivo Histórico del Congreso)

The People's Assembly

For Bolivian Trotskyism, the most far-reaching decision of May 1971 was the announcement that an Asamblea Popular (People's Assembly) would be convoked in June. This was especially important to Lora's POR-Masas, which made the Asamblea Popular a cornerstone of its strategy from 1971 through the present.

The decision to establish the Asamblea had been made after the failed January coup. A commission was set up to consider the issue, with representatives from the COB, union federations, MNR, PRIN, POR-Masas, PCB, Maoist PCML, and guerrilla-oriented PDCR. Filemón Escóbar referred to the assembly as a "people's parliament," while complaining that a boycott by the MNR and PRIN was delaying its convocation. The MNR was subsequently expelled from the Comando Político for opposing the "program and spirit of the anti-imperialist front," in Lora's words. His POR supported the expulsion, although it had previously "fought . . . to prevent the Comando from excluding the MNR," so rank-and-file MNR members could be won over. Lora argued that this had borne fruit, as "a leftist working-class tendency called the Labor Comando" had formed inside the MNR.[23]

On May Day, by arrangement with the COB, the government provided the Legislative Palace for a ceremony marking the foundation of the Asamblea Popular, chaired by Lechín, factory and teachers' union leaders, and two student representatives. Sixty percent of the assembly's 220 delegates would be representatives of working-class organizations. Middle-class and peasant groups would contribute 30 percent, political parties the remainder.[24] An Argentine daily predicted the Asamblea would be "a kind of 'little soviet,'" warning: "Sooner or later, this body can become a sword of Damocles over President Torres." However, "later" seemed to be the assembly's watchword, as it decided to reconvene almost two months afterward, on the anniversary of the San Juan massacre.[25]

The POR-Masas hailed the assembly as an "anti-imperialist front with soviet features" (i.e., resembling the workers' councils of the Russian Revolution), "an organ of power of the masses and the working class" that would "watch over the government's activities" but function "outside the existing juridical order" on the basis of "the masses' direct action." Instead of "wear[ing] itself out with speeches," the assembly would "carry out its decisions, thereby becoming the only authority for the masses."[26]

The POR-Combate was more skeptical. It initially characterized the Asamblea as "hardly more than a kind of national parliament." Delegates should be elected, "not hand-picked by the current bureaucratized leaderships." (Participants say delegates were elected by workers' meetings in Potosí and some other places, but this was the exception.) The POR-Combate's approach was influenced by the ELN, which declared that "Che's army, the People's army, will remain vigilant" but would support the Asamblea only if it adopted the perspective of armed struggle.[27]

Another Bolivian Trotskyist tendency reactivated in the new political climate: the Liga Socialista Revolucionaria (LSR) led by Chaco War veteran Carlos Salazar, a sculptor, historian, and able polemicist who had worked at the Warisata indigenous school. The LSR was first formed in 1949 when the left wing of Marof's PSOB "expelled" the leftist caudillo turned government adviser, then decided to found a new group with an untainted name. Its most prominent representative in the labor movement was the widely regarded factory workers' leader Constantino Camacho.[28]

The LSR opposed the idea that a bourgeois-democratic revolution was on the agenda, criticizing the Pulacayo Thesis for putting forward this concept. "The historical elimination of the bourgeois-democratic revolution imposes, as an immediate objective for all peoples, the realization of the socialist revolution, within which the pending bourgeois tasks will be converted into socialist tasks," it proclaimed. It also criticized the idea that the COB could become an effective instrument for the emancipation of the working class. During the Asamblea Popular period, the LSR appealed to the working class to follow a more revolutionary policy, saluting the assembly's formation but asking if it would be "a revolutionary or a bureaucratic organization," while complaining that legalistic arguments had been used to block the group from joining the assembly. Despite these efforts, the LSR "was unable to survive the blows inflicted by the military dictatorship installed in 1971."[29]

Salazar later wrote that the COB's "most original idea yet" was to ask that the government give permission "to set up the self-styled Workers' Parliament and issue a Supreme Decree legalizing its existence." Since the Comando Político had ousted the MNR, the latter "did not have official representation as a party, but its trade-union representation remained intact." As a result, the MNR "had a majority in the Asamblea, and no revolutionary action could be expected from such a composition."[30]

Tragedy of a Coup Foretold

When the Asamblea Popular reconvened on June 21, one of the first items on the agenda was its own composition. It decided to admit the Movimiento de la Izquierda Revolucionaria (MIR), just formed by Revolutionary Christian Democrats and other groups, as well as Marcelo Quiroga's new Partido Socialista (PS). The biggest bloc of labor delegates came from the MNR's Comando Laboral. The number of peasant delegates was the subject of sharp debates.

Acutely aware that right-wing officers had no intention of abandoning plans to seize power, the delegates decided to pass a motion. Noting that "the right wing is not going to stop conspiring," the assembly's Resolution No. 1 vowed: "in the event of a coup, the Asamblea Popular, as the expression of workers' power, will take over political and military leadership of the masses." The workers' "first response" to a coup would be "a general strike and the immediate occupation of workplaces."[31]

As leader of the Potosí miners, Julio García attended "all the sessions" of the Asamblea Popular. Asked what preparations were made against a coup, he said: "No, they decided that in September they would discuss the 'military question,' the arming of the masses. The coup came in August because the [right wing] feared this."[32] There was no real preparation, agree Daniel Campos, Edgardo Herbas, Jorge Echazú, and others who soon found themselves fighting desperate battles on the hills of La Paz.

"The right is preparing" a "night of the long knives," warned Salazar's LSR two months before the final *golpe* (coup). "They are going to attempt a definitive *golpe* against the entire Bolivian left. The People's Assembly must immediately . . . orient the workers and respond to the terror of the right." Based on secret police files, "which were never destroyed," lists had been drawn up of "thousands of revolutionaries to be liquidated at one stroke, as in Indonesia, Guatemala and Iran. . . . The extermination will be carried out . . . unless the revolutionary organizations stop it in time. We appeal to the People's Assembly: immediately adopt the necessary measures of defense against this deadly threat."[33]

But *later* was the assembly's watchword: the matter would be discussed sometime in September. In reality, Lechín relied on Torres's assurances that the army would remain loyal. Eventually, the left believed, he would even arm the people. The Asamblea met ten more times from June 23 to July 2. Lechín was elected chairman with the support of some union delegates, the Maoists, pro-guerrilla delegates, and those from his own "revolutionary nationalist" party, the PRIN. The POR-Masas, PCB, and other union delegates supported the opposing candidate, mine unionist Víctor López. Sessions debated the activities of a peasant group in Tarija, the need for "revolutionary tribunals" (given the courts' seeming inability to punish those responsible for crimes like the San Juan Massacre and the murder of Isaac Camacho), and other subjects. The bulk of the time went to proposals for "workers' comanagement" of Comibol and a "workers' university."[34]

Lora wrote extensively to support the focus on these issues, arguing that if the miners achieved majority representation in Comibol's administration, this would be a step toward workers taking power in the country as a whole. The POR leader defended this viewpoint against what he called the ultra-left group, which saw it as a return to MNR-style "cogovernment" and a distraction from a more direct struggle for power.

The last session of the Asamblea, on July 2, discussed several issues, including the importance of restoring the Miguel Alandia murals that Barrientos had destroyed. There was also some general talk about the need for popular militias. In mid-June, the COB had called on unions to organize workers' militias, but this remained at the level of intentions. Dutch journalist Jeroen Strengers notes that "the People's Assembly came to the conclusion that it still did not have concrete possibilities of putting this plan into effect."[35]

Remarkably, the assembly decided to adjourn for more than two months, then closed with the national anthem. The question of organizing armed militias was "referred to a commission." The next session was scheduled for September 7. Several participants said this was because delegates were running out of money and needed to return to their home areas for consultations. Sucre POR-Masas leader Eduardo Mendizábal remembers: "They all left, went home and thought the building would wait there for two months. They left nothing done, *pues*. But the right wing was not asleep." Asked how such a decision could have been made, he answered: "Maybe they were tired? I know that sounds absurd."[36]

Indeed, the right wing was not inclined to wait. It had powerful friends and was energetically encouraged by Brazilian and Argentine colleagues, while the Nixon administration promoted plots against the Allende government on the other side of the Andes. Banzer's followers in the armed forces joined with the Falange and MNR (now led by Paz Estenssoro) to prepare a coup. Supplementing their forces, they contracted gangs of young toughs called the *marqueses*. It was a *golpe anunciado*—a coup foretold—intensively prepared at least since early April. By late July, a *Masas* headline asked not *if* but "when is the coup going to happen?"[37]

They Fought at Laikacota

It began on August 19–20 in the rightist stronghold of Santa Cruz. Still, Lechín declared the rising would not spread because the army would remain loyal to Torres. When Banzer's forces took Cochabamba, the COB leader and other spokesmen for the recessed Asamblea Popular said the rightists would be stopped before they could reach Oruro. "When Oruro was taken, they said the [rightists] would not reach La Paz; when the insurgents reached the outskirts of the capital, Lechín said the garrison would remain loyal. Told that the Bolívar Regiment was marching on the city, he did not believe it."[38]

On August 20, up to one hundred thousand people gathered outside the Presidential Palace shouting at Torres and Lechín: "¡Armas, armas!" But "Torres said he was an officer of honor and could not permit a bloodbath of the people," Julio García remembers. "He did not want to give out arms." Lacking weapons to defend themselves, the miners of Potosí turned around and went home.[39]

Representatives of the Torres regime used Radio Illimani to call on the miners of Oruro to join loyal army units in "Operation Centipede—Flying Eagle," a battle to retake the historic mining center, repeating this call even as the military units went over to the coup (see figure 6.2). The miners marched to fight and were massacred. In La Paz, Salazar writes, resistance began to be organized only after local regiments revolted against Torres and

Figure 6.2 Miners mobilize against the Banzer coup. (Courtesy of Biblioteca y Archivo Histórico del Congreso)

the air force started bombing on August 21. "But now the Bolívar Regiment is advancing through El Alto, now it is no longer possible to build barricades or make Molotov cocktails to slow the tanks."[40]

There were "more than five thousand combatants, but 90 percent had no weapons," Hugo González reported after the coup. "At the last minute" civilians seized "1,300 old Mauser rifles from the Chaco War. Some worked, others didn't." Resistance was "completely disorganized, the Asamblea had done absolutely nothing to prepare," recalls Maoist activist Jorge Echazú. He was part of the group that attacked the Armory and seized the rifles. "The soldiers there surrendered, no problem. But the rifles were obsolete." Nonetheless, "long lines of volunteers" formed to get them, Salazar writes. Soon even these old guns ran out. Ammunition was so scarce that "every worker was given one or two bullets." Many could only stand by watching. Meanwhile, peasant leaders from Norte Potosí said eight thousand armed peasants were "waiting for instructions from the government as to where they should march in order to smash the coup."[41]

Students and factory workers searched for ways to resist. Receiving no direction whatsoever from their leaders, young Trotskyists like POR-Masas members Daniel Campos and Edgardo Herbas joined crowds clamoring for arms. Resistance to the coup was concentrating at the foot of Laikacota Hill, where civilians hoped to dislodge a pro-Banzer army unit that had seized this point overlooking the city. "We were the *elementos aguerridos,*" the hard core, says Alfonso Márquez; "we went to fight at Laikacota." He accompanied twenty or more factory workers, and they found Lechín and some MIR leaders at the foot of the hill.[42]

The crowd advanced up the hill, facing withering fire. Herbas remembers friends and comrades falling dead around him. Determined to dislodge the hostile troops, the young activists kept firing and, finally, to their surprise, succeeded in storming the army position. The frightened soldiers surrendered and were told to run away. "We *poristas* were the first to take Laikacota," recalls FSTMB activist Grover Alejandro. "Alfonso Márquez and I got some machine guns" when the troops surrendered.[43]

"Lechín had installed himself in a little soda stand. He told us the Air Force would provide back-up. We had to bring people down, because the planes were supposed to bomb the Army," recalls Echazú. Planes began flying overhead, but it was the young revolutionaries who were the targets of their strafing—the air force was supporting the coup. Echazú went to tell Lechín. "God damn it, they promised to support us," the COB leader exclaimed.[44] The hope that Torres would distribute weapons to the masses was a fatal illusion (see figure 6.3).

Just as false were the promises that the military would "defend the people." In July, General Reque Terán had categorically denied that officers were conspiring for a new coup d'état.[45] On August 20, he visited Torres to pledge his loyalty, only to join the mutiny the following day. Torres ordered him arrested, but he was then released. Reque resurfaced to command pro-Banzer troops in downtown La Paz, then became an important member of the new junta.

After the pro-Banzer Castrillo regiment retreated at Laikacota, the Tarapacá regiment—built up to bolster the Torres regime—joined the rightist coup. Its tanks took half an hour to arrive in downtown La Paz. When these World War II relics reached the presidential palace, Torres was gone, having left a lieutenant and six soldiers behind.[46]

René Poppe was in La Paz on August 21. He was famous for the "Miners' Stories" he published after "Filipo" Escóbar got him a job at Siglo XX. On the day of the coup, he was accompanying his friend Guillermo Lora on a walking tour around the city's combat zones. At one point, Poppe recounts, a bullet hit the wall right above Lora's head. "Plaster," remarked the POR leader, brushing dust out of his hair. Poppe says he walked with Lora for many hours but did not see him give orientation or instructions to any of his party's members. One woman activist claims Lora carried a brief-case on August 21, from which he carefully distributed five bullets each to various cadres—all of a different caliber.[47]

"We had been working very openly, thinking that whatever happened, we were not afraid of death, we had to do the work," remembers retired miner and POR-Masas supporter Pastor Peláez. "But the right is always stronger than us, really, because it has money and money talks. So they were able to frustrate the advance of the working class." Leftists and radical unionists "believed so much in our own power that we thought: with this mass upsurge they can't touch us," said Grover Alejandro.[48]

Activists of the González Moscoso POR also did their best to resist the coup. However, a report by United Secretariat supporters noted that "in spite of their prediction of the coup, it caught them totally unprepared." Among those who died was Central Committee member Tomás Chambi, reportedly killed while leading a column of poor peasants to fight the mili-tary takeover. Others escaped death. A former member recalled that she and another woman comrade tried to get away in a jeep belonging to the party. They found a peasant sitting in the vehicle, which contained a large machine gun the party had acquired. "I said, 'This is our jeep.' He said, 'No, it's mine.' We drove off with him still in it" and were able to avoid arrest.[49]

As evening drew near, several young Trotskyists decided to try to seize a building housing American Marines, but they were cut off by a column of Falangists. Wounded, Daniel Campos fell prisoner, the beginning of a years'-long inferno of imprisonment, torture, and exile.[50]

The late 1960s and early 1970s provided spectacular examples of Bolivia's institutional fragility, as one faction after another seized and then lost the presidency. The promises of nationalism were submitted to new tests as the left emerged from underground and aligned with populist military officers. Under the Torres regime, radical activists were swept to the fore in a new high tide of labor influence that brought new hopes after the defeats of the Barrientos years.

Bolivian Trotskyists reconfigured their alliances. Working with the pro-Moscow Communist Party, they returned to their role of generating ideology for the COB labor federation, in which Juan Lechín resumed his historic role. Lora's POR could truthfully call the People's Assembly its own, legitimate child.

a)

b)

Figure 6.3 21 August 1971. (*a*) Workers and (*b*) students fighting coup at Laikacota. (Courtesy of Museo de la Revolución) (*c*) Air force attacks civilians resisting coup, Laikacota. (Courtesy of Museo de la Revolución) (*d*) Manifesto of the Revolutionary Anti-Imperialist Front. (Courtesy of Biblioteca y Archivo Histórico del Congreso)

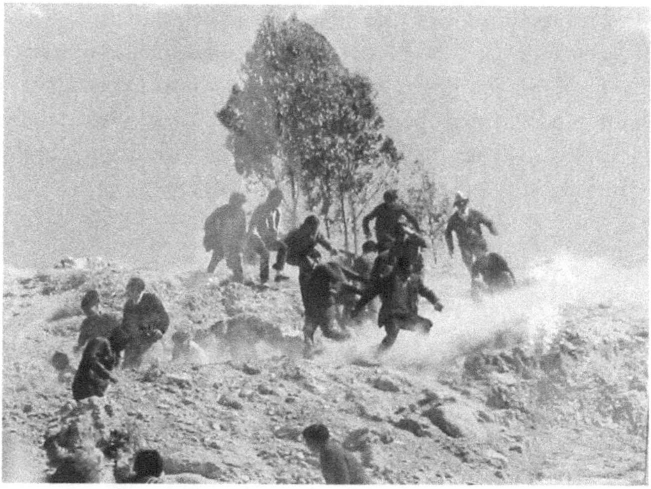

c)

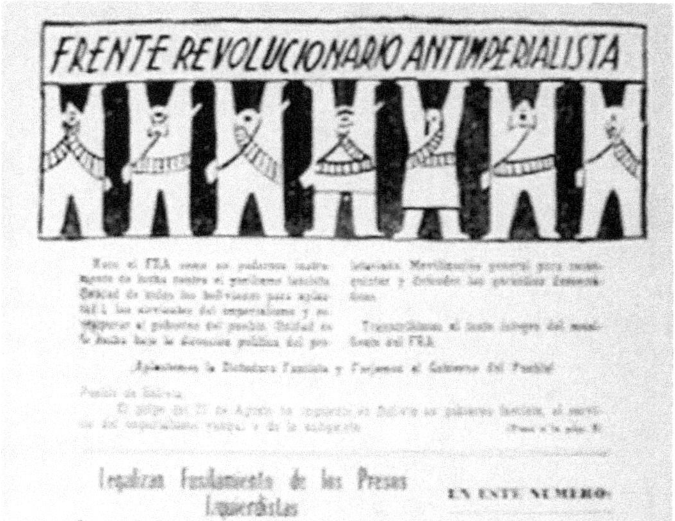

FRENTE REVOLUCIONARIO ANTIMPERIALISTA

Legalizan Fusilamiento de los Presos Izquierdistas

EN ESTE NUMERO

MASAS

PARTIDO OBRERO REVOLUCIONARIO

d)

Figure 6.3 (*Continued*)

So much more bitter was the new defeat dealt them by traditional enemies of labor and the left. Hopes that left-nationalist military officers would defend the working people, or arm them to defend themselves, proved suicidal. In the brief opening of 1969–71, Trotskyists had hoped to lead new victories. Instead, they were confronted with desperate defensive battles for the very survival of the workers' movement.

From Banzer to Evo

The Banzer coup placed power in the hands of a "Frente Popular Nacionalista" of right-wing officers, the Falange, and the MNR's Paz Estenssoro wing. In 1974, Banzer consolidated his power in an *autogolpe* ("self-coup").

"Under Banzer, we had to work clandestinely," says Pastor Peláez of Siglo XX. "We organized meetings at night outside town, in the Llallagua cemetery. Carrying out underground work, working at night, painting slogans on the wall, distributing pamphlets and leaflets—these were things we already knew how to do."[1] For eleven long years after the 1971 coup, Bolivian Trotskyists had to work underground. Only after new upheavals would Bolivia reemerge from dictatorship in the 1980s. The men and women of 1952 would then return, as the old MNR alliance bifurcated between popular-frontist "left" and "neoliberal" right. The president who had nationalized the mines, Víctor Paz Estenssoro, would come back to privatize them. The resulting social and political reconfiguration would then pave the way for a new indigenist movement and the presidency of Evo Morales.

The Revolutionary Anti-Imperialist Front

After Banzer's August 1971 coup, Lora's POR formed a political front to unite left parties with deposed nationalist president Torres and other political figures. Lora and other leaders took refuge in Allende's Chile, later joined by young activists like Campos and Herbas. They resumed publication of *Masas* and organized networks to get it back to Bolivia.[2]

Immediately after the coup, *Masas* published a declaration by military "chiefs, officers, junior officers, non-coms and soldiers." Titled "We Are with the People" and signed by Torres, Major Rubén Sánchez, and others, it announced: "We have joined the Revolutionary Anti-imperialist Front (FRA), a great popular alliance of all Bolivia's revolutionary sectors." "For our people, for our institutions, we must do our duty as Bolivians," it stated, calling on members of the armed forces and police to join in forging "a Sovereign and Free Fatherland."[3]

Addressed to "Patriots," the FRA Manifesto urged "fighting unity of all revolutionary, democratic and progressive forces" against the "fascist" Banzer regime, "to begin the great battle in conditions that offer a real perspective of popular, national power." This did not involve any one "sector of the exploited people, any class, institution or party alone"; thus "any form of sectarianism is counterrevolutionary." Under the "hegemony of the proletariat," the alliance sought joint struggle with "the revolutionaries of the Armed Forces and Police," for a "people's government." The appeal was signed by General Juan José Torres González, ex-President of Bolivia, and the "Revolutionary Armed Forces," a grouping led by Torres and Sánchez, together with the POR, PCB, Maoists, MIR, ELN, Lechín's PRIN, and others.[4]

Lora's POR insisted the FRA must "act as a unitary body on all fronts of social life" and "present joint slates in every kind of electoral event." The FRA soon broke into its component parts, but Lora's POR made the concept a key part of its program, repeatedly calling for the front's revival in subsequent decades. Lora stressed that although it included bourgeois nationalist groups, the FRA was "not a one-time front, but one for seizing power and building socialism." As for Torres's participation, "at a certain point, the nationalists in epaulettes become allies of the working class rather than its sworn enemies."[5]

News of the FRA hit the international Trotskyist movement like a bombshell. The explicit alliance with Torres was particularly controversial. Lora heatedly defended the FRA against critics who noted its likeness to the "popular front" advocated by Stalinist parties. The dispute divided the "International Committee of the Fourth International," whose French section, led by Pierre Lambert, took the POR's side against the British group of Gerry Healy.

The POR-Combate also joined the FRA. After public criticism from the United Secretariat, it concluded that it was an "error" to sign the FRA manifesto—"an unclear document that . . . leaves the impression that national unity-type governments are admissible"—without "simultaneously publishing our criticisms." The González group would remain in the FRA as a "tactical" measure while "reiterating its strategy of armed struggle and revolutionary war." From Paris, USec leaders joined in reaffirming the guerrilla strategy, claiming five days after Torres's fall: "already the revolutionary vanguard, especially our comrades of the POR (Bolivian section of the Fourth International), the ELN . . . and others, are continuing the struggle by organizing guerrilla war."[6]

Differences on the Torres period lay behind mine leader Filemón Escóbar's split from the POR-Masas, as he felt both the Lora and González groups had been ultra-leftist in their approach to the deposed regime. The popular student leader Víctor Sosa and some other young activists broke from Lora, eventually merging with the González POR, but "Filipo" formed his own organization, eventually called Vanguardia Obrera. Distancing himself from Trotskyism, he moved toward the indigenist political outlook known as Katarismo (after the 1781 Tupac Katari revolt). Cirilo Jiménez and other "remaining heirs of Trotskyism in Siglo XX," as Felipe Vásquez called them, established their own POR-De Pie (roughly, POR-Stand Up), whose differences with Lora focused largely on organizational issues. These splits significantly diminished POR-Masas's presence in the labor movement.[7]

On the international plane, the POR-Combate maintained its USec affiliation. Amadeo Vargas's POR-T represented the Posadas current, winning some followers at the La Paz university in the late 1970s.[8] Lora's POR aligned with Pierre Lambert's international tendency, later forming a short-lived international group of its own with an Argentine organization called Política Obrera.

The Banzer years were a period of dangerous, painstaking work to rebuild structures smashed by the dictatorship. In the mines, Trotskyist activists built "rank-and-file committees" (comités de base) to resist the government-appointed "intervenors" who took over the unions. POR miners usually worked with members of the PCB and other left groups to organize the comités, which tried to defend living standards and restore some measure of collective bargaining. The courage of Trotskyist militants who came forward to represent the embattled miners drew admiration even from adversaries on the left.

Edgar "Huracán" Ramírez was a worker at Potosí's Unificada mine and a long-time PCB leader; he eventually became general secretary of the COB. Now director of the Comibol archives in El Alto, he digs a 1975 photo out of a file. It shows the "heroic action" of a man who was "my ideological opponent," he explains. Accompanied by the press and diplomats from neighboring countries, Banzer had decided to "repeat" Simón Bolívar's triumphal visit to the Cerro Rico of Potosí. The comité de base, made up of four members each from the POR-Masas and the PCB, decided someone had to speak out in the name of the banned miners' union. "We drew straws," and POR-Masas member Grover Alejandro got the job of "greeting"

Figure 7.1 Cerro Rico, Potosí, 1975. Grover Alejandro presents workers'
demands to Banzer. (Courtesy of Archivo de Comibol)

the dictator with a speech of denunciation. The photo shows him presenting the miners' demands (see figure 7.1). The assignment was tremendously
dangerous, but Grover "agreed to go into the lion's den."[9]

Grover Alejandro remembers what he said: "I am here to denounce
to the whole world that we miners make less than sixty dollars a month,
that we eat only rice and noodles, that we live under tyranny, that Bolívar's
dream has been betrayed, as we are divided into little *republiquetas*. And here
a little dictator is trying to emulate the greatness of Bolívar." Responding
to Banzer's offer of a large check to "buy off" union leaders, he said: "That
money is stained with workers' blood!" As police agents closed in, he gave
Banzer the list of demands: "I am handing you this, the cry of rebellion of
the exploited of this country. We will bury your dictatorship!" As soon as he
finished speaking, workers hurried him off: "The comrades took me straight
to *interior mina*. I didn't come out for twenty days, because the repression was
terrible." His speech was reported by "all the miners' radio stations."[10]

POR-Masas activists were among the many facing harsh repression
throughout the Banzer years. In February 1973, police dynamited the
door at the home of Hugo González, who was fortunate not to be there at

the time. Four leaders of his party were imprisoned and tortured.[11] Edgar Ramírez was deported to Chile with POR-Combate member and San José miners' leader Paulino Joaniquina, who "gave me a *pullu*" (llama-wool blanket) because of the terrible cold.[12]

In January 1974, all the Trotskyist tendencies denounced Banzer's "Massacre of the Valley," when the army attacked a village near Cochabamba, killing up to two hundred peasants in a drive to crush protests against government austerity measures. The incident, which church spokesmen called "another My Lai," led to a resurgence of the peasant movement. Although the "Bolivian Indian Party" formed by the strident anti-communist Fausto Reinaga proved ephemeral, new indigenist political currents germinated in this period.[13]

The approaching centennial of the 1879 Pacific War diverted attention from the country's domestic strife. Chile, which won Bolivia's coastal regions in that war, was now embroiled in border disputes with Peru and Argentina. Banzer, who cultivated neighborly relations with Chile's Pinochet, raised the possibility of a "corridor" so Bolivia could regain some kind of outlet to the sea. *Masas* leapt at the chance to attack the dictator as a *vendepatria* (fatherland-seller), declaring: "The people's money paid to educate the generals, whose supposed mission was to regain Antofagasta [from Chile]. . . . Banzer is a demagogue [and] traitor to Bolivian sentiments. . . . He has done his utmost, in the service of Pinochet, to make the outlet to the sea impossible." When Banzer made a deal for Brazil to buy Bolivian gas, *Masas* wrote: "Banzer's Sellouts Anger the Army." The approach dovetailed with Lora's call for "Bolivianizing the Armed Forces" and increasing emphasis on the need to build a "revolutionary tendency" within the army.[14] In subsequent years *Masas* reprinted articles from *Vivo Rojo* (roughly, Red Hot), described as the underground publication of just such a tendency.

Women of the Mines Defy the Dictatorship

Banzer's government ended amidst dramatic developments in which Trotskyist militants played central roles. In mid-1976, miners' strikes swept the country under the leadership of Grover Alejandro and other radicals. After the June 1976 strike at Siglo XX, the junta offered a large cash reward for the capture, "dead or alive," of FSTMB and POR-De Pie activist Cirilo Jiménez. In December 1977, Jiménez issued a leaflet stating: "The executioners . . . who pursue, imprison, torture and exile us, will sooner rather than later pay for their crimes under proletarian justice. . . . Army out of the mines!"[15]

Almost a thousand miners were fired as a result of these strikes. In response, four miners' wives from Siglo XX launched an all-or-nothing struggle. They began a hunger strike to demand rehiring of the fired workers, freedom for political prisoners, the right of exiles to return, and withdrawal of troops from the mine camps. The government found itself unable to repress the protest, a display of determination that galvanized Bolivia's working people.

The hunger strike made Pulacayo-born Domitila de Chungara an international figure. Less known but crucial to pushing through the action was POR-Masas militant Aurora Villarroel de Lora.[16] Daughter of a miner fired twice for union activities, she joined the POR as a teenager in 1968 and later married Andrés Lora. Aurora was an active member of the Siglo XX Housewives' Committee. In a firm, animated voice she described how she and three other women traveled to La Paz with their children to begin the hunger strike in December 1977. "We had to decide what to do" in the face of the destitution caused by mass firings. "At a party meeting, Andrés said, 'This is the moment.' Some comrades said 'it's too risky.' But I said no, we need to do this."

> Nelly and Angélica, from Catavi, their husbands had been fired. They were ready to do the hunger strike with us. Our slogan was *todo por el todo*, we will go with our children, we cannot leave them, and we will continue *hasta triunfar*, even if we die. I invited Domitila. [At] assemblies in La Paz, some people got up and said we were intransigent, we were Trotskyists, *locas*, it was adventurist. We said we were going ahead. How could we bring our children into this, the priests asked. . . .
>
> I said it is a sacrifice but *it will win*. . . . I said we would *break the frontiers* and bring the message to the world! "How, who will do this?" they asked. "The POR, the POR," I said.[17]

The women entered the La Paz cathedral and began their fast. Attempts to break the hunger strike by force backfired. As Aurora Villarroel predicted, the women's heroism had a worldwide impact. The desperate tactic, "this discredited political recourse," in Salazar's words, became in this instance a "real means of domestic and international pressure," as the hunger strike grew to include a thousand people, lasting three weeks and touching off mass protests. Banzer denounced it as "a genuine extremist conspiracy" but was obliged to negotiate and finally to agree to the demands, except for withdrawal of troops from the mines.[18]

The upsurge hastened the end of his regime. Trade union freedoms and political amnesty opened the floodgates to left and labor organizations. In elections scheduled by the regime, Hernán Siles Zuazo, now head of the MNR-Izquierda (MNR-Left), ran as head of a new popular front, Unión Democrática y Popular (UDP), which included the pro-Moscow PCB, MIR, indigenist Movimiento Revolucionario Tupac Katari, and other groups. Lora's POR called for casting a blank ballot. The Socialist Party ran Marcelo Quiroga; and Lechín's PRIN, a Maoist group, and others formed the Frente Revolucionario de Izquierda (FRI), whose vice presidential candidate was former hunger striker Domitila de Chungara. The FRI was joined by the POR-Combate, Filemón Escóbar's group, and the "Posadasite" POR-T.

The elections ended in blatant electoral fraud. Citing the threat of international communism, a sector of the armed forces launched a new coup. Over the next two years, five presidents held office and two more elections were held. In the 1979 race, Escóbar's Vanguardia Obrera ran its own slate, as did Quiroga's Socialists. A new group claiming the Trotsky-ist legacy signed on to Quiroga's campaign: the Organización Socialista de los Trabajadores (OST), affiliated with the Latin American current led by Nahuel Moreno, whose slogan for Bolivia continued to be "COB to Power!" The "Morenoites" gained a foothold on the main La Paz university campus, and for a time served as advisers to a new Cochabamba peasant leader named Evo Morales. (Years later, as the nation's president, Morales made former OST leader Pablo Solón Bolivian Ambassador to the United Nations.)

The July 1979 vote yielded no clear winner. Bizarre bedfellows abounded, with Maoists supporting Paz Estenssoro and the remnants of the Stalin-ist PIR joining with the Falange to support Banzer's Acción Democrática Nacionalista. The standoff ended with Walter Guevara, former leader of the MNR's right wing and author of the "Anti-Thesis of Pulacayo," as one-year interim president pending new elections.

In November 1979, a new military coup placed the presidency in the hands of Colonel Alberto Natusch Busch. It was answered by the first general strike in almost a decade. The junta responded by shooting and "disappearing" large numbers of left and labor activists. Faced with wide-spread repudiation of the repression, Congress negotiated the turnover of the interim presidency to a civilian: Lidia Gueiler, a co-founder of Lechín's PRIN, ex-wife of "entrist" leader Edwin Möller, and author of a book on women's role in the Bolivian Revolution.

Mass protests erupted when Gueiler enacted IMF-prescribed austerity measures. Debates came to the fore at an FSTMB congress where Siglo XX Trotskyist Ascencio Cruz presented a resolution against support to bour-geois politicians and "parliamentary cretinism."[19] The motion drew fire from Lechín as well as the PCB, which sought to line up labor support for Siles's popular front.

As far-right groups escalated attacks on leftist and trade union militants, the COB, joined by both wings of the MNR, the MIR, PCB, and others, established the National Committee in Defense of Democracy (CONADE). Proclaiming itself "an important component" of CONADE, the González POR had moved away from the guerrilla warfare orientation, in line with a shift by Mandel's United Secretariat. The USec's Bolivian section held a congress in late 1980, that "confirmed that a great majority of the POR is made up of workers and peasants" and that the party had gained support among students. Delegates and guests included "trade union cadres from the main unions, miners, peasants from the La Paz region . . . and a comrade who is a member of the national leadership of the COB."[20]

Lora's POR argued the "non-viability of bourgeois democracy" in a semicolonial country like Bolivia. Criticizing the "electoralist" CONADE as an attempt at "'national unity' in the service of the bourgeoisie," it none-theless sought "CONADE's transformation on the basis of the rank and file, penetrating its committees to give them a revolutionary orientation." Events did not provide "enough time to test this tactic's merits," Lora wrote. Criticizing the UDP "popular front," the POR-Masas advocated "inde-pendent mobilization of the masses" but also "called on the parties of the left"—including "the components of the UDP"—to "establish a front which will unquestionably take on the characteristics of the FRA."[21] Thus the group continued its long-standing approach of criticizing existing leader-ships while trying to transform them through pressure.

A core of POR-Masas activists employed at various government insti-tutions began an intensive union organizing campaign. Alberto Bonadona, Sonia Sapiencia, and others began publishing a bulletin called *ARTE* (Acción Revolucionaria de Trabajadores del Estado—Public Employees' Revolution-ary Action). Despite the Labor Code's prohibition of white-collar govern-ment workers' unionization, they eventually established a federation with twenty thousand members, led by POR cells whose total membership was fifteen at most. Government repression, including the arrest and torture of Bonadona and others, did not destroy the organizing drive. However, disagreements over strategy and tactics led to conflicts between Lora and several ARTE leaders, who eventually left the party.[22]

Education workers became a bastion of POR-Masas influence (see fig-ure 7.2). Miguel Lora helped found URMA, the Revolutionary Union of Teachers, as a tendency within the teachers' federation, gaining fame in a hunger strike that nearly caused his death. In La Paz, URMA leader Vilma

Figure 7.2 La Paz, July 2004. Trotskyist-led teachers' union protests Mesa's "hydrocarbons referendum." (Photo by author)

Plata became the central leader of the city's teachers. A powerful speaker and indefatigable activist, defiant in the face of innumerable jailings, she became an important, though often dissident, figure in the COB, and eventually the best-known voice of Bolivian Trotskyism after Lora. *Los maestros trotskistas* (the Trotskyist teachers) became a catch phrase. Newspapers quote Plata during every episode of labor strife, portraying her in cartoons, sometimes with a sexist edge, as the embodiment of "unreasonable" radicalism. An ironic popular song reflects this idea: "The *trotskos* give their ranks/ A nice homework assignment / For a society without classes / Long live the teachers' strike!"

World Bank analysts cited the union, with "radical leaders, such as Vilma Plata and Miguel Lora," as one of the "emergent social actors that were able to paralyze the country" at the beginning of the millennium (see figure 7.3). URMA has led the La Paz union since the 1980s, winning significant improvements for the rank and file, "the majority of [whom] prefer an independent, radical leadership," according to an analysis of URMA's June 2006 reelection (won despite strenuous opposition from followers of Evo Morales).[23]

Figure 7.3 Vilma Plata. (Courtesy of José Luis Quintana)

"Cocaine Coup of the Narco Junta"

New elections held in June 1980 yielded a plurality for Siles Zuazo's UDP. The proliferating Trotskyist-derived groups were divided over electoral policy: Escóbar's joined the UDP; POR-Combate and the Moreno group supported the candidacy of Lechín, who withdrew in favor of the UDP; the "Posadas Trotskyists" joined a small coalition headed by the Christian Democrats, but their spokesman Carlos Flores was eventually elected to congress on the UDP ticket. Lora's POR-Masas called on voters to cast blank or spoiled ballots.

Shortly after the elections, the bloodiest military takeover in Bolivia's coup-ridden history was carried out by officers who became world-famous for the intensity of their violence and the astonishing scope of their corruption. The new junta was headed by colonels Luis García Meza (a cousin of Lidia Gueiler, who had appointed him army commander) and Luis Arce Gómez, a School of the Americas graduate. Paramilitary forces played a central role, most notoriously in the attack on COB offices in the downtown La Paz FSTMB headquarters. Marcelo Quiroga was among those murdered there, and Lechín and dozens of others were arrested. The building was demolished and reduced to a vacant lot, a gaping symbol of the junta's attempt to obliterate the labor movement. Inside, Alandia's mural "Strike and Massacre" was broken into pieces, later "rescued" by his son.

A foreign activist who worked with one of the Trotskyist groups recalls: "I went with comrades to try to get to the COB offices, but the military had already occupied the area. We went to El Alto and helped build some barricades, then had to go into hiding. It was felt there was no way I could do anything productive within the country." His job was to get word to the outside world. "Comrades gave me a list of political prisoners on onion-skin paper. We wrapped it in plastic and put it inside a tube of toothpaste. We weighed the toothpaste before and made sure we put enough back in so it would weigh about the same. It was easier than it sounds."[24]

The junta became notorious for its links to cocaine cartels that had developed a symbiotic relationship with death squads connected to Klaus Barbie, the Nazi "Butcher of Lyon." Spirited out of Europe by the "rat line" and protected by U.S. intelligence, Barbie arrived in Bolivia in 1951, received citizenship from Siles Zuazo in 1957, and was entrusted by Barrientos with funds for a phantasmagorical "warship for Bolivia," supposedly destined for Lake Titicaca. Settled in Santa Cruz, Barbie organized groups of Hitler admirers connected to neofascist groups in Europe. The POR-Masas helped take the lead in exposing these connections.[25]

The "narco-junta" bloodied but did not destroy Bolivian Trotskyism. The attempt to root radicalism out of the mines was a high priority for the colonels, as for their forebears. Military officers in charge of the Comibol national mine company kept close track of Trotskyist activists, receiving a stream of detailed reports from informers.[26] The security apparatus also paid renewed attention to attacking campus activists. Víctor Sosa, renowned since the University Revolution of 1970–71, was thrown in prison. Carlos Flores of the Posadas POR-T was among those killed at COB headquarters. Numerous others were hunted down, tortured, and often executed or "disappeared."

Bolivian Trotskyists speak stoically of imprisonment and torture, but many militants bear the scars of this experience today. A 1981 POR-Masas pamphlet, with militants' narratives of torture and resistance, makes difficult reading. "We will not present imprisonment as a great virtue of revolutionary militants," states the introduction. "The virtue consists of frustrating the plans of the police. . . . It is useful to read the testimony of Trotskyists who have become the personification of those hard-core militants who never talk, no matter what methods the torturers use."[27]

The extraordinarily high level of corruption and brutality exhibited by the military junta—including its cocaine business, summary execution of eight MIR leaders, and bloody disputes among its own adherents—brought it increasing international isolation. Working-class protests broke out against repression and IMF-inspired austerity measures, and the army was wracked by new splits. In August 1981, the military ousted the narco-dictators, replacing them with less flamboyant officers. The González POR reported: "In November 1981, our miner comrades, led by Felipe Vásquez, encouraged the Huanuni miners to organize . . . [to] confront the dictatorship. All our comrades, including Comrade Vásquez, were arrested and brutally tortured."[28] Nonetheless, the militant Huanuni strike dealt the death blow to the series of juntas as it spread to other mines and industries, forcing the government to legalize the COB.

From Junta to Popular Front

Discredited and "burned" by years in the Palacio Quemado, the military decided it would let the congress elected in 1980 decide the succession. The COB convoked a general strike, to last until the *gorilas* ceded power. At an enormous protest on September 14, 1982, Filemón Escóbar addressed the crowd. Though critical of the UDP, he insisted it be allowed to take office.[29] (See figure 7.4.) The next month, Hernán Siles Zuazo, MNR cofounder and nemesis of the miners' union in his first presidential term (1956–60), was installed anew in the presidential palace, populating the ministries with left-nationalists, MIR spokesmen, and PCB leaders.

It was not an auspicious time for popular front governments, as Latin America faced the Reagan White House and its anticommunist offensive. The UDP's difficulties were exacerbated by high inflation and fiscal crises inherited from its predecessors. Siles found himself caught between IMF austerity demands and the plebeian sectors that had swept him into office.

The combustible mixture of high expectations and harsh living conditions fueled increasing social unrest. Bolivia's Congress refused to back Siles's antinarcotics program, so he went on a hunger strike. Unable to satisfy workers' demands, the UDP was on a collision course with labor, placing left-wing members of the coalition in a highly vulnerable position, especially the PCB, which had one foot in the cabinet and the other in the FSTMB and COB leadership.

Given this opening, Bolivian Trotskyists made some gains but were unable to achieve a breakthrough. The POR-Masas youth group URUS recruited many activists and won student elections at the UMSA university campus. Still painstakingly typed and mimeographed, the weekly *Masas* attained a high press run and vigorous distribution in working-class neighborhoods,

Figure 7.4 Filemón Escóbar with ELN activist, early 1970s. (Courtesy of Cesar Escóbar)

factory zones, and universities. Militants also issued many other publications, including *Universidad Revolucionaria* and *Qué Hacer* (URUS), Local University Federation bulletins, and *Emancipación*, published by the "Women's Brigades of URUS, URMA, Professionals and Neighborhoods" under the slogan "Without Revolution There Is No Women's Liberation, Without Women's Participation There Is No Revolution." The Lora group's Revolutionary Trade-Union Brigade intervened at miners' congresses, sometimes winning a hearing from unionists repelled by the PCB's loyalty to Siles.[30]

Having built cells among factory workers, peasants, and other plebeian sectors, La Paz regional organizer Daniel Campos proposed that the POR-Masas open public offices and launch a large-scale recruitment campaign, especially among workers. Lora opposed this, a position Campos saw as condemning the party to sterility. The clash was one of a series between younger leaders and Lora, who at one point resigned dramatically from the Central Committee and launched his own personal journal, *La Colmena* (The Beehive). In late 1983, to the shock of Gonzalo Trigoso, Campos, and other cadres, Lora made a motion for the POR to dissolve, only to withdraw it at the last moment.[31] The party presented a two-tiered program in its daily agitation: the demand for a *salario mínimo vital* (living minimum wage) with an escalator clause to keep pace with inflation, and *Revolución y dictadura proletarias* (proletarian revolution and dictatorship of the proletariat). These phrases were painted on walls all over Bolivia, acquiring an almost ritual character as their connection, and the organizational forms for achieving them, were rarely concretized.

With a softer approach to the UDP, the POR-Combate worked to establish a visible presence and recruit new members as activists emerged from underground, "soap-boxing" in Aymara and Spanish on the UMSA campus and resuming open work in labor and peasant sectors. In July 1983, the group merged with former POR-Masas members led by Víctor Sosa in a congress attended by 150 delegates representing factory workers, teachers, peasants, students, and miners, "from La Paz, Huanuni, Siglo XX, Potosí, Oruro, Cochabamba, Santa Cruz, Escoma [and] San José." Adopting the name POR Unificado (POR-U) and launching the newspaper *Bandera Socialista,* it said "the workers are anxious to know what concrete steps will be made toward unity, unity in fronts, on the basis of blocs, or in relation to what might also be called a Higher Front of the Left."[32]

Soon, the group took another step toward this goal. At the September 1984 congress of the COB, the POR-U and POR-De Pie joined Lechín's PRIN in a new Unitary Revolutionary Directorate (DRU), which also included the Tupac Katari Revolutionary Movement, a pro-Albania Stalinist party, and others. Proclaiming opposition to the Siles regime, the DRU defeated the PCB slate.

The Days of March: "¡Obreros al poder!"

Conflicts between labor and the UDP government escalated as miners marched and struck repeatedly to protest austerity measures. In early 1984, I was walking in downtown La Paz when a detachment of riot police blocked the street. "What's going on?" I asked. "*Son los cascos café, protestando están*"—it's the brown helmets (miners), they're protesting again. I asked one miner who was resting on the curb what the protest was about. Seconded by his colleagues, he said: "We are the *proletarios*, this country runs from our work. This government, the UDP, they say they are a government of the people, but when we try to march to the presidential palace to state our demands, they send their police to stop us." They had come from Siglo XX.

Invited to their assembly in the rubble of the old FSTMB building, I was struck by what rank-and-file union members were most interested in discussing with a North American visitor: not the particularities of their situation, but the civil war in El Salvador and Nicaragua's resistance to Reagan's *contras*. Clearly, if labor sectors with a high level of political awareness and tradition of radical mobilization had turned against Siles's popular front, a new social explosion was only a matter of time.

It came in March 1985, as miners spearheaded mobilizations that once again posed the question of revolution on the altiplano. Twelve thousand mine workers occupied La Paz in revolt against UDP austerity measures and the 40 percent drop in wages that Bolivia's workforce had suffered since 1980. The nation's revolutionary history seemed to rear its head at every intersection: armed with dynamite, pickets took up position on the city's central arteries. Police and army troops abandoned the streets; now it was miners' detachments that patrolled the capital. The strikers met daily in mass assemblies in the Open Air Theater, a stone's throw from Laikacota hill. The slogan "*¡Obreros al poder!*" (Workers to power) resounded, over and over, at mass demonstrations.

The miners' "vanguard role," embedded in their class memory, asserted itself once again. Paralyzing the capital, their mobilization polarized its residents. Entire layers of the plebeian and middle-class populace came over to the workers' side. Market women organized to provide food for the strikers; other sectors took charge of giving them lodging.

To activists steeped in the imagery of Russia's Bolshevik Revolution, this was a classic revolutionary opportunity. What could be more like a "soviet" than the miners' daily mass assemblies? The parallels went further: mass working-class discontent challenged a popular front government; leaders linked to it had fallen into discredit and disarray; with increasing radicalization of labor and the poor, social forces polarized and realigned; the core of the nation's proletariat crystallized popular discontent—the situation was remarkably close to the original scenario for "permanent revolution." Had the "hour of Trotskyism" finally arrived?

President Siles, the former disciple of Aguirre Gainsborg, was afraid that it had. Stridently, he denounced the unions' "Trotskyist and neo-Trotskyist leadership" for planning "the seizure of power through violent actions."[33] Yet Bolivian Trotskyists had no clear orientation for transforming "*Obreros al poder*" from slogan to reality. Bound still to *El viejo Lechín*, they conceived their task as helping heat up labor militancy while providing general propaganda about the need for revolution.

Masas, published every day during the strike, centered agitation on a "living minimum wage with an escalator clause." Clearly, Siles was not going to agree. What then was to be done? Nobody had a concrete answer.

No systematic effort was made to link other labor, peasant, and impoverished urban sectors, which greeted the strike with hopeful enthusiasm, to the miners' mass assemblies. No one fought for them to elect delegates and transform the assemblies into an organizing center for taking power. Indeed, *Masas* had denounced "the ultra-leftist, ultimatist and subjectivist deviation that consists of decreeing that soviets should be built now, with this or that name," while stressing that "the POR was one of the architects of the FRA and has never flagged in its efforts to reestablish it."[34] The reference did not come out of the blue. At critical junctures, the "anti-imperialist front" took center stage as a recipe for blocs with the Lechinista labor officialdom and nationalist politicians.

Lechín let the miners continue with no clear direction until protests began to run out of steam. On March 24, Lora's POR, González's POR-U, and the Moreno group signed a statement with Lechín's nationalist PRIN and others, pledging to "join our forces and organize the political instrument that will lead to the achievement of the workers' historic objectives." What this meant in practice was this: as Lechín fulfilled his role of demobilizing radical struggle, Bolivian Trotskyists joined him in yet another bloc, avowing that he and they pursued the same "historical objectives." Yet Lora argued: "It was the masses themselves who, at the crucial moment in the class struggle, took from their heads their preconceived ideas, their prejudices, as a wall opposing itself to their own action," because they "required greater development of their consciousness."[35]

The majority of the COB leadership voted to lift the strike. When miners gathered at a farewell meeting, they vowed: *"Volveremos"*—We will return.

Revenge of the Criollo Thatcher

As none of the strike's central demands was met, demoralization spread in the labor movement. When Siles called early elections, sectors that had looked to the miners for a way out of a desperate situation swung sharply to the right. Large swathes of UDP voters switched to right-wing candidates, including Banzer and Paz Estenssoro. Now, history seemed to be cycling backward, as Siles was replaced in power by his aged ex-Jefe Paz.

Filemón Escóbar ran for vice president on the Tupac Katari slate of peasant leader Genaro Flores. His former comrade Lora ran an all-out campaign in the 1985 elections. Declaring "Our time has come" and "the prerevolutionary situation is deepening,"[36] the POR-Masas ran Lora for president and full slates across the country. Awash in the rightward tide, it received only 0.79 percent of the vote. Facing opposition, Lora expelled young critics, some of whom formed a group called Poder Obrero (Workers Power), which published a bulletin for a time before fading from the scene.

Víctor Paz returned to the Palacio Quemado as a *criollo* version of Margaret Thatcher, privatizer extraordinaire and determined enemy of the miners' union. Advised by Harvard economist Jeffrey Sachs and the young technocrat Gonzalo Sánchez de Lozada (himself a private mine owner), Paz was intent on structurally adjusting the mine union into oblivion. He seized on a drastic fall in the price of tin to shut down the majority of the mines that he had nationalized in 1952. The privatization measure, Decree 21060, became synonymous with misery and defeat for Bolivian workers, the subject of countless songs and chants as it gave private employers wide firing powers against strikers while turning infrastructure and one productive sector after another over to private, largely foreign capital.

El decreto maldito (the accursed decree) "relocalized" laid-off miners to regions far from their historic mine camps. Many went to the city of Cochabamba and coca-growing tropics nearby. One was Abraham Grandydier. Son of a peasant leader who went to work in Siglo XX, he too became a miner, then "relocated" to Cochabamba, where "two very important experiences" combined: "the Andean communitarian experience of people who migrated from the countryside . . . together with the union experience of the miners." Others moved to El Alto, where "today, ex-miners head many of the social organizations," notes former Siglo XX unionist Feliciano Muruchi Poma, who became a member of the Aymara city's Regional Labor Federation (COR) and of a local association of former political prisoners.[37]

In September 1985, miners, together with their wives and children, carried out a desperate "March for Life" on the highway to La Paz. The march was surrounded and turned back by the armed forces, ending in a new and bitter defeat. "The miners and other organized workers who brought Paz to power . . . in 1952 are now seen as the enemy," a British reporter noted. To dramatize their plight, some resorted to painful forms of self-sacrifice. Angel Capari invented the tactic he calls "self-crucifixion": he and others hung for days from huge crosses in downtown La Paz. A Spanish newsmagazine reported that "the Government . . . accused the Trotskyists of manipulating the poor devils" involved in the protest.[38]

In May 1988, Pope John Paul II brought his own crucifix to Bolivia. *Masas* proclaimed: "Down with the Oppressors' Religion! Long Live the Pachamama" (a female earth deity of the Andes). POR pamphlets declared "repudiation of the oppressors' religion and support to the affirmation of the culture and religion of the oppressed" Quechua, Aymara, and other indigenous peoples. As the U.S. "war on drugs" stepped up pressure against coca cultivation, Lora's party called for a struggle to "impose respect for the free cultivation, commercialization, and industrialization of coca, generating a powerful movement that uses direct action" in support of this demand.[39]

The new social movement that coca-growing peasants organized over the following years combined "defense of the coca leaf" with an affirmation of indigenous culture, history, and language. In Cochabamba's tropics, Filemón Escóbar ran seminars where coca growers related contemporary issues to documents like the Pulacayo Thesis. Having concluded that "the revolution will come from the Chapare, because it could not come from the mines," he became adviser to six peasant federations of the tropical zone.[40]

The combativity and organizational flexibility of coca growers' unions owed more than a little to "relocalized" miners who "'reinvested' their 'militant capital'" in the new organizations, "transmitting the accumulated experience of the most politicized sector" of Bolivia's plebeian population, as a recent book on Evo Morales put it.[41] Together with his "mentor" Escóbar, Morales formed the Movimiento Al Socialismo (MAS), a pragmatic group that spoke in general terms of "communal socialist" values. It soon became a force in parliament, with Senator Escóbar's colorful pronouncements spicing up the daily news and Representative Morales briefly expelled from the body, openly at the behest of the U.S. Embassy (see figure 7.5).

In the last decade of the millennium, as the Soviet bloc collapsed, many Latin America leftist movements fell apart. In Bolivia the effects of Washington's triumphalism were multiplied by Decree 21060's devastation of the mining proletariat. The Communist Party, which had long had a base among miners and factory workers, suffered a near-fatal crisis. However, world events generated a certain upswing of interest in the ideas of Bolivian Trotskyists. Declaring Marxism alive and well, they noted Trotsky's prediction that Stalin's "socialism in one country" set the stage for the USSR's destruction. Nonetheless, the movement was not immune to the impact of Washington's "New World Order" offensive. The González POR, in particular, experienced the defeat of Nicaragua's Sandinistas, in whom it had placed great hopes, as a major setback. The POR-U eventually stopped publishing its paper, folding as Hugo González fell ill and withdrew from politics.

Interest in class-based political challenges to capitalism declined among many Bolivian intellectuals, some of whom made their peace with the idea that "there is no alternative" to capital. Others argued for a shift toward an "Indianist" rather than Marxist outlook, most prominently Álvaro García Linera, who became the ideologue of a "Tupac Katari Guerrilla Army." After a spell in jail and a spate of books (one co-authored with former POR-Masas

Figure 7.5 Filemón Escóbar (left) with Evo Morales in 2003. (Courtesy of Cesar Escóbar)

youth leader Jaime Iturri), he joined forces with Evo Morales and is now Bolivia's vice president.

As the twentieth century came to a close, right-wing governments dominated Bolivia. A coalition headed by Banzer was followed by the first presidency of MNR technocrat Gonzalo Sánchez de Lozada, who deepened the privatization policy. In 1997, a new Banzer term was cut short when the ex-dictator succumbed, not to the "proletarian justice" radical miners had demanded, but to cancer. The following year, the IMF told Bolivia to privatize all remaining public enterprises, including oil refineries and water systems.

Lora's POR maintained its base in the teachers' union, while URUS remained active in La Paz and eventually grew at universities in Cochabamba and Sucre. However, the party was wracked by new rounds of internal crisis, most spectacularly the very public purge of Juan Pablo Bacherer, who had functioned as Lora's right-hand man. The talented and charismatic Bacherer joined an exile POR circle in France during the 1970s and became a history lecturer at UMSA while rising to the top leadership of the party. In 1995, as he prepared a document criticizing what he viewed as Lora's inability to translate abstract slogans into organizational progress, he was suddenly denounced as an "informer" by the long-time POR leader, who refused to provide any evidence for the inflammatory charge. Chaired by Trotsky's grandson Esteban Volkov, an "International Moral Tribunal" convened in La Paz, declaring the charge a baseless slander.[42]

Bacherer established a small group, the Oposición Trotskysta, which published a bulletin called *Trinchera* (Trench). Highly visible at the UMSA campus for several years, the "OT" lost members to the "new leftist" circle of Álvaro García Linera, functioning sporadically after Bacherer's death in 2001. Another group was founded in 1999: the Liga Obrera Revolucionaria por la Cuarta Internacional (LORCI; Revolutionary Workers League for the Fourth International), affiliated with a split from the Morenoite tendency. The LORCI carried out work on university campuses and later helped establish a warehouse workers' union at the El Alto airport.

Gas Wars on the Altiplano

As new realignments began to challenge the "Washington consensus," a range of ideologically diffuse movements arose to challenge the policies they called "neoliberal globalization." For many, the Cochabamba Water War of 2001 became a symbol. Massive opposition broke out against the city's water supply being turned over to the Aguas del Tunari company, a Bechtel subsidiary. Protests were led by a *Coordinadora* (coordinating committee) headed by factory workers' leader Oscar Olivera, a former supporter of the "Marxist-Leninist" (pro-Albania) party founded by Siglo XX miner Federico Escóbar (no relation to Filemón). The POR-Masas and URUS, long prominent at the local university, played an active role in the mass mobilizations.[43]

Zenovia Vásquez, widow of Trotskyist union leader Felipe Vásquez, recalls "transmitting" her experiences to neighbors during the struggle against water privatization, saying: "We women must not stay shut into our homes, we have to get out and join the fray, that's how we organized in Huanuni," the mine camp where she was a leader of the militant housewives' committee. A sign of this human continuity is the placard "The Huanuni Barrio Is Present Here Today," featured in a U.S. television special on the Cochabamba events.[44]

The Water War was followed by Gas Wars on the altiplano. After an election campaign managed by Clinton associate James Carville, Gonzalo Sánchez de Lozada—popularly known as "Goni"—returned to the presidency, supported by a "megacoalition" of right-wing, center, and center-left parties. Closely adhering to Washington's policy prescriptions, his government enjoyed an especially close relationship with the U.S. Embassy. In 2003, mass anger erupted after Goni signed what many viewed as sweetheart contracts with foreign energy conglomerates. Gas was to be exported through Chile, a country nationalist discourse depicted as a historic enemy. Protests reflected widespread popular perceptions about the country's history. Since colonial times, it had depended on the export of one commodity after another, enriching a few people, mainly very far away, while leaving the vast majority in poverty. First silver, then tin, now natural gas, of which Bolivia has the second largest reserves in Latin America.

Goni ordered the army to suppress the protests, whose epicenter was the working-class Aymara city of El Alto, home to many relocalized miners as well as thousands of small factories. Marksmen left the roads strewn with bodies. The role of miners, both active and relocated, as well as miners' wives and palliris (women who get ore from mine tailings) was reflected among the casualties. Zenobia Condori Ayra of Potosí recalls: "It was October 9 [2003] at nine in the morning when the miners arrived in Ventilla," a district in the south of El Alto. Soldiers "surrounded us, to torture all of us miners." "I want justice for my husband," demands the widow Alicia Cargas Condori. "He was a miner, they came out in defense of gas, they were marching from their work." He was killed on the highway to La Paz. "All those responsible for what happened in October must be put on trial," insists another woman from the Potosí mines, Justina Poma Coria.[45]

The massacre led to an outpouring of protest. The press cited Bolivian Trotskyists' calls for revolution, Evo Morales's Movimiento Al Socialismo denounced Goni's massacres, and affiliated peasant unions joined the protests. When the upheaval culminated in a miners' march on the capital, the president fled to Miami. Morales was the key figure in preparing the "orderly transition" of power to Vice President Carlos Mesa, then worked closely with him to design a referendum that envisaged higher government royalties and taxes on gas but not the "nationalization" many sectors were now demanding. The POR-Masas and La Paz teachers' union denounced "Evo" as a sellout.

The first Gas War was followed by a second after Bolivia's Congress passed a new Hydrocarbons Law in May 2005, rejected by peasant and labor groups as little more than a new version of Goni's policies. Carlos Mesa left the signing of the law to the rightist head of the Senate, Hormando Vaca Díez, but was unable to stave off a powerful new wave of protest. Workers struck; most of the country ground to a halt as slum dwellers' and peasants' organizations set up two hundred road blockades to paralyze transport. For the second time in less than two years, Bolivia reached the brink of civil war. Mesa resigned in early June, and Vaca Díez sought to fill the power vacuum. Enormous marches tried repeatedly to enter the Plaza Murillo, outside the presidential palace. Peasants, students, and teachers grouped around the disciplined ranks of *cascos café*—the mine workers in their brown *guardatojo* helmets. The streets of La Paz shook with dynamite blasts as miners battled police. *"Los mineros volveremos"*—a song based on the 1985 slogan, "We will return"—echoed through the streets. Fighting spread to Sucre, the country's second capital.

Lora's POR, seconded by the small LORCI and others, launched a campaign to form a "People's Assembly, like in 1971." The COB, FSTMB, and federations of El Alto Labor (COR) and Neighborhood Associations (FEJUVE) came together to convoke a "National Indigenous and People's Assembly," chaired by COB head Jaime Solares, who proclaimed it a countergovernment of the working class. The POR hailed the Assembly as the nucleus of a revolutionary government, calling it "a real organ of power" and "a powerful soviet [that] has begun to be born."[46]

Like the People's Assembly of 1971, however, the new body was more a forum for radical speeches than an organizing center for revolution. Unlike its namesake of 1971, the Assembly of 2005 was not destroyed by repression. Instead, it fizzled out after a few meetings when the MAS called a halt to peasant road blockades to facilitate a new "orderly transition." Morales played a central part in the negotiations that installed an interim president, Eduardo Rodríguez, head of the Supreme Court. The FEJUVE and COR leadership acceded to a "truce" organized by Rodríguez, Morales, and other political figures.[47]

¡Volveremos!

In the upsurge of 2005, patterns set half a century before continued to hold. The inability of Bolivian society to satisfy deeply felt mass aspirations led to an acute social crisis, sweeping one president after another from power. Mine workers returned to a leading role, despite privatizations that, twenty years earlier, led many observers to declare the proletariat's demise. When the time came for battles with the armed forces, peasants bearing indigenism's multicolored *wiphala* flag grouped around the compact force of dynamite-wielding miners. As protests radicalized, labor leaders adopted an increasingly leftist stance, with some calling to "return to the Thesis of Pulacayo."

In 2005, as in 1952, 1971, and 1985, Bolivian Trotskyists were in the thick of events. They had lost much of their working-class base in the repression, internal crises, and layoffs of the 1970s and 1980s, yet the "Trotskyist teachers" were prominent at rallies and mass protests, their leader Vilma Plata appearing in the daily papers as the very embodiment of radical protest.

Bolivian Trotskyists continued to play a central role as creators of ideology, concepts, and slogans for the broader labor movement. Their ideas did not remain on paper but found material expression in organizational regroupments carried out in response to mass mobilizations. In 1952 they had been fundamental to the organization of the Central Obrera Boliviana; in the 1960s and 1970s they were organizers of clandestine trade unions, housewives' committees, and other forms of resistance to military dictatorship. The ill-fated Asamblea Popular and Frente Revolucionario Antiimperialista of 1971 were largely their creation. The same was true of the National Indigenous and Popular Assembly of 2005.

Militants continued to proclaim the goal marked out when the POR was founded in the bloody aftermath of the Chaco War: to lead Bolivia's impoverished workers and indigenous peasants in a socialist revolution. Yet through the seven decades that followed that seminal event, they had been unable to resolve the "crisis of revolutionary leadership." In the blocs and alliances of the 1940s and 1950s, they had linked their fortunes to Juan Lechín and other labor leaders, who learned to "talk the talk" of proletarian revolution while pursuing very different goals. Repeatedly, Bolivian Trotskyists wound up reinforcing, not replacing, these nationalist leaders. In 2005, as civil war loomed, they found themselves again shoring up the left flank of union officialdom.

Bolivia may not be, as Guillermo Lora has boasted, a "Trotskyized country," but the movement made a deep impact on the ideology, identity, and organizing traditions of labor, peasant, student, women's, and artistic groups over the course of many decades. It survived because it filled a series of political needs: the miners' need to make sense of, and draw hope from, their central yet deeply oppressed status in national life; the need for vigorous intellectual creation that broke out of the rarified milieu of gente letrada ("lettered people," the small traditional intelligentsia); the need to integrate the country's indigenous culture and history with its place in the world economic system; above all, the need for a systematic critique of a starkly unequal society, linked to a vision of a different kind of future.

Did the movement fail because the idea of radical social transformation was irrelevant or impossible? Clearly, large numbers of Bolivians repeatedly seek fundamental changes in the way their society functions. The miners and peasants in whom Trotskyists placed their hopes launched one of the most extensive revolutions in Latin American history. One generation after another threw itself into tumultuous struggles against governments ranging from the far right to the popular front left. With new shifts in recent years, it remains to be seen how far and deep new processes of radicalization will go.

In reality, the proclaimed program of Bolivian Trotskyists remained *untested* because in practice the movement chained itself to nationalist labor leaders. Revolutionary opportunities presented themselves, not once but repeatedly—yet at each new stage they returned to their old ways of leaning on Lechín and his political heirs. Each new stage ended in new defeats and frustrations, as radical labor found itself unable to break free from the political framework bequeathed by the 1952 nationalist experience. At each new stage, social revolution remained a historic possibility, a potential that Bolivian Trotskyists found themselves unable to bring to fruition.

In the presidential elections of December 2005, MAS candidates Evo Morales and Álvaro García Linera called for a "democratic cultural revolution, with votes not guns," which would promote a specifically "Andean capitalism." While much of the domestic and international left applauded Morales's victory, he did not receive electoral support from the Bolivian Trotskyists. Lora's POR had stated that "history will show" that Morales betrayed "impoverished layers of the peasantry . . . particularly the coca-growers," who backed him "believing he would defend the positions and rights of the dispossessed from the countryside and urban slums." The Andean "Pucu-Pucu bird wakes people at dawn, and warns of approaching danger," added *Masas.* "It predicts that Evo will wear out his welcome and fall from his high perch into the mud."[48]

Morales and García Linera said they owed their election to Bolivia's social movements, which largely hailed the new regime. Yet expectations, raised by the election of South America's first indigenous president, clashed with his promise to cooperate with business elites and respect the "institutionality" of the armed forces. Sectors of those mass movements had already attacked Morales's role in ending the uprisings of October 2003 and May-June 2005 (see figure 7.6). In December 2005, activists from a range of urban and rural organizations were quoted voicing skepticism about his willingness or ability to meet their demands. On election day the *New York Times* quoted Rufo Yanarico, a 45-year-old community leader in an Aymara village. "What we really need is to transform this country," he said. "We have to do away with the capitalist system."[49] That fundamental idea had motivated José Aguirre Gainsborg and other young rebels to found the POR seventy years earlier.

Figure 7.6 La Paz, June 2005. Indigenous market women join miners' rally during second Gas War. (Photo by author)

After Morales took office, radical sectors criticized his proposed land reform, arguing that in key respects it favored the largest owners, as well as his government's renegotiation of gas contracts with multinationals under the rubric of ostensible nationalization. As right-wing business and civic leaders from Santa Cruz led an often violent campaign for "autonomy" against the indigenous altiplano, left critics accused Morales of conciliating reaction while clamping down on militant sectors of the peasant and labor movements.

Together with foreign analysts, Bolivia's politicians have often made the mistake of underestimating the resilience and combativeness of its working people. In the March days of 1985, the miners vowed, "We will return." In the Gas Wars twenty years later, they did. In October 2006, unionized miners at Huanuni defeated a violent assault by government-backed cooperatives. On August 5, 2008, the Morales government sent troops against a protest by Huanuni miners at Cuahuasi, killing two and wounding dozens. The following day in Oruro, 250 miners' wives battled young MAS members, who attacked the regional COB affiliate's headquarters.

That same day, the former head of the government's Comibol mine company, Guillermo Bedregal, wrote that the COB's historic outlook was "inspired in the dogma and almost messianic class-struggle exacerbation of the 'Thesis of Pulacayo' . . . whose ideology comes from Trotskyism."[50] Indeed, the ideals expressed at Pulacayo six decades ago have survived every attempt to root them out of the altiplano's rocky soil. Whether, and how, they will be attained remains very much an open question.

Appendix

Trotsky's Permanent Revolution and Latin America

The concept of "permanent revolution" advanced by Russian revolutionary Leon Trotsky (1879–1940) is central to understanding Trotskyism in Latin America. Too often the concept is misunderstood. For example, a recent survey of Latin America states that "Trotskyite believers in spontaneous global revolution . . . never developed an appreciable mass movement in Latin America."[1] However, permanent revolution refers neither to a "spontaneous" revolution (global or otherwise), nor, as is often believed, to an unending series of upheavals.

Instead, it is a theory and program regarding the nature of revolution in countries of "belated capitalist development." Here, revolution would have to become "permanent"—overthrowing capitalism itself and extending internationally—to triumph and survive. Trotskyism addressed questions of burning concern to Latin American activists: Was class struggle attenuated or accentuated in a nation oppressed by imperialism? Was the "national bourgeoisie" the leader of revolution, or its opponent? What was the political role of a working class central to national life but still a numerical minority, and its relation to peasants and other oppressed layers? How could Latin America contribute to a worldwide struggle to free humanity from exploitation and war?

The origins of the international Trotskyist movement lay in the "Left Opposition" that Trotsky formed in 1923 within the Communist Party of the Soviet Union, later spreading to other sections of the Communist International (Comintern). Its original objectives centered on defending the Soviet regime's internationalist, revolutionary foundations against the consolidating bureaucracy led by Joseph Stalin. After Lenin died in 1924,

Stalin declared that socialism could be built in a single country, at least in the Russian case. "Stalinism" and "Trotskyism" now took shape around two opposing banners: "socialism in one country" versus "permanent revolution." The counterposition sharpened as Stalinists advocated political alliances with nationalist politicians in China, India, and Latin America, and with liberal bourgeois parties in the Popular Fronts later formed in France, Spain, and elsewhere.

The Opposition sought to reform the Comintern until 1933, when the bankruptcy of its response to Hitler's rise led Trotsky to advocate formation of a Fourth International (FI), "World Party of Socialist Revolution," which he founded in 1938. Two years later, he was assassinated in Coyoacán, Mexico, by a Stalinist agent.

Permanent Revolution

Karl Marx introduced the concept of "permanent" revolution when he called on workers to draw lessons from the failed 1848 German revolution, "taking up their position as an independent party," instead of being "seduced . . . by the hypocritical phrases of the democratic petty bourgeois into refraining from the independent organization of the party of the proletariat. Their battle cry must be: The Revolution in Permanence."[2]

Trotsky revived the phrase in 1904. He agreed with other Marxists that a series of historic "tasks" remained pending in Russia because no bourgeois revolution had occurred there. However, he argued, a revolution beginning with such tasks would either put the working class into power or be defeated. Contrary to the view prevailing in the Socialist International, a workers' revolution could begin in an economically backward country like Russia, then spread to Europe.

The belated rise of capitalism in Russia caused "combined" development in which age-old social formations coexisted with the most up-to-date technology imported by European investors. Local capitalists, often members of land-owning families, operated under the wing of the czarist state and foreign capital from the few commercial powers already dominating the world market. Arriving on the historic scene too late to play an independent role, the local bourgeoisie saw any radical mobilization as a potential threat. Far from seeking to lead a thorough-going "bourgeois-democratic revolution," it would attempt to limit and defuse social upheaval.

The peasantry's heterogeneity, and the locally circumscribed nature of rural life, meant that periodic agrarian revolts would not generate a nationwide movement, much less one capable of seizing power. The necessary leadership would be provided not by the bourgeoisie but by the newly formed proletariat, whose concentrated, strategic position gave it a "specific weight" far exceeding its numbers, and the social power to lead the oppressed against the old order.

A thorough-going anti-czarist revolution would not respect the boundaries of capitalist property; its own logic would require capital's expropriation by a workers' state ("dictatorship of the proletariat") allied with the poor peasantry. However, Russia's relative economic backwardness could not be overcome at once, nor could an isolated workers' republic constitute a classless, socialist society. To defend the revolution and open the way for socialist development, it would have to be extended, particularly to the dominant industrial powers.[3] When Lenin launched the slogan "All Power to the Soviets!" in early 1917, Trotsky worked closely with him to put his program into practice in the October Revolution.

The issue of class relations in a "democratic revolution" was posed anew during China's 1925–27 upheaval. Arguing that China was in the first, bourgeois-democratic, phase of a two-stage revolution, the Comintern—now under Stalin's sway—ordered the Communist Party to remain within the nationalist Guomindang, whose leader, Chiang Kai-shek, allegedly headed a bloc of four "anti-imperialist" classes (bourgeoisie, proletariat, peasantry, urban middle class). A second, proletarian-socialist stage of revolution would be possible only later, after more intensive capitalist development.

Warning that the nationalist party would turn violently against the proletariat and poor peasants, Trotsky demanded Communists' exit from the Guomindang and an independent revolutionary program. When Chiang massacred workers in Shanghai and consolidated a right-wing dictatorship, Trotsky said the Stalinist policy of subordination to the national bourgeoisie had directly prepared this defeat. However, the Comintern applied its "two-stage" concept to countries from India to Brazil, throughout what is today called the Third World. Embracing the Popular Front in 1934–35, it added that "anti-fascist unity" meant anticolonial struggles would take a backseat if they risked alienating liberal sectors in France, Spain, Britain, and the United States.

In contrast, Trotsky extended his conception to all colonies and "semicolonies" (countries formally independent but still dominated by imperialist powers) where the working class was able to play a role in national life. Throughout these vast areas of the world, "bourgeois" revolutionary tasks "cannot be solved . . . under the leadership of the 'national' bourgeoisie, because the latter emerges at once with foreign support as a class alien or hostile to the people. Every stage in its development binds it only the more closely to the foreign finance capital of which it is essentially the agency." Instead, peasant unrest could fuel a nationwide struggle under the leadership of "the colonial proletariat, which, from its very first steps, stands opposed not only to the foreign but also to its own national bourgeoisie." The Chinese experience also led him to stress: *"Never and under no circumstances may the party of the proletariat enter into a party of another class or merge with it organizationally.* An absolutely independent party of the proletariat is a first and decisive condition for communist politics."[4]

Where Stalinists argued that imperialist domination justified an "anti-imperialist" bloc with the national bourgeoisie, Trotsky pointed out that in struggles against the tsarist empire's "prison house of peoples," Lenin had insisted on an *"irreconcilable* class policy," fighting national oppression *"with the methods of proletarian class struggle,* entirely rejecting the charlatan 'anti-imperialist' blocs with the numerous petty-bourgeois 'national' parties."[5]

Application to Latin America

In 1934, Trotsky wrote that the power of the United States was used to "disunite, weaken and enslave" South and Central America, whose emancipation required "uniting . . . into one powerful federation. But it is not the belated South American bourgeoisie, a thoroughly venal agency of foreign imperialism, who will be called upon to solve this task, but the young South American proletariat, the chosen leader of the oppressed masses." The struggle against imperialism and the local ruling classes posed the need for a Socialist United States of Latin America.[6]

In 1937, Trotsky was granted asylum in Mexico by President Lázaro Cárdenas. There, he helped launch *Clave* (Key), a Marxist journal for Latin America, which published articles on "The Class Struggle and the Indigenous Question" (by Diego Rivera), a critique of the Chilean Popular Front, a balance sheet of the Mexican Revolution, and an appreciation of José Carlos Mariátegui on the tenth anniversary of his death.[7]

Italy's assault on Ethiopia, Japan's invasion of China, and the threat of retaliation against Mexico's nationalization of foreign oil companies led Trotsky to emphasize that the interests of the international proletariat lay with "military defense" of colonial and semicolonial countries against imperialist attacks. However, the proletariat could give no "political support" to these countries' own capitalist rulers. Outspoken in defending Mexico's oil nationalization, Trotsky insisted at the same time that revolutionaries could have no confidence in the Cárdenas regime. Voting for any bourgeois politician was out of the question; what was required was "independent class politics."[8]

"The Kuomintang in China, the PRM [Cárdenas's Party of the Mexican Revolution] in Mexico and the APRA in Peru [the nationalist party of Haya de la Torre] are very similar organizations," he said. "Our organization doesn't participate in the APRA, Kuomintang, or PRM," which represented "the People's Front in the form of a party," subordinating workers to sectors of the bourgeoisie. Even in the struggle to achieve democratic tasks, "the independence of the proletariat . . . is absolutely necessary, and we especially oppose the proletariat to the bourgeoisie in the agrarian question, for [throughout Latin America] that class will rule . . . which has the peasants." When the bourgeoisie seeks "a bit more independence from the foreign imperialists," it is "obliged to flirt with the workers, with the peasants," giving rise to "semi-Bonapartist" or "strong man" regimes. Balancing between opposing forces to defend the overall interests of bourgeois rule, they often used peasant small proprietors to "discipline" the workers' movement.[9] These observations are relevant to Bolivia, where Toro and Busch in the 1930s and Villarroel in the 1940s sought an equilibrium between foreign capital and the working class at home, as did the MNR in the 1950s, also turning to the peasantry (after agrarian reform) as a bulwark against labor radicalism.

In a 1938 document for Latin American trade unionists, Trotsky argued that the region's proletariat should "attract to its side the tens of millions of Indo-American peasants" and "take the fate of Latin America into its hands." This called for "the closest possible ties [with] the proletariat of the United States of North America." The International expected its U.S. section to give active support to the fight against American imperialism, which was "inseparable from the class struggle of the American proletariat against the ruling bourgeoisie, and cannot be conducted apart from it." An "indispensable ally in this struggle" were the millions of "American Negroes . . . bound by many ties to the other groups of Negro peoples oppressed by American imperialism in the Caribbean and in Latin America."[10]

As World War II approached, the Popular Front policy of alliance with "progressive" capitalists was projected internationally. Backing colonial powers that stood to lose in a new division of the spoils, the Comintern had transformed its sections, "especially in Latin America, into a left agency of European and American imperialism," Trotsky wrote. Like Mexican labor leader Lombardo Toledano, Stalinists began (with the brief interlude of the Hitler-Stalin pact) portraying the United States as the defender of democracy. Some joined governments they had previously, and accurately, reviled as Yankee puppets.[11]

Trotsky argued that a real fight against fascism could be waged only through struggle against all imperialism. To call on workers and subject peoples to support their British, French, or U.S. rulers was to betray the most fundamental principles of internationalism. It was the duty of the international proletariat to defend the Soviet Union, a "bureaucratically degenerated workers' state," against Hitler's Germany and any other capitalist power, but revolutionaries could not bow to Moscow's capitalist allies. Roosevelt's "Good Neighbor" policy was the latest adornment of the Monroe Doctrine; the nature of "democratic" American capitalism was shown by its support to dictators like Brazil's Vargas and Cuba's Batista. Like "colonial slaves" from the Maghreb to Indochina, the peoples of Latin America should continue their struggles during the war. Upheavals against any one of the colonial powers could and should spread to regions dominated by its rivals, strengthening the position of workers and oppressed peoples internationally.

While calling the United States "the guardian of our liberty," APRA leader Haya de la Torre and other nationalists ruled out an alliance with workers in the United States and other imperialist countries. This, Trotsky wrote, was not only "suicidal," but reflected "the effort *not to frighten the 'democratic' imperialist bourgeoisie,* above all, the bourgeoisie of the United States."[12]

The Fourth International

For Trotsky, the FI's raison d'être was to resolve the "crisis of proletarian leadership" by building a powerful world party of socialist revolution. In this effort, Latin America could make a major contribution. If a "decisive revolutionary movement" emerged south of the Rio Grande, the workers of Mexico, for example, "can come to power before the workers of the United States"; and Marxist revolutionaries must "encourage them in this direction." This "does not signify that they will build their own [isolated] socialism." Instead, "giving the power to the workers' and peasants' soviets [councils] and fighting against the imperialists," they could give a powerful impetus to world revolution. "The future will depend upon events in the United States and the whole world."[13]

In a programmatic manifesto written four months before his death, Trotsky synthesized these ideas as follows:

> Only under its own revolutionary direction is the proletariat of the colonies and the semicolonies capable of achieving invincible collaboration with the proletariat of the metropolitan centers, and with the world working class as a whole. Only this collaboration can lead the oppressed peoples to complete and final emancipation, through the overthrow of imperialism the world over. A victory of the international proletariat will deliver the colonial countries from the

long-drawn-out travail of capitalist development, by opening up the possibility of arriving at socialism hand in hand with the proletariat of the advanced countries.

The perspective of the permanent revolution in no case signifies that the backward countries must await the signal from the advanced ones, or that the colonial peoples should patiently wait for the proletariat of the metropolitan centers to free them. Help comes to him who helps himself. Workers must develop the revolutionary struggle in every country, colonial or imperialist, where favorable conditions have been established, and through this set an example for the workers of other countries. Only initiative and activity, resoluteness and boldness can really materialize the slogan "Workers of the world, unite!"[14]

Trotsky does not seem to have written about Bolivia, but the Bolivian diplomat Alfredo Sanjines wrote a brief summary of his 1937 discussion with Trotsky on the agrarian question in Bolivia, particularly relations between latifundia and the indigenous ayllu. When Sanjines asked whether the Soviet system of collective farms might be applicable, Trotsky expressed the view that cooperative and collective farms could be formed voluntarily on lands seized from large estates, taking as the starting point "the Bolivian Indians' system of rural property," which, from Sanjines's description, struck him as "collectivist" in nature. He thought that even after joining a collective farm, Bolivian peasants would probably maintain small plots of their own to raise vegetables and animals for family consumption.[15]

In August 1940, the assassin Ramón Mercader put an end to the development of Trotsky's ideas on Latin America. Far from the house in Coyoacán, a movement inspired by these concepts was taking shape in Bolivia. He might have been surprised by the permutations his ideas would undergo there. Nonetheless, there is every reason to believe that he would have regarded Bolivia's altiplano not as foreign soil but as a very natural place for the program of permanent revolution to take root and grow.

Glossary

In Bolivia, some political figures are mainly known by both "paternal" and "maternal" last names (e.g., José Aguirre Gainsborg), others just by the former (e.g., Guillermo Lora).

Aguirre Gainsborg, José (1909–1938). Bolivian Marxist, co-founder of POR.

Alandia Pantoja, Miguel (1914–1975). Muralist, prominent in POR and COB.

Banzer, Hugo (1926–2002). General, led 1971 coup; president 1971–78, 1997–2001.

Barrientos, Oscar (1916–2001). Pseudonym: Warqui. Refounded POR in 1938.

Barrientos, René (1919–1969). Air Force general, led 1964 coup.

Beta Gama. Left-nationalist youth group in 1930s.

Bloque Minero Parlamentario (BMP). Miners Parliamentary Bloc, 1947–49.

Bravo James, Fernando (1912–1962). POR leader associated with Hugo González.

Buró Latinoamericano (BLA). Latin American Bureau of the Fourth International.

Central Obrera Boliviana (COB). Bolivian Labor Federation, founded in 1952.

Chaco War. Territorial conflict between Bolivia and Paraguay, 1932–35.

Cochabamba opposition. Mid-50s group within the POR, opposed to both main factions.

Comibol. Corporación Minera de Bolivia, state-owned Bolivian Mining Company.

Comité Central (CC). Central Committee.

Communist International (Comintern, CI). Third International, formed in 1919.

Ejército de Liberación Nacional (ELN). National Liberation Army guerrillas.

Entrists. Trotskyist leaders who joined MNR in late 1954.

Escóbar, Filemón (b. 1936). Trotskyist mine union leader; became "indigenist" senator, mentor to Evo Morales.

Fajardo, Leticia (d. 1978). Prominent Oruro leftist, joined POR in 1944.

Falange Socialista Boliviana (FSB). Far-right party.

Federación Obrera del Trabajo (FOT). La Paz labor federation in 1920s and 1930s.

Fourth International (FI). World Party of Socialist Revolution founded by Trotsky in 1938.

Fracción Obrera Leninista (FOL). Leninist Workers Faction in mid-50s POR, led by G. Lora and E. Möller.

Fracción Proletaria Internacionalista (FPI). Proletarian Internationalist Faction in mid-50s POR, led by H. González and F. Bravo.

Frente Democrático Antifascista (FDA). Anti-Fascist Democratic Front of PIR and Rosca parties, overthrew Villarroel, July 1946.

Frente Revolucionario Antiimperialista (FRA). Anti-Imperialist Revolutionary Front of POR, Torres, and others, formed in 1971.

FSTMB (Federación Sindical de Trabajadores Mineros de Bolivia). Nationwide Mine Workers Federation, founded in 1944.

Gamonales. Large landowners.

Goni: *see* Sánchez de Lozada, Gonzalo.

González Moscoso, Hugo (b. 1922). A central leader of POR and groups derived from split.

Grupo Tupac Amaru (GTA). Marof's exile group, became part of POR.

Indian. Most Bolivians identify themselves as *indios, indígenas,* or members of the *pueblos originarios* (original peoples), terms often used interchangeably.

International Committee of the Fourth International (IC). Formed in 1953 by Trotskyists opposed to M. Pablo.

International Communist League (ICL). Name ILO adopted in 1933; predecessor of FI.

International Left Opposition (ILO). Followers of Trotsky; predecessor of ICL and FI.

International Secretariat of the Fourth International (I.S.). Leading body of world Trotskyist movement, then of international tendency led by M. Pablo and E. Mandel.

Izquierda Boliviana. Exile group formed by Aguirre Gainsborg; joined with GTA to form POR.

Izquierda Comunista. Chilean Communist Left, broke with Trotskyism in 1936.

Lechín Oquendo, Juan. (1914–2001). Long-time leader of FSTMB, COB.

Liga Socialista Revolucionaria (LSR). Revolutionary Socialist League of Carlos Salazar Mostajo (1916–2004).

Lora, César (1927–1965). Trotskyist miners' leader; brother of Guillermo.

Lora, Guillermo (1922–2009). Best-known leader of Bolivian Trotskyism, early 1940s up to his death; head of POR-Masas after 1954–55 split.

Lucha Obrera (Workers' Struggle). Main POR newspaper until 1954–55 split, then of González's wing.

Mandel, Ernest (1923–1995). Leading member of I.S. after World War II, then of USec.

Mariátegui, José Carlos (1894–1930). Peruvian Marxist.

Marof, Tristán (1898–1979). Pseudonym of Gustavo Navarro, a founder of POR and then PSOB.

Masas (Masses). Newspaper founded by G. Lora in 1954.

Military socialism. Self-designation of post-Chaco regimes of colonels Toro and Busch.

Möller, Edwin (1924–1998). Leading POR member, prominent in COB; FOL coleader until late 1954, led "entrists" into MNR.

Morenoites. Followers of Argentine leftist "Nahuel Moreno" (Hugo Bressano, 1924–1987).

Movimiento Al Socialismo (MAS). Movement Toward Socialism of Evo Morales (elected president December 2005).

Movimiento de la Izquierda Revolucionaria (MIR). Movement of the Revolutionary Left of Jaime Paz Zamora (nephew of Paz Estenssoro, b. 1939, Bolivian president 1989–93).

Movimiento Nacionalista Revolucionario (MNR). Revolutionary Nationalist Movement, founded in 1941; ruling party after 1952 Revolution; overthrown in 1964 coup; later split between Paz Estenssoro and Siles wings.

National Revolution. MNR's name for 1952 Bolivian Revolution.

Pablo, Michel (1911–1996). Pseudonym of Michel Raptis, I.S. leader from end of World War II to early 1960s.

Partido Comunista Boliviano (PCB). Bolivian Communist Party founded in 1950 by former PIR youth members.

Partido de la Izquierda Revolucionaria (PIR). Pro-Moscow Party of the Revolutionary Left, founded in 1940.

Partido Obrero Revolucionario (POR). Revolutionary Workers Party founded in 1935; "refounded" in 1938; became FI's Bolivian section. Split in 1954–55 between Lora and González groups.

Partido Revolucionario de la Izquierda Nacional (PRIN). Revolutionary Party of the National Left formed by Lechín when he left the MNR in 1964.

Partido Socialista Obrero de Bolivia (PSOB). Bolivian Socialist Workers Party formed by Marof in 1938.

Paz Estenssoro, Víctor (1907–2001). MNR "Jefe," president 1952–56, 1960–64, 1985–89.

Permanent revolution. Trotsky's conception of revolution in countries of "belated capitalist development." *See* Appendix.

POR-Combate. Popular name for González's group beginning in the late 1960s, when it began publishing *Combate* (Combat).

POR-De Pie. "POR-Stand Up" founded by former POR-Masas members in 1977.

POR-Lucha Obrera. Popular name for González's group after 1954–55 POR split, when it took over publication of *Lucha Obrera*.

POR-Masas. Popular name for Lora group since 1954–55 POR split; publishes *Masas*.

POR-Trotskista. Name used by Posadas's followers after leaving González's group.

POR Unificado. "Unified POR" formed by González's group in 1983.

Porista. POR member.

Posadasites. Followers of Argentine leftist "J. Posadas" (Homero Cristalli, 1912–1981).

Republicans, Republican Socialists. Anti-communist followers of ex-president Bautista Saavedra (1869–1939).

Rosca. "Ring" of tin barons, landowners, and politicians dominant from early 1900s to 1952 National Revolution.

Sánchez de Lozada, Gonzalo (b. 1930). Known as Goni. Mine owner, MNR member, president 1993–97, 2002–03.

Siglo XX. Mine in Catavi-Llallagua region, a center of Trotskyist influence.

Siles Zuazo, Hernán (1914–1996). Son of Hernando Siles (president 1926–30); member Beta Gama; later MNR "Sub Jefe," president 1956–60, 1982–85.

Socialist Workers Party (SWP). U.S. Trotskyist party led by James P. Cannon, influential in world movement.

Thesis of Pulacayo. Radical program written by POR for FSTMB in 1946.

Torres, Juan José. (1921–1976). General, left-nationalist president 1970–71.

Trotskyism. *See* Appendix. Political outlook associated with Leon Trotsky (Lev Davidovich Bronstein, 1879–1940), coleader of Russian Revolution, exiled for opposing Stalin. In this book, "Trotskyist" describes those claiming adherence to this outlook; "Bolivian Trotskyism" is its nationally specific derivation.

Unión Democrática y Popular (UDP). People's Democratic Union of Siles Zuazo's MNR-Left, MIR, and PCB; governed 1982–85.

Unión Revolucionaria de Universitarios Socialistas (URUS). Revolutionary Union of Socialist University Students, a POR-Masas youth group.

United Secretariat of the Fourth International (USec or USFI). Formed by 1963 reunification of I.S. and most of ICFI.

Villarroel, Gualberto (1908–1946). Army major, president 1943–46.

Notes

Introduction

1. Anderson, *Che Guevara*, 105; Guevara, *América Latina*, 136–38.
2. Debray, *Che's Guerrilla War*, 51, 43–44.
3. Malloy and Gamarra, *Revolution and Reaction*, 59.
4. Report on speech by President Víctor Paz Estenssoro, *Lucha Obrera* (La Paz), 20 September 1953. Bolivia depended on "foreign countries" that would not tolerate a "Trotskyist government," he stressed.
5. Mesa Gisbert, "Introducción al tema," 20.
6. Guillermoprieto, "A New Bolivia?" 36–37.
7. Ibid., 36.
8. Interview, Cirilo Jiménez, 22 February 2007.
9. García Linera et al., *Sociología de movimientos*, 601. As Bolivian researcher Juan Manuel Arbona notes, "relocated mining families have become one of the driving forces behind the formation of a contestatory political identity that defines the city of El Alto," where their "histories and memories of organisation and struggle" have played a "crucial" role. Arbona, "Sangre de minero," 26, 40.
10. Goldenberg, *Kommunismus*, 96.
11. "Mineros quieren recuperar la Tesis de Pulacayo," *La Prensa* (La Paz), 24 March 2003; Cajías de la Vega, "Componente anarquista," 58; "Salt Route."
12. Guillermoprieto, "A New Bolivia?," 37; Guarachi Huanca, "Comunidades."
13. Whitehead, "Bolivia Since 1930," 528; *Time*, 16 March 1959, 40.
14. Carter, *Bolivia*, 61; Klein, *Parties*, 384; Debray, *Che's Guerrilla War*, 47, 58.
15. "La Révolution bolivienne entre Wall Street et Trotski," *Le Monde*, 24 October 1953.
16. See glossary in Poppe, *Interior mina*, 187–91.
17. See Nash, *We Eat the Mines* and "Interpreting Social Movements," and Poppe, *Compañeros del Tío*.
18. *La Razón* (La Paz, hereafter *Razón*), 7 July 2004, condensed from Thomson and Qayum, "Ahora que lo pienso"; interview, Alejandro Carvajal, 5 July 2004.

19. In June 2005 I watched members of the POR youth group practice a new version of an old miners' *huayño* to protest the army's killing of the miner Juan Coro Mayta as he led a march on Sucre to "shut down parliament." On miners' songs, see Youdale and Chire, *Cantan las minas.*

20. "1952: La Revolución."

21. See Dunkerley's *Bolivia: Revolution and the Power of History in the Present* and Thomson's "Revolutionary Memory in Bolivia."

22. Zavaleta Mercado, *Poder dual,* 84.

23. Interviews: Amadeo Vargas, 6 August 2004; Julio García, 30 July 2004; Pastor Peláez, 6 August 2004.

Chapter 1. Between Tupac Amaru and Trotsky

1. Mallon, "Decoding," 23.

2. Klein, *Bolivia,* 179; Dunkerley, "Origins," 141; Volk, "Class, Union, Party," 1:33.

3. Interview, Julio García, 30 July 2004; *New York Times* (hereafter *NYT*), 24 March 2003.

4. Interviews: Grover Alejandro, 16 July 2004; Felipe Vásquez, 4 October 1992; Dionicio Coca, 18 August 2007. Oruro's labor federation building is dedicated to the memory of Felipe Vásquez.

5. Iriarte, *Mineros,* 50–51.

6. Prada Alcoreza, "Perfiles," 41; Encinas, *Jinapuni,* 18.

7. Compañía Estañífera de Llallagua, 1923 report, 40–41, Patiño Collection, ADC; Pendle, *History of Latin America,* 212.

8. Montoya, "Crónicas."

9. *Bandera Roja,* 8 November 1926, 8.

10. Justo, *Bolivia,* 100.

11. *International Press Correspondence,* 17 October 1928; Comintern, *Matériaux et Informations,* Bulletin 4 (10 January 1930), pagination unclear.

12. Mariátegui, *Obras,* 2:171.

13. *Movimiento revolucionario latino americano,* 268–69, 282 (varies from *Obras* version).

14. Ibid., 303.

15. *Movimiento revolucionario latino americano,* 47; Justo, *Bolivia,* 100; Lora, *Historia de partidos políticos,* 187–88.

16. Knight, "Dynamics," 64; Whitehead, "Bolivia Since 1930," 528.

17. Lehman, *Bolivia and U.S.,* 72.

18. Klein, *Historia,* 232.

19. Comintern, *Matériaux et Informations,* Bulletin 4.

20. Zavaleta Mercado, *Crecimiento,* 22–24; Lehman, *Bolivia and U.S.,* 70; Rosalío Negrete, "Chaco: Imperialist Battleground," *The Militant* (New York), 6 January 1934.

21. Interview, Eduardo Arze, 2 October 1992; Aguirre Gainsborg, quoted in Lora, *Figuras*, 18.

22. Interview, Oscar Barrientos, 2 October 1992; Zavaleta Mercado, *Crecimiento*, 24.

23. Iriarte and Equipo CIPCA, "Sindicalismo campesino," 130.

24. Interview, Eduardo Mendizábal, 13 January 2007.

25. Klein, *Parties*, 196; *El Diario* (hereafter *Diario*), 21 September, 26 November, 4 December, 27 December 1932, 10 January 1933; *Ultima Hora* (La Paz), 26 November 1932.

26. Linke, *Viaje*, 276–77; interview, Eduardo Arze, 2 October 1992.

27. Lenin, "Defeat," 275.

28. Lora, *Figuras*, 7, 10; Abecia López, *7 políticos*, 77–78.

29. Díaz Machicao, *Bestia emocional*, 91–94, 102.

30. Lora, *Figuras*, 15, 16; Fernández (Aguirre), "Guerra del Chaco," 22; Ministerio de Gobierno, 10 August 1932, Archivo de la Paz/P-A. Prov. Sicasica, 1932–1937, C.7.

31. Díaz Machicao, *Bestia emocional*, 112–14, 118.

32. Interview, Eduardo Arze, 2 October 1992; Lora, *Contribución*, 1:74–75.

33. Saenz, "José Aguirre en Chile," 34–35.

34. Fernández (Aguirre), "Guerra del Chaco," 23, "Correspondencia del Chaco," 26.

35. *Nueva Internacional* (Mexico City), June 1934; Coggiola, *Trotskismo*, 22.

36. Lora, *Contribución*, 1:74.

37. Alexander, *Trotskyism*, 103; minutes, 14 February 1936, H-SWP, I.S. 1936 folder.

38. Interview, Eduardo Arze, 2 October 1992.

39. Lora, *Figuras*, 31.

40. U.S. Library of Congress, "Bolivia Country Studies"; Albarracín, *Sociedad opresora*, 31; Schelchkov, "Internacional Comunista," 4.

41. Klein, *Parties*, 191; Justo, *Bolivia*, 101; Baciu, *Marof*, 147.

42. Navarro, *Poetas-idealistas*, 130.

43. Ibid., 191–92.

44. Albarracín, *Sociedad opresora*, 297; Marof, *Novela de un hombre*, 165; "Historia de mis libros," in Baciu, *Marof*, 42; Asturias, "Suetonio Pimienta y otros libros," 198.

45. Albarracín, *Sociedad opresora*, 298.

46. Mella, *Mella en El Machete*, 160–64; Marof on muralists, Baciu, *Marof*, 69.

47. Mallon, "Decoding the Parchments," 25; Vanden, *National Marxism*, 53, 52.

48. Schelchkov, "Internacional Comunista," 6; Mariátegui, "Tristán Marof," 193, 195, and "Últimas aventuras"; Marof, "Política y economía," 16–17, "Espartacus y Sandino," 26.

49. Valencia Vega, *Desarrollo*, 92; Schelchkov, "Internacional Comunista," 6; Marof, *Justicia del Inca*, 39, 7, 9–10; Albarracín, *Sociedad opresora*, 302–13.

50. Thomson, "Revolutionary Memory," 127; *Amauta,* March 1928, 35; Klein, *Parties,* 97.

51. Marof, "Bolivia y la nacionalización de las minas," 90, 92; *Labor Defender,* September 1929 (page unclear); Marof, "Oil and Blood," 75.

52. Schelchkov, "Internacional Comunista," 8; Arriola Woog, *Sobre rusos y Rusia,* 333; Marof, *Wall Street,* 9, 12, 36–37, 141, passim.

53. Mariátegui, *Correspondencia* 2:408–9; Marof, *México,* 22–24, 146–50.

54. Baciu, *Marof,* 131; Klein, *Parties,* 125–6, 195; Lora, *Figuras,* 32–34.

55. Fernández (Aguirre), "Falta un partido," 36; Lora, *Contribución,* 1:85; Klein, *Orígenes,* 167.

56. Marof, *Tragedia,* 6, 214, 217–19.

57. Ibid., 53, 60, 220–22.

58. Ibid., 119, 209.

59. Interview, Eduardo Arze, 2 October 1992.

Chapter 2. Return to an Early Grave

1. "Informe general sobre el primer congreso del P.O.R. al Secretariado de la L.C.I.," unsigned, n.d. Attached to Partido Obrero Revolucionario, letter to Leon Trotsky, 26 July 1935, Leon Trotsky Exile Papers, bMS Russ 13.1 (1046), by permission of the Houghton Library, Harvard University.

2. Marof, *Tragedia,* 222; Lora, *Historia de partidos políticos,* 199–200.

3. Fernández (Aguirre), "Falta un partido," 35–36.

4. "Informe general."

5. Linke, *Viaje,* 277.

6. "Informe general"; interview, Eduardo Arze, 2 October 1992.

7. Interview, Eduardo Arze, 2 October 1992.

8. POR letter to Trotsky, 26 July 1935, Leon Trotsky Exile Papers, bMS Russ 13.1 (1046), by permission of the Houghton Library, Harvard University.

9. "Informe general." These resolutions are not attached to the report.

10. Klein, *Parties,* 195–96; Mariano Baptista, quoted in Justo, *Bolivia,* 99.

11. Lora, *Marxismo en Bolivia,* 34, "Crise," 2–3; Baciu, *Marof,* 163.

12. Lora, *Figuras,* 34–35, *Contribución,* 1:104; "Informe general"; Trotsky, *Stalin's Gangsters,* 58–61.

13. Justo, *Bolivia,* 102.

14. Lora, *Contribución,* 1:92–93.

15. Justo, *Bolivia,* 102; Marof, *Habla un condenado,* 18, 91.

16. Marof, *Habla un condenado,* 37–38, 168, 173.

17. Ibid., 43.

18. Ibid., 178, 183–84.

19. Ibid., 137, 147–48.

20. Ibid., 187. This is presumably the same General Quintanilla who became president in 1939.

21. Trotsky, *Spanish Revolution,* 236.

22. Fernández (Aguirre), "POR y Toro."

23. Klein, *Parties*, 196; Lora, "Crise," 4–5. Lora later denounced those who "irresponsibly say that the POR disappeared from the political scene after its foundation" (*Contribución*, 1:133).

24. Villa, *Orígenes*, 5; interviews: Eduardo Arze, Oscar Barrientos, 2 October 1992.

25. Alvarez España, *Memorias*, 82, 111; Lora, *Contribución*, 1:227.

26. Interviews: Eduardo Arze, Oscar Barrientos, 2 October 1992.

27. Valencia Vega, *Desarrollo*, 101.

28. *Diario*, 29 October and 31 October 1935 (compare Klein, *Parties*, 212); Lora, *Contribución*, 1:106. Earlier, Lora wrote more critically in "Crise."

29. Lora, *Figuras*, 39–40.

30. *Diario*, 9, 17, 18, 25 and 26 October, 12 and 24 November 1935; Villa, *Orígenes*, 7.

31. Marof letter to *La Fragua* (La Paz, hereafter *Fragua*), 5 May 1936; *Diario*, 20 October 1935, 13 March 1936; see also Alvarez, *Memorias*, 72.

32. *Fragua*, 11 March 1936; *La República* (hereafter *República*), 29 March 1936.

33. *El Ex-Combatiente*, 23 February 1936.

34. Interview, Oscar Barrientos, 2 October 1992.

35. *Ultima Hora*, 21 May and 25 July 1936.

36. Miranda, *Crisis de poder*, 61.

37. See "Bolivia y su petróleo," *Clave* (Mexico City), 1 June 1939.

38. Miranda, *Crisis de poder*, 63; *El dictador suicida* (1956) is Augusto Céspedes's celebrated book on Busch.

39. Alvarez, *Memorias*, 98; "Un Voto de Apoyo al Ministro señor Waldo Alvarez," *Diario*, 27 May 1936.

40. *República*, 7 June 1936; *Diario*, 9 August 1936; *La Calle* (hereafter *Calle*), 2 October, 26 August, and 12 September 1936; *Ultima Hora*, 26 August 1936. I have kept the "z" in "trotzkista."

41. *Calle*, 1, 20, 22, and 27 August, 9, 10, and 11 September 1936.

42. *Calle*, 22 September and 3 December 1936.

43. Fernández, "POR y Toro."

44. Lora, *Figuras*, 55–56; Alvarez, *Memorias*, 148, 150–51.

45. *República*, 29 and 31 March 1936; *Fragua*, 19 and 20 March, 17 April 1936. A subhead, possibly added by the editors, states: "My communism is economic nationalism."

46. Schelchkov, "Internacional Comunista," 12–14.

47. Interview, Eduardo Arze, 2 October 1992; Baciu, *Marof*, 50; Marof, *Verdad socialista*, 52, 61, 66–69.

48. Lora, *Obras*, 3:302; interview, Eduardo Arze, 2 October 1992; Lora, *Contribución*, 1:192–93.

49. Interview, Eduardo Arze, 2 October 1992. Oscar Barrientos was present and did not contradict Arze's account.

50. Baciu, *Marof,* 163; Peñaloza in *Razón,* 27 October 1938.

51. *Calle,* 3 and 6 November 1938.

52. *Calle,* 25 October 1938.

53. *Calle,* 25 and 28 October, 1 November 1938; *Diario,* 27 October 1938; *Razón,* 25 October 1938.

54. Díaz Machicao, *Bestia emocional,* 92; *Diario,* 25 October 1938; *Calle,* 27 October 1938.

55. *Razón,* 26 October 1938.

56. Salazar, *Gesta,* 82.

57. Interview, Eduardo Arze, 2 October 1992.

58. Salazar, *Gesta,* 11. Elizardo's niece Ana, shown with Salazar in figure 2.3, later joined Lora's POR. (Personal communication from Cecilia Salazar de la Torre, 13 June 2008.)

Chapter 3. Under the Sign of Pulacayo

1. Interview, Oscar Barrientos, 2 October 1992.

2. Cornejo, *Programas,* 364–69, 373, 378–83 (original emphasis).

3. Lora, "Crise," 5, 16, *Contribución,* 1:297; interviews: Modesto Sejas, 2 October 1992; Guillermo Lora, 1 August 2003.

4. Interview, Jorge Abelardo Ramos, 30 January 1992. Ramos left the Fourth International and, after decades leading the pro-Peronist "national left," was appointed ambassador by Carlos Menem.

5. Lora, *Figuras,* 164; Cornejo, *Programas,* 297–312.

6. Lora, *Figuras,* 164–65; *Documentos* (La Paz), December 1978, 29.

7. Interview, Oscar Barrientos, 2 October 1992.

8. POR letter to Trotsky, 26 July 1935, cited above; minutes, 17 May 1938, H-SWP, AAPB folder.

9. Circular letter, 1 April 1938, H-SWP, I.S. Corresp. 1935–45 folder; Prager, *Congrès,* 1:215, 241; *Socialist Appeal* (New York), 22 October 1938.

10. Cornejo, *Programas,* 383 (original emphasis); interview, Oscar Barrientos, 2 October 1992; *Documents of the FI,* 381.

11. Lora, *Contribución,* 1:298.

12. IKD report, untitled bulletin, H-SWP, emergency conference folder; Abramo, "Construire," 91–92.

13. Document dated 2 May 1907, Copiador de la Cía. Porvenir de Colquechaca, ADC; interview, Elio Vásquez, 17 July 2004.

14. Interviews: Guillermo Lora, 1 August 2003, 26 July 2004; Lora, *Figuras,* 80–84, 119–21.

15. Interviews: Oscar Barrientos, 2 October 1992; Jorge Abelardo Ramos, 30 January 1992.

16. Lora, *Figuras,* 83; interview, Oscar Barrientos, 2 October 1992.

17. *Razón,* 20 February 1942.

18. *Tierra* (La Paz), 24 February 1942; *Diario*, 22 February 1942; *Razón*, 20 and 21 February 1942.

19. *Calle*, 21 February 1942; *El País*, 25 February 1942; *Calle*, 1 March 1942.

20. Interviews: Guillermo Lora, 1 August 2003, 26 July 2004; Volk, "Class, Union, Party," 2:190.

21. Ruiz González, *Prometeo de los Andes*, 97; Le Bot, "Mineurs boliviens," 13; Whitehead, "Bolivia Since 1930," 528; article on "progressive bourgeoisie," *La Chispa* (La Paz), 15 February 1947.

22. Interview, former POR member (anonymous), 18 January 2007.

23. *Lucha Obrera* (Mexico City), July 1943.

24. Interviews: Alberto Aguilar, 16 July 2004; Juan Perelman Fajardo, 5 July 2004; L. Fajardo, *A los trabajadores*, October 1944, Carmen and Francisco Bedregal collection.

25. Interviews: Juan Perelman Fajardo, 5 July 2004; Andrés Soliz Rada, 29 September 1992.

26. Interview, former POR member (anonymous), 18 January 2007; Fajardo, *Pampa, metal y sangre.*

27. Núñez to I.S., 14 January 1947, BDIC F. rés 457/1–2 (Dossier Bolivie, IV Internationale, Correspondance), 1947 folder (hereafter "BDIC 457/1–2" and folder); interview, Hugo González, 5 October 1992.

28. Interview, Hugo González, 5 October 1992.

29. *Minneapolis Star Journal*, 10 January 1945; Villa, *Orígenes*, 13.

30. Cajías de la Vega and Jiménez Chávez, *Mujeres en las minas*, 82, 85.

31. Interview, former POR member (anonymous), 18 January 2007.

32. Lora, *Obras*, 1:87–91, 27:71; *The Militant*, 1 May 1943, 1 January 1944.

33. MNR program, in Baptista Gumucio, *Cuadros Quiroga*, 195–99, 201–2 (signatories included Paz, Siles, Walter Guevara, Augusto Céspedes, and Carlos Montenegro); contract with Víctor Paz Estenssoro, 30 July 1937, Patiño Collection, ADC.

34. *The Militant*, 1 January 1944.

35. These manifestos were later reprinted in the POR's *Lucha Obrera* (La Paz), 2 March 1947.

36. Interview, Hugo González, 5 October 1992.

37. Chávez Guzmán, *Muerte de Enrique Ferrante*, 26–27.

38. Interview, Hugo González, 5 October 1992.

39. Undated leaflets, BDIC 468/1, 1945 folder; Volk, "Class, Union, Party," 2:190.

40. Hence the title of Augusto Céspedes's *El presidente colgado* (The Hanged President).

41. Lora, *Contribución*, 2:42–43; interview, Modesto Sejas, 2 October 1992; *Manifiesto del Frente Universitario de Izquierda*, 6 August 1946, BDIC 468/1, 1946 folder; interview, Edwin Möller, 29 September 1992.

42. *Lucha Obrera* (La Paz), 29 October 1946; untitled resolution, 6 August 1946, FBEC; manifesto, 4 September 1946, BDIC 468/1, 1946 folder.

43. *Tribuna Socialista* (Mexico City), 21 September 1946; *Fourth International* (New York), March 1947, 79–81; Rey, *En Bolivia*, 125.

44. *Revolución Proletaria* (Havana), 1 April 1946.

45. Interview, Hugo González, 5 October 1992.

46. *Noticias*, 25 August 1946; *The Militant*, 21 September 1946.

47. Encinas, *Jinapuni*, 31; Lora, *Contribución*, 2:5–6.

48. Cajías, *Historia de una leyenda*, 63; *Los Tiempos* (Cochabamba, hereafter *Tiempos*), 3 January 1947; Lora, *Vigencia*, 14, *Contribución*, 2:47.

49. Interviews: Hugo González, 5 October 1992; Gloria Lora, 18 August 2007.

50. Lora, *Contribución*, 2:25–26, 50.

51. Malloy, *Uncompleted Revolution*, 146–47.

52. Lora, *Figuras*, 85, *Historia, 1933–1952*, 47, *Contribución*, 2:57.

53. Miguel Núñez (then POR general secretary) to I.S., 14 January 1947, BDIC 457/1–2, 1947 folder; *Razón*, 19 March 1946.

54. *Razón*, 20 March 1946; *Tiempos*, 20 March 1946; *Cumbre* (La Paz), 21 March 1946; *Ultima Hora*, 21 March 1946.

55. *Razón*, 19 March 1946; *Diario*, 23 March 1946; Lora, *Contribución*, 2:26, 31. The "Transitional Program" is Trotsky's 1938 pamphlet *The Death Agony of Capitalism and the Tasks of the Fourth International.*

56. Minutes and resolutions of POR Fifth Congress, 25 September 1946, FBEC.

57. "Salt Route."

58. During the lead-up to Goni's overthrow, union spokesmen called to "return to the Thesis of Pulacayo"; "Mineros quieren recuperar la Tesis de Pulacayo," *La Prensa* (La Paz), 24 March 2003.

59. Interviews: Guillermo Lora, 3 August 2004; Emma Bolshia Bravo, 4 August 2003; Hugo González, 5 October 1992.

60. Interview, Julio Bardales, 28 June 2004.

61. "Tesis Central Aprobada en el Primer Congreso Extraordinario de Trabajadores Mineros de Bolivia," *Razón*, 8 December 1946 (hereafter cited as "Tesis de Pulacayo").

62. "Tesis de Pulacayo."

63. *Política Obrera* (Buenos Aires), 23 October 1974.

64. "Tesis de Pulacayo." This aspect was later critiqued by Salazar's LSR; see his *Caducidad de una estrategia.*

65. Zapata, *Autonomía*, 54; compare Volk, "Class, Union, Party." A former comrade claimed the Bolivian Trotskyists "were always half-anarchists, you know"; conversation with Adolfo Gilly, 13 March 2008.

66. Interview, Julio García, 30 July 2004; Lora, *Figuras*, 85.

67. Klein, *Parties*, 384; Candia G., *Experimento comunista*, 89; *Bolivia* report (1947), 6, Max Shachtman Papers, Box 4, Folder 42, Tamiment Institute;

Diario, 26 August 1949; *Manifiesto Obrero* leaflet, PURS, La Paz, May 1947; BAHC-SCC.

68. *Diario,* 11 November 1946; *El Imparcial* (Cochabamba), 29 April 1947; *Ultima Hora,* 11 November 1990; article on W. Guevara, http://www.voltairenet .org/article120493.html (accessed 2 February 2006); *Siempre Abril* (La Paz), 24 February 1984.

69. *La Noche* (La Paz, hereafter *Noche*), 23 May 1947; *Razón,* 9 June 1947.

70. *Noche,* 22 May and 9 June 1947.

71. *El Comercio* (La Paz), 27 June 1947; *Diario,* 24 June 1947.

72. POR leaflet, December 1946, BAHC-SCC; introduction to 1980 edition of *Tesis de Pulacayo,* 4; Canciones del POR and recording, kindly provided by Emma Bolshia Bravo.

73. *Bolivia* report (1947), 6, Shachtman papers, Tamiment.

74. Scali (Broué), *Révolution bolivienne,* 14.

75. *Razón,* 10 November 1946; Scali, *Révolution bolivienne,* 15.

76. Zavaleta Mercado, *Caída,* 66.

77. Klein, *Bolivia,* 222.

78. Núñez to I.S., 14 January 1947, BDIC 457/1–2, 1947 folder; *Manifiesto del Comité Sindicalista del Banco Central,* 25 April 1946 (signed by POR militant Guillermo Guerrero as Secretary General), BDIC 468/1, 1946 folder; Möller Pacieri, *Dios desnudo,* 35.

79. *Tiempos,* 31 January 1947.

80. *Razón,* 7 and 9 February 1947.

81. Communiqué, La Paz, 31 January 1947, BAHC-SCC; leaflet, 6 February 1947, BDIC 468/1, 1947 folder; *Tiempos,* 1 February 1947; Lora, *Crímenes del PIR,* 3.

82. *Manifiesto Obrero* (see note 67); *La Batalla* (La Paz), 1 May 1947; *Tiempos,* 1 February 1947.

83. *Noticias* article reprinted in *Tiempos,* 30 January 1947.

84. *Lucha Obrera* (La Paz), 3 April 1947.

85. Antezana, *Historia secreta,* 1167–72. Antezana states that Lechín had joined the MNR four years previously at Siles Zuazo's invitation, but he rejected the proposal to run some official MNR candidates in mine districts.

86. *Noche,* 3 January 1947; POR manifesto, December 1946, Archivo y Biblioteca de la Nación. Núñez to I.S., 14 January 1947, BDIC 457/1–2, 1947 folder.

87. Interviews: Grover Alejandro, 16 July 2004; Guillermo Lora, 26 July 2004; *Razón,* 19 January 1947.

88. *Razón,* 3 August and 18 September 1947.

89. *Redactor–Diputados,* 1947, 1:141, 143; interview, Jorge Abelardo Ramos, 30 January 1992.

90. Lora, *Obras,* 2:93, 492–93; *Razón,* 29 March 1947; Cajías, *Historia de una leyenda,* 92.

91. *Tribuna Socialista* (Mexico City), 10 March 1947; *The Militant*, 14 July 1947.

92. *Contra la Corriente* (Montevideo), February 1947. The paper reported that Ernesto Ayala, Fernando Bravo, and three other POR members were elected as alternate deputies (*suplentes*), while referring to Lechín, Torres, and others as "pro-POR miners" in the BMP. Although "against Lechín's will," it stated, the MNR had tried to claim him as its vice presidential candidate.

93. *Bolivia* report, 1947, 6, Shachtman papers, Tamiment.

94. "Lettre de Lima," 25 November 1947, BDIC 468/1–2, 1947 folder.

95. Interview, Hugo González, 5 October 1992; resolutions, Sixth POR Conference, 16 October 1947, FBEC.

96. Interview, Hugo González, 5 October 1992; Lora, *Contribución*, 2:193, *Obras*, 3:456–58; Céspedes letter, n.d., BDIC 457/1–2, 1948 folder; Villa, *Orígenes*, 28.

97. Leaflet on BMP, November 1947, BAHC-SCC.

98. Interviews: Hugo González, 5 October 1992; Jorge Abelardo Ramos, 10 January 1992; I.S. *Internal Bulletin*, December 1947, 3; *The Fourth (Trotskyite) International—Its Structure and Personnel*, 5 December 1949, declassified in 1976, 18, H-WER, Box 14, Folder 2. Providing lists of alleged leaders and membership figures for FI sections, this inaccurate, often lurid document is one of the declassified intelligence reports in the papers of a witness for the government in the SWP's 1973–86 lawsuit against FBI spying.

99. *The Militant*, 14 July 1947; *Tribuna Socialista*, 16 July 1947; FI report on Bolivia, 10 July 1947, BDIC 468/1, 1947 folder; Céspedes to SWP, 13 October 1947, H-SWP, Bolivia 1941–47 folder.

100. Lora, *Estado y Rosca*; *Diario*, 22 June, 10 June, 12 June, and 2 July 1948; *Noche*, 28 June 1948; *Lucha Obrera* (La Paz), 6 March 1948.

101. *Diario*, 17 May and 4 June 1949.

102. CC resolution, 28 July 1949, FBEC (original emphasis); POR manifesto, August 1949, BAHC-SCC.

103. *Razón*, 29 and 30 May 1949.

104. *Diario*, 1 June 1949. Many front-page cartoons featured the POR during this period.

105. *Razón*, 31 May 1949. Lora recalled (interview, 26 July 2004) that years later he was barred from entering the United States, accused of complicity in the hostages' deaths, although he had not been present. When an immigration official offered him a cup of coffee, "I threw it at him and called him a gringo shithead."

106. *Diario*, 6 and 26 August 1949. Former Trotskyist Max Shachtman's *Labor Action* (New York) published several dispatches that year warning that the MNR and POR sought a "totalitarian," "Stalinazi" takeover.

107. Interview, Julio Bardales, 28 June 2004; *Junta Revolucionaria*, Pulacayo, 10 September 1949, Julio Bardales papers, ADC; interviews: Grover Alejandro, 16 July 2004; Julio García, 30 July 2004.

108. Lora, "Class Struggles," 127; Chávez Guzmán, *Muerte de Enrique Ferrante,* 53, 55; interview, Eduardo Mendizábal, 13 January 2007; *Documentos* (La Paz), December 1978, p. "b."

109. Lora, *Contribución,* 2:220; *Internacionalismo proletario,* 6; interviews: Elio Vásquez, 17 July 2004; Edwin Möller, 29 September 1992.

110. Interview, Hugo González, 5 October 1992.

111. Taboada Terán, *Revolución desfigurada,* 649; Encinas, *Jinapuni,* 28.

112. This coincidence is discussed in Debray, *Che's Guerrilla War,* 93–94.

113. *Diario,* 14 September 1949; Chávez Guzmán, *Muerte de Enrique Ferrante,* 71–72.

114. *Ultima Hora* and *Diario,* 11 April 1950.

115. *Service Presse Internationale (4)* (Paris), July–August 1950, 10–11. *Ultima Hora* (23 May 1950) reported "extremely high casualties," in Villa Victoria.

116. *Razón,* 28 May 1950.

117. *Razón,* 29 and 30 May 1950; interview, Eduardo Mendizábal, 13 January 2007; Chávez Guzmán, *Muerte de Enrique Ferrante,* 3–10, 20.

118. Céspedes to SWP, 13 October 1947, H-SWP, Bolivia 1941–47 folder; I.S. minutes, 2 December 1946, CERMRTI; *Bolivia* and *Chile* reports (1947), Shachtman papers, Tamiment; interview, Hugo González, 5 October 1992; Lora, *Contribución,* 2:200–201.

119. *Boletín latino-americano,* March 1949, 31–33, H-SWP, "International Bulletins, Spanish-language 1949" folder.

120. Wald, *Revolutionary Imagination,* 207–15; *Masas,* 10 February 1962.

121. Interview, Hugo González, 5 October 1992; I.S. *Bulletin intérieur,* September 1951, 5.

122. Interviews: Hugo González, 5 October 1992; Guillermo Lora, 1 August 2003.

123. Prager, *Congrès,* 4:27, 36, 47.

124. *Cuarta Internacional* (Buenos Aires), August–October 1951, 60–61.

125. I.S. *Boletín interno,* September 1951, 11; *La Vérité* (Paris, date illegible), CERMTRI; *Cuarta Internacional,* August–October 1951, 61.

126. *Cuarta Internacional,* August–October 1951, 60–61 (emphasis added).

127. Lora, *Contribución,* 2:196–97, 225.

128. Interview, Hugo González, 5 October 1992.

129. Cited in *Latin American Facts* (New York), May 1952, 6; Mitchell, *Legacy of Populism,* 33.

130. Alexander, *Trotskyism in Latin America,* 124; Villa, *Orígenes,* 33; Mitchell, *Legacy of Populism,* 31; Malloy, *Uncompleted Revolution,* 152; Lora, *Contribución,* 2:224–25; interviews: Edwin Möller, 29 September 1992; Hugo González, 5 October 1992.

131. Sergio (Möller) to regional committees, 14 March 1952, BDIC 457/1–2, 1952 folder (original emphasis); *Noticias,* 1 April 1952; Villa, *Orígenes,* 34.

132. Interview in *The Militant,* 12 and 19 May 1952, which translated it from *La Vérité,* 17 April–7 May 1952.

Chapter 4. Trotskyism and the Revolución Nacional

1. Knight, "Domestic Dynamics," 60.
2. Ribeiro, *Américas,* 199; *La Nación* (La Paz, hereafter *Nación*), 18 August 1954.
3. Interview, Hugo González, 5 October 1992.
4. "Defend the Bolivian Revolution!" *The Militant,* 5 May 1952.
5. Interview, Gonzalo Trigoso, 19 July 2004 (compare Roberts Barragán, *Revolución del 9 de abril* and Irusta Medrano, *Lucha armada*); Selbin, *Modern Latin American Revolutions,* 39.
6. Sapiencia, "Factor conspirativo," 13; interview, Grover Alejandro, 16 July 2004; Encinas, *Jinapuni,* 37–38.
7. *Tiempos,* 15 April 1952.
8. Encinas, *Jinapuni,* 38; *NYT,* 19 April 1952.
9. Encinas, *Jinapuni,* 38.
10. Ibid., 49.
11. *The Militant,* 5 May 1952; *Revolución en Bolivia* (Buenos Aires), May 1953, 9, H-LSH, Box 18, "Bolivia Miscellaneous" folder.
12. *NYT,* 10 April and 4 May 1952.
13. Möller, *Dios desnudo,* 40.
14. Interview, former POR member (anonymous), 18 January 2007; Malloy, *Uncompleted Revolution,* 75.
15. *Le Monde* (Paris), 24 October 1953.
16. *Le Monde,* 21–22 August 1955.
17. Prado, *Populismo,* 77.
18. Paz Estenssoro, "Fundamentos científicos de la Revolución Nacional," 63–64, 67–68.
19. Ibid., 62–64, 67; Chávez Ortiz, *Cinco ensayos,* 43.
20. *Lucha Obrera* (La Paz), 20 September 1953.
21. Velarde, *Nacionalismo y acción demagógica,* 4, 19. Comibol chief Guillermo Bedregal, Ernesto Ayala (after he left the POR for the MNR), Luis Antezana, Carlos Serrate Reich, and Roberto Jordán Pando also polemicized extensively against Trotskyism.
22. *Nación,* 7 March 1953.
23. Klein, *Bolivia,* 238, 118.
24. *Extrait d'un document intérieur du P.O.R. bolivien* (21 April 1952), H-SWP, Bolivia 1952–1953 folder; Lora, *Revolución Boliviana,* 38.
25. Interview, Edwin Möller, 29 September 1992; Justo, *Bolivia,* 145.
26. Interview, Hugo González, 5 October 1992.
27. Interview, former POR member (anonymous), 18 January 2007.
28. Interview, Modesto Sejas, 2 October 1992.

29. Interview, Julio García, 30 July 2004.

30. Interview, Hugo González, 5 October 1992.

31. *Tiempos*, 16 April 1952.

32. *Extrait d'un document*, 21 April 1952, cited above.

33. "Lenin telegraphed . . . 'Our tactic; absolute lack of confidence; no support to the new government'"; quoted in Trotsky, *History of the Russian Revolution*, 1:292.

34. *The Militant*, 19 May 1952; *Lucha Obrera* (La Paz), 18 May 1952.

35. Report on Ninth Conference, October 1952, BDIC 468/1, subfolder 1952; *Lucha Obrera* (La Paz), 11 November 1952, quoted in *The Militant*, 19 January 1953; *Tiempos*, 16 May 1953.

36. *International Information Bulletin* (SWP), January 1953, 24; *Fourth International* (New York), January–February 1953, 16.

37. *Economist*, 23 May 1953, 528.

38. *Tiempos*, 13 May 1953.

39. Interview, Edwin Möller, 29 September 1992; *NYT*, 3 May 1952.

40. Salazar Mostajo, *Pintura contemporánea*, 131–35; Lora, *Figuras*, 122–33, 157; Salazar de la Torre, "Identidad nacional"; *Presencia*, 13 November 1983 and 10 July 1984; Cordero, "Alandia"; Montoya, "Pinturas rebeldes."

41. "El Mural de Alandia Pantoja en el Palacio de Gobierno," *Nación*, 1 January 1953. Together with Carlos Salazar (whose brother Jorge, a POR leader, was his intimate friend), Alandia established a Union of Revolutionary Painters (*Nación*, 12 January 1953).

42. Cited in an untitled brochure (1961) presenting Alandia's Legislative Palace mural, "The Bourgeois Parliament and the Revolution."

43. Interview, Edwin Möller, 29 September 1992; *Economist*, 23 May 1953, 528; *Nación*, 8 January 1953.

44. Interview, Hugo González, 5 October 1992; Lora, *Contribución*, 2:228; *Así lucharon*, 85.

45. I.S. *Bulletin intérieur* on Bolivia, April 1953, 3; *Nación*, 27 February 1953; I.S. *Bulletin intérieur*, January 1953, 1–4; *Lucha Obrera* (La Paz), 5 July 1953; Rosas to Dobbs, 30 November 1953, H-SWP, Bolivia 1952–53 folder; interviews: Alejandro Carvajal, 5 July 2005; Grover Alejandro, 16 July 2004.

46. "Tesis de Pulacayo"; Lazarte, *Movimiento obrero*, 7; Lora, *Revolución Boliviana*, 282; *The Militant*, 19 May 1952; Lora, *Contribución*, 2:252; *Revolución en Bolivia* (Buenos Aires), May 1953, 24.

47. POR to I.S., 7 February 1953, H-SWP, Bolivia 1952–1953 folder. *The Militant* (5 May 1952) had also questioned Lechín's decision to join "a capitalist government."

48. *Nación*, 14 October 1952; *Bulletin d'Information*, 1 November 1952, 5–6, and *Bulletin intérieur*, January 1953, 5.

49. Lora, *Obras*, 4:166–67.

50. *Lucha Obrera* (La Paz), 5 July and 2 August 1953.

51. *Lucha Obrera* (La Paz), 23 August 1953.

52. *Lucha Obrera* (La Paz), 30 August 1953. The POR advanced similar positions in a resolution for the Second COB Congress, reprinted in César Lora, *Escritos*, 5.

53. Undated leaflet, BDIC F. rés 468/2 (Dossier Bolivie, IV Inter., Archives du SI [puis SU], 1954–1965)(hereafter "468/2"), 1954 folder.

54. Linke, *Viaje*, 296–97.

55. Lora, "Anti-trotskismo," 163.

56. MNR program, in Baptista Gumucio, *Cuadros Quiroga*, 201–2.

57. Patch, "Restrained Revolution," 129; Dunkerley, *Rebellion*, 73.

58. Leaflet, *El POR llama a las masas campesinas a luchar organizadamente por la conquista de las tierras*, 1953; Antezana, *Reforma agraria*, 71.

59. Interview, Edwin Möller, 29 September 1992; *Nación*, 5 July 1953.

60. *Lucha Obrera* (La Paz), 1 and 31 May 1953.

61. *Lucha Obrera* (La Paz), 5 July and 23 August 1953.

62. *Nación*, 19 March 1953.

63. Sinforoso Rivas in Gordillo, *Arando*, 100.

64. *Tiempos*, 31 January and 1 February 1953; manuscript of Cochrane lecture, 24 April 1953, 21–22, Cochrane Papers, Box 2, Folder 18, Tamiment; interview, Modesto Sejas, 2 October 1992.

65. Iriarte and Equipo CIPCA, "Sindicalismo campesino," 154–55; *Tiempos*, 25 April 1953; *NYT*, 8 February 1953.

66. Ortiz, *Amanecer en Bolivia*, 42, 164.

67. Iriarte and Equipo CIPCA, "Sindicalismo campesino," 153; Ponce Arauco, "Insurgencia campesina," 19–20.

68. I.S. *Bulletin intérieur*, February 1954, 23; appeal by "Walker," 27 January 1954, BDIC 468/2, 1954 folder.

69. Interview, Modesto Sejas, 2 October 1992. The Carlos Bayón recalled by Sejas and the Carlos Bayá recalled by Lora (see chapter 3) may have been the same person.

70. Interview, Guillermo Lora, 1 August 2003. In reality, Lenin and Trotsky, like Marx, consistently characterized smallholding peasants (as distinct from landless rural laborers) as proprietors.

71. Political Bureau circular (7 February 1953), in I.S. *Bulletin intérieur* on Bolivia, April 1953, 4, 6–7.

72. Resolution on Cochabamba (17 February 1953) in ibid., 9–10.

73. Letter to I.S. (undated), in ibid., 1.

74. *El POR en defensa de las tierras ocupadas*, Comité Local del POR, Ucureña, 9 April 1954, anonymous collection (original emphasis).

75. Lora, *Contribución*, 2:258–59; "Etapa actual de la Revolución Boliviana y tareas del P.O.R.," *¿Qué Hacer?* December 1953, 24–27. Lora (*Obras*, 4:366) notes that *¿Qué Hacer?* reproduced the original. However, the text in *Obras* includes several changes.

76. "Etapa actual," 32.

77. Ibid., 34, 36.

78. Lora, *Contribución*, 2:261.

79. Interview, Hugo González, 5 October 1992.

80. I.S. letter in *Bulletin d'information*, January 1954, 16–17 (original emphasis).

81. Lora, *Contribución*, 2:257, 263–73, 285, *Obras*, 5:124–26.

82. Lora, *Contribución*, 2:264–66, 271, *Obras*, 5:128; I.S. circular, 15 March 1954, BAHC-SCC.

83. Documents reproduced in Lora, *Obras*, 5:80, 84–85; letter from L. to Gaby, 22 December 1953, BDIC 457/1–2, 1953 folder; POR CC resolution, 5 January 1954, Prometheus Research Library. A March 1954 letter to SWP from Cochabamba opposition member "J." (H-SWP, Bolivia 1954 folder) said Lora was the only CC member to vote against condemning the SWP, arguing insufficient information, but proposed the POR ranks not be informed of the I.S./IC split; the CC agreed.

84. Lora, *Contribución*, 2:269. H-SWP (Bolivia 1954 folder) contains correspondence between Lora and "Smith" (Dobbs) in March–April 1954, after French Trotskyists forwarded Lora's contact information. Lora wrote on the POR crisis, asking that the information not be publicized, as opponents accused him of supporting the IC, whose formation he considered premature, although he sympathized with some of its views.

85. Lora, *Contribución*, 2:279.

86. Interview, Eduardo Mendizábal, 18 January 2007; Peñaranda, "Participación de la mujer" and *Obras de Agar Peñaranda*; Marcel to BP de la FOL, 5 January 1955, anonymous private collection.

87. Warqui, *La Revolución Boliviana—Proyecto de Tesis Política*, 20 April 1955, H-SWP, Bolivia 1955–56 folder.

88. Three decades earlier, Trotsky's Left Opposition denounced the similar "thesis" that "the Communists must enter [China's] National government to support the Left wing in its struggle against the feeble and wavering policy of the Right"; Isaacs, *Tragedy of the Chinese Revolution*, 121.

89. Lora, *Obras*, 4:187, 246; Lora letter, 22 October 1954, H-SWP, Bolivia 1954 folder; Lora, *Contribución*, 2:282–83.

90. Lora, "Bolivia: Control del MNR," 143; Lora letter, 19 October 1954, H-SWP, Bolivia 1954 folder (includes a critique of Nahuel Moreno's Peronist party entrism). Archives show no response from the SWP.

91. Huguembert, "Informe" (9 December 1954), *Boletín de discusión sobre Bolivia* (Buenos Aires) [1955], H-LSH, unboxed section, nonsequential pagination; interview, Edwin Möller, 29 September 1992. Möller (*Dios desnudo*, 48) lists 17 POR leaders who entered the MNR with him, including Ayala, Sinforoso Cabrera, Guillermo Guerrero, Jorge Salazar, and José Zegada. Möller's "expulsion" from the POR is reported in *Diario*, 15 October 1954.

92. Interview, Hugo González, 5 October 1992.

93. *Diario*, 9 November 1954; undated report by Arroyo (Gilly), BDIC 468/1, 1955 folder. Compare *Labor Action*, 10 January 1955.

94. Interview, Modesto Sejas, 2 October 1992. This account's main features were confirmed by Hugo González (interview, 5 October 1992), who claimed raids affected the Cochabamba group and FPI, but not the FOL.

95. Letter to Pablo (15 April 1954), Lora, *Obras*, 5:83; Warqui to I.S., 13 June 1955, H-SWP, Bolivia 1954 folder.

96. J. López, *La tesis de la X* Conferencia del POR a la luz del leninismo*, February 1954, BAHC-SCC, and *Hacia la revolución proletaria!* (*Proyecto de Tesis para la Conf. Regional de Cochabamba y la XI Conf. Nacional*), n.d., BDIC 468/2, 1954 folder.

97. López, *Hacia la revolución proletaria!*

98. José Rodríguez et al., *Democracia proletaria o encuestas?* 1 March 1954, BDIC 468/2, 1954 folder.

99. Célula Manuel Cruz Vallejos, *El Partido al borde del precipicio*, March 1954, BDIC 468/2, 1954 folder; José Rodríguez et al., *¿Buró Político del POR = servidor del MNR?*, February 1954, BAHC-SCC.

100. Buró de la FPI, *Autocrítica*, 23 June 1954, BDIC 468/1, 1954 folder.

101. Ryan, "Letter on the Bolivian Revolution," "Bolivia—Class Collaboration Makes a Recruit," and "Bolivian Revolution and the Fight against Revisionism."

102. M. Stein to POR, 2 July 1952, H-SWP, Bolivia 1952–53 folder.

103. See Magri, "Moreno y la revolución boliviana"; E. González, *Trotskismo obrero*; unsigned, undated Morenoite polemic *Dos líneas: La oportunista y la revolucionaria frente a la Revolución Boliviana*, H-LSH, unboxed section.

104. *Dos líneas*, 9, 12.

105. José Valdez, "Etapa actual" ("approx. December 1953"), "Poder dual" (19 July 1954), and "Afinando la puntería" (21 December 1954); "Memorándum" (n.d.); Moreno, "Afinemos" (n.d.), all in above-cited *Boletín de discusión sobre Bolivia*, nonsequential pagination.

106. Valdez, "Etapa actual."

Chapter 5. Cold War Calculus

1. Sergio Almaraz, quoted in Lehman, *Bolivia and U.S.*, 143–44.

2. *Lecciones del proceso guatemalteco*, 2, 3.

3. Lehman, *Bolivia and U.S.*, 97–110, 120.

4. "About 50% of the first hundred issues" of Lora's newspaper were "seized totally or partially"; *Masas*, 15 November 1959.

5. "50 años de Masas," *El Juguete Rabioso*, 28 November 2004, http://www.voltairenet.org/article123324.html (accessed 12 February 2006).

6. Escóbar, *Testimonio*, 22–23; interview, Filemón Escóbar, 23 September 1992.

7. Interview, Miguel Lora, 6 August 2004; "Congreso gorkysta," *Trinchera de la Juventud Revolucionaria* (La Paz), 7 November 1959; interview, Dionicio Coca, 18 August 2007.

8. Interview, Andrés Lora, 6 August 2004.

9. Interview, Elsa Cladera de Bravo, June 1977. The POR-LO's Catavi-Siglo XX, Potosí, and Huanuni committees published *Lucha Minera*, *Socavón* (Mineshaft), and *La Voz del Minero*, respectively. Fernando Bravo published *¡A Luchar!* in the teachers' union. Also see his *Revolución Boliviana y educación*.

10. *Lucha Minera*, 1st fortnight January 1962.

11. Undated report (1958 or 1959) and Achacachi documents, 24 February and 30 December 1959, FBEC; Oruro communiqué, 30 March 1959, BAHC-SCC.

12. Interview, Alejandro Carvajal, 5 July 2004; *El Harinero* (La Paz), September 1958. Sánchez, then thirty-four, was on the POR-LO's list of candidates for the Chamber of Deputies (20 June 1958, FBEC), which included González (37), Carvajal (28), Villegas (36), and ten others for La Paz district; eight for Cochabamba, including Encarnación Colque (30), Modesto Sejas (34), and Amadeo Vargas (30); and six for Oruro, including Bravo (40), Florentino Calustro (30), Cardenio Vásquez (30), and former BMP alternate deputy Ismael Pérez (40).

13. Interviews: Alejandro Carvajal, 5 July 2004; Elio Vásquez, 17 July 2004; Felipe Vásquez, 4 October 1992.

14. Interviews: Miguel Lora, 6 August 2004; Andrés Lora, 6 August 2004; Angel Capari, 5 August 2004; Dionicio Coca, 18 August 2007; Pastor Peláez, 6 August 2004; Alejandro Carvajal, 5 July 2004; Elio Vásquez, 17 July 2004. See F. Escóbar, "César Lora," in Barnadas, *Diccionario histórico*, 2:112 for useful background.

15. Salazar Mostajo, *Caducidad*, 144–45. Salazar's LSR had formed an electoral alliance with the POR-LO and protested this last-minute policy.

16. Interview, Elio Vásquez, 17 July 2004; POR, *¿Qué es y qué quiere el POR?* 1.

17. Miscellaneous items in H-WER; provenance explained above.

18. CIA, *Fourth International: Its Structure, Activities, Personnel*, 89–91, H-WER, Box 14, Folder 1.

19. *Masas*, 18 August 1956.

20. Eder, *Inflation and Development*, 87 (also see Lehman, *Bolivia and U.S.*, 123; Dunkerley, *Rebellion*, 86); Lora, *Estabilización*, 1.

21. I.S. *Internal Bulletin*, 1 May 1959, 14.

22. Cajías de la Vega, "Deterioro," 100–104; *NYT*, 29 December 1956; *Masas*, 9 August 1958.

23. Daily reports in *Diario*, 3–13 June 1957.

24. Dunkerley, *Rebellion*, 90; POR, *Huelga general y crisis*, 2–5.

25. Lora et al., *Masacre de Huanuni*, 7; *Lucha Minera*, 2nd fortnight May, 1959 (original emphasis).

26. Cajías de la Vega, "Deterioro," 136–38; *Masas*, 12 December 1957.

27. *Lucha Minera*, 12 May 1958; Catavi mine union declaration, 27 January 1958, FBEC; *NYT*, 5 April 1959.

28. Report by Lucero (Gilly), 18 December 1959, FBEC.

29. *NYT*, 10 March and 3 April 1959; *Time*, 16 March 1959, 40, 42; *Life*, 30 June 1960, 69.

30. This was also the case around the same time in Potosí and Colquiri; Cajías de la Vega, "Deterioro," 168–69.

31. Interview, Felipe Vásquez, 4 October 1992; Lora et al., *Masacre de Huanuni*, 19–20; Dunkerley, *Rebellion*, 98–99.

32. Siles, *Mensaje-informe*, 26, 27, 34.

33. Zavaleta Mercado, "Ampliado minero," 3–4.

34. Zavaleta Mercado, *Caída*, 105.

35. Salazar Mostajo, *Caducidad*, 67; communiqué in *Nación*, 26 March 1960; *Lucha Minera*, 3 June 1960.

36. *Internacionalismo proletario*, 1, 3, 5.

37. Rabe, *Most Dangerous Area*, 17, 24.

38. Dunkerley, *Rebellion*, 108, 114; Lehman, *Bolivia and U.S.*, 150–51, who states Kennedy increased military assistance to Bolivia by 800 percent.

39. Gill, *School of the Americas*, 78, 97–99.

40. *Estaño* (La Paz), April–May 1961, 58.

41. Interview, Filemón Escóbar, 23 September 1992. The POR-LO's leaflet for the occasion (22 December 1960, FBEC) appealed for Khrushchev to "rehabilitate" Trotsky.

42. Guevara, *América Latina*, 418.

43. Debray, *Strategy*, 53, *Revolution in the Revolution?* 116, 38.

44. Debray, *Strategy*, 38.

45. *Fourth International* (Amsterdam), Winter 1960–61, 61; leaflets, 21 June 1961, April 1961, 1 January 1962, FBEC.

46. *Cuaderno de canciones*; May Day 1970 leaflet, "Arms in Hand, Push Forward the March to Socialism!" FBEC.

47. Lora, *Lección cubana*, 3, 17, *Obras*, 4:150.

48. *Masas*, 29 August 1964; interview, Guillermo Lora, 3 August 2004.

49. See Lora, *Revolución y foquismo*, 8–12.

50. Lora, *Las guerrillas*, 18–23.

51. Salazar Mostajo, *Caducidad*, 60–63.

52. Interviews: Alejandro Carvajal, 7 July 2004; Francisco Bedregal, 5 July 2004; Gilly et al., "Trotskyism and the Cuban Revolution."

53. The letter drew U.S. intelligence agents' attention; report, 16 June 1961, H-WER, Box 14, Folder 7.

54. L.M. report, 15 October 1962, anonymous collection; Pablo to CC, 27 March 1962, FBEC; report on POR-LO division, 8–9 December 1962, H-WER, Box 14, Folder 5.

55. Interviews: Amadeo Vargas, 27 July 2003; Francisco Bedregal, 5 July 2004; Emma Bolshia Bravo, 4 August 2003.

56. Interview, Alejandro Carvajal, 7 July 2004.

57. *NYT,* 30 May 1964; *Masas,* 22 February 1964, 15 November 1963; *Time,* 2 April 1965, 36.

58. *Vistazo* (La Paz), 27 October 1964, 5; Zavaleta Mercado, *Caída,* 115.

59. Escóbar, *Testimonio,* 52; *New Leader* (New York), 6 June 1966, 7; *Vistazo,* 8 November 1964, 15.

60. Interview, Andrés Lora, 6 August 2004.

61. Interviews: Elio Vásquez, 17 July 2004; Filemón Escóbar, 23 September 1992; *International Socialist Review* (New York), Winter 1965, 27.

62. Interview, Alejandro Carvajal, 7 July 2004; Escóbar, *Testimonio,* 54; *La junta militar usurpa la victoria del pueblo,* 3, 8.

63. 1956 memo quoted in Lehman, *Bolivia and U.S.,* 148–49; Weiner, *Legacy of Ashes,* 281.

64. Salazar Mostajo, *Caducidad,* 183.

65. POR, *XXI Congreso Nacional,* 26–30.

66. *Masas,* 14 November 1964; *Vistazo,* 14 November 1964, 12.

67. Tom E. Robles, "Situation in Bolivia," 23 November 1964, H-JL, Box 426, Folder 18. On the AIFLD, a joint venture of U.S. labor leaders and intelligence agencies, see Agee, *CIA Diary.*

68. *Vistazo,* 14 November 1964, 4.

69. *Wall Street Journal,* 12 January 1966.

70. César Lora, *Escritos,* 24–26. On the clandestine unions, see: FSTMB, *Conferencia Nacional de Comités Sindicales Clandestinos; Masas,* 21 August 1965; *Lucha Obrera* (La Paz), 30 November 1965.

71. Interviews: Angel Capari, 5 August 2004; Andrés Lora, 6 August 2004.

72. Interviews: Guillermo Lora, 3 August 2004; Miguel Lora, 6 August 2004.

73. Interviews: Angel Capari, 5 August 2004; Pastor Peláez, 6 August 2004.

74. Recording provided anonymously to author.

75. Interview, Andrés Lora, 6 August 2004. *Chicherías* are bars that sell corn beer.

76. Poppe, *Cuentos mineros,* 56–57.

77. *Newsweek,* 4 October 1965, 58.

78. Interview, Elio Vásquez, 17 July 2004; *Lucha Obrera* (La Paz), 30 November 1965.

79. Lora, *Obras,* 17:18.

80. Ibid., 17:396.

81. *Masas,* March 1966. Calling the junta a fascist regime was a departure from the term "military bonapartist" traditionally used by Trotskyists to describe dictatorships arising from the armed forces, in contrast to mass-based fascist movements.

82. S. to Livio, 5 March 1966, H-JH Box 40, Folder H24.

83. Guevara, *América Latina,* 504–6.

84. Debray, *Che's Guerrilla War,* 51.

85. *Presencia* (La Paz), 23 February, 8 and 14 June 1967; *Ultima Hora*, 21 June 1967; interviews: Miguel Lora, 6 August 2004; Alejandro Carvajal, 15 July 2004; Jorge Echazú, 7 July 2004.

86. Interviews: Hugo González, 5 October 1992; Elio Vásquez, 17 July 2004; reports from "Foreign City" on "Bolivia/Peru" (late November 1965) and "Bolivia, Argentina, Peru" (12–15 August 1966), declassified in 1976, H-WER, Box 14, Folder 5.

87. *Intercontinental Press*, 10 June 1968, 11 May 1970.

88. Interview, Dionicio Coca, 18 August 2007; Lora, *Obras*, 7:327.

89. Lora, *Revalorización*, 26, 38–43.

90. Lora, *Obras*, 17:395, 351, 102.

91. *Presencia*, 8 and 17 June 1967; *Ultima Hora*, 16 June 1967.

92. Interviews: Angel Capari, 5 August 2004; Pastor Peláez, 6 August 2004.

93. *Presencia*, 25 and 26 June 1967; *Jornada* (La Paz), 26 June 1967.

94. Interview, Angel Capari, 5 August 2004.

95. Lora, *Obras*, 7:362.

96. Interview, Daniel Campos, 14 July 2004. On Monje's relations with Che, see Anderson, *Che Guevara*, 696–96, 704–5.

97. *Intercontinental Press*, 22 September 1969. Another Peredo brother, Antonio, was Evo Morales's running mate in 2002.

98. *Report on Bolivia and Argentina*, n.d., 4–5, H-JH, Box 57, Folder 9.

99. Lora, *Obras*, 25:361–62; interview, Hugo González, 5 October 1992.

100. Mujeres de Bolivia, 1 May 1968, FBEC.

Chapter 6. "The First Soviet of the Americas"

1. Escóbar, *Testimonio*, 192.

2. Sacchi, *Torres*, 122.

3. *Ibid.*, 125; USec, *Boletín de información*, October 1970, 8.

4. Lora, *Obras*, 25:347, 26:21–23.

5. Interview, Andrés Soliz Rada, 29 September 1992; Pinto Parabá, *1970*, 82–89, 108; interview, Francisco Bedregal, 5 July 2004.

6. Interview, Alfonso Velarde, 10 August 2004.

7. Strengers, *Asamblea Popular*, 27–35; leaflet to miners' congress, Oruro, 9 April 1970, BAHC-SCC.

8. Lehman, *Bolivia and U.S.*, 160.

9. COB thesis reproduced in 1980 *Tesis de Pulacayo* edition, 80–81.

10. *Diario*, 21 and 29 October, 1 November 1970.

11. Strengers, *Asamblea Popular*, 84–85.

12. Interview, Alfonso Márquez, 7 August 2004.

13. Lora, *De la Asamblea*, 48. Cf. Escóbar, *Testimonio*, 154–55; *Diario*, 9 October 1970; *Masas*, 17 August 1971.

14. USec, *Boletín de información*, October 1970, 8. Also see *Diario*, 1 November 1970; Torres, *Defensa*, 67–69.

15. *Diario*, 9 October 1970.

16. *Bocamina* (La Paz), 1st fortnight December 1970, 14–18; 2nd fortnight December 1970, 3; 1st fortnight January 1971, 8.

17. Escóbar, *Testimonio*, 215–18.

18. Interview, Julio García, 30 July 2004; *Intercontinental Press*, 6 September 1971.

19. Interview, Edgardo Herbas, 1 July 2005.

20. Lora, *De la Asamblea*, 82, 97.

21. *Intercontinental Press*, 23 November 1970; Maitan quotation from Blanco et al., "Argentina and Bolivia," 13.

22. *Masas*, 9 May 1971.

23. Strengers, *Asamblea Popular*, 127–29; *Masas*, 22 April 1971.

24. Strengers, *Asamblea Popular*, 141. The FSTMB stressed that the assembly should be "predominantly working-class"; *Presencia*, 22 January 1971.

25. *Intercontinental Press*, 12 April 1971; *Presencia*, 2 May 1971.

26. *Masas*, 9 May 1971.

27. Blanco et al., "Argentina and Bolivia," 19; USec *Boletín de información*, June 1971, 18; *Diario*, 1 July 1971.

28. Interview, Carlos Salazar Mostajo, 3 August 2003.

29. *Liga Socialista Revolucionaria* journal, November 1962, 3, 21, and June 1971, 13; Salazar Mostajo, *Caducidad*, 14.

30. Salazar Mostajo, *Caducidad*, 188.

31. *Diario*, 23 June 1971; *Presencia*, 22 June 1971.

32. Interview, Julio García, 30 July 2004.

33. Salazar Mostajo, *Caducidad*, 212–13.

34. *Diario*, 27 June 1971; *Presencia*, 29 and 30 June 1971; Strengers, *Asamblea Popular*, 146–67.

35. "Workers Will Smash Coup," headlined *Diario*, 19 June 1971; Strengers, *Asamblea Popular*, 160–61. On eventual restoration of Alandia's murals, see *Presencia*, 7 November 1982.

36. *Diario*, 3 July 1971; interview, Eduardo Mendizábal, 18 January 2007.

37. *Masas*, 24 July 1971. Coup supporter Kieffer Guzmán gives details in *De cara a la Revolución del 21 de agosto*.

38. Salazar Mostajo, *Caducidad*, 189.

39. Interview, Julio García, 30 July 2004.

40. Salazar Mostajo, *Caducidad*, 190.

41. USec *Boletín de información*, October 1971, 24; interview, Jorge Echazú, 7 July 2004; Salazar Mostajo, *Caducidad*, 190; *Presencia*, 21 August 1971. As COB Secretary of Militias, Miguel Alandia gave out some weapons, according to Grover Alejandro (interview, 16 July 2004).

42. Interviews: Daniel Campos, 14 July 2004; Edgardo Herbas, 1 July 2005; Alfonso Márquez, 7 August 2004.

43. Interviews: Edgardo Herbas, 1 July 2005; Grover Alejandro, 16 July 2004.

44. Interview, Jorge Echazú, 7 July 2004.

45. *Presencia*, 7 July 1971.

46. *Intercontinental Press*, 13 September 1971.

47. Interviews: René Poppe, 28 June 2005; anonymous, La Paz, 5 August 2004.

48. Interviews: Pastor Peláez, 6 August 2004; Grover Alejandro, 16 July 2004.

49. *Report on Bolivia and Argentina*, n.d., H-JH, Box 57, Folder 9, 6; interview, anonymous, La Paz, 10 July 2003.

50. Interview, Daniel Campos, 14 July 2004.

Chapter 7. From Banzer to Evo

1. Interview, Pastor Peláez, 6 August 2004.

2. Interviews: Daniel Campos, 14 July 2004; Edgardo Herbas, 1 July 2005.

3. *Masas*, December 1971. The November and December 1971 issues also printed appeals by Major Sánchez.

4. *Intercontinental Press*, 6 December 1971. Torres refers to his participation in interview, *Intercontinental Press*, 25 June 1973. Former POR exiles say Sánchez also participated in FRA meetings in Santiago.

5. *Masas*, May 1972, December 1971; Lora, *Frente antiimperialista*, 17–18, *De la Asamblea*, 97.

6. POR-Combate resolution, April 1972, and associated materials, H-JH, Box 41, Folder H-26; *Intercontinental Press*, 20 September 1971.

7. Interviews: Filemón Escóbar, 23 September 1992; Juan Perelman Fajardo, 5 July 2004; Felipe Vásquez, 4 October 1992.

8. Interview, Francisco Bedregal, 5 July 2004.

9. Interview, Edgar Ramírez, 29 June 2004.

10. Interview, Grover Alejandro, 16 July 2004.

11. POR-Combate statement, *Intercontinental Press*, 26 February 1973.

12. Interview, Edgar Ramírez, 3 January 2007.

13. Rivera Cusicanqui, *Oprimidos*, 156–67; Dunkerley, *Rebellion*, 212. In his 1971 *Tesis india* (85, 122–34), Reinaga called for continuing the Military-Peasant Pact and accused the left of trying to turn Bolivia into a colony of the USSR, Cuba, and Allende's Chile.

14. *Masas*, 30 September and 18 August 1977. See Lora, *Causas de la inestabilidad*, 86, 109–12.

15. Dunkerley, *Rebellion*, 232; Jiménez leaflet, 2 December 1977, FBEC.

16. Villarroel de Lora's crucial role is confirmed by the detailed study in Lavaud, *Dictadura minada*, 84–102.

17. Interview, Aurora Villarroel de Lora, 6 August 2004.

18. Salazar Mostajo, *Caducidad*, 192; Lavaud, *Dictadura minada*, 239; Dunkerley, *Rebellion*, 240–41.

19. Cruz described his decades of activism in an interview at his Tío de la Mina bookstore in Oruro, 30 July 2003.

20. *International Viewpoint*, 21 March 1983, 17; *Intercontinental Press*, 21 January 1981.

21. Lora, *Electoreros*, 45, *Autopsia del gorilismo*, 106; *Masas*, 7 August 1981.

22. Interviews: Alberto Bonadona, 30 July 2004; Sonia Sapiencia, 3 August 2003 and 10 August 2004.

23. Interviews: Vilma Plata, 31 July 2003 and 28 June 2004; Rico, *Luis Rico y su Banda*; *Voice of the Poor and Taming of the Shrew*, 87; "El trotskismo gana la Federación de Maestros" (4 June 2006), http://www.bolpress.com/art.php?Cod=2006060401 (accessed 10 June 2006). Also see Miguel Lora, *Luchemos por una nueva educación*.

24. Interview, Fernando, 25 May 2006.

25. "Klaus Barbie and the Bolivian Navy," *Workers Vanguard* (New York), 20 May 1983; Lora, *Nuestra posición frente al narcotráfico*.

26. For example, confidential Comibol report on POR "agitation" in the mines, 22 July 1981 (anonymous source).

27. *Testimonios de la represión*, 1.

28. *International Viewpoint*, 21 March 1983, 17.

29. Dunkerley, *Rebellion*, 343.

30. Interviews: Jaime Iturri Salmón, 3 September 1999; Ascencio Cruz, 30 July 2003.

31. Interviews: Daniel Campos, 14 July 2004; Gonzalo Trigoso, 19 July 2004; Sonia Sapiencia, 3 August 2003. Also see Bacherer Soliz, *Represión*, 28–29.

32. *Bandera Socialista*, July 1983.

33. *Cambio 16* (Madrid), 22 April 1985, 96.

34. *Masas*, 23 November 1984.

35. *Masas*, 24 March 1985; *La Colmena* (La Paz), 1 November 1985.

36. *Masas*, April 1985.

37. Interview, Abraham Grandydier, 23 March 2007; Muruchi Poma, "Urban Social Movements."

38. *South* (London), November 1986, 30; interview, Angel Capari, 5 August 2004; *Cambio 16*, 29 May 1989, 84.

39. *Masas*, 11 and 25 May 1988.

40. Guarachi Huanca, "Comunidades."

41. Stefanoni and Do Alto, *Evo Morales*, 29. After a falling-out in 2004, Morales expelled Escóbar from the MAS.

42. Magri, *En Defensa del Marxismo*, December 1995, 34–44.

43. Olivera and Lewis, *¡Cochabamba!*, 2; interview, Ariel Román, 5 August 2004.

44. Interview, Zenovia Vásquez, 13 March 2007; "Bolivia: Leasing the Rain."

45. Auza, *Memoria testimonial de la "Guerra del Gas,"* 167–68, 149.

46. *Masas*, 10 and 17 June 2005; *El Marginal*, June 2005.

47. "El Alto and the 'People's Assembly,'" *The Internationalist,* Summer 2005, http://www.internationalist.org/elaltoapno050620.html (accessed 10 March 2008).

48. *Masas,* 16 July 2004.

49. *NYT,* 19 December 2005.

50. *Razón,* 6 August 2008, http://www.la-razon.com/versiones/20080806_006356/nota_244_645919.htm (accessed 8 August 2008).

Appendix

1. Wiarda, *Soul of Latin America,* 233.

2. Marx and Engels, "Address of the Central Committee," 185.

3. Trotsky, *History of the Russian Revolution,* 3:419–27.

4. Trotsky, *On China,* 583, 403.

5. Trotsky, *Writings 1934–35,* 251 (original emphasis).

6. Trotsky, *Writings 1933–34,* 306.

7. See appendix to Trotsky, *Escritos latinoamericanos.*

8. Trotsky, *Writings 1938–39,* 176.

9. Trotsky, *Writings, Supplement (1934–40),* 784–85.

10. Ibid., 84; *Documents of the Fourth International,* 249–50.

11. Trotsky, *Writings 1938–39,* 73, 91. Cuban Communist Carlos Rafael Rodríguez, for example (later vice president under Fidel Castro), joined Batista's cabinet in 1944.

12. Ibid., 101–3. Emphasis in original.

13. Trotsky, *Writings, Supplement (1934–40),* 786.

14. *Documents of the Fourth International,* 333–34.

15. Trotsky, *Writings 1936–37,* 276–79.

References

Archives and Collections

Those appearing frequently are identified by abbreviations.

ADC: Archivo de Comibol (Corporación Minera de Bolivia). El Alto, Bolivia.

BAHC: Biblioteca y Archivo Histórico del Congreso de la Nación. La Paz, Bolivia.

BAHC-SCC: Sinforoso Cabrera Collection.

BDIC: Bibliotèque de Documentation Internationale Contemporaine. Université de Paris X, France.

CERMTRI: Centre d'Études et Récherches sur les Mouvements Trotskystes et Révolutionnaires Internationaux. Paris, France.

FBEC: Fernando Bravo and Elsa Cladera papers. Private collection. La Paz, Bolivia.

H: Hoover Institution, Stanford University. Palo Alto, California.

H-JH: Joseph Hansen Papers.

H-JL: Jay Lovestone Papers.

H-LSH: Library of Social History Collection.

H-SWP: Socialist Workers Party Records.

H-WER: William E. Ratliff Collection.

Archivo de La Paz. La Paz, Bolivia.

Archivo Nacional. Santiago, Chile.

Archivo y Biblioteca de la Nación. Sucre, Bolivia.

Carmen and Francisco Bedregal, private collection. La Paz, Bolivia.

Leon Trotsky Exile Papers. Houghton Library, Harvard University.

Private anonymous collections. Cochabamba, El Alto, La Paz, Oruro, and Sucre, Bolivia.

Prometheus Research Library. New York City.
Tamiment Library, New York University. New York City.

Internal Bulletins

Boletín de discusión sobre Bolivia, Partido Obrero Revolucionario de Argentina (Buenos Aires).

Boletín de información, USec (Paris).

Boletín informativo latino-americano, Bulletin d'Information, Bullétin Intérieur, Internal Bulletin, I.S. (Paris).

Boletín interno del Secretariado Internacional de la Cuarta Internacional, Grupo Cuarta Internacional (Buenos Aires).

Bulletins and circulars (misc.), COB, Cuerpo Nacional de Milicias Armadas de la COB, FSTMB.

Discussion Bulletin, Internal Bulletin, International Information Bulletin, and *International Internal Discussion Bulletin,* SWP (New York).

Matériaux et Informations, Latin American Secretariat, Executive Committee of the Communist International (Moscow).

Untitled preparatory bulletin for 1940 Emergency Conference of the Fourth International (n.p.).

Interviews

I have cited each participant's name as he or she is publicly known; they are alphabetized by paternal surname. Unless otherwise indicated, interviews were carried out by the author.

Aguilar, Alberto. La Paz, 16 July 2004. Former POR leader.

Alejandro, Grover. La Paz, 16 July 2004. Retired miner, COB leader, and former POR-Masas activist.

Anonymous. La Paz, 10 July 2003. Former POR sympathizer.

Anonymous. Sucre, 2 August 2004. Activist.

Anonymous. La Paz, 18 January 2007. Former POR member.

Anonymous. La Paz, 20 January 2007. Former POR sympathizer.

Arze Loureiro, Eduardo. Cochabamba, 2 October 1992. Founding member of POR and PSOB.

Bardales, Julio. La Paz, 28 June 2004. Former president of the Pulacayo miners' union.

Barrientos, Oscar. Cochabamba, 2 October 1992. Former POR leader.

Bedregal, Francisco. La Paz, 5 July 2004. Former POR-T activist.

Bonadona, Alberto. La Paz, 30 July 2004. Head of Bolivia's pension system when interviewed and former POR-Masas activist.

Bravo Cladera, Emma Bolshia. La Paz, 4 August 2003, 11 July 2004. Daughter of POR leader Fernando Bravo.

Campos, Daniel. La Paz, 3 August 2003, 14 July 2004. Former leading member of POR-Masas.

Capari, Angel. Cochabamba, 5 August 2004. Former miner; POR-Masas activist.

Carvajal, Alejandro. La Paz, 5 July 2004, 7 July 2004, 15 July 2004. Former factory union, POR-Lucha Obrera, and POR-Combate leader.

Cladera de Bravo, Elsa. Fribourg, Switzerland, 9 June 1977. Teachers' union activist and widow of Fernando Bravo. Interview by Marcelo Quezada and Alfonso Gumucio.

Coca, Dionicio. Stockholm, 18 August 2007. Former miner and POR-Masas activist. Interview conducted for author by Nadezhda Bravo Cladera.

Cruz, Ascencio. Oruro, 30 July 2003. Former miner; POR-Masas activist.

Del Nuevo Mundo, Juan. El Alto, 29 July 2004. Poet and former POR-Masas activist.

Echazú, Jorge. La Paz, 7 July 2004. Maoist leader.

Echazú, Luis Alberto. La Paz, 7 July 2004. Maoist leader who became Vice Minister of Mining in Morales government.

Escóbar, Filemón. La Paz, 23 September 1992. Former FSTMB and POR-Masas leader, indigenist congressman, and MAS leader.

Fernando (pseudonym). New York City, 25 May 2006. Foreign activist who worked with a Bolivian Trotskyist group from the late 1970s to early 1980s.

García Colque, Julio. La Paz, 30 July 2004. Secretary General, retirees' association, former president Potosí miners' union, and former POR-Masas activist.

Gilly, Adolfo. Discussion with author, New York City, 13 March 2008. Former BLA representative.

González Moscoso, Hugo. Cochabamba, 5 October 1992. Leader of POR, POR-LO, POR-Combate, and POR-U.

Grandydier, Abraham. Cochabamba, 23 March 2007. Retired miner. Interview by Sarah Hines.

Herbas, Edgardo. La Paz, 1 July 2005. Former URUS and POR-Masas activist.

Iturri Salmón, Jaime. La Paz, 3 September 1999. Former POR-Masas activist.

Jiménez, Cirilo. Cochabamba, 22 February 2007. Former POR-De Pie leader. Interview by Sarah Hines.

Lora, Andrés. Cochabamba, 6 August 2004. Former FSTMB and POR-Masas activist.

Lora, Gloria. Stockholm, 18 August 2007. Sister of Guillermo. Interview conducted for author by Nadezhda Bravo Cladera.

Lora, Guillermo. La Paz, 1 August 2003, 26 July 2004, 3 August 2004. POR and POR-Masas leader.

Lora, Miguel. Cochabamba, 6 August 2004. Teachers' union and POR-Masas leader.

Márquez, Alfonso. La Paz, 7 August 2004. POR-Masas activist.

Mendizábal, Eduardo. Sucre, 13 January 2007. POR-Masas activist.

Möller, Edwin. La Paz, 29 September 1992. Former POR, COB, and PRIN leader.

Peláez, Pastor. Cochabamba, 6 August 2004. Retired miner and POR-Masas activist.

Perelman Fajardo, Juan. La Paz, 5 July 2004. Son of Leticia Fajardo.

Plata, Vilma. Oruro, 31 July 2003; La Paz, 28 June 2004. Teachers' union leader and POR-Masas spokesperson.

Poppe, René. La Paz, 28 June 2005. Writer.

Ramírez, Edgar "Huracán." El Alto, 29 June 2004; La Paz, 3 January 2007. Director, Comibol Archives, and former PCB activist, FSTMB leader, and COB secretary general.

Ramos, Jorge Abelardo. Mexico City, 30 January 1992. Argentine ambassador to Mexico and former Trotskyist.

Román, Ariel. Cochabamba, 5 August 2004. URUS leader.

Salazar Mostajo, Carlos. La Paz, 3 August 2003, 5 August 2003. Former Warisata teacher and LSR leader.

Sapiencia, Sonia. La Paz, 3 August 2003, 10 August 2004. Former public workers' union organizer.

Sejas, Modesto. Cochabamba, 2 October 1992. Peasant leader and POR and POR-Masas activist.

Soliz Rada, Andrés. La Paz, 29 September 1992. Congressman and former Octubre leader who became Energy Minister in Morales government.

Trigoso, Gonzalo. La Paz, 19 July 2004, 20 July 2004. Former POR-Masas activist.

Vargas, Amadeo. Oruro, 29 July 2003; Cochabamba, 6 August 2004. Former POR, POR-LO, and POR-T leader.

Vásquez, Felipe. Oruro, 4 October 1992. Huanuni mine union, POR-LO, and POR-Combate leader.

Vásquez, Zenovia. Cochabamba, 13 March 2007. Huanuni and Cochabamba activist. Interview by Sarah Hines.

Vásquez Condori, Elio. El Alto, 17 July 2004. Retired Comibol worker and POR-LO, and POR-Combate activist.

Velarde Alfonso. La Paz, 10 August 2004. POR-Masas spokesman and founding member of URUS.

Villarroel de Lora, Aurora. Cochabamba, 6 August 2004. Former House-wives' Committee leader and POR-Masas activist.

Newspapers and Magazines

Alianza Obrera (Santiago, Chile).

¡A Luchar! (La Paz).

Amauta (Lima).

América India (Santiago).

Bandera Roja (La Paz).

Bandera Socialista (La Paz).

La Batalla (La Paz).

Bocamina (La Paz).

La Calle (La Paz).

Cambio 16 (Madrid).

La Chispa (La Paz).

Clave (Mexico City).

La Colmena (La Paz).

Combate (La Paz).

El Comercio (La Paz).

Contra la Corriente (Montevideo).

Cuarta Internacional (Buenos Aires).

Cultura Política (La Paz).

Cumbre (La Paz).

El Diario (La Paz).

Documentos (La Paz, Lima, and Santiago).

The Economist (London).

Emancipación (La Paz).

Estaño (La Paz).

El Ex-Combatiente (Sucre).

Fourth International (I.S.), (Amsterdam).

Fourth International (SWP), (New York).

La Fragua (La Paz).

El Harinero (La Paz).

El Imparcial (Cochabamba).

Intercontinental Press (New York).

International Press Correspondence (Berlin).

International Socialist Review (New York).

International Viewpoint (Amsterdam).

The Internationalist (New York).
Jornada (La Paz).
Labor Action (New York).
Labor Defender (New York).
Latin American Facts (New York).
Life (New York).
Liga Socialista Revolucionaria (La Paz).
Lucha Minera (Catavi-Siglo XX).
Lucha Obrera (La Paz).
Lucha Obrera (Mexico City).
El Marginal (La Paz).
Masas (La Paz).
The Militant (New York).
Minneapolis Star Journal.
Le Monde (Paris).
La Nación (La Paz).
New Leader (New York).
New York Times. Abbreviated *NYT*.
Newsweek (New York).
La Noche (La Paz).
Noticias (Oruro).
Nueva Internacional (Mexico City).
El País (Cochabamba).
Política Obrera (Buenos Aires).
La Prensa (La Paz).
Presencia (La Paz).
Quatrième Internationale (Paris).
Qué Hacer (La Paz).
¿Qué Hacer? (Mexico City).
La Razón (La Paz).
La República (La Paz).
Revolución en Bolivia (Buenos Aires).
Revolución Proletaria (Havana).
Service Presse Internationale (4) (Paris).
Siempre Abril (La Paz).
Socavón (Potosí).
Socialist Appeal (New York).
South (London).
Los Tiempos (Cochabamba).

Tierra (La Paz).
Time (New York).
Tribuna Socialista (Mexico City).
Trinchera (La Paz).
Trinchera de la Juventud Revolucionaria (La Paz).
Ultima Hora (La Paz).
Universidad Abierta (La Paz).
La Vérité (Paris).
Vistazo (La Paz).
Vivo Rojo (La Paz).
La Voz del Minero (Huanuni).
Wall Street Journal (New York).
Workers Vanguard (New York).

Other Sources

"1952: La Revolución." Presented by Carlos Mesa Gisbert. *Detrás de las Noticias* (PAT), 2002.

Abecia López, Valentín. *7 políticos bolivianos.* La Paz: Juventud, 1986.

Abramo, Fúlvio. "Construire la IVᵉ Internationale en Amérique latine." Interview. *Cahiers Léon Trotsky* 11 (September 1982), 83–93.

Agee, Philip. *CIA Diary: Inside the Company.* New York: Bantam, 1986.

Albarracín Millán, Juan. *La sociedad opresora.* La Paz: Empresa Editora Universo, 1979.

Alexander, Robert J. *Trotskyism in Latin America.* Stanford: Hoover Institution Press, 1973.

Alvarez España, Waldo. *Memorias del primer ministro obrero.* La Paz: Renovación, 1986.

Anderson, Jon Lee. *Che Guevara: A Revolutionary Life.* New York: Grove Press, 1997.

Antezana Ergueta, Luis. *Historia secreta del Movimiento Nacionalista Revolucionario,* vol. 5. La Paz: Juventud, 1986.

———. *Proceso y sentencia de la reforma agraria en Bolivia.* La Paz: Ediciones Puerta del Sol, 1979.

Arbona, Juan Manuel. "'Sangre de minero, semilla de guerrillero': Histories and Memories in the Organisation and Struggles of the Santiago II Neighbourhood of El Alto, Bolivia." *Bulletin of Latin American Research* 27:1 (January 2008), 24–42.

Arriola Woog, Enrique, ed. *Sobre rusos y Rusia: Antología documental.* Mexico City: INAH, 1994.

Así lucharon los hombres del M.N.R. La Paz: ECEGE, n.d.

Asturias, Miguel Ángel. "'Suetonio Pimienta' y otros libros de Tristán Marof," in Baciu, *Tristán Marof de cuerpo entero,* 198–200.

Aubron, Yannick. *Fiesta y revolución.* La Paz: Ediciones Masas, n.d.

Auza, Verónica, coord. *Memoria testimonial de la "Guerra del Gas."* La Paz: Cepas-Caritas, 2004.

Bacherer Soliz, Juan Pablo. *Represión política en el Partido Obrero Revolucionario.* La Paz: Ediciones Trinchera, 1994.

Baciu, Stefan. *Tristán Marof de cuerpo entero.* La Paz: Ediciones Isla, 1987.

Baptista Gumucio, Mariano, comp. *José Cuadros Quiroga: Inventor del Movimiento Nacionalista Revolucionario.* La Paz: Mariano Baptista Gumucio, 2002.

Barnadas, Josep M. *Diccionario histórico de Bolivia,* vol. 2. Sucre: Grupo de Estudios Históricos, 2002.

Bethell, Leslie, ed. *The Cambridge History of Latin America,* vol. 8. Cambridge: Cambridge University Press, 1991.

Blanco, Hugo, et al., "Argentina and Bolivia—the Balance Sheet," SWP *International Internal Discussion Bulletin,* January 1973, 5–55.

"Bolivia: Leasing the Rain." *Frontline/World* (PBS), 5 July 2002.

Boynton, Rachel, dir. *Our Brand Is Crisis.* Koch Lorber Films, 2005.

Bravo Cladera, Emma Bolshia, Andrés Gautier, Susana Bacherer Debreczeni, et al. *La represión de la "Marcha por la Sobrevivencia."* La Paz: ITEI, 2003.

Bravo James, Fernando. *La Revolución Boliviana y la educación.* Uncía: n.p., 1954.

Cajías, Lupe. *Historia de una leyenda. Vida y palabra de Juan Lechín Oquendo, líder de los mineros bolivianos.* 2nd ed. La Paz: Ediciones Gráficas EG, 1989.

Cajías de la Vega, Magdalena. "El componente anarquista en el discurso minero del pre-52," *Estudios Bolivianos* (La Paz) 12 (2004), 15–78.

———. "El deterioro de una alianza: Mineros y MNR en Bolivia, 1952–1958." Master's thesis, FLACSO, Quito, 1987.

———, and Iván Jiménez Chávez. *Mujeres en las minas de Bolivia.* La Paz: Ministerio de Desarrollo Humano, 1997.

"Canciones del POR." Recording provided to author by Emma Bolshia Bravo Cladera.

Candia G., Alfredo. *Bolivia: Un experimento comunista en América.* La Paz: n.p., n.d.

Carter, William. *Bolivia: A Profile.* New York: Praeger, 1971.

Central Intelligence Agency. *The Fourth International: Its Structure, Activities, Personnel.* n.p., 1964.

Céspedes, Augusto. *El dictador suicida.* La Paz: Juventud, 2002.

———. *El presidente colgado.* Buenos Aires: Editorial Jorge Alvarez, 1966.

Chávez Guzmán, Arnaldo. *La muerte de Enrique Ferrante Callaú (Remembranzas)*. Monteagudo (Chuquisaca): n.p., 2006.

Chávez Ortiz, Ñuflo. *Cinco ensayos y un anhelo*. La Paz: Burillo, 1963.

Coggiola, Osvaldo. *O Trotskismo na América Latina*. São Paulo: Brasiliense, 1984.

Cordero G., Carlos. "Alandia, el Inmortal." *Cultural* 37 (December 2005) (La Paz), 8–18.

Cornejo S., Alberto, comp. *Programas políticos de Bolivia*. Cochabamba: Imprenta Universitaria, 1949.

Cuaderno de canciones del Comité Local de Catavi del POR. Catavi: Ediciones Lucha Minera, n.d.

Debray, Régis. *Che's Guerrilla War*. Middlesex: Penguin Books, 1975.

———. *Revolution in the Revolution?* New York: Grove Press, 1967.

———. *Strategy for Revolution*, ed. Robin Blackburn. London: Jonathan Cape, 1970.

Díaz Machicao, Porfirio. *La bestia emocional*. La Paz: Editorial Juventud, 1955.

Documents of the Fourth International. New York: Pathfinder Press, 1973.

Dunkerley, James. *Bolivia: Revolution and the Power of History in the Present*. London: Institute for the Study of the Americas, 2007.

———. "The Origins of the Bolivian Revolution in the Twentieth Century," in Grindle and Domingo, *Proclaiming Revolution*, 135–63.

———. *Rebellion in the Veins: Political Struggle in Bolivia, 1952–1982*. London: Verso, 1984.

Eder, George Jackson. *Inflation and Development in Latin America*. Ann Arbor: University of Michigan, 1968.

Encinas, Enrique, with Fernando Mayorga and Enrique Birhuet. *Jinapuni: Testimonio de un dirigente campesino*. La Paz: Hisbol, 1989.

Encinas A., Hipólito. *Estado, clase obrera y sociedad civil: La Asamblea Popular de 1971*. La Paz: Punto Cero, 1996.

Escóbar, Filemón. *Testimonio de un militante obrero*. La Paz: Hisbol, 1984.

Fajardo de Perelman, Leticia. *Pampa, metal y sangre*. La Paz: Maceda Cáceres, 1959.

Federación Sindical de Trabajadores Mineros de Bolivia. *Conferencia Nacional de Comités Sindicales Clandestinos de la Minería*. n.p., 1965.

Fernández, M. [José Aguirre Gainsborg]. "La Guerra del Chaco está próxima a su fin" and "Correspondencia del Chaco," *Hojas de mi archivo* (La Paz), June 1992, 22–27.

———. "Falta un partido," *América India* (Santiago), July–September 1972, 35–36.

Fernández, M. [José Aguirre Gainsborg]. "El Partido Obrero Revolucionario en Bolivia y el gobierno de Toro," *Alianza Obrera* (Santiago), 2nd fortnight of November 1936.

Fourth (Trotskyite) International—Structure and Personnel. Anonymous U.S. government report. n.p., 1949.

García Linera, Álvaro, Marxa Chávez León, and Patricia Costas Monje. *Sociología de los movimientos sociales en Bolivia.* La Paz: Diakonía/Oxfam, 2005.

———, Jaime Iturri, et al. *Las armas de la utopía.* La Paz: Punto Cero, 1996.

Gill, Lesley. *The School of the Americas.* Durham: Duke University Press, 2004.

———. *Teetering on the Rim.* New York: Columbia University Press, 2000.

Gilly, Adolfo, Angel Fanjul, and José G. Pérez. "Trotskyism and the Cuban Revolution." http://www.whatnextjournal.co.uk/Pages/History/Cuba .html (accessed 4 January 2008).

Goldenberg, Boris. *Kommunismus in Lateinamerika.* Stuttgart: Kohlhammer, 1971.

González, Ernesto, coord. *El trotskismo obrero e internacionalista en la Argentina,* vol. 1. Buenos Aires: Antídoto, 1995.

Gordillo, José M., coord. *Arando en la Historia: La experiencia política campesina en Cochabamba.* La Paz: Plural, 1998.

———. *Campesinos revolucionarios en Bolivia: Identidad, territorio y sexualidad en el Valle Alto de Cochabamba, 1952–1964.* La Paz: Plural-Promec, 2000.

Grindle, Merilee S., and Pilar Domingo, eds. *Proclaiming Revolution: Bolivia in Comparative Perspective.* Cambridge and London: Harvard University Press, 2003.

Guarachi Huanca, Paulino. "Las comunidades rurales y urbanas festejan el triunfo de Evo Morales," in *Bolivia: escenarios futuros.* (2006), http://www .democraciapartidos.org.bo/libro/escenarios%20futuros.pdf (accessed 17 February 2006).

Guevara, Ernesto Che. *América Latina. Despertar de un Continente,* ed. María del Carmen Ariet García. Melbourne: Ocean Press, 2003.

Guillermoprieto, Alma. "A New Bolivia?" *New York Review of Books,* 21 September 2006, 36–38.

Hacia la liberación de la mujer. Catavi-Siglo XX: Ediciones Lucha Minera, 1959.

"Homenaje a César Lora." Recording of funeral march (n.d., 1965), provided anonymously to author.

El internacionalismo proletario y el renegado Lora. Catavi-Siglo XX: Lucha Minera, 1960.

Iriarte, Gregorio. *Los mineros*. La Paz: Ediciones Puerta del Sol, 1983.

———, and Equipo CIPCA. "El sindicalismo campesino en Bolivia," *Revista Mexicana de Ciencias Políticas y Sociales*, January–March 1981, 127–81.

Irusta Medrano, Gerardo. *La lucha armada en Bolivia*. La Paz: Calama, 1988.

Isaacs, Harold R. *The Tragedy of the Chinese Revolution*, 2nd ed. New York: Atheneum, 1966.

La junta militar usurpa la victoria del pueblo para salvar dominio imperialista. La Paz: Lucha Obrera, 1964.

Justo, Liborio. *Bolivia: La revolución derrotada*. Cochabamba: Editorial Serrano, 1967.

Kieffer Guzmán, Fernando. *De cara a la revolución del 21 de agosto de 1971*. La Paz: Editorial Offset Boliviana, 1999.

Klein, Herbert S. *Bolivia: The Evolution of a Multi-Ethnic Society*, 2nd ed. New York: Oxford University Press, 1992.

———. *Historia general de Bolivia*. La Paz: Librería Editorial Juventud, 1982.

———. *Orígenes de la revolución nacional boliviana*. Mexico City: Editorial Grijalbo, 1993.

———. *Parties and Political Change in Bolivia, 1880–1952*. London: Cambridge University Press, 1969.

Knight, Alan. "The Domestic Dynamics of the Mexican and Bolivian Revolutions Compared," in Grindle and Domingo, *Proclaiming Revolution*, 54–90.

Lavaud, Jean-Pierre. *La dictadura minada. La huelga de hambre de las mujeres mineras*. La Paz: Plural, 2003.

Lazarte R., Jorge. *Movimiento obrero y procesos políticos en Bolivia*. La Paz: ILDIS, 1989.

Le Bot, Y. "Les mineurs boliviens et le marché mondial de l'étain." *Le Monde Diplomatique*, February 1981, 13.

Las lecciones del proceso guatemalteco. La Paz: Comité Regional del POR, 1954.

Lechín Oquendo, Juan. *Memorias*. La Paz: Litexsa Boliviana, 2000.

Lehman, Kenneth D. *Bolivia and the United States: A Limited Partnership*. Athens, Georgia: University of Georgia Press, 1999.

Lenin, V.I. "Defeat of One's Own Government in the Imperialist War," *Collected Works*, vol. 21. Moscow: Progress Publishers, 1964, 275–80.

Linke, Lilo. *Viaje por una revolución*. Quito: Casa de la Cultura Ecuatoriana, 1956.

Lora, César. *Escritos*. La Paz: Ediciones Masas, 1969.

Lora, Guillermo. "El anti-trotskismo del gobierno boliviano," *¿Qué Hacer?* (Mexico City), November 1954, 162–64.

———. *Autopsia del gorilismo*. La Paz: Ediciones Masas, 1984.

Lora, Guillermo. "Bolivia: El control del MNR sobre las masas," *¿Qué Hacer?* (Mexico City), October 1954, 140–43.

———. *Causas de la inestabilidad política y de la crisis de las FF.AA.* La Paz: Ediciones Masas, 1983.

———. "Class Struggles in Bolivia," *Fourth International* (New York), July–August 1952, 125–28.

———. *Contribución a la historia política de Bolivia,* 2 vols. La Paz: Ediciones Isla, 1978.

———. *Los crímenes del PIR. Masacre de Potosí.* n.p., n.d. [1948].

———. "La crise du Parti Ouvrier Révolutionnaire bolivien," *Bulletin Intérieur du Secrétariat International de la IVᵉ Internationale,* No. VI, November 1950, 1–26.

———. *De la Asamblea Popular al golpe fascista.* Buenos Aires: El Yunque, 1972.

———. *Los electoreros sirven a la burguesía y al golpismo.* La Paz: Ediciones Masas, 1980.

———. *La estabilización, una impostura.* La Paz: Ediciones Masas, 1960.

———. *Estado y Rosca: Impugnación del Decreto de Estado de Sitio.* La Paz: Acción Obrera, 1948.

———. *Figuras del trotskysmo boliviano.* La Paz: Ediciones Masas, 1983.

———. *El frente antiimperialista.* La Paz: n.p., 1984.

———. *Las guerrillas.* La Paz: Ediciones Masas, 1963.

———. *Historia del movimiento obrero boliviano, 1900–1923.* La Paz: Los Amigos del Libro, 1969.

———. *Historia del movimiento obrero boliviano, 1933–1952.* La Paz: Los Amigos del Libro, 1980.

———. *Historia de los partidos políticos de Bolivia.* La Paz: Ediciones La Colmena, 1987.

———. *Lección cubana.* La Paz: Ediciones Masas, 1962.

———. *El marxismo en Bolivia.* La Paz: n.p., 1985.

———. *Nuestra posición frente al narcotráfico.* La Paz: Ediciones Masas, 1982.

———. *Obras completas.* La Paz: Ediciones Masas, 67 volumes, 1994–2002.

———. *Revalorización del método de las guerrillas.* La Paz: Ediciones Masas, 1967.

———. *La Revolución Boliviana.* La Paz: Difusión S.R.L., 1964.

———. *Revolución y foquismo: Crítica marxista al ultra izquierdismo aventurero,* 2nd ed. La Paz: n.p., 1978.

———. *Vigencia de la Tesis de Pulacayo.* La Paz: Ediciones Masas, 1984.

———, Tomás Aguirre, Alejandro Bustamante and A. Sáenz. *La masacre de Huanuni.* La Paz: Ediciones Masas, 1960.

Lora, Miguel. *Luchemos por una nueva educación*. La Paz: n.p., 1991.

Magri, Julio. "Nahuel Moreno y la revolución boliviana," *En Defensa del Marxismo*, December 1991, 95–96.

Mallon, Florencia E. "Decoding the Parchments of the Latin American Nation-State," in James Dunkerley, ed., *Studies in the Formation of the Nation-State in Latin America*. London: Institute of Latin American Studies, 2002, 13–53.

Malloy, James M. *Bolivia: The Uncompleted Revolution*. Pittsburgh, PA: University of Pittsburgh Press, 1970.

———. *El MNR boliviano*. University of Pittsburgh, 1970.

———, and Eduardo Gamarra. *Revolution and Reaction: Bolivia, 1964–1985*. New Brunsick, NJ: Transaction Books, 1988.

Mariátegui, José Carlos. *Correspondencia (1915–1930)*, vol. 2. Lima: Biblioteca Amauta, 1984.

———. *Obras*, vol. 2. Havana: Casa de las Américas, 1982.

———. "Tristán Marof," in Baciu, *Tristán Marof de cuerpo entero*, 193–96.

———. "Últimas aventuras de la vida de don Ramón del Valle Inclán" (1928), http://www.elpasajero.com/espejo.htm (accessed 20 April 2008).

Marof, Tristán [Gustavo Navarro]. "Bolivia y la nacionalización de las minas," *Amauta*, February–March 1929, 84–93.

———. "Espartacus y Sandino," *Amauta*, April 1928, 26.

———. *Habla un condenado a muerte*. Córdoba, Argentina: Editorial Logos, n.d.

———. *La justicia del Inca*. Brussels: La Edición Latino Americana, 1926.

———. *México de frente y perfil*. Buenos Aires: Editorial Claridad, n.d.

———. *La novela de un hombre. Memorias–I*. La Paz: n.p., 1956.

———. "Oil and Blood," *Labor Defender*, April 1930, 75.

———. "Política y economía bolivianas," *Amauta*, May 1927, 16, 29.

———. *Suetonio Pimienta (Memorias de un diplomático de la República de Zanahoria)*. Madrid: Librería de Alejandro Pueyo, 1926.

———. *La tragedia del altiplano*. Buenos Aires: Editorial Claridad, n.d. [1934?].

———. *La verdad socialista en Bolivia*. La Paz: Editorial Trabajo, 1938.

———. *Wall Street y hambre*. Montevideo: Impresora Uruguaya, 1931.

Marx, Karl, and Frederick Engels. "Address of the Central Committee to the Communist League," *Selected Works*, vol. 1. Moscow: Progress Publishers, 1973, 175–85.

Mella, Julio Antonio. *Julio Antonio Mella en El Machete*, ed. Raquel Tibol. Mexico City: Fondo de Cultura Popular, 1968.

Mesa Gisbert, Carlos D. "Introducción al tema," in Toranzo Roca, *Desafíos para la izquierda*, 15–26.

Miranda Pacheco, Mario. *Crisis de poder en Bolivia*. La Paz: Librería Editorial Juventud, 1995.

Mitchell, Christopher. *The Legacy of Populism in Bolivia*. New York: Praeger, 1977.

Möller Pacieri, Edwin. *El Dios desnudo de mi conciencia revolucionaria*. La Paz: Plural, 2001.

Montoya, Víctor. "Crónicas mineras," http://www.fundacionjuanmunizzapico .org/CronicasVictorMontoya/index.htm (accessed 6 July 2008).

————. "Las pinturas rebeldes de un muralista latinoamericano," http://www .margencero.com/montoya/miguel_alandia.htm (accessed 5 July 2008).

El movimiento revolucionario latino americano. Versiones de la Primera Conferencia Comunista Latino Americana, Junio de 1929. Buenos Aires: La Correspondencia Sudamericana, n.d. [1929?].

Muruchi Poma, Feliciano. "Urban Social Movements as Engines of Political Change." Lecture, CUNY Graduate Center, 5 April 2006.

Nash, June. "Interpreting Social Movements: Bolivian Resistance to Economic Conditions Imposed by the International Monetary Fund," *American Ethnologist* 19:2 (May 1992), 275–93.

————. *We Eat the Mines and the Mines Eat Us*. New York: Columbia University Press, 1979.

Navarro, Gustavo A. *Poetas-idealistas e idealismos de la América hispana*. La Paz: Editorial Los Andes, n.d.

Olivera, Oscar, and Tom Lewis. *¡Cochabamba! Water War in Bolivia*. Cambridge, MA: South End Press, 2004.

Ortiz, Alicia. *Amanecer en Bolivia*. Buenos Aires: Hemisferio, 1953.

Para que no se olvide: La dictadura de Luis García Meza. La Paz: ASOFAMD, 1997.

Partido Obrero Revolucionario. *XXI Congreso Nacional del Partido Obrero Revolucionario*. La Paz: Ediciones Masas, 1964.

————. *La huelga general y la crisis de la dirección obrera*. La Paz: Lucha Obrera, 1957.

————. *¿Qué es y qué quiere el POR?* La Paz: Ediciones Masas, 1959.

————. *Resolución del ampliado del CC del POR: El POR llama a las masas campesinas a luchar organizadamente por la conquista de las tierras*. La Paz: n.p., 1953.

Patch, Richard W. "Bolivia: The Restrained Revolution," *Annual of the American Academy of Political and Social Science* 334 (1961), 123–32.

Paz Estenssoro, Víctor. "Fundamentos científicos de la Revolución Nacional," *Cultura Política* (La Paz) 1:1 (April 1954), 56–68.

Peñaranda Oropeza, Agar. *Obras de Agar Peñaranda*. La Paz: Brigada Revolucionaria de Mujeres, 1988.

————. "Participación de la mujer," *Monografía de Bolivia*, vol. 1. La Paz: Biblioteca del Sesquicentenario de la República, 1975.

Pendle, George. *A History of Latin America*. Middlesex: Penguin Books, 1971.

Pinto Parabá, Miguel. *1970: Cuando los periodistas se enfrentaron al poder*. La Paz: CEDLA, 2005.

Ponce Arauco, Gabriel. "Insurgencia campesina y respuesta estatal en el período 1952–1953," *Estudios Sociales* 1:1 (June 1987), 1–22.

Poppe, René. *Compañeros del Tío (cuentos mineros)*. La Paz: Plural, 1997.

————. *Cuentos mineros*. La Paz: Ediciones ISLA, 1985.

————. *Interior mina: Testimonio*. La Paz: Plural, 2003.

Prada Alcoreza, Raúl. "Perfiles del movimiento social contemporáneo," *Revista del Observatorio Social de América Latina (OSAL)* 4:12 (September–December 2003), 35–46.

Prado, Maria Lígia. *O populismo na América Latina*. São Paulo: Editora Brasiliense, 1986.

Prager, Rodolphe, comp. *Les Congrès de la Quatrième Internationale*, vols. I and IV. Paris: Éditions La Brèche, 1978.

Rabe, Stephen G. *The Most Dangerous Area in the World: John F. Kennedy Confronts Communist Revolution in Latin America*. Chapel Hill and London: University of North Carolina Press, 1999.

Redactor de la H. Cámara de Diputados. La Paz: n.p., 1947.

Reinaga, Fausto. *Tesis india*. La Paz: Ediciones PIB, 1971.

Rey, Esteban. *En Bolivia la revolución empieza ahora*. Buenos Aires: La Vanguardia, 1947.

Ribeiro, Darcy. *Las Américas y la civilización*. Mexico City: Extemporáneos, 1977.

Rico, Luis. *Luis Rico y su Banda Show Caracol*. Compact disc. La Paz: Discolandia, 2005.

Rivas Antezana, Sinforoso. *Los hombres de la Revolución: Memorias de un líder campesino*. La Paz: CERES/Plural, 2000.

Rivera Cusicanqui, Silvia. *"Oprimidos pero no vencidos": Luchas del campesinado aymara y quechwa 1900–1980*. La Paz: Hisbol, 2003.

Roberts Barragán, Hugo. *La Revolución del 9 de abril*. La Paz: Burillo, 1971.

Ruiz González, Raúl. *Bolivia, el prometeo de los Andes*. Buenos Aires: Editorial Platina, 1961.

Ryan, Sam. "A Letter on the Bolivian Revolution" (June 1952), reprinted in *Documents of the Vern-Ryan Tendency*, [Los Angeles?]: Communard Press, 1983, 41–44.

————. "Bolivia—Class-Collaboration Makes a Recruit," SWP *Internal Bulletin*, August 1953, 40–51.

Ryan, Sam. "The Bolivian Revolution and the Fight against Revisionism," *SWP Discussion Bulletin,* October 1954, 1–20.

Sacchi, Hugo M. *Torres: El nacionalismo revolucionario en Bolivia.* Buenos Aires: CEAL, 1985.

Saenz, Alberto. "José Aguirre en Chile," *América India* (Santiago), July–September 1972, 32–35.

Salazar de la Torre, Cecilia. "Identidad nacional y conciencia reflexiva." BA thesis, UMSA, 2004.

Salazar Mostajo, Carlos. *Caducidad de una estrategia,* 2nd ed. La Paz: Juventud, 2003.

————. *Gesta y fotografía: Historia de Warisata en imágenes.* La Paz: Lazarsa, 2005.

————. *La pintura contemporánea de Bolivia.* La Paz: Juventud, 1989.

"The Salt Route," http://www.andes-salt-uyuni.com.bo/pc11c.htm (accessed 3 August 2005).

Sapiencia, Sonia. "El factor conspirativo en el golpe del 9 de abril de 1952," *Universidad Abierta* (La Paz), 4 May 1992, 13–15.

Scali, Pierre [Pierre Broué]. *La révolution bolivienne.* Paris: La Vérité, 1954.

Schelchkov, Andrei. "La Internacional Comunista y Tristán Marof," *Anuario,* Archivo y Biblioteca Nacionales de Bolivia (Sucre), 1998, 3–18.

Selbin, Eric. *Modern Latin American Revolutions.* Boulder, CO: Westview Press, 1993.

Siles Zuazo, Hernán. *Mensaje-informe dirigido a la VIII Convención del M.N.R.* La Paz: Burillo, 1960.

Stefanoni, Pablo, and Hervé Do Alto. *Evo Morales, de la coca al Palacio.* La Paz: Malatesta, 2006.

Strengers, Jeroen. *La Asamblea Popular: Bolivia '71.* La Paz: SIDIS, n.d.

Taboada Terán, Néstor. *Bolivia: la revolución desfigurada.* Buenos Aires: CEAL, 1974.

Tesis de Pulacayo. La Paz: Ediciones Masas, 1980.

Testimonios de la represión en Bolivia. Célula Central en Europa del POR, n.p., 1981.

Thomson, Sinclair. "Revolutionary Memory in Bolivia," in Grindle and Domingo, *Proclaiming Revolution,* 117–34.

————, and Seemin Qayum. "'Ahora que lo pienso, cincuenta años después . . .'" (Adolfo Gilly interview), *Historias* (La Paz) 6 (2003), 239–58.

Toranzo Roca, Carlos, F., ed. *Desafíos para la izquierda.* La Paz: ILDIS, 1991.

Torres, Juan José. *En defensa de mi nación oprimida.* La Paz: ISLA, 1985.

Trotsky, Leon. *Escritos latinoamericanos.* Buenos Aires: CEIP León Trotsky, 2000.

―――. *History of the Russian Revolution*, 3 vols. Ann Arbor: University of Michigan Press, 1932.

―――. *Leon Trotsky on China*. New York: Monad Press, 1976.

―――. *The Spanish Revolution (1931–39)*. New York: Pathfinder, 1973.

―――. *Stalin's Gangsters*. London: New Park, 1977.

―――. *The Transitional Program for Socialist Revolution*. New York: Pathfinder, 1977.

―――. *Writings of Leon Trotsky*, 14 vols. New York: Pathfinder, 1971–1978.

United States Library of Congress Federal Research Division Country Studies, "Bolivia Country Studies," http://www.country-studies.com/bolivia (accessed 19 July 2005).

Valencia Vega, Alipio. *Desarrollo del pensamiento político en Bolivia (bosquejo)*. La Paz: Editorial Trabajo, 1953.

―――. *Historia política de Bolivia*. La Paz: Editorial Juventud, 1987.

Vanden, Harry E. *National Marxism in Latin America: José Carlos Mariátegui's Thought and Politics*. Boulder, CO: Lynn Rienner, 1986.

Velarde, Alfredo. *Historia de URUS*. La Paz: URUS, 1986.

Velarde, Carlos [Juan Fellman Velarde]. *El nacionalismo y la acción demagógica y proimperialista del trotzkismo*. La Paz: MNR/S.P.I.C., n.d.

Villa, José. *Los orígenes de la revolución de 1952 y del trotskismo boliviano*. Ediciones Poder Obrero, n.p., n.d.

Voice of the Poor and Taming of the Shrew: Evidence from the Bolivia Public Officials' Survey. February 2001 draft by World Bank analysts, http://info.worldbank.org/etools/docs/library/206605/bol_po_results01.pdf (accessed 1 April 2007).

Volk, Steven S. "Class, Union, Party: The Development of a Revolutionary Union Movement in Bolivia (1905–1952)," *Science and Society* 39:1&2, 26–43, 180–98.

Wald, Alan M. *The Revolutionary Imagination: The Poetry and Politics of John Wheelwright and Sherry Mangan*. Chapel Hill and London: University of North Carolina Press, 1983.

Weiner, Tim. *Legacy of Ashes: The History of the CIA*. New York: Doubleday, 2007.

Whitehead, Laurence. "Bolivia Since 1930," in Bethell, *The Cambridge History of Latin America*, vol. 8, 1991, 509–83.

―――. "The Bolivian National Revolution," in Grindle and Domingo, *Proclaiming Revolution*, 25–53.

Wiarda, Howard J. *The Soul of Latin America*. New Haven and London: Yale University Press, 2001.

Youdale, Roy, and Vimar Chire. *Cantan las minas*. Oruro: CEDIPAS, 1992.

Zapata, Francisco. *Autonomía y subordinación en el sindicalismo latinoamericano.* Mexico City: Fondo de Cultura Económica, 1993.

Zavaleta Mercado, René. "El ampliado minero y la clandestinidad," *Hojas de mi archivo* (La Paz), June 1992, 3–13.

―――. *Bolivia: Crecimiento de la idea nacional.* Havana: Casa de las Américas, 1967.

―――. *La caída del M.N.R. y la conjuración de noviembre.* La Paz: Los Amigos del Libro, 1995.

―――. *El poder dual en América Latina.* Mexico City: Siglo Veintiuno Editores, 1974.

Index

POR role in, 126, 131–37, 140,
160, 167–68, 171, 211, 222–23;
re-emergence, 198, 226; Second
Congress, 170; Sixth Congress,
228; and Torres, 201–2. *See also*
cogovernment; Lechín Oquendo,
Juan; Lora, Guillermo; Möller,
Edwin; worker ministers
Central Obrera Departamental
(COD), 132, 198, 202
Centro Obrero Revolucionario, 79
Céspedes, Augusto, 57, 259n38,
261n33, 261n40
Chaco War, 9–10, 27–33, 29(fig.),
40–44, 52, 63, 249, 251; impact,
15, 46, 48–49, 53–55, 57, 67, 237;
veterans, 15, 57–58, 76, 77, 92,
107, 133, 205; weapons from, 119,
209
Chávez, Ñuflo, 124, 140, 170, 202
Chiang Kai-shek, 24, 174, 243. *See
also* Guomindang
Chile: Chaco War and, 28–29, 33;
Comintern and, 27; Communists,
9, 32, 34; exiles in, 23, 32, 34,
44, 48, 109–11, 215, 219; Gas
War and, 235; popular front, 34,
244; Trotskyists, 103, 111, 113,
153. *See also* Aguirre Gainsborg,
José; Allende, Salvador; Izquierda
Comunista; Pinochet, Augusto;
War of the Pacific
China, 124, 155, 243–44, 269n88. *See
also* Chiang Kai-shek; Guomindang
Civil War of 1949, 105–11
Cladera, Elsa, 92, 166
clandestine unions, 185, 188, 273n70
class: and ethnicity, 5, 11, 24–27;
and language, 11; relations, 21
Clinton, Bill, 234
Coca, Dionicio, 20, 165, 167
coca/coca growers, 1,2, 7, 9, 11, 18,
21, 231–32, 238

cocaine cartels, 225
Cochabamba: peasant upheaval, 138–
47; relocated miners, 7–8, 231–32.
See also Ucureña; Water War
Cochabamba opposition, 153–57,
249, 270n94
Cochabamba Regional Committee,
146, 155–56
Cochrane, Bert, 142
CODEP (People's Democratic Coun-
cil), 188–89
cogovernment, 120, 126, 131, 135,
137, 170–71, 183, 207. *See also*
worker ministers
Cold War: Cuban Revolution and
MNR, 175; overview, 162–63;
Washington boundaries, 118
collective memory, 4, 12–15, 187,
255n9
Colque, Encarnación, 145, 180(fig.),
271n12; candidate, 271n12
Comando Obrero, 127
Comando Político, 201–2, 204, 206
Combate (publication), 195
Comibol. *See* Corporación Minera
Boliviana
Comintern. *See* Communist
International
communist movement: early years,
23–28, 30–32. *See also specific related
topics*
Communist International (Comin-
tern or CI), 249; and Bolivia,
23–28; on Chaco, 28, 33; on indig-
enous peoples, 24–27; and Marof,
61–62; Sixth World Congress, 26;
and two-stage revolution, 9, 243;
and WWII, 245. *See also* popular
fronts; Stalinism
Communist Party. *See specific countries*
Control Político, 125, 135
Corporación Minera Boliviana
(Comibol), 121, 158(fig.), 167,

16, 119–20, 122(fig.), 127, 157,
158(fig.), 160, 163, 171; Asamblea
Popular and, 207; calls for, 53, 108,
132, 137, 202; at Catavi-Siglo XX,
171–72, 182, 185; and Cochabamba upheaval, 144–45
miners: collective memory, 4, 13–15,
187, 229, 255n9; culture and
identity, 1–5, 11–13, 21, 23, 26;
early strikes, 23; Che Guevara on,
2–3, 190; Morales government
and, 240; and peasant unions, 11,
21; radio stations, 11, 163, 171,
182, 185, 190, 218; role in national life, 2, 6–10, 14, 17–21, 27,
76–77, 229, 237–38; songs, 12–13,
187, 236, 256n19; and Trotskyism, 7–10, 13–16, 79–80, 87, 117,
237–38; wages, 20–21, 101, 202;
working conditions, 18. *See also*
April 9 uprising; Bloque Minero
Parlamentario; Federación Sindical de Trabajadores Mineros de
Bolivia; housewives' committees;
massacres; militias; National Revolution; occupational health and
safety; relocalization; *sexenio rosquero*; Thesis of Pulacayo; *and other
specific events, groups, and individuals*
Miners Parliamentary Bloc. *See* Bloque Minero Parlamentario
mines. *See* miners; *specific mines*
Mine Workers Federation of Bolivia.
See Federación Sindical de Trabajadores Mineros de Bolivia
mining: lexicon, 11; role in nation,
21, 22(fig.)
Miranda, Mario, 58
Miranda, Rogelio, 201
Mistral, Gabriela, 35
mita, 11, 20–21, 192
Möller, Edwin, 251; on agrarian
question, 140; and April 9 uprising,

127; in Civil War (1949), 108; in
COB, 132–35, 143, 149, 153, 171,
181; and Comando Político, 202;
entrism, 152–53, 269n91; Gueiler
husband, 189, 221; on 1951
elections, 115; in 1951 general
strike, 110; and POR faction fight,
148–54, 156; and PRIN, 153, 181,
202; union activism, 97, 110, 133;
and Villarroel overthrow, 85–86
Le Monde (publication), 10, 123
Monje, Mario, 195, 274n96
Montenegro, Carlos, 57–58, 261n33
Montoya, Víctor, 23
Morales, Evo, 1, 6–9, 16–17, 221,
232–38, 233(fig.), 250, 277n41
Moreno, Nahuel (Hugo Bressano),
113–14, 159–60, 221, 251, 269n90
Morenoites, 159–60, 221, 251
Movimiento Al Socialismo (MAS),
6–7, 232, 235, 251
Movimiento de la Izquierda Revolucionaria (MIR), 206, 210, 216, 221,
222, 226, 251
Movimiento Nacionalista Revolucionario (MNR), 251; and agrarian
question, 123,138, 142–45;
April 9th uprising, 118–23, 127–
29; and Asamblea Popular, 204,
206; and Banzer, 201, 208, 215;
and Barrientos coup, 117, 181–82,
196; Beta Gama and, 55–56, 65;
BMP and, 101–2; Civil War (1949),
92, 97, 105–8; and CODEP, 189;
and Comando Político, 201–2,
204; and CONADE, 222; and
Cuba, 175–78; description, 10, 28,
251; disenchantment with, 180,
183, 196; in elections, 99–100,
104, 115–16, 167–69, 174; founding of, 28, 46, 58, 83; ideology
and program, 52, 83, 94, 118, 121,
124, 138, 261n33; I.S. on, 113–15;

About the Author

S. Sándor John received a BA in history from the University of Chicago, a master's in Latin American studies from the Universidad Nacional Autónoma de México, and a PhD in history from the City University of New York, where he is an adjunct assistant professor specializing in Latin American and labor history. In addition to Bolivia's radical history, his research interests include the African diaspora in Latin America and intersections between radicalism and immigrant labor. Most recently, he wrote the Bolivia entry for the *International Encyclopedia of Revolution and Protest* and an article on Bolivian miners "rescuing history" at the Mining Archives in El Alto.

www.ingramcontent.com/pod-product-compliance
Lightning Source LLC
Chambersburg PA
CBHW021850020426
42334CB00013B/262